SEEKING THE BEST MASTER

SEEKING THE BEST MASTER

*State Ownership
in the Varieties of Capitalism*

Edited by
MIKLÓS SZANYI

Central European University Press
Budapest–New York

© 2019 the editor and contributors

Published in 2019 by the

Centre for Economic and Regional Studies, Hungarian Academy of Sciences
Tóth Kálmán u. 4. H-1097
Budapest, Hungary
http://www.krtk.mta.hu

and

Central European University Press
Nádor utca 9, H-1051 Budapest, Hungary
224 West 57th Street, New York NY 10019, USA
Tel: +36-1-327-3138 or 327-3000
http://www.ceupress.com

All rights reserved. No part of this publication may be reproduced, stored in a retrieval system, or transmitted, in any form or by any means, without the permission of the Publisher.

ISBN 978-963-386-321-3

The research and the publishing of this book was sponsored by the OTKA Grant No. 112069 "Varieties of Capitalism—Varieties of Direct Economic Intervention of the State."

Library of Congress Cataloging-in-Publication Data

Names: Szanyi, M., editor.
Title: Seeking the best master : state ownership in the varieties of capitalism / edited by Miklós Szanyi.
Description: Budapest ; New York : Central European University Press, [2019] | Includes index.
Identifiers: LCCN 2019011501 (print) | LCCN 2019012867 (ebook) | ISBN 9789633863213 (hardcover)
Subjects: LCSH: Government ownership. | Capitalism.
Classification: LCC HD3850 .S795 2019 (print) | LCC HD3850 (ebook) | DDC 338.6/2—dc23
LC record available at https://lccn.loc.gov/2019011501
LC ebook record available at https://lccn.loc.gov/2019012867

Printed in Hungary

Contents

Introduction: The Revival of the State
MIKLÓS SZANYI 1

Chapter 1: Crisis Management in Europe: Nationalizations and Privatizations
ÉVA VOSZKA 13

Chapter 2: The Changing Role of the State in France: from Crisis to Crisis
MIKLÓS SOMAI 53

Chapter 3: The Involvement of the State in the German Economy
ZSÓFIA NASZÁDOS 79

Chapter 4: The Relationship between State and Private Enterprise in the Austrian Economy
ISTVÁN KŐRÖSI 101

Chapter 5: Some Aspects of State Ownership in East-Central European Transition
MIKLÓS SZANYI 137

Chapter 6: Listed Companies with State Ownership: The Case of Poland
ÉVA OZSVALD 163

Chapter 7: The Changing Role of the State in Slovenia:
Privatizations and Banks' consolidations
MIKLÓS SOMAI 189

Chapter 8: The Role of State Ownership in and after Hungary's
Transition to Market Economy
MIKLÓS SZANYI 213

Chapter 9: The Changing Role of the State in Development in
Emerging Economies: The Developmental State Perspective
JUDIT RICZ 237

Chapter 10: A Successful Model of State Capitalism: Singapore
KATALIN VÖLGYI 275

Chapter 11: The Changing Role of the State in Turkish Economy
TAMÁS SZIGETVÁRI 297

Chapter 12: Strong State Influence in the Brazilian Economy:
Continuity or Change?
JUDIT RICZ 325

Concluding Remarks and Further Research Agenda
MIKLÓS SZANYI 363

List of Contributors 375
Index 377

INTRODUCTION
The Revival of the State

MIKLÓS SZANYI

Throughout the history of mankind, the state has always been an important actor in social life. The arenas and tools of state intervention have changed substantially over time in connection to social perceptions and political institutions. The role of the state, including its involvement in the economy, has always been a political issue. The state is an embedded social institution. Therefore, state performance can be analyzed not only from the technical but also from the political perspective. It is an important dimension of a state's effectiveness, but also whose interests are mostly served and how state actions affect other social institutions. In the age of modern capitalism, three periods of intensive state activity may be observed. As Nölke (2014) rightly indicates, after late-nineteenth-century economic nationalism and the Keynesian (and corporatist) decades of the twentieth century, the new period of statism in the first decades of the twenty-first century has already become the third state-led paradigm of the capitalist world. Obviously, the three periods had very different features even from the technical standpoint (the usage of economic policy tools). Therefore, it is not self-evident that these periods have so much in common that direct comparisons between them are possible, especially without proper analysis of both state policies and the global economic environment and political conditions in which they developed. Obviously, the state's policy toolkit depended on both internal and external political conditions as well as on prevailing political concepts and social perceptions.

Based mainly on the experience of late twentieth-century transition economies, Kornai (2016) differentiated between two main types of economic and political systems. Liberal democracy goes together with the free market economy principle. Dictatorship is bound together with bureaucratic control and coordination of the economy. Of course, most market economies are somewhere in between. In the group of countries with more stable and long traditions of political democracy and free market economies, there are countries that traditionally have more state influence in the economy (France) than others (Britain). The political scene also shows different institutional systems. Market economic institutions are sometimes coupled with weak democratic institutions and influential charismatic leaders. In such autocracies, we can usually see a high level of centralization in decision making that provides the state with stronger control over the economy. Historically we can also observe an oscillation between basic state concepts in some countries: autocracy (dictatorship) and liberal democracy (Kornai 2016).

Countries are diverse in terms of their historical and cultural heritage, natural and human endowments, and level of development. Therefore, Kornai's dichotomy can be applied only with fairly high levels of abstraction. The "Varieties of Capitalism" (VoC) literature (see Hall and Soskice 2001; Amable 2003, and many others) identifies significant differences among capitalist models within the relatively homogenous group of countries of core Europe. This is despite the fact that the countries of core Europe are regarded as liberal democracies and free market economies. Moreover, their political orientation and institutional systems are streamlined according to the foundational documents of the European Union. Basic principles of economic integration describe the potential benefits of increased homogeneity in the single European market. The globalization process has also triggered important spontaneous as well as institutionally initiated economic streamlining in many areas from consumerism enforced by multinational corporations to financial market liberalization proposed by international organizations. Yet Gerschenkornian diversity has prevailed. Relatively little attention has been paid until now to an important object of study within the theme of capitalist diversity: the economic role of the state.

Over time, the development of economics as discipline has produced important insights that permit a better understanding of economic systems. Theoreticians and policy makers generally accepted these new insights, thus creating economic policy paradigms. Two important paradigms of the twentieth century, the Keynesian and the monetarist, delivered conceptually contradictory perceptions of the role of the state in the economy. In the background, we can see the long-lasting effects of liberal economic thought (Keynes wished to reform the liberal approach to the economy). Later, the neo-liberal agenda developed into a pervasive principle that claimed exclusive influence in economics, economic policy, and education (see, e.g., Csaba 2009 and Stiglitz 2010).

The neo-liberal approach to the role of the state is fairly conservative and emphasizes the principle of minimal state. Due to strong pressure from the monetarist school starting in the mid-1980s, pervasive state intervention was scaled back drastically. Ronald Reagan's America and Margaret Thatcher's Britain took the lead in the liberalization and deregulation of markets. In Britain, massive privatization of state-owned companies also took place, and direct state intervention was curtailed. Similar policies were applied in many developed economies to a lesser extent. Moreover, international organizations (strongly influenced by the United States and its economic policy paradigm) suggested similar policies to countries with different levels of development and distinctive cultural and institutional heritages. "Minimal state" became the buzzword of the last two decades of the twentieth century. Liberalization, deregulation, and privatization was reinforced in many developing countries and emerging market economies, including the transition economies of Central and Eastern Europe (CEE).

This agenda produced a rather smooth development pattern in developed market economies. The period of "Great Moderation" from the 1990s to the 2007 financial crisis showed fairly stable and significant economic growth in the developed part of the world. One could conclude that the minimal state concept could work if proper market economic institutions effectively regulated markets and the economy in general. Warning signs of recurrent currency crises in Latin America and Southeast Asia were neglected due to the belief that, in the long run, the reasons for these problems could disappear if market institutions were properly developed. The concept was only slightly amended to consider local circumstances in the implementation of proposed policies. The fundamental goal of introducing the liberal market economy in every country remained unchanged.

The neo-liberal agenda also moved full steam ahead during the transition process in Central and Eastern Europe (CEE). The stabilization and modernization of Central European transition economies was based on these concepts. However, the pervasive economic decline of Russia during the Yeltsin era could not be considered a true success story. Yet, the chaos in the Russian economy did not shake mainstream economists' belief in the omnipotent minimal state concept (see Fukuyama 1992). It was shaken only by the 2007 financial crisis, which showed the limits of liberal market economic institutions' regulatory effect on the global economy.

Economic concepts were reconsidered in many countries after the 2008–09 global economic crisis. The devastating effects of the unexpected financial crisis could be mitigated only by massive state intervention. The meltdown of the global financial system was prevented through bailouts of the largest global financial institutions in the United States and Europe. Various techniques were applied, but the outcome was generally a massive increase of state ownership in the financial sector (see Voszka in Chapter 1). In some cases, "too big to fail" corporations received the same treatment. The myth of omnipotent self-regulating markets was destroyed. The state had to come back in for even the most developed advocates of the neo-liberal concept.

The starting point of this book is the state's rapidly increasing economic intervention. The revival of the state has been a general phenomenon in the world economy. However, this change has affected various regions and countries differently. The depth and direction of changes in policy concepts regarding direct state intervention has very much depended on historic and cultural heritage. While broad state intervention in the economy has had a long tradition in France (see Somai in Chapter 2), British and German traditions suggest a more rapid and potentially fuller retreat from state intervention (to take just two examples from the developed world). Emerging market economies in the Third World and also in CEE possessed much weaker market institutions and had already become rather skeptical about the application of the minimal state concept in their countries prior to the 2008–09 crisis. Most countries in these regions did not hesitate to take the now much easier opportunity to increase state economic intervention in the long term.

Diffusing empirical evidence of economic policies shows increasing diversity parallel with weakening neo-liberal principles. For example, the European Union continues to reinforce the paragraphs of the Maastricht Treaty in its neighborhood policy (e.g., in the Western Balkans), but meanwhile, a significant group of EU member states (with Hungary and Poland taking the lead) openly question the validity of the political and institutional fundamentals of the same agreement and try to prevent the application of the Treaty. State permeated economies (Nölke 2014, 2015) have emerged and played roles in the global division of labor that mainstream economic thought reserved only for highly developed economies (e.g., foreign direct investment). For decades, economic development in Africa could not be triggered successfully by policies recommended by mainstream international financial institutions but rather only by new policy approaches from the past decade that better understood and considered local realities (see Diao et al. 2017).

The interpretation of post-crisis development patterns is not at all straightforward. This is the reason for increased research interest in comparative economics. For example, the evolving concept of state capitalism (Nölke 2014 and Kurlantzick 2016) regards increased state intervention as the main driver of the current changes in the world economy. Recent studies on state capitalism emphasize not only the role of the state in economic coordination, but also the multifaceted interplay of social, political, and economic institutions affecting various dimensions of state activity.

The predecessors of this complex political economy approach (e.g., Nordhaus's political budget cycle) dealt with many issues that became fashionable research topics after the 2008-09 crisis. Yet, the early results were usually interpreted as variations of the basic model in comparison with the mainstream approaches. This has changed recently. Earlier research on the development of China, for example, repeatedly treated the Chinese model as a specific type of market economy. But it can be also regarded as a rather specific model, which is very far from any version of a Western market economic model described in the VoC literature. The Chinese themselves treat their economic and social development pattern as a unique model (e.g., Guangdong Xu 2015) that can serve as yardstick for other countries in the Third World. What remains clear, however, is the possibility of the parallel existence and development of several capitalist models that have their own internal logic, are not necessarily interchangeable, and should not be exported in a "one size fits all" manner. In this regard, the conceptualization in VoC literature that describes variations within the Western world's free market economic models requires further development.

Special interest has been devoted to increased state intervention in the economy, especially the increasing role of state-owned companies. Earlier, the VoC literature (based on the analytical framework laid down by Hall and Soskice 2001 and Amable 2003) did not tackle this issue. Analysis of the state's role was restricted mainly to market regulations, the size of the central budget, and the degree of income redistribution (see, e.g., Sapir 2006). Research on increased state intervention is in an early stage. Scholars concentrate on various aspects. Nölke (2014 and 2015) put the main emphasis on the development of globally successful national champion companies in large emerging market economies. In so doing, he concentrated on the technical dimensions of state intervention only in four large emerging market economies: Brazil, India, China, and South Africa (BICS). Kurlantzick (2016) compared countries with high shares of state-owned enterprises (SOEs) in GDP production (a rather heterogeneous group of countries that include, among others, Norway, Singapore, and Thailand).

State ownership is just one aspect of increasing state intervention. The current revival of the state in matters of the economy represents a rather complex systemic change that also involves changes in economic and market regulations, development policy, social policies. It also possesses strong linkages to political institutions. Therefore, the comprehensive political economy approach to the role of the state in the economy is applicable. An important aim of this book is to interpret increased state activity in various capitalist models within and beyond the countries usually covered in the VoC scholarship.

We can list some typical features that were frequently observed in countries where state involvement in the economy increased during the 2000s and especially after the 2008–09 crisis. In addition to the high share of SOEs in GDP production, Kurlantzick (2016) listed the general decline of free market policies (as listed by the Fraser Institute). Economic regulation in general became selective, discriminatory, and nationalist (about the advance of economic patriotism see also Gerőcs and Szanyi 2019). Selective policies thwart competition in selected markets, mainly in finance and banking, public utility services, energy, and the gas and oil industry and supply. These are branches of strategic importance from the political perspective: through manipulated prices, governments can successfully influence consumption. Imprints of state paternalism from the pre-Washington Consensus period are still strongly felt in many emerging market economies. Therefore, cheap public utility prices are important dimensions of political competition.

This of course also means a deliberate detour from the classic liberal democratic principles of political competition. Nordhaus (1975) developed the theory of the political budget cycles (PBC), a predecessor to the theory of economy-polity interactions of emerging market economies. The theory argued that average voters were short-sighted and learned slowly about negative long term impacts of excessive state spending in periods of election campaigns, after several elections. Thus, they provided opportunities for the manipulation of elections through excessive public spending. Though some empirical evidence (for a summary, see Halász 2014) suggested that over several election periods the effect might flatten because of social learning, the 2008–09 crisis seemed to reverse this tendency. Moreover, recent election campaigns showed an escalation of populism in highly developed countries of the world. Therefore, there is a worldwide departure from the classic liberal principle of economic and polity separation.

Because of these empirical facts, the analysis of state capitalism should not necessarily be limited to emerging market economies, which has been the case until now. Therefore, case studies of highly developed countries are also included in this volume.

Another important goal of increased state intervention is the development of national champions. These projects may also have important political implications because they increase national pride and boost the popularity of those politicians and governments who contribute to them. The economic development agenda is, of course, not new. Historic evidence (e.g., Somai in chapter 2 or Szanyi in chapter 8 of this volume) puts this motive into the broad context of core-periphery and developmental state literature (see Ricz in chapter 9). This ambition gained new impetus after the crisis. One important new feature is the changed international environment where large multinational enterprises increased entry barriers to most markets. It is therefore more difficult to successfully implement national champion development projects (some successful cases are covered in the third section of this volume). An open question in this context is country size. Large countries can allocate significantly more resources to typically state-owned national champions. Stable long-term financing of such projects is a primary condition of success. Nevertheless, the mounting evidence of unsuccessful cases calls for caution. Money alone cannot create miracles. On the other hand, there are also successful cases with small countries like Singapore (see Völgyi in chapter 10).

The long-term stability of national champions is connected to their successful integration in world trade. The well-known success stories of the East Asian developmental state model are based on international trade success and export-led growth patterns, among other things (see Ricz in chapter 9). The concept of economic patriotism is based on the temporary protection of all national firms in a given branch against global competition (Clift and Woll 2012). The idea is to enhance the accumulation of capital, expertise, and technological knowledge in national companies so they may become competitive internationally. Competition in the national market plays important role during the protected period, and after opening to world markets, also internationally; this is the infant industry development concept. More recent examples, like Chinese practices, are rather mixed concerning the role of competition in development policies.

National champion development programs, and excessive state ownership can fall easy prey of rent seeking too. Kurlantzick (2016) states that the success of state development programs very much depends on the level of corruption. No country is absolutely free of corruption, and there is a significant range of corruption levels displayed by state capitalist regimes, from Singapore, on the one hand, with very little state corruption, to many post-Soviet countries with high corruption levels on the other. Systemic corruption has many levels, but the most damage is caused by public procurement tenders directed to cronies. There is ample evidence from various countries of big government projects that cost several times more in public expenditure than similar projects in countries with better public and institutional controls on corruption. This practice highlights the danger that "elite enrichment becomes the primary purpose of state enterprises" (39). Besides SOEs, partisan firms' massive involvement in public procurement also raises worries about increasing corruption and the deteriorating efficiency in the usage of public money (see Szanyi in chapter 8). The second part of this volume deals with these issues using case studies from three transition economies in Central Europe.

Usually, the slow social learning described in PBC theory substantially deteriorated after the 2008–09 crisis. The Washington Consensus promised welfare returns attached to increasing political and economic freedoms that would favor the middle class. But voters' dissatisfaction with political freedom increased due to increasing inequalities. After the 2008–09 crisis, benefits realized by the middle class were also reduced. Increased state intervention therefore challenged the model of democracy and free market economics with promised welfare gains through increased state activity instead. This new attitude was perceived and welcomed by the societies of many countries as the revival of older paternalistic traditions. Changes in the perception of neo-liberal concepts were also reinforced by political elites who lacked a personal commitment to democracy and a free market economy. Kurlantzick (2016) listed many examples of elected political leaders-turned-autocrats who effectively rolled back democratic institutions with voters' support in order to strengthen their political positions. The robustly expanding state sector played a significant role in this process.

The short list of successful state led development models (mainly in East Asia) can not overshadow the potential flaws of excessive state intervention. These are connected to high levels of moral hazard, especially if business and polity relationships are not under institutional and social control. As was mentioned earlier, there have been many attempts to roll back democratic institutions in emerging market economies, and thus the danger of moral hazard is growing. There have been corruption scandals in many countries from China to Hungary to Brazil. Some of these cases reached the highest political circles, such as the imprisonment of former Brazilian president Lula. But besides corruption and outright theft, there is also widespread political rent seeking, like overspending on social welfare for political support (PBC) or on prestigious national programs like the World Cup or Olympic games (Brazil, Russia, South Korea). State-owned firms played an outstanding role in rent seeking and overspending.

This book concentrates on issues of public (mainly state) ownership as it relates to the economy-polity relationship. SOEs are the primary tools of market and price manipulation for political purposes. They can also be used for outright rent seeking. They play important roles in prestigious national development programs like major construction works and the organization of social or sporting events. Many of the national champions are also state owned. After the 2008–09 crisis, a general increase in public ownership was observed worldwide. Hence, the main support tool of state capitalist systems was present in countries with very different development levels and institutional systems. The main aim of the book is to highlight the differences in treating and using increased state property in various capitalist models. The national case studies will provide examples of successful state capitalist models (Singapore) and less impressive results (Brazil). They will also highlight the struggle between democratic institutions and interested political parties (Central European countries). In case of highly developed countries (the first part of the volume), state ownership did not significantly change the institutional framework of the liberal market economy model.

The approach of the book is fresh in a variety of ways. First, all of the case studies include substantial explanations of the cultural and institutional heritage of their chosen countries. This feature adds a new aspect to the existing VoC literature. We also would like to emphasize that the economic systems of countries in regions with heritages that differ from the classic Euro-Atlantic development paradigm cannot be regarded as variations of the mainstream capitalist model. The usual classifications that stem from the seminal works of Hall and Soskice (2001) or Amable (2003) cannot properly describe economic systems of other regions. Nölke (2014 and 2015) took an important first step in defining one of the alternative capitalist systems in large emerging market economies (state-permeated capitalism in BICS). However, this concept describes the usage of sophisticated new toolkits to enhance the economic convergence of economies in the periphery on the practice of only a few large emerging markets. But increased state intervention has been observed more generally and with potentially very different intentions and effects.

In my view, active state development policies pursued by BICS are best described by Clift and Woll's concept of economic patriotism (Clift and Woll 2012). In the age of globalization and the liberalized world, covert protection is provided. The concepts are old, and the toolkit is amended. However, BICS as well as many other countries increased state economic intervention for various political reasons. I believe that the types of policies that were placed in the foreground depended heavily on decision makers' political purposes ranging from economic development to the monopolization of political power. In these rather diverse aims and policies, the common denominator was state ownership. SOEs are crucial tools for achieving the most diverse political goals.

In the discussion of this topic, we will concentrate on the political relevance and effects of increased state ownership. The first section contains three case studies (France, Germany, Austria) from core Europe that highlight how stable democracies handled the problem of increased state ownership. The second section includes essays on three Central-European transition economies. The main theme in this section is the role of privatization in strengthening market institutions and the interplay between economy and polity, which was sharply altered after the 2008–09 crisis by increasing nationalization. The third section is about Third World countries and compares the classic success stories of catching-up (the East Asian developmental state model as illustrated by Singapore) with more recent and less successful attempts (Brazil and Turkey). Throughout the book, the role of state ownership is discussed mainly in relation to various political goals. Although we do not intend to provide a thorough definition or description of the state capitalist model, all of the essays contribute to a better understanding of some of the most common features in the field of economy-polity interplay.

The main hypothesis of the book is that the weakening of the neoclassical paradigm after the 2008–2009 crisis and the resulting increase in state intervention affected countries with different economic and democratic development levels differently. The social control and institutional embeddedness of the competition state concept prevented more developed countries from directly slipping into more autocratic system solutions. In countries with weaker and less traditional market economic and democratic political institutions, erosion of these has begun. Emerging state capitalist systems used increased state ownership for their own political legitimation and rent seeking. SOEs can be developed into globally competitive national champions, and they can participate in politically-motivated, large development projects. They can also serve political rent seeking (in new forms of state paternalism) and the enrichment of influential political lobbies. The balance between social goals and personal or partisan goals also depends on the strength of social control. Stronger control will encourage policies targeting more social goals that serve political self-interests (e.g., reelection) indirectly through rising popularity. This effect is not much different than the excessive budgetary spending of PBC. However, the deliberate rolling back of social institutions and increasing populism works in the opposite direction, giving way to more direct forms of rent seeking. This book has collected case studies that test these processes and assumptions.

REFERENCES

Amable, Bruno. 2003. *The Diversity of Modern Capitalism*. Oxford: Oxford University Press.
Clift, Ben, and Cornelia Woll. 2012. "Economic Patriotism: Reinventing Control over Open Markets." *Journal of European Public Policy* 19 (3): 307–23.
Csaba, László. 2009. "Orthodoxy, Renewal and Complexity in Contemporary Economics." *Zeitschrift für Staats- und Europawissenschaften* 7 (1): 51–82.
Diao, Xinshen, Kenneth Harttgen, and Margaret N. McMillan. 2017. "The Changing Structure of Africa's Economies." Policy Research Working Paper 7958. The World Bank.
Fukuyama, Francis. 1992. *The End of History and the Last Man*. London: Penguin.
Gerőcs, Tamás, and Miklós Szanyi. 2019. *Market Liberalism and Economic Patriotism in the Capitalist World-System*. London: Palgrave MacMillan.
Halász, Ágnes. 2014. "Political Budget Cycles: An Empirical Analysis on Hungary." In *Crisis in the West and the East: Economic Governance in Times of Challenge*, edited by István Benczes, 184–204. Vienna: Wiener Verlag für Sozialforschung.
Hall, Peter A., and David Soskice, eds. 2001. *Varieties of Capitalism: The Institutional Foundations of Comparative Advantage*. Oxford: Oxford University Press.
Kornai, János. 2016. "The System Paradigm Revisited: Clarification and Additions in the Light of Experiences in the Post-Socialist Region." *Acta Oeconomica* 66 (4): 547–96.
Kurlantzick, Joshua. 2016. *State Capitalism: How the Return of Statism Is Transforming the World*. New York: Oxford University Press.
Nordhaus, William D. 1975. "The Political Business Cycle." *Review of Economic Studies* 42 (2): 169–90.
Nölke, Andreas. 2015. "Domestic Structures, Foreign Economic Policies and Global Economic Order: Implications from the Rise of Large Emerging Economies." *European Journal of International Relations* 21 (3): 538–67.
———, ed. 2014. *Multinational Corporations from Emerging Markets: State Capitalism 3.0*. Basingstoke: Palgrave MacMillan.

Sapir, André. 2006. "Globalization and the Reform of European Social Models." *Journal of Common Market Studies* 44 (2): 369–90.
Stiglitz, Joseph. 2010. "Needed: A New Economic Paradigm." *Financial Times*, August 19.
Xu, Guangdong. 2015. "The Institutional Foundations of China's Unbalanced Economy." *Europa-Asia Studies* 67 (9): 1351–70.

CHAPTER 1
Crisis Management in Europe: Nationalizations and Privatizations

ÉVA VOSZKA

In the years following the 2008 crisis, the developed countries of Europe experienced a massive wave of nationalization. At the same time, a wave of privatization began, but on a smaller scale than in the preceding decades. This paper analyzes the drivers and movements of this complex process. It reveals how quiet and hidden privatization techniques became increasingly important, while nationalizations also took place discreetly, without attracting much publicity or even without statistical review. As part of this process, along with the fortification and foreign expansion of state-owned entities and funds, a new type of public ownership emerged, which, by disregarding the intentions of governments in destination countries, may significantly differ from its traditional form in terms of its operation, objectives, and impact. All of this plays a role in blurring the boundaries between public and private ownership and nationalization and privatization. The dichotomous approach is, therefore, worthy of replacement by new analytical methods.

In spite of the long wave of privatization in the past decades, state ownership has remained significant both in the developed countries of Europe and globally. In 2008–9, the scope of state ownership broadened spectacularly before the sale of some smaller and larger entities, which took place in the years that followed.[1] However, this was just a milestone on a long and twisting path, "one of endless adventures" (Lewis 1965). How

---

[1] An earlier version of this paper analyzing the case of the U.S. and also some economic policy issues appeared in *Annals of Public and Cooperative Economics* (Voszka 2017).

should we interpret the changes of this period and the opposite processes of privatization and nationalization occurring simultaneously?

This paper, focusing on developed regions of Europe, puts the developments of the post-crisis management into historico-institutional context. It also draws attention to some new and unusual characteristics of ownership changes. It argues that although privatization as well as nationalization seems to be useful tools to address crisis-related restructuring needs, many decades of experience have shown the disadvantages of both of them. That is why both the expansion and contraction of state ownership became unpopular, and forced politicians to strike the right balance between short-term constraints and once generally accepted principles.

The first part of the essay presents the size of state ownership in developed European countries, and provides a short summary of major developments leading to the current situation. After this, the essay turns to an investigation of the crisis-related nationalizations and privatizations. All along, we must keep in mind that, beyond basic European trends, each country has its own distinct pattern.

The Function of State Ownership and Its Historical Changes

In Europe, public ownership had been growing steadily since the nineteenth century, especially in the years immediately after 1914. This process, covering several countries in more or less harmonized waves, intensified during the two World Wars, the Great Depression, post-1945 reconstruction, and the oil crisis of the 1970s.[2]

In its early days, the rise of public ownership in Europe was linked with the concept of the developmental state, the most important objectives of which were to supplement scarce private capital, build infrastructure as well as markets, and, in several cases—most spectacularly in Germany and Italy—create a unified nation state (Millward 2011). As a general rule, state ownership became widespread in public services, transportation, and—in order to finance all of this, especially in the continent's less developed countries—financial institutions.

Later, in peacetime, the state appeared as an alternative to the market, able to correct market failures. The target system became more complex,

---

[2] For a concise history of nationalizations, see, e.g., Aharoni (1986), Toninelli (2000), Millward (2011), and Voszka (2018).

comprising efforts that sought to: mitigate unfavorable effects related to private ownership and monopolies; reduce negative externalities; help under-developed regions; improve employment; and drive down prices. During years of economic crises, sustaining the economy, saving banks and companies from bankruptcy, and reducing unemployment had been turned into justification for even more state ownership, which was expanding across economic sectors considered to be strategic, as well as part of the manufacturing industry.[3]

Hence, state ownership was destined to meet a multitude of often-conflicting objectives. According to contemporary and ex-post facto analyses, governments considered it to be a panacea, a remedy for all of the evils of capitalism (Ward 1946; Aharoni 1986). In times of wars and crises, as well as during the emergence of welfare states, one could assist with the expansion of public property, which went hand-in-hand with the state's growing role and the strengthening of market regulation.

At the turn of the 1970s and 1980s, when state ownership probably reached its apex, the public sector accounted for an average of 12 percent of GDP in developed countries of Europe by Shirley's estimate (1983).[4] Data, however, are—as also observed in her paper —incomplete and far from reliable, as the definition and registration of, and accounting system for public property differ from country to country. Hence, the table below only provides a rough estimate of the importance of the public sector in the economy.

Table 1
Share of non-financial SOEs (state-owned enterprises) in the economy of some European countries, at the turn of the 1970s and 1980s (percent)

Country	GDP	GFCF	Employment (excl. agric.)
Portugal	25.0	52.0	12.0
France	17.0	12.1	–
Austria	14.5	19.2	–
Sweden	14.4^x	11.4	3.4
United Kingdom	10.9^{xx}	17.0	8.5
Germany	10.2^{xxx}	10.8	4.2

---

[3] A fine summary of objectives can be found in, e.g., Aharoni (1986), Vickers and Wright (1989a), Megginson and Netter (2003).
[4] Financial enterprises are excluded.

Country	GDP	GFCF	Employment (excl. agric.)
Ireland	8.0	11.8	8.8
Italy	7.4	15.2	2.5
Denmark	6.3	–	2.6
Belgium	6.0 xxxx	13.1	7.5
Spain	4.1	15.6	...
The Netherlands	3.6	12.6	1.1
Average of developed countries of Europe	12	–	–

Note: Most data relate to the period of 1978–81
x 1982 data, only referring to central state level (Carlsson 1988)
xx Financial enterprises included. By the account of Parris (1985), it does not contain non-corporate entities (e.g., of local public services), or those having the same legal status as private companies.
xxx Data corrected on the basis on Pontusson (1989) referring to IMF data.
xxxx 1961 data, not comprising local governments' interests (Langer 1966)
Source: own composition based on Shirley (1983); data for Portugal comes from The Library of Congress (1993)

In spite of uncertainties, we can ascertain that there was a wide range of state-owned enterprises' (SOE) share of GDP in individual countries: between 4 and 25 percent of GDP; 10 and 52 percent of gross fixed capital formation (GFCF), and 1 and 12 percent of employment. State ownership was most significant in Portugal for all examined indicators,[5] with France, Austria, Sweden, the United Kingdom, and Germany also claiming top positions. At the other end of the spectrum are Spain and the Netherlands. Differences may be explained partly by socio-cultural heritage or specific factors.

In France, the state has intervened in the economy for centuries. The relationship between government and business, which was also based on the common cultural background of public and corporate elites, has always been strong. The first state owned manufactures were developed in the seventeenth century through the initiative of Louis XIV's powerful finance minister, Jean-Baptiste Colbert. Later, public ownership increased in waves following the Great Depression, both World Wars, and—as a deviation from trends in Europe—at the beginning of the 1980s. In this

---

[5] Finland was not included in the survey and comparable statistics were not available. According to Willner's data (2003), before the big wave of privatization, SOEs represented an 18–22 percent share in industrial value added, and 12–15 percent in industrial employment, which leads us to the assumption that Finland occupied a prominent place in the ranking at the time.

latter moment, it embraced approximately 3000 companies producing almost one-fourth of French GDP (Somai 2017). In Austria, public companies (of which three big banks) produced one-fifth of the national economic output even before the Anschluss. After 1945, both firms founded by the Germans and Austrian businesses they had previously acquired were made public. The goal was to prevent Soviet ownership (Kőrösi 2016). In nineteenth-century Germany, greater state involvement in the economy had been regarded as a key factor in the catching up process; public ownership (i.e., the creation of a common infrastructure) also enabled the creation of the unified nation-state. Public arms companies established during World War One, were joined by new ones following the Great Depression. Although in Germany no extensive nationalization took place after World War Two, a significant proportion of industrial production came from the six huge groups of companies that were mainly involved in heavy industry and operated with the government as the majority shareholder. Besides central state ownership, the role of federal states remained substantial (Naszádos 2017). In contrast, the U.K. initially had relatively few public properties due to their free market traditions. Following some large-scale nationalizations in the oil and electricity industries at the beginning of the twentieth century, public ownership became significant only after 1945, and covered all strategic sectors (Aharoni 1986; Millward 2000).

In the shadow of consecutive waves of nationalization, privatization also appeared, but remained sporadic for a long time. The change of direction occurred as a consequence of the failure in crisis management at the turn of the 1970s and 1980s. At that time, in order to save companies and preserve jobs, a majority of European states resorted to further nationalizations. Nevertheless, this led to a sharp rise in both losses and subsidies and, therefore, a deterioration of macroeconomic balances, while the state remained unable to cope either with the rising prices or recession. This is why the big wave of privatization was launched—first in England where expanded public ownership was the furthest from the traditionally free market conception of the economy—and lasted, with varying intensity, as late as 2008.

The goals of the process were still multifaceted and controversial. Some of them related to political ideology, like strengthening market orientation at the expense of state intervention, depoliticizing the economy, boosting private ownership (democratizing ownership), and expanding electorate for the parties in power. Other goals related to the economy, such as remedying government failures, enhancing economic restructuration and modernization, improving corporate governance and companies' competitiveness, reducing budget subsidies and risk, and restoring financial equilibrium.[6] All this means that governments' deemed privatizations accompanied by the opening of market and deregulation to be a comprehensive solution for all difficulties, just as in the case of earlier nationalizations.

During the big wave of privatization that took place between 1977 and 2004, Western Europe emerged as a leader in sales, and it was responsible for nearly half of global revenues and almost one-third of all transactions (Bortolotti and Milella 2006). However, differences between the individual countries remained significant.

Table 2
Privatization performance in Western Europe, 1977–2002

	Total number of privatizations	Revenues (USD Bn)	Revenues/ GDP (%)	SOE/GDP (%)	Revenues/SOE
Portugal	78	25.4	19	15	1.87
United Kingdom	183	145.5	11	11	1.40
The Netherlands	29	19.2	4	6	1.15
Spain	74	46.6	6	9	1.01
Italy	103	96.4	8	9	0.86
Germany	150	73.3	3	10	0.79
Sweden	56	18.6	6	10	0.73
Belgium	10	5.7	2	4	0.69
Austria	51	11.5	4	14	0.52
France	97	59.9	3	11	0.48
Finland	56	16.3	10	–	–
Average	81	47.1	7	9	0.95

Notes:
In USD 1995 values.
Revenues: total revenues cumulated within the investigated period.
Revenues/GDP: the ratio of total revenues cumulated in the period up to 2002 GDP.
SOE/GDP is the ratio of SOEs' value added to GDP reported the year before the first privatization.
As for the uncertainty of data, the authors themselves draw attention to it.
Source: own calculation based on Bortolotti-Milella (2006)

---

[6] For a good overview of the objectives of privatization, see e.g., Aharoni (1986), Yarrow (1986), Vickers and Wright (1989a), Toninelli (2000), Megginson and Netter (2003), and Parker (2003).

The study cited in Table 2 deserves special attention as—unlike the usual approach—it also includes the initial size of public assets.[7] On this basis, countries can be grouped into categories according to the size and accomplishment of privatization.

Table 3
Relationship between the magnitude of public assets and that of privatization

		Initial size of state assets	
		big (greater than or equal to 10% of GDP)	small (less than 10% of GDP)
The magnitude of privatization	big (revenues greater than 1% of public assets)	"big privatizers": Portugal United Kingdom	"countries of selling-out" Netherlands Spain
	small (revenues smaller than 0.8% of public assets)	"reluctant countries": France Austria Germany Sweden	"moderate privatizer": Belgium

Source: Calculated on the basis of Bortolotti-Milella (2006)

In Table 3, "big privatizers" emerge as one of the main types, represented here by the United Kingdom and Portugal, which considerably reduced their huge state assets. The group of "reluctant countries" consists of France and Austria, and, less justifiably, Germany and Sweden, which sold relatively few of their large shares. As for the two other groups, the Netherlands and Spain sold out the majority of their relatively small assets, while Belgium, the "moderate privatizer," generated small revenues from the sale of its shares in small public sector.[8]

---

[7] Although the economic incorrectness of the "assets-to-GDP ratio" had been pointed out by several studies, this remains, for the simple reason of data accessibility, one of the most commonly used indicators. (To measure SOEs, value added or revenues from privatization or costs of nationalizations to GDP are all less problematic.) One the one hand, indices calibrated to GDP can only mitigate, rather than eliminate the effects of changes in assets' value. On the other hand, their advantage is to make comparisons in space and time more robust by negating both size differences between countries and the impact of inflation. Therefore, wherever possible, we will disclose this (asset-to-GDP) indicator in addition to those in absolute terms at current prices.

[8] The rest of the countries cannot, either for lack of data or overpassing the thresholds, be put in any of these categories displaying extreme cases.

Cross-country differences are influenced by institutional and historical conditions (i.e., state system, political structure, constitutional characteristics, closeness of relations between cabinet and companies, attitudes of voters towards central government and public ownership), and by prevailing economic and political circumstances: the degree of imbalance or growth, the need for restructuring, the strength of the central executive, and the balance of forces between stakeholders supporting and opposing the administration (e.g., opposition parties, trade unions, SOEs' CEOs, public opinion).[9] The more the government perceives that there are strong short-term economic constraints and pressure coming from supporters, the more they feel urged to make firm decisions. Obviously, these decisions are simpler to adopt and consistently execute if governments may rely on a comfortable majority and do not have to bargain with their coalition partners (see, e.g., the position of the British cabinet, which was also bolstered by the successful outcome of the Falklands War, versus that of the Belgian one). It is easier to proceed when the political structure is built on cooperation rather than a sharp rivalry between parties (e.g., in Austria and the Netherlands versus Germany), or when everything is in the central governments' hands rather than dispersed among different levels of administration, creating a situation in which the cabinet has to reach agreement with regional or local authorities (e.g., in France versus Germany). Privatization is easier if you can sell state assets without having to dismantle constitutional safeguards (e.g., as in Spain, Portugal, France or Germany), and if public companies are not as narrowly interwoven with political parties as, for instance, in Italy or Austria. It is also helpful if both constituents and businessmen keep distance from the state as in Britain, rather than cultivating close ties with it (as in France or Austria). Possibilities are also dependent upon the composition of the state's property portfolio: it is easier to privatize companies in the manufacturing sector than monopolies in public services. The same holds true for profitable, market-oriented subsidiaries of some huge corporations versus large entities working under the direct control of a Ministry.

Despite the long-standing process of privatization, the state has remained an important player globally in the field of corporate ownership. According to 2014 data (OECD 2016), 326 out of the 2000 biggest companies in the world had the government as a majority or minority

---

[9] These aspects are detailed in Vickers and Wright (1989b), Boix (1997), Bortolotti-Pinotti (2003), Bortolotti and Milella (2006).

shareholder. Although only twenty-six of them were of European (French, German, Italian and British) origin, while one-third of them were Chinese. But as we will see, the size of other regions' public property, as well as the "hows" and "whys" of its rapid expansion, are not irrelevant for the EU.[10] In 2012, public assets represented over 10 percent of GDP and the sector made up 3.5 percent of the labor force, in developed countries of Europe (Table 4).

Table 4
SOEs' weight in EU's old member states in 2012

Country	Number of companies	Employees/total employees (%)	Asset value/GDP (%)
Finland	53	9.7	67.3
Sweden	52	4.7	35.0
Belgium	12	3.2	34.1
Ireland	25	2.4	19.4
France	68	10.0	14.2
Italy	17	2.4	14.1
Austria	11	3.0	10.9
The Netherlands	26	1.0	9.9
Denmark	19	1.5	8.3
Greece	56	5.0	6.8
United Kingdom	18	1.5	5.8
Germany	75	2.8	4.6
Portugal	84	4.1	3.5
Spain	55	0.6	1.0
Average of old EU Members	41	3.5	10.5

Source: For SOEs: OECD (2012); For employment: Eurostat http://appsso.eurostat.ec.europa.eu/nui/show.do
For GDP: http://appsso.eurostat.ec.europa.eu/nui/submitViewTableAction.do, and
https://data.oecd.org/gdp/gdp-long-term-forecast.htm#indicator-chart

---

[10] In the list of Fortune's Global 500, during the period between 2003–2014, the share of publicly owned companies has increased from 9 to 23 percent, which was due mainly to China (PWC 2015).

Data contained in Table 4, even if more detailed than other sources', are only a snapshot of the situation, and, to our knowledge, there are no long-term data series comparable to them. If we take a look at earlier data (Table 1), the regional average ratio of public property to GDP appears to have risen back to its prevailing level at the turn of the 1970s and 1980s. At that time, it was 12 percent, and in 2012, it was 10.5 percent. The comparison is, however, distorted by uncertainties in both data collection and data management methods, which is also a problem for more recent figures.

OECD data are of a smaller magnitude than those cited in the country case studies of our volume. Somai (2017), referring to the French statistical office, claims that 1632 French firms were under state control at the end of 2014, while the OECD only reported on 68 companies. In Austria, according to Kőrösi's sources, state, provinces, and municipalities have shares in approximately 3,500 firms, versus the 11 that appear in the international survey. For the last twenty years, the state has constantly maintained around 40 percent of shareholdings in Austrian economy either directly or indirectly through the banking system (Kőrösi 2016, 15). Naszádos (2017), referring to another OECD paper (2011), writes that in Germany, there were 15,127 public companies (most of them in the hands of the municipalities), 111 of which had majority or minority state ownership, *versus* 75 in Table 4. According to Biedermann, Orosz, and Szijártó (2017), there are 70 public companies in Italy (as opposed to the 17 indicated by OECD) representing 27 percent in total sales, and 19 percent of employment. The above differences may arise from differences in definitions and data records. We mention here just two examples. The first one is about the giant companies that provide French postal and telecommunication services. They only appeared in the register of SOEs transformation from administrative entities into independent public companies. This increased the number of public employees by more than 400,000 and their share of total employment to 8 percent (Somai 2017). Likewise, the Austrian state railways were reported to be part of the public sector until 1993, after which they were transformed into a holding company, and then fully privatized (Kőrösi 2016). Assuming national statistics to be close to reality, the weight of the public sector as reported in international sources is still significantly underestimated. Those sources can, at most and only with reservations, provide some clues for cross-country comparisons.

Longer-term data sets are further biased, in that statistics and commonly used indices cannot separate the impact of an increase in state ownership from that of stock price fluctuations. Finally, indicators for 2012 reflect not only the effects of nationalizations, but also those of post-2008 asset sales, which were significant in many countries.

Crisis Management by Nationalizations

According to global data, there was a jump in nationalizations in 2008 and 2009, amounting to a value of $270 and $325 billion in these two years respectively, as compared with the average of $53 billion in the previous two decades.[11] Beyond absolute figures, in order to obtain a better comparison, it is worth looking at indices expressed in terms of GDP. Calculated by either method, the majority of global growth came from Europe and the United States.

Table 5
Growth in state ownership from 2008 to 2012

	Nationalizations (in USD bn)	In percentage points of GDP 2012
Globally	1010	1.35
of which in USA	356	2.20
of which in EU	390	2.26

Source: For nationalizations in the U.S. see: TARP (2016); for nationalizations in the EU: author's estimation. See for for GDP data (based on December 2012 EUR/USD exchange rate): http://data.worldbank.org/indicator/NY.GDP.MKTP.CD?end=2015&start=1960&view=chart.

In Europe as well as overseas, the bulk of nationalizations took place in the financial sector.[12]

Saving the banks

Fearing a total meltdown of the financial system and a decline in the economy to a level unprecedented for decades, and also referring to lessons learned from the Great Depression, banks that got into trouble were systematically saved in developed countries. As a combined effect of the

---

[11] Calculation based on Megginson (2013).
[12] Hereafter, for the sake of brevity, the term "banks" is often used. But it always relates to the whole financial sector.

subprime mortgage crisis—spreading quickly in the globalized system—the liquidity shortfall, and recession, even those financial institutions that could not to be blamed for having purchased a massive amount of "toxic assets" were shaken. Thus, it became important to stop the contagion and avoid the domino effect.

In 2007, at the beginning of the crisis, several financial institutions in Europe—like those of the United States—tried to solve their problems by raising private capital. Then governments attempted to enhance mergers, which resulted in ever higher subsidies and ultimately nationalizations rather than success stories.[13] It quickly became obvious that, at a time of market turmoil, capital shortage could only be overcome and market confidence could only be restored with public funds.

Decisions on grants were taken by national governments, but these also had to be approved by the EU's competition authority on the basis of European rules of procedure. By upholding the fundamental principles of EU competition law, the Commission stated that the assistance should, in general, be exceptional and of temporary nature; that the institutions in question, as well as their owners, should contribute to bearing the costs; furthermore, that it is important to limit competition distortions through, for example, restraining expansion or setting up strict requirements for reorganization (European Commission 2009a). The framework for state aid measures to support bailouts was set at €5.763 trillion, 44 percent of the EU's 2013 GDP. Just over one quarter of these funds were used as guarantees, liquidity measures, impaired assets measures and recapitalizations (European Commission Directorate-General for Competition 2014).

From the perspective of nationalizations, recapitalizations are of special interest, for nationalization had not originally been listed as an approved method for rescuing banks. This option was only tolerated by the Commission starting in early 2009, after several precedents had occurred in member states (European Commission 2009b).[14] However, no particular rules of procedure or criteria for decision making were prescribed. In practice nationalizations had been interlinked with other forms of state assistance.

This "hidden nationalization" involved an increase in capital and the purchase of impaired assets. It often took the form of acquiring preferential, non-voting shares with extra rights, or other securities which could

---

[13] See details in Voszka (2017).
[14] Besides, the Union generally upholds the principle of neutrality in the ownership of companies. Hence, the power of determining and changing the ownership structure is reserved to the nation-states.

then become convertible into freely negotiable shares, that is, shares that would be available also for the banks themselves to buy back.[15] Due to the manifest reticence in using this method, the Union has never even published any summary statistics on the size of nationalizations, hence the need for estimation.

One of our methods of estimation consists of approximating the upper limit through capital injection, and the lower one through a sum of individual decisions. When determining the maximum value, our point of departure was the supposition that, although recapitalization was not necessarily followed by ownership changes, public property usually emerged through recapitalization after 2008. From the €821 billion originally approved for this aid scheme, €448 billion was used (Table 6), which thus indicates the maximum extent of bank nationalization. Table 6 shows high regional concentration: half of the recapitalization came from three member states and over 90 percent from ten. Country differences might be explained by the size of the economy and the banking system, along with the depth of involvement in the turbulence and some other special features.[16]

Table 6
EU member states using the highest capital injections, in 2008–2013
(Countries using amounts higher than €10 billion)

Countries	Capital injection (€ bn)	As a percentage of 2013 GDP
United Kingdom	100.1	5.0
Germany	64.2	2.3
Ireland	62.8	38.3
Spain	61.9	6.1
Greece	40.9	22.4
France	25.1	1.2
Belgium	23.3	6.1

---

[15] A similar method was in use in the United States as well. See it in detail in Voszka (2017).

[16] In the EU's new member states for example, banks had only sporadically been bailed out by governments, owing to the low level of contamination by toxic assets in their portfolios and the peculiarities of their ownership structure. Here it was the foreign parent banks that helped out their subsidiaries located outside the Eurozone—the notable exception being Slovenia, where financial institutions had primarily been in domestic hands.

Countries	Capital injection (€ bn)	As a percentage of 2013 GDP
The Netherlands	23.0	3.8
Austria	11.1	3.5
Denmark	10.8	4.3
Total of the 10 countries	423.2	4.4
EU 27	448.2	3.4

Source: European Commission Directorate-General for Competition (2014), GDP: http://ec.europa.eu/eurostat/tgm/refreshTableAction.do?tab=table&plugin=1&pcode=tec00001&language=en.

Nominal amounts are highest in the U.K. and Germany, the countries with the largest financial sectors, and those that are also the most tightly connected to U.S. security markets. A special feature in Germany is the federal states' *(Bundesländer)* extensive ownership, which reached 40 percent of pre-crisis banking assets (Hüfner 2010). Most banks owned by these states *(Landesbanken)* hoarded toxic assets and were badly in need of government assistance. Other German financial institutions were also nationalized. Ireland—a country highly ranked by the GDP-related index—saw its financial institutions, saddled with toxic assets, in urgent need of state aid immediately after the escalation of the crisis; four of the country's six largest banks had to be nationalized. State ownership in the banking sector is significant also in Greece, which holds the second position in the abovementioned index, and, even if to a lesser extent, in Spain, although these countries had barely been hit by the mortgage crisis. For them, this was the second wave of the crisis, which came as a shock. Meanwhile, stress tests, the reassessment of capital adequacy on a regular basis, also stimulated recapitalization, which under the prevailing market conditions could only mostly be financed from public sources.

At the end of 2008, Greek banks were stabilized with a package of emergency state aid worth €28 billion, while there was no nationalization until 2011 (Visvizi 2012). But when financial institutions, which already had to suffer the effects of resource shortages and deep recession, also had to agree to a more than 50 percent cut of Greek government bonds in their portfolios, nationalization became inevitable. In 2012, the second bailout scheme for Greece included a bank recapitalization package worth €48 billion, 27.5 billion of which was earmarked to support the four biggest banks (European Commission Directorate-General for Economic and Financial Affairs 2013). Three of them—the National Bank of Greece, Alpha and Piraeus—were able to raise 10 percentage of new equity from private investors, thus avoiding falling under majority state control. The Eurobank failed to do so, and the state, thanks to a capital injection of €5.8 billion, gained almost full ownership of it (Hellenic Financial Stability Fund 2014). The prudent operation of traditionally well-capitalized Spanish banks had been loosened during the real estate boom, but problems were swept under the rug, first by concealing the losses and then via mergers and budgetary subsidies (The EU 2012). By 2012, public assistance for the recapitalization of Spanish financial institutions became imperative, a project to which the European Union had given €100 billion. Four major loss-producing banks, accounting for one-quarter of the Spanish banking sector and having lost most of their equity, were nationalized.[17]

As a contrast, in France, thanks above all to structural and regulatory peculiarities, only a little money had to be spent on rescuing financial institutions. Here, a concentrated banking system emerged from the context of large-scaled privatizations in the 1990s. Apart from relatively strict public control, the common cultural (i.e., educational and civil service) backgrounds of the banks' top executives has also played a role in those companies' involvement in relatively few risky businesses and, cautiousness about derivatives. (Somai 2017).

Our estimations of the lower limit of nationalizations were based on individual decisions of the Union's competition authority regarding the recapitalization of nearly one hundred financial institutions. This was facilitated by the fact that the concentration of recapitalization was high not only regionally, but also on the level of individual banks. More than half of the €448 billion was allocated to just 17 beneficiaries.

To give a couple of examples: more than one member state took part in rescuing Fortis and Dexia. The financial situation of the latter, established by a merger of Belgian and French banks in 1996, became aggravated by its American subsidiary FSA and a multi-billion loan to the troubled German-Irish bank Depfa. Later in 2011, Dexia had to post a loss of €4 billion after writing down the value of its Greek debt. The bank was split up, with the Belgian state taking over the part of the business operating on its territory for €4 billion, while French banks purchasing smaller parts. The remaining troubled assets were placed in a "bad bank," covered by a guarantee of €90 billion by the states concerned (Second 2008; Dalton and Gauthier-Villars 2011). As for Fortis, its liquidity position was weakened following the acqui-

---

[17] Fondo de Reestructuración Ordenada, available at http://www.frob.es/es/Documents/20141223Presentaci%C3%B3n%20FROB%20prot.pdf.

sition of Dutch ABN AMRO in 2007, bloated—as it became obvious later on—with toxic assets. This was a take-over mounted, after fierce price competition, by a member of a consortium together with Spanish Santander and the Royal Bank of Scotland (RBS), which also got into trouble because of this deal (RBS 2007). Valued at more than a hundred billion Euros, this was the world's biggest bank takeover at the time. A year later, the governments of Belgium, the Netherlands, and Luxemburg had to save the bank, but this time it had to disburse only €11 billion altogether, in exchange for a 49 percent stake each in the three different subsidiaries of Fortis that were in their respective jurisdictions. For a further €13 billion, the Dutch government became the 100 percent owner of the Dutch business of Fortis, including its ABN AMRO business (Netherlands 2008).

The abovementioned cases of bank bailouts were not the most complicated ones. The bailout process of Hypo Real Estate (HRE) holding entailed seven rounds of approval of the Commission's competition authority from autumn 2008 to 2011 (Buder et al. 2011). The problems of HRE also got worse due to a 2007 acquisition of the originally Prussian Depfa Bank, which had been relocated into Ireland in the 1990s. HRE—just like RBS and Dexia—finally received more support than the whole Spanish banking sector Keeping these big entities afloat proved to be more expensive than the controversial first Greek rescue package.

When looking closely at this narrower group, we found that for institutions receiving the highest support, capital injection meant effective nationalization.[18] Adding the cost of nationalization of the relatively smaller Greek and Spanish banks to the sum of €253 billion injected into the 17 big banks, we can price European bank nationalizations at a minimum of €296 billion.

As another method of estimation, we used the Eurostat dataset about the impact of government interventions to support financial institutions on budget deficits and public debt (European Commission Eurostat 2016). From the expenditure lines of the statistical tables derived from member states' reports, we summarized those concerning capital investments (e.g., capital increases), other capital transfers (e.g., purchases of shares), and other expenditures (including special government bodies like "bad banks") for the period between 2007 and 2015. In this case, we can only give approximate estimates, because the data are not about the increase of public ownership, and furthermore, the content of the cells, as it is also clear from the member states' notes, is often ambiguous.

---

[18] See details in Voszka (2017).

Table 7
State capital investment in EU member states from 2007 to 2013
(€ billion)

	2008	2009	2010	2011	2012	2013	Total
United Kingdom							53.1[x]
Germany	3.7	4.0	34.4	2.5	4.6	1.9	51.1
Ireland	0	4.0	35.4	7.3	0.6	0.5	47.8
Spain	0	0	0.4	5.1	39.1	3.0	47.6
Greece	0	0	0	0.4	9.4	21	30.8
Austria	0	2.7	0.7	1.7	1.6	2.0	8.7
Belgium	0	0	0	0.8	2.9	5.0	8.7
The Netherlands	0	2.2	1.0	0.04	0.03	1.3	4.6
Portugal	0	0	1.8	0.6	0.9	0.7	4.0
Slovenia	0	0	0	0.2	0.06	3.6	3.9
Denmark	0	0	0	2.5	0.3	0.2	3.0
France	0	0	0	0	2.6	0	2.6
Bulgaria							0.9
Latvia	0	0.2	0.4	0.1	0.1	0	0.8
Cyprus	0	0	0	0	0.1	0	0.1
Lithuania	0	0	0.03	0	0	0.09	0.1
Luxemburg	0.03	0	0	0	0	0	0.0
Total of 17 countries							**267.8**

[x] until 2015

Note: In ten member states, there was no such expenditure in the scrutinized period. For countries outside the Eurozone, whose data were available in national currencies, we only displayed a total amount using the average exchange rate of the year with the highest expenditure.
Source: author's calculation based on European Commission Eurostat data (2016)

The figure in the "Total of 17 countries" line of Table 7 only slightly differs from the one we arrived at by our first minimum estimation method. This confirms that our calculations are, by and large, correct: bank nationalizations in Europe roughly cost somewhere between €300 and €400 billion.

Nationalization as an ultimate solution was, unlike in previous times, unpopular in many European countries. People did not consider it to be a matter of public interest. They rather interpreted it as a way of rescuing the financial elites and socializing their losses. The process was no triumph for other affected parties either. Management was generally removed, their bonuses limited, and high remunerations dropped throughout the sector. Governments acquired non-voting preference shares in some cases, but in others, they received the right to veto, and their representatives appeared on boards. Shareholders and creditors had to write off a certain proportion of their claims. States acquired banks' assets mainly at low prices, devalued to a fraction of their pre-crisis worth. Or it was the nationalization itself, which caused falling share prices. Therefore original owners often debated the methods and compensation levels applied.

Rules for restructuring were strict and required the banks to repay state aid (with all premiums and accumulated interest) by predetermined deadlines, and, partly in order to do so, to sell branches and subsidiaries, close offices, terminate hundreds and thousands of employees, reduce costs, assets, and balance sheets, and forbid acquisitions. For example, the Union's competition authority prescribed the breaking up of three big banks out of the 17 top beneficiaries. Several giant banks had to sell their subsidiaries; six of them were forced to cut back their balance sheet by 40 to 60 percent; and one of them by 85 percent. The fulfillment of these obligations was strictly controlled by authorities (Voszka 2017).

New ways of nationalization?

In Europe, nationalizations had not been restrained to the financial sector but also covered other activities, especially public services and energy industries. This was only indirectly linked to the crisis through the increased need for security and disruption in the once unambiguous direction of privatization policy. At times, the process started with the tightening of regulations and price caps, also called the nationalization of incomes or "creeping nationalization" (De Clercq 2014).

One of the methods used was re-municipalization, that is, restoring the role of local governments as owners or direct service providers in order to reduce subsidies, cut steeply rising private profits, and lower prices. Another method was the state repurchase of companies especially in sectors considered to be strategic, such as electricity, gas, or petroleum. However, governments also used stealthy ways of nationalization by increasing state ownership in partially privatized companies, setting up subsidiaries for large state-owned companies or launching new public investment programs.[19]

These methods, stealthy ones included, are not new in themselves. As for the order of magnitude of such nationalizations, it cannot even be

---

[19] See details in Voszka (2017).

estimated, but several sources suggest that the expansion of SOEs gained momentum again in the years of the global financial crisis. According to Somai (2017), the number of public companies in France, majority owned by the state, increased by around one third between 2009 and 2014, pushing up the number of those employed in such concerns by 400,000, or 2 percentage points. This was mainly due to the expansion of the large companies associated with the electricity industry (EdF) and the national railways (SNCF).

A similar trend can be observed in the case of mergers and acquisitions (M&A). While this type of activity for exclusively state-owned enterprises accounted for less than one percent of all transactions in 1996, it jumped close to 20 percent in 2009, and then fell to half of this proportion later on (OECD 2016).[20] Although SOEs made most of their investments in domestic markets—part of which certainly fell under the so-called stealthy nationalization—their international expansion had been quite noteworthy. The latter grew 14 times between 2003 and 2009, rising to a peak never ever reached prior to the crisis. This is obviously linked to the fact that public firms depend much less on financial markets for their funding than do their private counterparts. Hence, because the crisis had less of an effect on them, they could take advantage of their rivals' weaknesses. The latter statement holds true not only for companies, but also for countries. If investor countries are divided into those that are developed (consisting mostly of EU members) and those in the process of developing, we can find very similar transformation curves, but it must be noted that developing countries are responsible for two-thirds of transactions.[21]

Sovereign Wealth Funds (SWF) are often found in the background of acquisitions by governments and state-owned entities in the international arena. The investment of these major institutions tripled between 2008

---

[20] The other data cited here are from this very same study. If we took into account not only one hundred percent ownership, this proportion would probably be much higher.

[21] China's role here is significant but, contrary to public opinion, not as important as in the case of global companies, at least according to OECD (2016). (While one-third of the two thousand largest SOEs are Chinese, as for M&A, they were responsible for only 14 percent of the transactions in the peak year of 2009—and for one half of them in 2014, when the global trend was already falling.) The Asian country announced their "Go Global Strategy" in 2000. The strategy urged, among other recommendations, SOEs to invest in foreign companies in order to boost their own competitiveness (OECD 2010).

and 2013, through acquisitions that included well-known North American and European companies.[22]

The treatment of SWFs in statistics on international changes in corporate ownership is far from consistent.[23] But the relationship between mergers and acquisitions on one hand, and privatizations and nationalizations on the other, is not clear either. As for the latter, the picture has been further blurred by the emergence of state-owned firms and other governmental bodies as buyers.

For example, *Privatization Barometer Report* listed when the state-owned Electricité de France (EdF) sold its minority package in EnBW Energie to the German Federal State of Baden-Württemberg as privatization, because the buyer expressed his intention to let the company enter into private hands in the long-run (Megginson 2011, 9–10). Similarly, the sale of part of the French postal service (La Poste), which was originally owned by the French Ministry of Finance, to the sovereign wealth fund of the French national government was also listed as privatization, arguing that the buyer acted as a commercially oriented investor rather than a politically motivated actor (Megginson and Bortolotti 2011, 11.). Surely these were not small transactions: the former accounted for 14 percent of the total annual income from privatization in the EU, and for the latter it was 10 percent.

SOEs' domestic and international expansion together with statistical uncertainties deserve special attention because two important conclusions can be drawn from them in our analysis. First, the involvement of public companies and funds in ownership changes points to the interconnection of nationalization and privatization, and also the blurring of their boundaries in the same transaction. For example, when a government sells stock market shares, it may start as a privatization, but if the buyer happens to be another state, a public company, or a SWF, the size of state property will not really change, only the identity of the public owner does. Second, in the case of cross-border transactions, nationalization may arise independently

---

[22] For example, Abu Dhabi Investment Authority (ADIA) acquired 4.9 percent of Citigroup after 2008, and then Chrysler HQ in New York. And as Singapore Wealth Fund acquired 10.7 percent of Merrill Lynch, Qatar SWF did likewise with 15 percent of Volkswagen and the entire Manchester United Football Club (Guedhami 2013; *The Rise* 2012).

[23] *Privatization Barometer* first considered foreign purchases of funds (and other public finance organizations) as privatization (but it did not do the same with the domestic purchase). In the following year, all SWF investments were listed as nationalization (Megginson and Bortolotti 2012, 11; Megginson 2013, 20).

from the intentions of the government of the destination country. Public ownership expands, but under the influence of another state, its goals, mode of operations, and effects may fundamentally differ from those of traditional nationalization, one purpose of which is to keep out foreign investors. This already happened earlier, but investors at the time would come (e.g., to the regions of Central and Eastern Europe in transition) largely from developed countries. Nevertheless, the expansion of the developing world in Europe's core countries has been considered a genuine novelty.

This obviously raises concerns in developed host countries.[24] Also, many fear that the level playing field in international trade competition (or at least the status quo) is endangered by SOEs' large and growing role in foreign investments, as it is assumed that publicly-owned companies have easier access to resources and subsidies than private ones. No wonder that in recent years, this issue has been kept on the agenda by large international organizations and advisers. As the process is difficult to control because of respect for the sovereignty of nation-states and the framework of liberal principles, multilateral agreements and the strengthening of rules came to the forefront. Instead of pushing for privatization, the focus is shifting towards taking these big and expanding SOEs for granted. Several studies published by OECD, the World Bank, or PricewaterhouseCoopers recently admit that there are legitimate economic and other reasons related to social-value creation for the establishment and maintenance of public companies. According to them,[25] it is important, however, to undertake thorough reform of the management of these SOEs' in order to make their operations transparent and compliant with market principles.

The institutions of corporate governance have been transformed in many European countries in recent years, with market-based operations as the main objective everywhere. The French SWF (named Agence des participations de l'Etat, or APE) was established in 2004 with the aim of separating the state's functions as shareholder from its other functions, transforming the firms in its portfolio into joint-stock companies (i.e., bringing them into conformity with private law and opening them to outside investors), and ensuring that their operations are effective. In 2014, APE, managing nearly €110 billion in shareholdings, paid €4.1 billion in dividends into the state budget. In the years of the Great Recession the government

---

[24] As, e.g., in Greek privatization.
[25] See e.g., OECD (2016); World Bank (2006); Kowalski et al. (2013); PWC (2015).

considered public companies viable and crisis-resistant. Thus in spite of some privatization following the crisis, the diminution of the public sector came to a halt, and an opposite process even began (Somai 2017). In Italy in the 2000s, under the treasury's trusteeship, Cassa Depositi e Prestiti was set up under the control of the Ministry of Economy and Finance (Biederman, Orosz, and Szijártó 2017). In Germany after 2008, several new regulations were introduced and codified in the so-called Public Corporate Governance Codex (Naszádos 2017). Austria expects to improve the efficiency of control (and companies' operation) by centralizing decision-making. In 2015, Austria's public property fund, operating as a joint-stock company, was replaced by a limited company, Österreichische Bundes- und Industriebeteiligungen, or ÖBIB, which was formally obliged to follow the instructions of the Finance Minister, who exercised property rights (Kőrösi 2016).

Several international analyses suggest that governments may also have a strong influence on private companies (generally in the form of regulation, including subsidies).This has been and continues to be true for all European countries.

Austria appears as a good example of traditional symbiosis between state and market. This is reflected in the complicated ownership and part-ownership schemes, profit-sharing, and investments. In a broad range of infrastructure projects, public and private investments are so completely interwoven in practice that there is virtually no exclusively private ownership in this sector. The Austrian "close-to-the-state" category includes all private companies regularly supplying at least one public actor. Their number exceeds two thousand (Kőrösi 2016). The close relationship between state and companies has always been characteristic of France too, not least because of the interconnecting elites. Here the creation of national champions by giving direct subsidies and supporting their acquisitions abroad has been fairly widespread in manufacturing, energy and the financial sector (Somai 2017).

Meanwhile, state-owned companies do not form a homogeneous group, not only because of their sectoral affiliation or profitability, but also because of the ratio of public ownership, and the ways in which ownership rights are exercised. According to PWC, there is a continuum of models spanning the public–private interface: at one end, there are executive agencies (as part of the administration), while at the other end, we can find private companies; in between, there are eight versions that differ partly according to the right of disposal (PWC 2015, 15).

In light of the new approach to the role of public companies, privatization ceased to be as unambiguous and exclusive solution proposed by experts as it used to be in the 1980s and 1990s. Great Recession produced arguments in favor of this option, too, but the measures have been more moderate than twenty years ago.

Crisis Management by Privatization

The post-2008 privatizations can be divided into two groups: privatization of banks nationalized during the crisis—hereafter referred to as re-privatization—and privatization in other parts of the economy. The analytical separation of the two categories is justified by the motives behind these policies rather than by sectoral differences.

PRIVATIZATION OF BANKS

With the easing of the crisis, the withdrawal of the extraordinary measures was soon placed on the agenda. The consensus around a Keynesian approach based on state intervention quickly disappeared (Farrell and Quiggin 2017), and debates began over whether it would be possible to return to free market policies, or if the global financial crisis marked the end of liberal capitalism, therefore brand new approaches became necessary

In principle, there was general agreement about the need for both re-privatizing the banks and tightening their regulation. Politicians had to look at nationalizations as a temporary measure not least because of the EU's own principles, and could not ignore the aforementioned unpopularity of bank nationalizations. Also, financial institutions wanted to get out from government tutelage as quickly as possible. They tried to repurchase their preferred stocks, and involve private capital (by selling a percentage of the equity on the stock market or issuing new shares) in order to restore their business reputations, reduce interest and fees related to (state) capital injections, and loosen restrictions on executive pay.

International statistics show that bank privatizations got off to a quick start. In 2009, two-thirds of global privatization revenue (the latter amounting to $265 billion) came from selling preference shares, acquired previously by governments in return for their re-capitalization support to banks (based on Megginson 2010). A decisive part (more than 80 percent) of this revenue, however, resulted from the re-privatization of a small but systematically important group of American banks. For them the whole process was terminated by 2011. In Europe, this process took much longer. In 2009, the share of revenues from bank re-privatization among all privatizations was higher than in the following three years, but the process gained momentum in the period between 2013 and 2015, only to start falling again (as did other privatizations) after 2016 under the shadow of Brexit and terrorist attacks.[26]

Table 8
Revenues from privatization and re-privatization in the European Union in 2009–2016
(€ billion and percent)

	Total revenues from priv.	Priv. revenues/ GDP	Revenues from re-priv.	Share of revenues from re-priv.	Revenues from non re-priv.	Non-re-priv./ GDP
2009	38.8	0.32	20.4	52.6	18.4	0.15
2010	33.1	0.26	2.3	7.0	30.8	0.24
2011	19.5	0.15	4.2	21.5	15.3	0.16
2012	28.5	0.21	7.0	24.3	21.5	0.16
2013	50.7	0.37	22.1	43.8	28.6	0.21
2014	58.3	0.42	26.0	44.2	32.3	0.23
2015	80.0	0.54	33.1	41.4	46.9	0.32
2016	34.0	0.23	2.6	7.6	31.4	0.21
Total EU 2009–2016	342.9	0.30	117.7	34.1	225.2	0.21
Total EU 1996–2008	633.8	0.48	–	–	–	–

Re-privatization: sale of banks nationalized after 2007
Note: The magnitude of both nationalizations and privatizations remained below one percent of GDP per year in all countries or regions (except for the extreme cases of transition countries).
Source: revenues computed on the basis of Privatization Barometer Reports.
GDP: http://ec.europa.eu/eurostat/tgm/refreshTableAction.do?tab=table&plugin=1&pcode=tec00001&

Privatization revenues during this period amounted to €343 billion, roughly equalvalent to the costs of bank nationalizations. However, only one-third of the sum came from the re-privatization of the banks nationalized during the crisis (see Table 8).[27] The fifty-two transactions registered during the

---

[26] The U.K. government announced a pause in ongoing sales of many companies and assets, e.g., in case of the Royal Bank of Scotland or Lloyds (Meggingson 2017).

[27] This data may be slightly underestimated as they do not include the revenues from the sale of overseas (especially American and Asian) divisions of European banks. Global lists of our sources (the annual issues of *Privatization Barometer*) only contain transactions above $500 million. As a result, sales of subsidiaries most likely were overlooked without, however, much affecting magnitudes.

eight years (2009–2016), involved twenty-nine banks, out of the ninety-two had been affected by previous nationalizations. The resulting revenues amount to less than 40 percent of the (minimum) €296 billion government spending (previous capital injections), while the U.S.'s largest banks have repaid their bailouts, with interest.[28]

The prolongation of the re-privatization process in Europe might be explained by the fact that nationalization took place in several steps: after 2008–9, there was a second wave of both the crisis and nationalizations in 2011–12. Moreover, public ownership in this sector has always been well known in most countries. Here, only six banks (BNP Paribas, BPCE/Natixis, Société General, Lloyds, Alpha Bank, ING) were able to repurchase (partly or entirely) their preference shares in 2009. However, for the majority of the banks the chances for repurchase were greatly reduced in Europe as opposed to the United States. Reorganization, required as a condition of state support, has often meant breaking up large financial institutions, or the forced sale of branches and subsidiaries.

Among major beneficiaries, the Anglo Irish Bank came off the worst: after liquidation its assets were transferred to the portfolio of the National Asset Management Agency (Watson 2013). ING has gradually divested its overseas insurance division, regrouped its similar European activities into Nationale-Nederlanden Group, and sold all of its NN-shares on the stock market between 2014 and 2016 (ING 2016). Lloyds, Royal Bank of Scotland and Bayerische Landesbank also sold some of their branches (Williams-Grut 2015).

In other cases it were the states who sold certain parts or shares of financial institutions, thus revenues flowed into the treasury rather than to the banks themselves. Half of Fortis was privatized, not for cash but by way of changing shares.[29] It was after dismemberment that Bradford & Bingley was sold to Spanish Santander, and the marketable part of

---

[28] Taking into account only the nationalization-related investments made through TARP in banks and the automotive industry, net profit rate resulting from re-privatization and other (e.g., fees, interests, dividend) revenues to the U.S. federal treasury amounted to 6.6 percent by August 2016 (computed on the basis of TARP 2016). According to Eurostat's survey, government interventions to support financial institutions has, in every year from 2008 to 2015, affected member states' budgets negatively, causing a peak deficit of close to €70 billion in 2010, and still a €17 billion in 2015.(European Commission 2016).

[29] While remaining minority shareholders, the governments of Belgium and Luxemburg sold 75 percent of the bailed-out Fortis local businesses to BNP Paribas. In return, they obtained 12 percent in Paribas, in which they became the largest

Northern Rock to Virgin Money, the latter having been unsuccessful in its attempt to take control of the former in 2007 (BBC News 2012, UK Financial Investments Ltd. 2012). In 2015, American Cerberus Group bought mortgages issued by Northern Rock—once seen as highly toxic— for €18.4 billion (Parker and Dunkley 2015), which was the largest deal of that year and the largest ever sale of financial assets in the history of English privatization.

Lloyds is the stock market champion, having issued several packages of shares (for a total value of €13.4 billion), but in this field Greeks were also on top. In 2013, the biggest transaction in Europe was the privatization of Piraeus Bank at a price of €7.1 billion, completed by the sale of its further stakes of €2.4 and €1.3 billion during the following two years. Almost €7 billion of privatization revenue was raised by the sale of assets of the National Bank of Greece, Eurobank, and Alpha combined. They were closely followed, with items ranging from €1 to €3 billion by Spanish Bankia and Novaglicia, Commerzbank, the English branch of Ally Financial, and the Bank of Cyprus. Sales of entire banks in their original form proved to be rare, confined to small institutions like the German IKB, the Spanish Valencia, or Irish Life.

As Table 8 indicates, most of the privatization revenue was generated in other sectors, that is, the focus of the process in Europe was not re-privatization of financial institutions.

The expansion of privatization

A crisis can be mitigated not only by nationalizing but also by privatizing. The argument that privatization might reduce public deficits and debt, which had skyrocketed in relation to banks bailouts in the first years of the crisis, became central now (Megginson 2010; Bartsch and Ng 2010). Selling assets can also be considered a good supplement to spending cuts or tax increases, as it stimulates growth and foreign investment rather than deepening the downturn.

In Europe, privatization in the post-crisis years has remained less intense than it was in the previous period. Revenues stemming from the sale of state assets were of €43 billion per year on average between 2009

---

shareholders (Webb 2013). Privatization resulted in replacing full public control with minority state ownership in two financial institutions.

and 2016, as compared to €49 billion between 1996 and 2008 (see Table 8). The significant distortion of data reported at current prices for as long as two decades can be reduced by computing GDP-related indices. This shows an even bigger difference: privatization revenues of the earlier period amounted to 0.48 percent of GDP, compared to only 0.3 percent since 2009. Although in absolute terms 2005 was the peak year of the last two decades, the corresponding index (of 0.54 percent measured in GDP) was smaller than that of 2005 or the years from 1996 to 2000.

If looking only at sales other than bank re-privatization, post-crisis yearly average revenues amount to 0.21 percent of GDP, less than half of what they were in the pre-2009 period. This modest rate, however, represents almost two-thirds of the 2009–2016 revenues (Table 8). Hence, the more dynamic part of the privatization process has been found outside the financial sector.

The European Union has played an important role in promoting privatization just as in the early 1990s. Although the EU does not prescribe how to shape ownership structure, it influences the process indirectly. In Europe, neoliberal-inspired austerity measures have widely been introduced to address the surge in government deficits and the threat of sovereign debt crises. In 2011, new and more stringent requirements and sanctions regarding macroeconomic balances came into force (European Commission 2012), encouraging governments to increase revenues by continuing privatization beyond the banking sector. The EU has sometimes called attention to specific sectors, the privatization of which it strongly supported, including rail transport and public services, especially water supply. Those suggestions were, however, not met with enthusiasm everywhere.

In the field of transport, almost all member states concerned—Ireland, Bulgaria, Estonia, and Luxemburg—proved to be reluctant to take this step (Artner 2015). Further, plans for privatization of water supply have provoked a public outcry in Ireland, Greece, Portugal, and Italy. In 2011, the Italians rejected such a plan in a referendum, and yet a few months later, the liberalization and comprehensive privatization of all local public services were prescribed by the European Commission as key points of the reform. However, the Constitutional Court declared unconstitutional the prescription regarding the privatization of local public services in Italy (Zacune 2013). In 2013, a semi-public water supply company was established in Ireland, with the parallel introduction of a water-charge, which did not exist before. the general tax revenues financing consumption thus far. The measure, widely seen as the anteroom of austerity policy and "pushing up prices even further" privatization, provoked civil disobedience in which more than half of the population refused to pay their water bill in the summer of 2015 (Artner 2015).

These examples already show that the EU's influence on state ownership issues has not been strong everywhere during the last eight years. In nearly half of member states, including most new members, no or very few public assets have been privatized.

Table 9
Revenues from privatization in EU member states, 2009–2016
(above €5 billion)

Country	Revenues (€ bn)	Revenues/ GDP 2016 (%)	Revenues from non-banking privatization (€ bn)	Non-banking priv. revenues /GDP 2016 (%)	Difference of costs of re-capitalization and priv. revenues (€ bn)x/
United Kingdom	69.5	2.9	17.1	0.7	−30.6ˣ
France	43.7	1.96	29.7	1.3	18.6
Italy	27.5	1.6	25.5	1.5	+ˣˣ
Greece	25.2	14.3	5.3	3.0	−15.7
The Netherlands	24.7	3.5	13.4	1.9	1.7
Ireland	18.6	7.3ˣˣˣ	11.2	4.4	−58.4
Sweden	18.3	3.96	18.3	3.96	+
Portugal	17.4	12.4	11.9	6.4	+
Poland	16.7	4.3	16.7	3.9	+
Spain	15.0	1.3	11.0	1.0	−46.9
Germany	12.3	0.4	7.2	0.2	−51.9
Total of 11 countries	288.9	4.0	167.3	2.3	−

ˣ The negative sign (-) means that costs of re-capitalization exceeded revenues from privatization (see Table 6)
ˣˣ Recapitalization remained under €10 billion, so the balance is surely positive.
ˣˣˣ Computation based on 2015 GDP
Source: Revenues: based on *Privatization Barometer Reports*; GDP: http://ec.europa.eu/eurostat/tgm/refreshTableAction.do?tab=table&plugin=1&pcode=tec00001&language=en.

In absolute terms, the rankings are led by two big countries: the United Kingdom and France. But if we set aside banks' reprivatization, Italy, Sweden and Poland also hold leading positions, covering a wide spectrum of sectors: they have sold companies in sectors like energy, public services, civil aviation, and manufacturing. In Poland, a country that experienced no recession since well before 2008, a decisive role was played by liberals, who came to power not much earlier, and held the conviction that privatization revenues were needed both to reduce the deficit and boost the economy (Kozarzewski and Bałtowski 2016). Between 2013 and 2015, the U.K. was a European leader in selling public assets, primarily aimed at reducing public deficits and debt (Parker and Dunkley 2015). Italy announced a major privatization program as part of its structural reforms in 2014, including the launch of privatization for ENAV (aviation services) and Poste Italiane, and the continuation of the privatization program for several other big companies (ENI, ENEL, Fincantieri) (Biederman, Orosz, and Szijártó. 2017). Part of this program was successfully completed in the following years, which placed Italy second in the European rankings of privatization revenues in 2015 and fourth in 2016 (Megginson 2017).

Most of these countries made their own decision on privatization. In other member states, however, the impact of external pressure can be assumed. This is demonstrated in lists considering the size of the countries. Compared to the total national product, besides Poland three countries have earned significant income from privatization: Greece, Ireland, and Portugal.[30] Since all these countries were in need of international financial assistance, it is clear that the European Commission, together with the European Central Bank and the International Monetary Fund, was able to exert strong influence on them. Apart from fiscal austerity, a key requirement of the rescue packages was that governments continued privatizing, which was considered to be a useful reform element and a stimulus for growth (Visvizi 2012; Borrman et al. 2014).

Post-crisis situation has an ambivalent effect on privatization. On the one hand, the lasting recession and the subsequent economic and social uncertainties may discourage investors, while on the other hand, the artificially inflated supply of low-cost assets offers great opportunities for buyers from rich countries and well-capitalized companies. Greece deserves special attention also because of the variability of its story.

Initially, plans for privatization in Greece were to produce revenues of €1 billion per annum, but under pressure from international creditors the target was raised to €50 billion. The implementation of the plans, however, has—just as in many other countries—been postponed due to the falling prices on stock markets (Megginson and Bortolotti 2012). Later on, these plans, considered unrealistic due to long-lasting economic decline and lack of investors' confidence, had to be scaled back to €20 billion.

---

[30] Nevertheless, in the first two countries, revenues from privatization did not cover the cost of nationalizations, as the last column in Table 9 indicates.

There were loud protests not only by workers in the companies concerned but also by powerful labor unions organizing extensive strikes against most of the sales.

The political costs of privatization are high—says Visvizi (2012)—not least because public opinion links them immediately to neoliberal economic policy and austerity measures accompanying the rescue packages. According to public opinion polls, the majority of the population fears a sell-off of public assets and the growing role played by foreign investors (Poggioli 2013).

By 2012, actual sales revenues were far behind schedule, in spite of some major deals. Apart from bank re-privatization, the majority share of a gas pipeline was taken by the Azerbaijani public company, a 33 percent stake of the national lottery was sold to domestic investors, and Deutsche Telekom increased its stake in Greek telecoms by 10 percentage points. International organizations have been participating in the work of Athens's privatization agency. What is more, when they considered the process to be too slow, they have threatened to take over management. But when well-capitalized buyers from outside the group of the most developed countries made their bids—like Gazprom for the gas utility company, or Chinese firms on ports and railways—European governments as well as Washington expressed their concerns over the issue and the privatization agency had to delay the decision (Poggioli 2013). The privatization of real estate, fields, islands, and monuments has also been impeded by the inadequacies of different registries (Bräuninger 2013).

In 2013–14, the Greek government made significant steps towards generating more revenues from privatization primarily by selling consolidated and unified banks; in 2014, the country became the third largest privatizer in Europe (Megginson 2017). Following the general elections of early 2015, the new left-wing cabinet announced the suspension of the privatization program. But in July, Eurozone prime ministers imposed even more stringent demands on the Syriza government.[31] A new privatization and asset management agency has been set up into which Athens transferred companies with asset value 50 billion euros that were either being sold or run profitably. Apart from paying debt, revenues would be used for bank recapitalization and public investments (Cosgrave 2015). According to the agreement, the management is Greek but works under EU tute-

---

[31] Euro Summit Statement (July 12, 2015), available at www.consilium.europa.eu/en/press/.../2015/.../20150712eurosummit-statement-greece.

lage; a French expert has been named as the fund's executive chairman (Hope 2016). The quantitative target for revenues from privatization was restored to its original (2011) level of €50 billion. It was a relief, however, that Greece now has ten years to achieve it. As first steps, Piraeus port and its supervisory authority, as well as that of regional airports has been successfully privatized, even if only for a few billion euros (Megginson 2017).

As an important feature of privatizations in this period, the bulk of the transactions meant partial privatizations, not only for banks but also in other sectors of the economy. According to my calculations based on the lists of the *Privatization Barometer*, sales of entire companies (including banks) represented one-tenth to one-third of all transactions in Europe in the period of between 2009 and 2016.[32] In Poland for example, in transactions generating three-quarters of privatization revenues, the sale of assets left ownership control unchanged (Kozarzewski and Bałtowski 2016).[33] In France, the system of double-voting- rights shares was generalized in 2014, rewarding all long-term investors (including the government) for holding their shares for at least two years. The declared goal here was to protect firms against speculative attacks, but obviously the state's long-term ownership also doubled its influence. (Somai 2017).

Partial privatizations give the opportunity to governments to sell shares without losing their control over the company. This method was not exceptional even in the past decades. Large firms are never and nowhere being sold in one fell swoop but in stages, taking into account the absorption capacity of capital markets and aspects of price optimization as well. In times of crisis or strong fiscal pressure, however, it might be especially important for governments to achieve two goals at once: raising incomes without relinquishing control. The consequence is hybridization, based on mixing public and private ownership. This phenomenon had already been strengthened by the earlier big wave of privatization (Bortolotti-Faccio 2004), but it remained typical in the years after 2008.

---

[32] The data might be underestimated, considering that the lists often only include transactions over €10 or €100 million, while full privatization may be typical for smaller firms. Moreover, the lists do not show the initial share of the state. Therefore it is possible that the sale of a relatively small package represents the final phase of the privatization of an entire company.

[33] According to the estimates of the authors for the year 2012, if formal ownership data were corrected with actual control position, public sector's weight in GDP would amount to 15–20 percent instead of the official 10 percent, and 16 percent in employment instead of 13 percent.

It is also well-known, that revenues from privatization on their own can never solve macroeconomic imbalances (see their share in relation to GDP in Table 9). This is demonstrated by recent calculations: when assessing the "privatization potential," it became clear that revenues would cover only a fraction of the public debt, even in the least probable case of selling all state assets.

One of the first comprehensive analyses on the issue estimated the potential revenue for the EU15 to be around 2.5 percent of GDP, and ten percent for Finland (Bartsch and Ng 2009). The International Monetary Fund estimated the value of privatizable assets for 32 countries to reach 4 to 7 percent of GDP (Bova et al. 2013), while gross government debts were typically higher than 50 or even 100 percent of it. The Economica Institute in Vienna assessed all marketable (public) assets in the largest 10 Eurozone member states and 4 non-Eurozone ones, putting it at a total of €511 billion. The sale of this wealth could yield more than €100 billion for France, €76 billion for Germany, and €59 billion for both Italy and the Netherlands. Expected proceeds could, however, cover only 4.4 percent of the debt burden on average - Finland ranked first with 14.5 percent. (Borrmann et al. 2014).

Therefore, in most European countries, a new wave of privatization could only temper government deficits in the short term, and might potentially have a positive effect by improving the income generating capacity of national economies.

Summary: Boundaries and Directions are Getting Blurred

As presented in our analysis, there has been a significant wave of nationalization in developed countries of Europe in the post-crisis period of 2008. In a couple of years, governments spent an amount equivalent to 2 to 3 percent of GDP on expanding public assets in the financial sector without considering the growth in municipal, central or federal, and also foreign public assets. For comparison, the earlier wave of privatization had funneled to the treasuries roughly 7 percent of GDP over twenty-five years. The average for the public property share of GDP in Europe seems to turn towards the peak of the late 1970s (12 and 10.5 percent respectively),[34]

---

[34] These figures are subject to caution because of uncertainties about definitions and methodology.

which because of uncertainties about definitions and methodology must be viewed with reservations.

Parallel with nationalizations, a wave of privatization has also started. Its order of magnitude reached 3 percent of GDP for the period between 2009 and 2016 equaled that of recent nationalizations. However, only one-third of the revenues stemmed from bank re-privatization, the rest was generated in other sectors of the economy.

Although both policies aimed at addressing the crisis, the motives behind them were different. The purpose of nationalization was, as it had been decades ago, to save companies from bankruptcy, avoid domino effects, minimize social losses, and restore trust, which was considered a prerequisite for recovery. As before, privatization focused on improving macroeconomic imbalances in the short run, and on promoting strong and healthy growth by strengthening the role of both market and private ownership in the longer run.

Thus, the aims of post-2008 ownership changes were similar to the earlier waves. Different national patterns regarding the methods and scales are not unusual either. Some EU members (Portugal, Poland, Sweden) excelled in only privatization, while others (Spain, Belgium) in nationalization; certain countries (Greece, Ireland) were at the forefront of both policies, while others were not significantly involved in either process (Italy, France, Germany).

The recent wave of ownership changes, however, is characterized also by unusual features. The most striking one was the almost parallel emergence and strengthening of nationalization and privatization in Europe and even within single countries. This phenomenon is closely related to several other new features. First, the rapid change and parallel existence of the two processes prove that today, neither nationalization nor privatization is deemed to be a panacea. Disadvantages and side effects of both policies have already been widely discussed in the political arena and in scientific papers; the belief that either of them could be a long-term solution to economic difficulties has been shaken. The nationalization of banks had originally been considered a temporary move, and most of the governments have only reluctantly undertaken privatization in other sectors

Second, the nationalization of banks, a policy directly contradicting the highly praised free market principles and privatization, has been executed in a hidden, stealthy way, concealed by other methods like bank bailouts (re-capitalization, the purchase of impaired assets), which could be evidenced by the complete lack of relevant statistical records. The non-financial public sector has also often expanded due to such "silent methods": capital increases by the government, large public investment projects, or the expansion of—partly foreign—state-owned companies and funds through the acquisition of private companies. Privatization itself has often meant the sale of minority holdings without the transfer of control.

Third, these procedures resulted in a further blurring of borders between public and private property, as well as between nationalization and privatization. The former process manifests itself not only through the expansion of mixed-ownership in joint-stock companies, but also through the ongoing tightening of financial regulation, the limitation of price increases, and the increase in tax burdens, all of which pointing towards a limitation of private property rights. Small wonder that companies concerned called these steps the "expropriation of incomes." As for privatization, the clear identification of the direction of changes in ownership has been made difficult by the fact that the buyer of a public company often— regardless of the seller's intention—is another public corporation, or investment fund.

Growing uncertainties among politicians and in expert's evaluations indicates that, in the last few years, the evergreen debate about "nationalization or privatization" seems to have been replaced by a push to steer a middle course: improve governance in public companies and create conditions for their market-based activities. This keeps the old debate alive about whether or not ownership is more important than regulation. Moreover, there is the recognition that dichotomous approaches may be simplified: both public and private ownership involves a variety of companies and operation models.

If this approach becomes dominant, the dividing lines between the two sectors will be even more blurred.

REFERENCES

Aharoni, Yair. 1986. *The Evolution and Management of State Owned Enterprises*. Pensacola: Ballinger Publishing.
Artner, Annamária. 2015. "The Role of State in Ireland." Unpublished manuscript.
Bartsch, Elga and Edmund Ng. 2010. "Towards Fiscal Tightening and Privatization: Implications for Equities." In *The Privatization Barometer Report 2009*, 19–27. Milan: Fondazione ENI.
BBC News. 2007. "RBS Woos ABN with £49bn Bid Plan." April 25. http://news.bbc.co.uk/2/hi/business/6590741.stm.
BBC News. 2008. "Second Belgian Bank Gets Bail-out." September 30. http://news.bbc.co.uk/2/hi/business/7643638.stm.

BBC News. 2012. "Barclays to acquire ING Direct UK." October 9. https://www.bbc.com/news/business-19880659.
Biedermann, Zsuzsánna, Ágnes Orosz, and Norbert Szijártó. 2017. "The Role of State in Italy, State-owned Enterprises through History: Nationalization and Privatization Periods in Italy." Unpublished manuscript.
Boix, Carles. 1997. "Privatizing the Public Business Sector in the Eighties: Economic Performance, Partisan Responses and Divided Governments." *British Journal of Political Science* 27 (4): 473–96.
Borrmann, Julia, Markus Fichtinger, Christian Helmenstein, and Georg Neumüller. 2014. "Privatisation Potential in the European Union." Research Report. Economica.
Bortolotti, Bernardo, and Mara Faccio. 2004. "Reluctant Privatization." Note di lavoro. Fondazione Eni Enrico Mattei, October. https://www.feem.it/en/publications/feem-working-papers-note-di-lavoro-series/reluctant-privatization/.
Bortolotti, Bernardo, and Valentina Milella. 2006. "Privatization in Western Europe Stylized Facts, Outcomes, and Open Issues." Note di lavoro. Fondazione Eni Enrico Mattei, July. https://www.feem.it/en/publications/feem-working-papers-note-di-lavoro-series/privatization-in-western-europe-stylized-facts-outcomes-and-open-issues/.
Bortolotti, Bernardo, and Paolo Pinotti. 2003. "The Political Economy of Privatization." Note di lavoro. Fondazione Eni Enrico Mattei. https://papers.ssrn.com/sol3/papers.cfm?abstract_id=418020.
Bova, Elva, Robert Dippelsman, Kara C. Rideout, and Andrea Schaechter. 2013. "Another Look at Governments' Balance Sheets: The Role of Nonfinancial Assets." IMF Working Papers. International Monetary Fund, May 2. https://www.imf.org/en/Publications/WP/Issues/2016/12/31/Another-Look-at-Governments-Balance-Sheets-The-Role-of-Nonfinancial-Assets-40503.
Bräuninger, Dieter. 2015. "Privatisation in the Euro Area: Differing Attitudes towards Public Assets." Research Briefing. Deutsche Bank AG. https://www.dbresearch.de/PROD/RPS_DE-PROD/PROD0000000000463937/Research_Briefing%3A_Privatisation_in_the_euro_area_.pdf.
Buder, Matthäus, Max Lienemeyer, Marcel Magnus, Bert Smits, and Karl Soukup. 2011. "The Rescue and Restructuring of Hypo Real Estate." *Competition Policy Newsletter* (3): 41-44. http://ec.europa.eu/competition/publications/cpn/2011_3_9_en.pdf.
Carlsson, Bo. 1988. "Public Industrial Enterprises in Sweden: Searching for a viable structure." *Annals of Public & Co-operative Economy* 59 (2): 175–95.
Cosgrave, Jenny. 2015. "Greece's $55B Privatization Fund: How it will Work." *CNBC News* July 14. http://www.cnbc.com/2015/07/14/greeces-55b-privatization-fund-how-it-will-work.html.
Dalton, Matthiew, and David Gauthier-Villars. 2011. "France, Belgium Reach Pact on Ailing Dexia." *The Wall Street Journal.* October 10. http://www.wsj.com/articles/SB10001424052970203633104576620720705508498.
De Clercq, Geert. 2014. "Insight: Europe's Utilities Squeezed by Creeping Nationalization." *Reuters Business News*, January 19. https://www.reuters.com/article/us-utilities-unplugged-renationalisation/insight-europes-utilities-squeezed-by-creeping-nationalization-idUSBREA0I03720140119.

Economist. 2012. "The Rise of State Capitalism." January 21. https://www.economist.com/leaders/2012/01/21/the-rise-of-state-capitalism.European Commission. 2008. "State aid: Commission approves UK rescue aid package for Bradford & Bingley." Press Release, October 1. http://europa.eu/rapid/press-release_IP-08-1437_en.htm.

———. 2009a "Communication from the Commission: The recapitalisation of financial institutions in the current financial crisis: limitation of aid to the minimum necessary and safeguards against undue distortions of competition." January 15. *Official Journal of the European Union 2009.*

———. 2009b "Communication from the Commission on the Treatment of Impaired Assets in the Community Banking Sector." March 26. *Official Journal of the European Union.*

———. 2012. " Treaty on Stability, Coordination and Governance in the Economic and Monetary Union." Press Release, February 1. https://europa.eu/rapid/press-release_DOC-12-2_en.htm.

European Commission Directorate-General for Competition. 2014. "State Aid Control. State Aid Scoreboard 2014. Aid in the Context of Financial and Economic Crisis." Accessed 15. Sept. 2015. European Commission Directorate-General for Economic and Financial Affairs. 2013. "The Second Economic Adjustment Programme for Greece—Third Review." *European Economy: Occasional Papers* (159) July. https://ec.europa.eu/economy_finance/publications/occasional_paper/2013/pdf/ocp159_en.pdf.

European Commission Eurostat. 2016. *Eurostat Supplementary Table for Reporting Government Interventions to Support Financial Institutions.* http://ec.europa.eu/eurostat/web/government-finance-statistics/excessive-deficit/supplemtary-tables-financial-crisis.

Farrell, Henry, and John Quiggin. 2017. "Consensus, Dissensus and Economic Ideas: Economic Crisis and the Rise and Fall of Keynesianism." *International Studies Quarterly* 61 (2): 269–83.

Guedhami, Omrane. 2012. "Characteristics of Government Acquisitions over Time: International Evidence and Crisis Effect." In *The Privatization Barometer Report* 2012, 30–43. Milan: Fondazione ENI.

Hellenic Financial Stability Fund. 2014. "Interim Financial Statements for the nine month period ended 30/09/2014." December 11. http://www.hfsf.gr/en/financialinformation.htm.

Hope, Kerin. 2016. "Athens Approves Fund to Speed up Privatisation Programme." *Financial Times*, September 27. https://www.ft.com/content/81dc1d54-84f5-11e6-8897-2359a58ac7a5.

Hüfner, Felix. 2010. "The German Banking System: Lessons from the Financial Crisis." OECD Economics Department Working Papers. OECD, July 1. https://www.oecd-ilibrary.org/economics/the-german-banking-system-lessons-from-the-financial-crisis_5kmbm80pjkd6-en.

ING. 2016. "Brief Background on the Divestment Process of NN Group." https://www.ing.com/Investor-relations/Divestment-of-NN-Group/Brief-background-on-the-divestment-process-of-NN-Group.htm. Accessed 12 May 2017.

Kowalski, Przemysław, Max Büge, Monika Sztajerowska, and Matias Egeland. 2013. "State-Owned Enterprises: Trade Effects and Policy Implications." OECD Trade Policy Papers 147. OECD. http://dx.doi.org/10.1787/5k4869ckqk7l-en.

Kozarzewski, Piotr, and Maciej Bałtowski. 2016. "Formal and Real Ownership Structure of the Polish Economy: State-owned versus State-controlled Enterprises." *Post-Communist Economies* 28 (3): 405–19.
Kőrösi, István. 2016. *Az állam és a magánvállalatok viszonya az osztrák gazdaságban* [Relations of the state and private companies in Austrian economy]. MTA Közgazdaság- és Regionális Tudományi Kutatóközpont Világgazdasági Intézet Műhelytanulmányok 111., 1–35. http://mek-oszk.uz.ua/16000/16028/16028.pdfLanger, Edmond I. 1966. "The Economic Importance of Public Enterprise in Belgium." *Annals of Public & Co-operative Economy* 37 (1): 65–77.
Lewis, Ben W. 1965. "British Nationalization and American Private Enterprise: Some Parallels and Contrasts." *American Economic Review* 55 (2): 50–75.
Megginson, William L. 2010. "Privatization Trends and Major Deals in 2009." In *The Privatization Barometer Report 2009*, 7–18. Milan: Fondazione ENI.
Megginson, William L. 2011. "Privatization Trends and Major Deals in 2010." *The Privatization Barometer Report 2010*, 6–22. Milan: Fondazione ENI.
———. 2013. "Privatization Trends and Major Deals in 2012 and 1H2013." In *The Privatization Barometer Report 2012*, 3–24. Milan: Fondazione ENI.
———. 2017. "Privatization Trends and Major Deals in 2015 and 2016." In *The Privatization Barometer Report 2015–16*, 5–32. Milan: Fondazione ENI.
Megginson, William L., and Bortolotti, Bernardo. 2012. "Privatization Trends and Major Deals in 2011." In *The Privatization Barometer Report 2011*, 7–22. Milan: Fondazione ENI.
Megginson, William L., and Netter, Jeffry. M. 2003. "History and Methods of Privatization." In *International Handbook of Privatisation*, edited by David Parker and David Saal, 25–40. Cheltenham: Edward Elgar.
Millward, Robert. 2011. "Public Enterprise in the Modern Western World: An Historical Analysis." *Annals for Public and Corporative Economics* 82 (4): 375–98.
Naszádos, Zsófia. 2017. "The Involvement of the State in the German Economy." Unpublished manuscript.
Netherlands. 2008. "Netherlands Govt Buys Fortis Units for 16.8 bn Euro." *Business Standard* October 4. http://www.business-standard.com/article/finance/netherlands-govt-buys-fortis-units-for-16-8-bn-euro-108100400011_1.html.
OECD. 2010. "SOEs Operating Abroad: An Application of the OECD Guidelines on Corporate Governance of State-Owned Enterprises to the Cross-border Operations of SOEs." Paris: OECD Publishing. http://www.oecd.org/corporate/ca/corporategovernanceofstate-ownedenterprises/44215438.pdf.
———. 2011. "State-Owned Governance Enterprise Reform. An Inventory of Recent Change." Paris: OECD Publishing. https://www.oecd.org/daf/ca/corporategovernanceofstate-ownedenterprises/48455108.pdf.
———. 2012. "Dataset on the Size and Sectoral Composition of National SOE Sectors." Paris: OECD Publishing. https://www.oecd.org/corporate/ca/Dataset%20size%20and%20composition%20SOEs%202012.xlsx. Accessed 15 January 2015.
———. 2016. "State-Owned Enterprises as Global Competitors. A Challenge or an Opportunity?" Paris: OECD Publishing. http://www.oecd.org/corporate/state-owned-enterprises-as-global-competitors-9789264262096-en.htm.

Parker, David. 2003. "Privatization in the European Union." In *International Handbook of Privatisation*, edited by David Parker and David Saal, 105–28. Cheltenham: Edward Elgar.
Parker, David, and David Saal. 2003. *International Handbook of Privatisation*. Cheltenham: Edward Elgar.
Parker, George, and Emma Dunkley. 2015. "Sale of NRock's 'Toxic' Loans Heralds further Privatizations." *Financial Times*, November 13. https://www.ft.com/content/942B42C8-8A19-11E5-9F8C-A8D619FA707C.
Parris, Henry. 1985. "Public Enterprises in Great Britain." *Annals of Public and Cooperative Economics* 56 (3): 393–410.
Poggioli, Sylvia. 2013. "Privatization of Greek Assets Runs behind Schedule." *NPR*, February 7. http://www.npr.org/2013/02/07/171294406/privatization-of-greek-assets-runs-behind-schedule.
Pontusson, Jonas. 1989. "The Triumph of Pragmatism: Nationalization and Privatization in Sweden." In *The Politics of Privatisation in Western Europe*, edited by John Vickers and Vincent Wright, 129–40. London: Frank Cass.
PricewaterhouseCoopers. 2015 "State-Owned Enterprises: Catalysts for public value creation?" PwC report. https://www.pwc.com/gx/en/psrc/publications/assets/pwc-state-owned-enterprise-psrc.pdf.
Robinett, David. 2006. "Held by the Visible Hand—The Challenge of SOE Corporate Governance for Emerging Markets." Working Paper 37711. The World Bank, May. http://documents.worldbank.org/curated/en/396071468158997475/pdf/377110Corporate0Governance0SOEs01PUBLIC1.pdf.
Shirley, Mary M. 1983. "Managing State-Owned Enterprises." Working Paper 577. Management and Development Series 4. World Bank Staff. http://documents.worldbank.org/curated/en/378431468740430088/Managing-state-owned-enterprises.
Somai, Miklós. 2017. "Állami befolyás a francia gazdaságban: válságtól válságig" [State interference in the French economy: From crisis to crisis]. *Külgazdaság* 61 (3–4): 51–73.
The Library of Congress. 1993. "Portugal. The Nonfinancial Public Enterprises." Country Studies; http://countrystudies.us/portugal/66.htm
Toninelli, Pier Angelo, ed. 2000. *The Rise and Fall of State-Owned Enterprise in the Western World*. Cambridge: Cambridge University Press.
UK Financial Investments Ltd. 2012. "UKFI Confirms Completion of Northern Rock Sale to Virgin Money." News release, December 11.
U.S. Department of the Treasury. 2016. "Monthly TARP Update for 08/01/2016." https://www.treasury.gov/initiatives/financial-stability/reports/Documents/Monthly_TARP_Update%20-%2008.01.2016.pdf.
Vickers, John, and Vincent Wright, eds. 1989a. *The Politics of Privatisation in Western Europe*, London: Frank Cass.
———. 1989b. "The Politics of Industrial Privatization in Western Europe: An Overview." In *The Politics of Privatisation in Western Europe*, edited by John Vickers and Vincent Wright, 1–30. London: Frank Cass.
Visvizi, Anna. 2012. "The Crisis in Greece and the EU–IMF Rescue Package: Determinants and Pitfalls." *Acta Oeconomica* 62 (1): 15–39.
Voszka, Éva. 2017. "Nationalization or Privatization? The Fragmentation of the Mainstream." *Annals of Public and Cooperative Economics* 88 (1): 91–120.

———. 2018. *Az állami tulajdon pillanatai. Gazdaságtörténeti és tudománytörténeti nézőpontok.* [Moments of state ownership: Economic historical and theoretical perspectives]. Budapest: Akadémia Kiadó.

Ward, Barbara. 1946. "Europe Debates Nationalization." *Foreign Affairs*, October. https://www.foreignaffairs.com/articles/western-europe/1946-10-01/europe-debates-nationalization.

Watson, Leon. 2013. "Failed Anglo Irish Bank that Had £24billion Bailout to be Liquidated after Politicians Work through the Night to Sign Deal into Law." *Daily Mail*, February 7. http://www.dailymail.co.uk/news/article-2274902/Failed-Anglo-Irish-Bank-liquidated-politicians-work-night-sign-deal-law.html.

Webb, Sara. 2013. "ABN AMRO Cuts 400 Jobs as Prepares for Eventual Sale." *Reuters*, May 17. http://www.reuters.com/article/us-abnamro-earnings-idUS-BRE94G05D20130517.

Weil, Jonathan. 2012. "The EU Smiled While Spain's Banks Cooked the Books." *Bloomberg*, June 15. http://www.bloomberg.com/view/articles/2012-06-14/the-eu-smiled-while-spain-s-banks-cooked-the-books.

Williams-Grut, Oscar. 2015. "TSB is now officially Spanish." *Business Insider*, June 30. https://www.businessinsider.in/TSB-is-now-officially-Spanish/articleshow/47879247.cms.

Willner, Johan. 2003. "Privatisation and Public Ownership in Finland." CESifo Working Paper 1012. Center for Economic Studies, University of Munich. https://ssrn.com/abstract=436607.

CHAPTER 2

Changing Role of the State in France: from Crisis to Crisis

Miklós Somai

Introduction

In times of great socio-economic crises, considerations about the role of the state in the economy and the optimal size of the public sector always come to the forefront of public debates. So it happened following the outbreak of the 2008 global financial crisis. Although the neoliberal paradigm did not collapse and privatization continued (both worldwide and in France)[1] after Lehman Brothers filed for bankruptcy, the strengthening of state intervention in the economy, which took place parallel to privatization, has also been noticeable since then: first, through measures reinforcing the state's shareholder position; and second, through the expansion of state-owned enterprises, often across national borders.

This paper presents the role played by the state in the French economy thanks to its ownership in and control over the corporate world. Following some relatively short sections devoted to France's tradition(s) of centralization and the different waves of nationalization and privatization—the background of which is the crucial turning point in 1983, it gives an overview of the period since the global financial crisis with special focus on two main topics: public wealth management and the banking sector's crisis resistance.

---

[1] During the five years following Lehman's filing for bankruptcy protection (on September 15, 2008), public property worth of almost $40 billion has been privatized in France (*Privatization Barometer* 2016 online).

Centralization Traditions

Due to the reigns of Louis IX "the Saint" and Louis XI "the Prudent" among other things, France was known to be a fairly centralized state as early as the fifteenth century. The centralization of the country's economic resources intensified during the Great Century[2] with the rise of absolutism and Colbertism,[3] as well as the implementation of fiscal austerity under both Richelieu and Mazarin.

Since the early seventeenth century, French governments have traditionally been closely linked to the big players of the economy; a practice introduced by Sully, the Minister of Finances under Henri IV. Power and business developed hand in hand, as the state had a continuous interest in maintaining a high level of intervention in economic affairs. Unlike in Germany or the United Kingdom where the nature of state influence on economy has changed with the political climate, the French people have a strong tradition of favoring big government and have great pride in their public sector.[4]

Taken more generally and somewhat simplifying our analysis of France's unique perspective on the role of government, there are two main differences compared to other developed countries' approach to state intervention. The first one is structural, based on the long-standing and steady tradition of centralization, which has led to the formation of permanent and powerful public administrations ("Grand Corps de l'État"), whose members have remained in their posts throughout changes of government. The second one is rooted in history and relates to the revolution of 1789, that is, a permanent search for the best public action for the sake of the French people's happiness, liberty, and fair treatment (Kolm 2010, 90–91).

---

[2] The period lasting from 1589 to 1715 (i.e., from Henri IV to Louis XIV), was when France both politically and culturally exerted the greatest influence on the development of Europe and the world.

[3] The royal manufactures developed by Colbert in France can be considered the first state-owned enterprises (Chevallier 1979, 16).

[4] It is typical that although people during the French revolution were desperate and upset about unbearably high taxes (especially those on peasants), it was not the state but the aristocracy and the clergy they blamed for the economic problems of the country (Meisel 2014, 81–82).

Waves of Nationalizations

Temporary increases in the intensity of the state's direct economic intervention during the twentieth century can be interpreted as responses to the socio-economic shocks of the century. Nationalization typically took place at the end of crisis periods when the political and economic climate made them not only possible but often necessary.

Already during the period after World War I, mixed public-private companies were established to implement large scale hydro-energy projects and create "commercial and industrial public establishments" for running autonomous ports like those of Le Havre, Strasbourg, and Bordeaux (Chevallier 1979, 17–19). But the first big wave of nationalizations was linked to the establishment of the Popular Front (1936–1938), a left-wing party alliance. The policy mainly focused on learning the lessons of the Great Depression (1929–1933) and was intended to ameliorate its consequences (e.g., capital shortages). Several mixed companies such as Air France and SNCF were created by swapping debt (actually state subsidies) for equity, but the establishment of the first supervisory/regulatory authorities (e.g., the national Grain Board)[5] and the democratization of the Bank of France also took place during this period.[6]

In the aftermath of the great destruction caused by World War II, the political push behind nationalization dated back to the Resistance's 1943 program.[7] Also, it is necessary to remember that the Communist Party was the most important political force of France in the period during and right after the Liberation (Brucy 2001, 67). German businesses and business shares and those of French people who collaborated with them—for instance, the automobile company Renault and the Havas news agency—

---

[5] By way of price regulation and monopolizing warehousing and export/import activities, the Board tried to protect small farmers from the abuse of trusts'/big mills' dominant position (Bajomi 1938).

[6] The reform of the central bank changed the composition of the General Assembly. Unlike earlier, when it had been the privilege of the 200 largest shareholders to be present, all shareholders with French citizenship became entitled to participate in it, and each had one vote, irrespective of the number of shares he or she held (Banque de France 2016 online, 207).

[7] "The means of production incorporated in sources of energy, treasures of earth, banks and insurance companies must return to the Nation." In the text of the program, because of fears of dividing the movement, expressions of nationalization/socialization of the means of production had to be avoided (Andrieu 2014).

were nationalized. The economic reasons behind nationalization could be explained by the enormous need for the reconstruction of infrastructure (like railroads, roads, energy, and pipelines) in the environment of general capital shortage. The political and economic motives behind the nationalization of most of the financial and insurance sector—that is, big saving banks, real estate, and agricultural lending—mutually reinforced each other as state ownership enabled savings to go towards the massive investment projects undertaken by the state companies operating infrastructure networks.

The duality of political and economic motives can also be found beyond the twentieth century's third major wave of nationalizations initiated by Mitterrand. By taking over 100 percent of all firms to be nationalized, the Socialists sought to deprive the country's industrial and financial elite (i.e., the heirs of Bank of France's main shareholders) of their economic power base, and curb the expansion of foreign capital in France. At the same time, at least in the case of industrial firms, nationalizations only concerned groups that were in need of urgent state aid (Cohen 1993, 794).

While post-World War II nationalizations had not yet involved commercial banks, the Nationalization Act of February 11, 1982 transferred the entirety of thirty-nine registered banks and two important financial groups to the state, in addition to 100 percent of the shares of the above-mentioned major industrial groups.[8] The state also acquired a blocking minority stake in the giants of the steel industry and in French and foreign-owned companies in certain high-tech sectors (e.g., IT, telecommunications, pharmaceuticals, aviation, aerospace, the nuclear and military industry) (Vessilier 1983, 467). Along with the already mentioned political and ideological motivations, the latter move may also have been justified on the grounds of national security.[9]

As a result of this third wave of nationalizations, the number of public companies rose to 3000, representing 23 percent of France's GDP in 1982

---

[8] A financial group is a group of companies in the center of which there is a bank that combines traditional commercial banking and investment banking, holds a highly diversified portfolio in various sectors, and therefore is able to exert pressure on a large part of the real economy (Harbula 1999, 246–48). In the case of three other banks, indirect state ownership was converted into direct (Loi 82-155 du 11 février 1982 de nationalisation, Article 12).

[9] Protecting strategic sectors is far from a French specialty. In the United States, the *1988 "Exon-Florio" amendment* to "Defense Production Act" gave the president a broad mandate to limit foreign investments in strategic sectors. Since neither France nor the EU has such legal instrument, state ownership continues to play an important role in protecting industries deemed strategic for national security (Cour des comptes 2013, 28).

(*Vie Publique* 2018). A total of 670,000 jobs had been transferred from the private to the public sphere, and the total number of employees working in the public sector thus rose to a historic high of 2.3 million, representing more than 10 percent of the total workforce in the period between 1982 and 1985.[10]

When assessing the waves of nationalization, on the positive side, one can mention that public companies contributed to the country's postwar modernization (e.g., the development of gas supply, high-speed rail networks, and nuclear power industry), and the effective organization of public services by the managers of nationalized companies, who shared an educational background in France's top universities. Even if the 1981–82 nationalizations ultimately proved to be short-lived, they, nevertheless, facilitated the timely restructuration of French industry.

On the negative side, anxieties about the expansion of the public sector stem from the double risks associated with first, the government's intervention in day-to-day business operations ("manual control"), and second, the regulatory agency's eventual domination by the state-owned company that needs to be regulated ("regulatory capture").[11]

Crisis and Turning Point

After World War II, the state's regular and substantial intervention typically concentrated on a few large, so-called crisis industries. Shipbuilding benefited from regular subsidies starting in 1951, as did coal mining

---

[10] The percentage share of the public sector rose from 6.1 to 18.6 in terms of industrial jobs, from 8.0 to 22.5 in value added, from 9.2 to 23.8 in investments, and from 12.2 to 32.1 in exports (Bizaguet 1983, 455). The credit sector in the strict sense of the word—that is, excluding broker and financial advisory activities—nearly became completely controlled by the government: 90 percent of the liquid assets, 84.7 percent of loans to the economy, and 89.9 percent of those employed in the sector (458).

[11] Such capture has, in the literature, been typically linked to two major state-owned companies in France. One of them is EDF, which, by virtue of its accumulated knowledge concerning the sector, alone determines and executes the current French energy policy and defines the structure of energy production with the predominance of nuclear power (Kissler and Pautrat 2007, 33). The other company is SNCF, which, by pushing the concept of TGV (high-speed trains) to the extreme and thus contributing to the dereliction of regional railways, "captured" not only the regulator but also the infrastructure manager and the regional decision makers (Doumayrou 2007, 222).

throughout the 1960s and the steel industry from 1966 onwards, although these subsidies were, by then, mostly based on industrial policy considerations and emerged in the context of (or as quasi-catalysts for) territorial development policy. The period between 1974 and 1984, which was burdened with oil and financial crises, did, however, bring strong constraints on structural change for French industry.[12]

While the crisis expanded to other segments of industry (textiles, printing, leather and footwear, machine tool manufacturing), the left-wing government that came to power in 1981 tried, if only for a couple of years, to return to previous voluntarist industrial policy. The old toolkit for rescuing companies had been significantly enhanced to incorporate sometimes even violent elements such as forced co-operation between banks and local authorities; the compulsory reorganization of management (that is, stuffing boards and filling leadership positions with political appointees); the imposition of special taxes on companies' public customers, etc. The former "catalyst function" of government support was replaced by the "protecting state function": economic rescue operations became increasingly costly for the national budget (Cohen 2007, 10–12).

In France, the neoliberal turn had to be postponed until 1983. In addition to three consecutive minor devaluations of the Franc and the introduction of a price and wage freeze in the public sector as of June 1982, drastic austerity measures were announced in March 1983.[13]

---

[12] In order to understand how harmful the crisis was, it is enough to remember that nearly one-third of French industrial jobs had been lost between 1978 and 1985 (Cohen 2007, 20).

[13] Apart from significant cuts in public expenditures, there were new taxes imposed, the wealthy were obliged to purchase state bonds, and restrictions were placed on foreign currency outflow (Souriac 1996, 141–42). *Note*: The three mini-devaluations may, at first glance, seem meaningless. It should, however, be remembered that within the framework of the European Monetary System (EMS), which has been in place since 1979, only minor exchange rate adjustments were permitted if agreed upon with partners beforehand. The real choice was between leaving the EMS, thus permitting the Franc to depreciate, which would have slowed down imports and protected French industry and jobs, or remaining in the EMS and avoiding—by means of austerity (a policy so credible in the eyes of the mainstream elite)—the need for further devaluations, giving a chance to structural change and industrial modernization. And indeed, the policy of a "strong Franc" and low inflation has followed since 1983, and eventually led to low interest rates, structural consolidation, and sustained growth. The three "mini-devaluations" could ultimately be judged as the strong commitment of France to European integration (Asselain 2002).

There were also radical changes made to economic rescue policy: the procedures for bankrupt companies were reorganized (reshaped) on a market basis (as opposed to a power politics basis) and their cases were assigned to commercial courts. The number of expensive state interventions decreased substantially, providing space for consultative, professional advisers and analysts. In cases where interventions still did take place, it was the territorial administrative level that had increasingly been charged with footing the bill. Moreover, if a troubled company needed life breathed into it, central authorities were becoming less and less reluctant to solve the problem by turning to foreign investors.

Reprivatization

The quarter century following the left's neoliberal shift in 1983 and lasting up to the 2008 crisis saw a continuous decrease in the economic role of the state. Regardless of their political affiliation, and on the basis of the growing inclination to implement neoliberal economic policies, all French governments have felt it their duty to continue reprivatization. As a result, the weight of SOEs[14] in the French economy has decreased substantially. Since 1985, their share shrank to one-third in fixed capital, one-fourth in employment, and one-fifth in GVA (Figure 1).

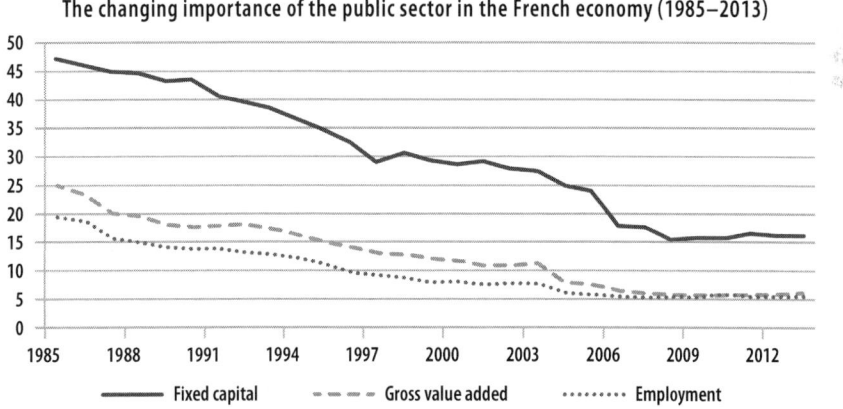

Figure 1
The changing importance of the public sector in the French economy (1985–2013)

Source: INSEE, 2016a. Note: The significant downturn in the public sector fixed capital share after 2005 was due to the privatization of motorway companies in 2006.

---

[14] State owned enterprises are defined as companies in which the public has majority ownership (*Vie Publique* 2018).

The fact that the public sector has been diminishing in importance can also be observed in the decline of the number of SOEs and employment in the state sector (Figure 2). Between 1986, the last year before the formal privatization process began, and 2007, the last year before the global financial crisis had been felt fully, the number of SOEs fell by three-fourths, and the number of people employed by them fell by more than half. In the same period, the share of SOEs' employees in the total employment figures fell from 10 to 3.5 percent.

Figure 2
Number of SOEs (triangles, lhs), number of people employed in SOEs (spots, x1000, lhs), and their share of total employment (bars, percent, rhs)

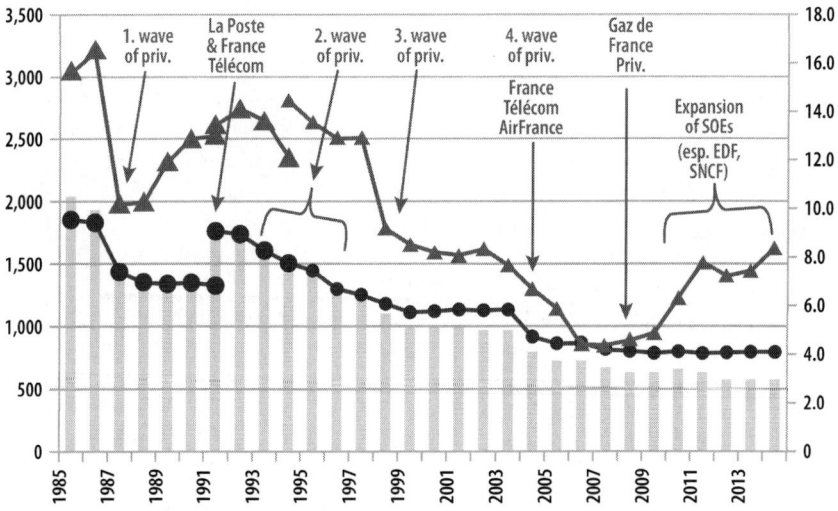

Source: Author's own compilation based on INSEE 2016b.
Note: Discontinuities in series for the bars and spots were due to the 1991 split of PTT, a former government department, into two public law corporations: La Poste and France Télécom, which caused an increase of 400,000, or 2 percent of SOEs' employees. The discontinuity for the graph's triangles in 1994 was due to a change in methodology.

As a result of the privatization process, French corporate structure (especially concerning the largest firms) has significantly changed and has been fortified. The incumbent government had actually been free to decide on the shareholder structure in companies slated for privatization. As a defensive move against potential hostile takeovers, so-called "stable nuclei" were formed with the participation of around ten to twelve larger shareholders— i.e., institutional investors who were often slated for privatization as well—who individually acquired between 0.5 and 5.0 percent of the corporation's capital.

Although the Minister of Finance tried different combinations of large investors when preparing "stable nuclei" in order to prevent accusations of corruption, top managers and members of boards in the privatized firms were almost exclusively people from right-wing politicians' and their friends' and relatives' circles, members of the French establishment who graduated from ENA[15] or Polytechnique, the most prestigious and elitist high schools, or those who came straight out of the Grand Corps of the State.[16]

Because the big French companies purchased each other's shares, even if in relatively broad circles, a complex network of cross ownership was established, which, by its mere existence, ruled out any possibility of hostile takeovers. This practice (common educational background plus cross-ownership) enabled a high level of coordination and protection of both business and political interests (Harbula 2007, 5). As a result, instead of creating a new economic system based, as originally planned, on masses of small shareholders and the primacy of market forces,[17] the reprivatization process bolstered the system of "establishment solidarity," a French tradition of "capitalism without capital" and a financial market without sanctions; in short, a sort of "capitalisme à la française" (Bauer 1988, 59–60).

The process of privatization lasted so long not only because of the large number of companies to be privatized, but also because all along, the deregulation/privatization of certain sectors (e.g., telecommunication) was defined by two different approaches to public services that had been competing with each other: the American approach based on Anglo-Saxon legal traditions (focusing on the "product"), and the Latin-European tradition based on Roman law.[18] Additionally, for the French, public services have traditionally been part of their history, culture, and rule of law; something connected to the elimination of feudalism; a sort of republican value. In French public services, the principle of equality prevails, and a system of

---

[15] École nationale d'administration (National School of Administration).
[16] Already mentioned under the subheading Centralizations Traditions.
[17] "Market forces were involved neither as an actor in the privatisations, nor as a regulator of the privatized groups" (Bauer 1988, 60).
[18] With some simplification, the obvious differences in approaches are attributed to the assumption that while English common law was the product of judges, Roman private law was the work of jurists (Watson 1990, 249).

differentiated tariffs allows transfers among social strata and geographical regions, which enhance social, economic and territorial cohesion.

In contrast, through deregulation, this enhanced (French) interpretation of public services has inevitably been restricted to an Anglo-Saxon concept of "universal service," which has eventually come to mean nothing more than an obligation to provide everybody a certain minimum set of services (at decent prices). Collective utility and related positive externalities were all ignored by this new concept of public services. By pushing back the role of the state, there was a limit placed on income redistribution through tariffs and equalization payments, which had long been a traditional element of French territorial cohesion.

Breaking up monopolies, taking apart segments of the market, separating network infrastructure from services, all of this weakened the positions of both the state and historical service providers, while at the same time, under the pretext of competition, it provided global market actors with open access to national infrastructure, which had previously been built and operated with taxpayers' money. The result was that instead of a monopoly, an oligopolic system emerged (Musso 2008, 15–18).

While on the eve of the global financial crisis, the scope of centrally managed financial institutions only included the CDC,[19] the BPI,[20] and the Banque Postale, some other sectors of the economy still remained under significant state control. In the case of operators of natural monopolies and some major public service providers (the post and railways)—fearing social conflicts and/or due to low profitability—as well as some businesses of strategic importance (e.g., Areva, the worldwide player in nuclear energy), Paris has continued to abstain from privatization (Fournier 2014).

---

[19] The *Caisse des dépôts et consignations* [Deposits and Consignments Fund] is a special French public financial institution under parliamentary control that is responsible for collecting tax-free retail deposits (so-called *Livret A*) and financing social housing, local government investments, and especially those slow-return economic development projects (in the field of infrastructure, urbanization, and environment) that are of little interest to the private sector. Its role has recently been questioned because of the archaic monopoly it enjoys concerning mandatory deposits of some regulated professions (like notaries, trustees, liquidators, bailiffs), real estate deposits, and minor mannequins' and actors' salaries, which, because of economic inertia, present stable sources for its medium- and long-term investments and the opportunity to engage in risky financial market transactions (*Generationlibre* 2016 online).

[20] The *Banque publique d'investissement* [Public Investment Bank] is a public investment bank aimed at supporting national and regional development policies and the participation of small and medium-sized enterprises in them.

Crisis = Change?

In France, the 2008 global financial crisis cannot be considered a landmark for the role of the state in the economy. There was neither a break nor a change in the prevailing paradigm. There have, of course, been pros and cons to increasing or decreasing the scope of public intervention, but there was no major change in the overall trend. The privatization process already slowed down well before the crisis, and in the life of the biggest SOEs, 2004, the year the Government Shareholdings Agency (APE[21]) was established, was more important than 2008.

There is, however, a relationship between the crisis on one hand, and public thinking about the role of the state—or rather the changing role of the state—in the economy on the other. As a matter of fact, the crisis, which caused millions of people to lose their jobs and homes, has given further impetus to the trend of implementing increasingly stringent (i.e., private-sector-style) management practices in public companies.

French Banks and the Financial Crisis

The 2008 global financial crisis hit the banking system in France much less severely than in other European countries with similarly sized economies, because, due to various reasons such as regulatory and structural features to be explored later in this chapter, it was relatively less exposed to shocks from abroad. The French have indeed spent comparatively little on bailing out their financial institutions—5.6 percent of GDP (i.e., €119 billion) between 2008 and 2014, which was a very low level in the EU, especially among the old member states. Out of the EU's six largest economies, France ranks last (Figure 3). Of this amount, 21.1 percent went to recapitalize banks, and 1 percent went to finance impaired asset measures. The remaining 77.9 percent consisted of *de facto* state guarantees given to cover part of the liabilities, originally amounting to EUR 319.8 billion, of which only €92.7 billion was used.[22]

---

[21] *Agence des participations de l'Etat.*

[22] A significant part of the support was given to the two banks that suffered the most from the U.S. subprime mortgage crisis: Natixis, a bank formed through the cooperation of *Banque Populaire* and *Caisse d'Épargne* set up in 2006, and the French-Belgian *Dexia.* Both of them got into trouble because of their subsidiaries (FSA

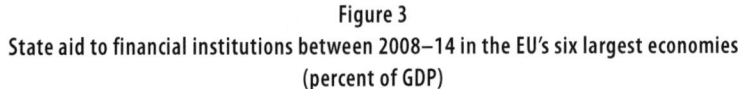

Figure 3
State aid to financial institutions between 2008–14 in the EU's six largest economies
(percent of GDP)

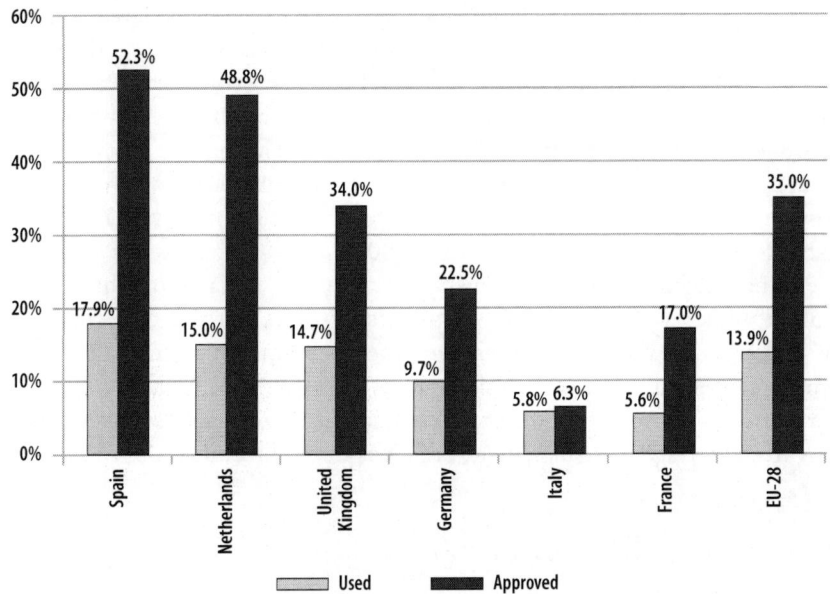

Source: author's own compilation based on data from *EC, DG Competition* (2016 online).

Eventually, French taxpayers were fairly content with the relatively low costs incurred by them when facing the consequences of the global financial crisis on their banking system. Also, public subsidies, most of which were concentrated in the early years of the crisis, did not need to be significantly increased later.[23]

---

and CIFG respectively) were two of the biggest American "monoline" insurance companies. The latter institutions were originally narrowly focused on providing financial guarantees to municipal bond investors—that is why they were called "monolines": to distinguish them from "multi-line" insurance companies, which also offer life or property and casualty insurance. After 1985, however, in a search of higher profit, the "monolines" began to diversify themselves by taking on lucrative RMBS (residential mortgage-backed securities) and other structured products, which, because they were heavily leveraged through the U.S. housing boom (2002–2006), put their whole business model at risk (Lautier and Simon 2008).

[23] At the same time, it should not be forgotten that French banks were heavily exposed—both at home and, via their subsidiaries, abroad (especially in South Europe)—to the secondary effects of the global financial crisis, i.e., the slowdown in economic growth and the sovereign debt crisis (Howarth 2013, 381).

When examining the background of the above events, it is important to be clear about the significant changes in the French financial system triggered by the neoliberal turn and the subsequent privatization process starting in the mid-1980s. The dominance of state (public) ownership ended quickly, when the largest commercial banks were listed on the stock exchange. All French banks, which were covered by the same (unified) legal framework starting in 1984, were allowed to become universal banks: this made it possible for them to diversify in ways that moved them away from their former core activities towards more profitable ones. The stock market was flourishing, and the MATIF[24] began trading futures in 1986. The removal of credit market restrictions spurred competition in the internal market. Links between French banks and non-financial firms, which had never been as tight as in Germany, became even looser, especially for CAC40's blue chips, which relied increasingly on the financial market. The French economy had "moved from a financial network to a financial market form of capitalism" (Hardie–Howarth 2009, 1020). But this change was not unreasonably fast. The "built-in brakes" of the old model worked, and they eventually helped shelter the French financial system from suffering as much as its British or German counterparts from the global financial crisis.

What were the 'built-in brakes' mentioned above? First, it was the very structure of the financial system. As a result of the privatization process in France, a highly concentrated financial system emerged around a small number of giant banks: these banks were interconnected in a complex cross-ownership network together with large corporations in other sectors of the economy. And although in the decade preceding the crisis—parallel to the growing internationalization of French economy and stock exchange—the extensive network of cross-ownership had begun to unravel, the economic model based on financial networks continued to exist in many respects. On the one hand, financial institutions, like most of the giant corporations, continued to have large shareholders with (in most cases) blocking minority control (Harbula 2007, 448). On the other hand, there was still the overrepresentation of people from the Ministry of Finance or bank supervision authority and other senior officials of major state bodies —that is, the so-called elite network—on the companies' boards, all of whom had pursued relatively standard careers and all knew each other from school (Schmidt 2003, 542).

---

[24] Marché à terme international de France [International futures market of France] (now Euronext Paris S.A.).

Managers' common "cultural" background (in public administration) prevented financial companies from engaging in overly risky transactions, or at least gaining too much importance from them in their business turnover. In this respect, it is typical that when financial liberalization broadened the scope of activities, French banks began to establish strongholds in retail banking services, especially in Southern Europe, since these same countries had long been France's financial hunting grounds.[25] In contrast to the British and German examples where the internationalization of financial activities was almost exclusively in corporate lending and investment banking, the French banking sector gained international prominence by investing in retail banking, which was deemed to be a relatively low-risk business line. Undoubtedly, the strong retail component (both domestic and international) of the French banks helped lessen the overall impact of the global financial crisis (Hardie and Howarth 2009, 1023).

A similar cautiousness with regard to the use of derivatives in trading activities can also be observed. French banks mostly specialized in equity, interest, and exchange rate derivatives, from which record earnings mitigated the impulse to extend into more risky credit derivatives.

On the whole, for their size, and thus their ability to resist market turmoil, French banks:

a.) invested little in assets that later became toxic (notably products based on American subprime mortgages);
b.) were less involved in setting up off-balance sheet vehicles (OBSV, like SPVs/SPEs),[26] securitizing property-based financial products (especially billions of dollars' worth of risky U.S. subprime mortgages), i.e. wrapping them and selling them to investors in tranches;
c.) were, in general, less engaged in the securitization of lending; and
d.) were less reliant on short-term interbank lending (Howarth 2013, 376–77).

The above listed features of the French financial system may partly be explained in terms of banking strategy. But this uniformity of all or most of the largest French banks could also be described as systemic, and as such, ultimately linked to some permanent elements of French economic policy.

---

[25] As a result of their rapid expansion in Italy, both *BNP Paribas* and the *Crédit Agricole* counted the country as their second "domestic" market by 2006–7 (CECEI 2007, 127).

[26] Special Purpose Vehicles or Special Purpose Entities.

It is no wonder that the state action to boost investments and replace traditional funding sources for NFCs (such as retail deposit and commercial papers) through encouraging banks to engage in securitization was unsuccessful, if on the other hand, laws and regulations like those limiting the type of assets to be securitized or the maintenance of red tape surrounding the creation of OBSVs endured. Furthermore, in order to create and strengthen big banks as market leaders (so-called national champions), a number of laws and regulations remained in place for decades—such as the limitation on the distribution of certain types of accounts (like *Livret A*) with fiscal advantages for their holders to a small number of financial institutions; the preservation of the privileged role of the CDC; and the strengthening of the regulation thwarting hostile takeovers of large national companies.[27] The maintenance of those laws and regulations provided French banks with effective protection as well as a kind of guiding framework.

Although the French financial system has become extremely open, the "internationalization" of the market did not lead to a significant expansion of foreign banks in France. In fact, the opposite happened. In response to increased competitive pressure, there was strong concentration in the financial sector, with the ever-larger French banks expanding to foreign markets. This expansion could not even be stopped by the global financial crisis. The contemporary problem is that certain banks have grown too big, and four out of the five largest financial institutions in France have already appeared in the list of the FSB[28]. This list identifies the thirty Global Systematically Important Banks (G-SIB) which, by their problems, size, complexity, and interconnections, pose systemic risk to the global financial system (FSB 2015, 2016).

The state has played a prominent role in the development, internationalization, and increasing market orientation of the French banking

---

[27] As of 1989, the former regulation about the requirement to notify the relevant (financial market) authority in case any person's or entity's shareholding reached a certain threshold (5 percent, 10 percent, 15 percent, 20 percent, 25 percent, 30 percent, one-third, 50 percent, two-thirds, 90 percent or 95 percent) in a listed company, was supplemented by a new provision which has since proven to be most effective in the protection of big banks. According to the provision, beyond the threshold of 33.3 percent, there was an obligation to make a public bid of up to at least 66.6 percent, making it prohibitively expensive to venture into any hostile takeovers against large French corporations (Borgomano et al. 2016 online).

[28] The Financial Stability Board is a Swiss-based international body that monitors and makes recommendations about the global financial system.

system, and has done a great deal to keep the sector afloat in the worst period of the global financial crisis, even without directly intervening in the market. As of the beginning of the 2000s, the preference for indirect tools of economic policy over direct ones has gained ground in other strategic sectors too. Successive governments made increasing use of market methods.

Government Asset Management

Although the (re)privatization process that started at the mid-1980s has, in several waves, substantially narrowed the government's latitude to influence the economy, this did not mean that debates about how the remnants of the public sector should most effectively operate were over. The analyses forming the basis for these debates developed principles and recommendations, and also exposed the unsustainability of the situation. Let us start with the latter.

As markets became increasingly open to international competition; European competition policy became less and less permissive with regard to the finances of public-sector companies; the amount of profits available in the financial sector clearly rose to well above those in the real economy; and radical changes occurred in shareholders' role and management methods of private companies —the state was unable to reconstruct itself at such a fast pace, and companies of the public sector remained partially regulated by rules and laws dating back to the 1950s (!) (Minefi 2003, 7).

As for the principles and recommendations contained in the analyses, it is worth mentioning the need for:
- a clear separation of the state's shareholder function from its other functions;
- operational and contracting transparency;
- the outsourcing of public services via a transparent and accountable concession contract administration process;
- a clear distinction between public services and services of public interest;
- the separation of public sector activities from market sector activities;
- opening up the latter for private investment by transforming utilities into joint-stock companies;
- and finally, setting up a state wealth agency.

All analyses agreed that the government must seek to establish policies and institutions by which it would able to pursue a responsible asset management policy, thus promoting the development of the companies in its portfolio (Minefi 2001, 2003; Barbier de la Serre et al. 2003).

Finally established by decree in 2004, the Government Shareholding Agency's mission, main objectives, and guidelines concerning its operational functioning are as follows:

- the APE acts as a prudent and well advised long-term equity investor in companies deemed to be of strategic importance for the country;[29]
- revenues generated by the APE should be reinvested in wealth management or used to pay down public debt[30] (APE 2016 online/a,b);
- for the APE, four main objectives are identified as necessities:
  - to maintain a sufficient level of control in strategic companies—such as 100 percent in electricity grid management, 70 percent in gas and electricity service providers, and 50 percent in the Paris airports operator ADP (Aéroports de Paris) (Sénat 2016);
  - to preserve strong public services operators able to meet France's basic needs;
  - to help consolidate and develop businesses in sectors driving economic growth both in France and Europe;[31]
  - to proceed with *ad hoc* bailouts of companies whose failure could lead to systemic risk (*APE*, 2016 online/c).

---

[29] Companies of strategic importance are, e.g., those that enjoy a natural or market monopoly, or operate in the field of security, defense or the nuclear industry, whose investments are to be financed by the state through capital increases (i.e., not by indebting them) in accordance with Article 107 of the Treaty on the Functioning of the EU relating to state aid (Boillon 2014, 41).

[30] In 2015, €800 million of the proceeds of disposals was used in this way (APE 2016).

[31] In order to achieve this goal, it is not necessary for the state to be a majority owner. Depending on the shareholder structure, 5 to 30 percent of public ownership may generally be sufficient (APE 2016 online/c). Note, however, that although the success of companies and their value creation is dependent on the economic sector they are in rather than their shareholder structure, research shows that companies with controlling shareholders generally outperform their counterparts with fragmented ownership. Nevertheless, corporate performance improves with increases in controlling shareholders' shares until the latter reaches an optimum level (at about 25 to 30 percent), and then it gets progressively weaker (Harbula 2007, 449).

The APE 2014–15 annual report revealed that this small agency, which has a staff of slightly more than fifty, manages a portfolio worth €90 billion (including €60 billion in listed companies alone). The eighty-one businesses belonging to its portfolio generated an annual revenue of €147 billion and employed almost 1.7 million people in 2015. In that year, APE paid dividends worth €3.9 billion into the general budget. APE's portfolio, which contains both direct and indirect shareholdings, is extremely diverse both in terms of the sectors covered—though with the prominence of aerospace/defense, energy, transport, automobile manufacturing, services (particularly telecom, postal, and banking), and audio-visual—and the size of the government's stake in the individual companies (for the main elements of the portfolio, see Figure 4).

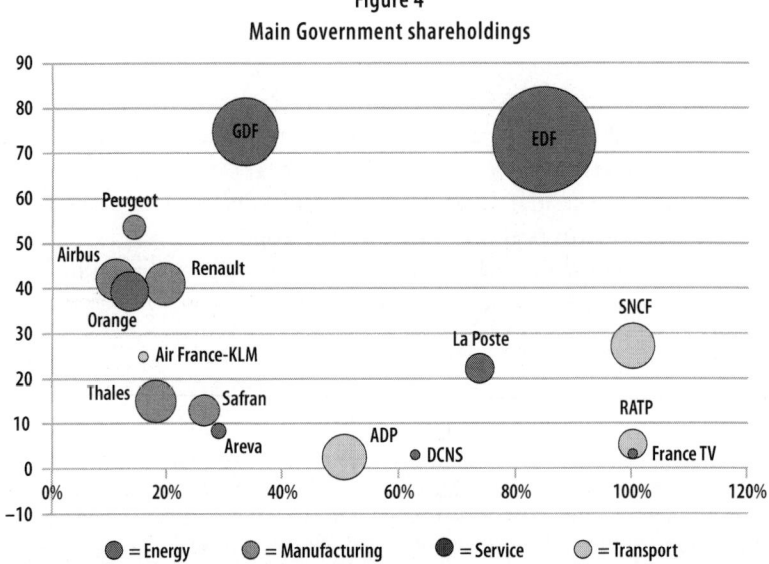

Figure 4
Main Government shareholdings

Source: author's own computation based on *APE* 2015. Listed companies (circles) and non-listed companies (shadowed circles: SNCF, La Poste, RATP, DCNS, and France TV). The size of each circle is proportional to the Government's equity stake (calculated on the basis of stock market value in the case of listed companies). In this figure, there are companies with more than 10,000 employees. X-axis: share of state ownership. Y-axis: annual turnover (€ billion)

As for the above-mentioned recommendations preceding the establishment of the APE, most of them—for instance, the separation of shareholding from other state functions; the contractualization of public services and their transformation into concessions; the separation of commercial activities (from those under public service obligations); and the opening of SOEs' capital to private investors—were taken into account and put into practice by the government. The one related to the transformation of state-owned entities was so widely supported that by mid-2014, the vast majority (68 percent) of the firms in the government's portfolio (of which several symbolic ones like ADP, EDF or GDF since 2004–5) have operated as public limited companies[32] (Boillon 2014, 46). The advantage of being a PLC resided in the fact that it was much easier for enterprises to raise funds, and they could more effectively mitigate risks and losses associated with business cycle volatility and market fluctuations than if they remained in their former legal form.

At the same time, recommendations concerning transparency of operation and contracting have not been fully implemented yet, or more precisely, there has been some controversy surrounding government intentions and actions. On the one hand, legal changes (a law from January 2014 and a decree from August 2014) have taken effect, which simplify life for public companies, making it similar to that of private companies by relaxing the rules on the composition of both management and supervisory boards.[33] On the other hand, apart from the remnants of French protectionism present in some out-of-date laws and regulations, a new wave of economic patriotism has recently arisen and been institutionalized in a law from March 2014, the so-called *Law Aimed at Recapturing the Real Economy*. This law initially made it more difficult to shut down factories and initiate mass layoffs in companies employing over 1,000 people in France by slowing down and rendering the process more expensive. Second, through the generalization of double voting rights in listed companies[34] for those

---

[32] The portfolio also encompasses other legal forms: government-funded industrial and commercial institutions (e.g., RATP, SNCF network), government-funded administrative institutions (e.g., National Highway Authority), government-funded institutions (mainly sea ports), and semi-public companies (e.g., Semmaris, the operator of Paris-Rungis, the world's largest wholesale food (fresh produce) market) (APE 2016).

[33] In the wake of the changes—as board members, instead of being appointed from a limited group of senior civil servants, could be drawn from a larger pool of experts, a method more suited to companies' interests—the number of political nominees reduced substantially. While in 2013, the state still participated in the nomination of 936 administrators, of which 366 represented the state directly, in 2015 these numbers fell to 765 and 272 respectively (APE 2016 online/c; APE 2013, 7; APE 2016, 17).

[34] More than half of the CAC 40 companies have as yet introduced double voting rights. The French government now has double voting rights in Renault,

holding their shares for at least two years, it strengthened the state's controlling role.³⁵

Certainly, there were one or two cases when the law helped to preserve jobs.³⁶ But the law was more about the Socialist Party's (governing France between 2012 and 2017) desire to expand its electoral base by appealing to voters receptive to the idea of economic patriotism. Experience shows, however, that the pursuit of consensus or the implementation of methods borrowed from the private sector, like APE's asset management, can be more effective than pushing through laws in the interests of domestic players.

An example of the consensus-seeking approach was when Peugeot SA (or PSA), Europe's second largest carmaker, Dongfeng Motors, its Chinese partner, and the French government agreed to collectively invest €3 billion in capital increases—providing €1.4, 0.8, and 0.8 billion respectively, much-needed cash to keep PSA afloat—in return for each receiving a 14 percent stake in the company.³⁷ The agreement made it possible to simultaneously avoid factory shutdowns, keep three quarters of research and development activity in France, and help the company expand internationally.

The efficiency of APE's asset management can be confirmed through the post-2009 expansion of both EDF and SNCF (as shown in Figure 2), which was made possible by the introduction of modern corporate governance methods borrowed from the private sector. Because of its extensive subsidiary network, the acquisition of Dalkia alone by EDF in 2014 increased the number of SOEs by almost 200.³⁸

Air France, Safran, Thales, PSA Peugeot Citroën, Orange, Aéroports de Paris, CNP, Areva, EDF and ENGIE (APE 2016, 22).

³⁵ The legislators' proclaimed intention with the law was to protect companies against speculative attacks, but in practice, it made possible for the state—in order to reduce general debt or finance other investments—to sell its shares without having to reduce its influence in those companies (Errard 2015).

³⁶ See e.g. the capital increase in Renault, by which the influence of the state has grown so that it will certainly be able to prevent plans for endangering jobs in France. (*Le Monde* 2015) At the same time, the deal was rated differently by the stock market: Renault shares dropped by a third in the short term, and have been since then fluctuating approximately 10–15 percent below their former value (*Euronext* 2016 online http://www.boursedeparis.fr/products/equities/FR0000131906-XPAR).

³⁷ Before the savings deal, the Peugeot family had 25.4 percent of the capital and 38.1 percent of the voting rights (*HuffPost* 2014).

³⁸ If the number of employees seems not to keep up with the increase in the number of state-owned companies (in Figure 2), this is due to the continuous "rationalization" of staff at the major public sector employers (e.g. railways, post and energy) (INSEE 2016b).

Final Remarks

Regarding the economic role of the state through state-owned enterprises, today's France does not provide much of a contrast to its main partners anymore.[39] If it still seems to be different, this comes partly from the common educational and cultural background of the French elite (see French banks' effective crisis resistance) and partly from the efforts of the Socialist government (in power from 2012 to 2017) to maintain at least the semblance of its commitment to economic patriotism in order to enlarge its electoral basis. But against the reality of globalized competitive markets, all of those efforts are worthless. If the prospects for return on capital are higher outside of France, investments will take place abroad.

What is positive (or promising) is that two-thirds of SOEs in France already operate as plc, in conditions increasingly similar to those of private companies. Several SOEs have even changed their names to separate themselves from the old-fashioned, paternalistic culture their former names connoted.[40] However, in companies that have not yet been transformed, there is still the risk of "manual control," that is, the intervention of the "owner state" in day-to-day business operations.[41]

Although the global financial crisis did not cause a paradigm shift regarding the role of the state in the economy, the ideological foundations of the previous (re-privatization) policy have been shaken. In certain functions, state (public) ownership proved to be viable and crisis resistant, thereby justifying its existence. The privatization process did not come to a halt—currently the sale of the airports is on the agenda—but the time of the state's continuous withdrawal from the economy is over. Some of the ongoing processes—e.g., challenges related to climate change, to be

---

[39] According to data from the French statistical office (INSEE), at the end of 2014, 1,632 French companies were under state control, with a total of workforce of 795,000 people. 85 percent of employees worked in the field of transport, transportation, or warehousing (60.7 percent), power generation and supply (16.7 percent) or science (7.6 percent) (INSEE 2016b). In 2012, the book value of equity of SOEs relative to GDP was lower in France than in the Netherlands, Sweden, Finland, Italy, the Baltics, Czechia, Poland, or Ireland (EC 2015, 25).

[40] That's how Gaz de France became *Engie*, and France Télécom became *Orange*.

[41] Boillon raises several examples including when the already heavily indebted SNFC was forced into the purchase of 40 TGV trains from Alstom to preserve jobs in the latter's factories (Boillon 2014, 67–68).

addressed as a major priority for the coming decades—already suggest that demand for public intervention in certain sectors of the economy may be rising (Fournier 2015).

REFERENCES

Andrieu, Claire. 2014. "Le programme du CNR dans la dynamique de construction de la nation résistante." *Histoire@ Politique* 3 (24): 5-23.
Agence des participations de l'État. 2016. "Notre Mission Statement." http://www.economie.gouv.fr/agence-participations-etat/notre-mission-statement.
———. 2016. "Lignes directrices de l'État actionnaire." http://www.economie.gouv.fr/files/files/directions_services/agence-participations-etat/Documents/Textes_de_reference/Lignes_directrices_de_l'Etat_actionnaire_-_17_03_2014.pdf.
———. 2016. "Notre stratégie." http://www.economie.gouv.fr/agence-participations-etat/notre-strategie.
———. 2013. "L'État actionnaire." http://www.economie.gouv.fr/files/directions_services/agence-participations-etat/Documents/Rapports-de-l-Etat-actionnaire/2013/RA_APE_complet.pdf.
———. 2014-5. "L'État actionnaire: Énergie, industrie, services et finance, transports." economie.gouv.fr. http://www.agefi.fr/sites/agefi.fr/files/migrate/etudereference/PKPWYLGPSY_Rapport_Web_APE_2014-15.pdf.
———. 2015-16. "Rapport d'activité 2015/2016." economie.gouv.fr. http://www.economie.gouv.fr/files/files/directions_services/agence-participations-etat/RAPPORT_D'ACTIVITE_APE_2015-2016.pdf.
Asselain, Jean-Charles. 2002. "Le siècle des dévaluations." In *Conferences du Ministère de l'Economie et des Finances de France* (Vol. 4). http://champdespossibles.blogspot.com/2011/10/le-siecle-des-devaluations_18.html.
Bajomi, Endre. 1938. "A francia gabonahivatal" [The French Grain Board]. *Korunk* 13: 536–38.
Banque de France (online). *Loi tendant à modifier et à compléter les Lois et statuts qui régissent la Banque de France.* Histoire, Institution https://www.banque-france.fr/sites/default/files/arrete.pdf#page=207.
Barbier de La Serre, René, Jacques-Henri David, Alain Joly, and Philippe Rouvillois. 2003. *L'Etat actionnaire et le gouvernement des entreprises publiques.* Paris: Ministère de l'Economie, des finances et de l'industrie.
Bauer, M. 1988. "The Politics of State-directed Privatisation: The Case of France, 1986–88." *West European Politics* 11 (4): 49–60.
Bizaguet, Armand. 1983. "L'importance des entreprises publiques dans l'économie française et européenne après les nationalisations de 1982." *Revue économique* 34 (3): 434–465.
Boillon, Christophe. 2014. *La gouvernance des entreprises à participations publiques: L'Etat comme actionnaire privé.* Paris: Université Paris-Sud. http://memoire.jm.u-psud.fr/index.php?id=4400.
Borgomano, Cyril, Olivier Hoen, Aarnaud Mora, and Caroline Tetelboum. 2016. "Prise de controle de sociétés et moyens de defense." Jeulin. http://www.jeulin.net/ScPo/OPA.htm.

Brucy, Guy. 2001. "La doctrine de la CGT sur la formation des adultes: entre pragmatisme et lutte de classes (1945–1955)" *Travail et emploi* (86): 65–86.
Comité des établissements de crédit et des entreprises d'investissement (CECEI). 2007. *2007, Rapport annuel du Comité des établissements de crédit et des entreprises d'investissement* https://acpr.banque-france.fr/sites/default/files/media/2017/10/30/cecei_ra_2007.pdf.
Chevallier, François. 1979. *Les entreprises publiques en France. Notes et Études documentaires.* Nos. 4507–4508, March 9, 1979. Paris: La documentation française.
Cohen, Elie. 1993. "Représentation de l'adversaire et politique économique: nationalisation, politique industrielle et Acte unique européen." *Revue française de science politique* (5): 788–806.
———. 2007. "Le CIRI ou l'ingénierie sociale du déclin industriel." *Actes du Colloque du Creusot 2007.* http://elie-cohen.eu/IMG/pdf/Creusot3.pdf.
Cour des comptes [Court of Audit]. 2013. *Les faiblesses de l'État actionnaire d'entreprises industrielles de défense, rapport public thématique.* Paris: La Documentation française.
Doumayrou, Vincent. 2007. *La fracture ferroviaire: pourquoi le TGV ne sauvera pas le chemin de fer.* Ivry-sur-Seine: Editions de l'Atelier.
European Commission. 2015. "Macroeconomic imbalances Country Report—Slovenia 2015" *Occasional papers* 224 (June). https://ec.europa.eu/economy_finance/publications/occasional_paper/2015/pdf/ocp224_en.pdf.
European Commission, DG Competition. 2016. "State Aid Scoreboard 2015—Aid in the Context of Financial and Economic Crisis."
Fournier, J. 2014. "L'entreprise publique." Lecture held at the conference "Actualité du droit de l'entreprise," Collège de France, Amphitéâtre Marguerite de Navarre, Paris, June 13.
———. 2015. "L'évolution de l'action publique en France." Lecture held at École Nationale des Travaux Publiques de l'Etat, Vaulx-en-Velin, April.
Financial Stability Board. 2015. "2015 Update of List of Global Systematically Important Banks (G-SIBs)." November 3. http://www.fsb.org/wp-content/uploads/2015-update-of-list-of-global-systemically-important-banks-G-SIBs.pdf.
Financial Stability Board. 2016. "2016 List of Global Systematically Important Banks (G-SIBs)." November 21. http://www.fsb.org/wp-content/uploads/2016-list-of-global-systemically-important-banks-G-SIBs.pdf.
Fondazione Eni Enrico Mattei. 2019. „PB Database." privatizationbarometer.com. http://www.privatizationbarometer.com/database.php.
Generationlibre. 2014. "La Caisse des Dépôts et Consignations: Visage de la finance folle?" March. https://www.generationlibre.eu/wp-content/uploads/2018/03/2014-03-CDC-visage-de-la-finance-folle-_-GenerationLibre.pdf.
Harbula, Péter. 1999. "Tulajdonosi és nagyvállalati struktúra a francia gazdaságban." [Ownership and corporate structure in the French economy] *Közgazdasági Szemle* 46 (3): 245–65.
———. 2007. "Francia vállalatok tulajdonosi szerkezete, felelős irányítása és felelőssége." [Ownership structure, responsible management and responsibility in French companies] *Hitelintézeti szemle* 6 (5): 429–52.
Hardie, Iain. And David Howarth. 2009. "Die Krise but not La Crise? The Financial Crisis and the Transformation of German and French Banking Systems." *Journal of Common Market Studies* 47 (5): 1017–39.

Howarth, David. 2013. "The Legacy of State-led Finance in France and the Rise of Gallic Market-Based Banking." *Governance* 26 (3): 369–95.
Huffington Post. 2014. "PSA officialise l'arrivée de l'Etat et du chinois Dongfeng au capital." February 19. http://www.huffingtonpost.fr/2014/02/19/psa-dongfeng-etat-officiel_n_4813116.html.
Institut national de la statistique et des études économiques. 2016a. "Entreprises publiques." *Insee Références* 15 (5) https://www.insee.fr/fr/statistiques/1906721?-sommaire=1906743..
———. Institut national de la statistique et des études économiques. 2016b. „Les entreprises contrôlées majoritairement par l'État au 31 décembre 2014." Insee. fr. https://www.insee.fr/fr/statistiques/1913867?sommaire=1914057#consulter-sommaire.
Kißler, Leo, René Lasserre, and Marie-Hélène Pautrat, eds. 2007. *Modernisation des services publics et management social en France et en Allemagne.* Cergy-Pontoise: CIRAC.
Kolm, Serge-Christophe. 2010. "History of Public Economics: The Historical French School." *European Journal of the History of Economic Thought* 17 (4): 687–718.
Lautier, Delphine, and Yves Simon. 2008. "Les rehausseurs de credit anatomie d'une crise." In "Crise financière: analyses et propositions," special edition. *Revue d'économie financière* (7): 305–14.
Errard, Guillaume. 2015. "Actionnaires: pourquoi l'État veut imposer le droit de vote double." *Le Figaro,* April 14. http://www.lefigaro.fr/societes/2015/04/14/20005-20150414ARTFIG00210-actionnaires-pourquoi-l-etat-veut-imposer-le-droit-de-vote-double.php.
Le Monde Économie. 2015. "Qu'est-ce que le droit de vote double que l'Etat veut défendre chez Renault?" April 8.
Meisel, Chris. 2014. "The Role of State History on Current European Union Economic Policies." *Towson University Journal of International Affairs* 47 (Fall 1): 78–97.
Ministry of the Economy and Finance. 2001. "L'État actionnaire: rapport 2001." https://www.youscribe.com/catalogue/documents/ressources-professionnelles/fiscalite/l-etat-actionnaire-rapport-2001-2369541
Ministry of the Economy and Finance. 2003. "L'État actionnaire: rapport 2003." https://www.ladocumentationfrancaise.fr/var/storage/rapports-publics/034000640.pdf
Musso, Pierre. 2008. "III. La dérégulation du système des télécoms," in *Les télécommunications,* edited by Pierre Musso, 38–59. Paris, La Découverte, "Repères." https://www.cairn.info/les-telecommunications--9782707150165-page-38.htm
Schmidt, Vivien. 2003. "French Capitalism Transformed, Yet Still a Third Variety of Capitalism." *Economy and Society* 32 (4): 526–54.
Souriac, René, ed. 1996. *Histoire de France, 1750–1995: Société, culture.* Vol. 2. Toulouse: Mirail University Press.
Vessilier, Elisabeth. 1983. "Aspects financiers des nationalisations." *Revue économique* 34 (3): 466–95.
Vie Publique. 2018. "L'évolution du périmètre du secteur publique d'entreprises." https://www.vie-publique.fr/decouverte-institutions/institutions/approfondissements/evolution-du-perimetre-du-secteur-public-entreprises.html

Vincent, Maurice. 2015. "Projet de loi de finances pour 2016: Compte d'affectation spéciale: participations financières de l'État." Report. *Senat.fr*, November 19. http://www.senat.fr/rap/l15-164-321/l15-164-321.html.

Watson, Alan. 1990. "Roman Law and English Law: Two Patterns of Legal Development." *Loyola Law Review* 36 (2): 248–68. http://digitalcommons.law.uga.edu/cgi/viewcontent.cgi?article=1844&context=fac_artchop.

CHAPTER 3
The Involvement of the State in the German Economy

Zsófia Naszádos

The Birth of the Unified German Nation State and Its Economic System

As is well known, modern Germany had a significantly different path of development than its Western neighbors both politically and economically. The first detailed studies and plans to comprehensively improve the economy of the considerably fragmented German-speaking areas, which were divided into a number of principalities and duchies, and help them catch up with contemporary centralized states (Great Britain and France) were completed in the 1840s and 1850s. Scientific discourse evolving around this topic was strongly related to nationalist movements, which emerged at the time and sought to create a unified German (nation) state. Several different paths and aims were widely known, and they resulted in a series of political and military conflicts.[1]

Until the creation of the unified German Empire in 1871, several states at different levels of development competed and coexisted with each other while Prussia gradually became dominant. Cooperation among states had already started in 1834, when the German Customs Union (*Zoll-*

---

[1] Those dedicated to a *smaller Germany* imagined the nation-state as the unification of the Northern and Western principalities with the leadership of Prussia, while the Habsburg Empire would be excluded. As opposed to this, a *greater Germany* favored by Austria would include the multiethnic Habsburg Empire.

As a result of the firm policy of Otto von Bismarck, in the end, the first version was realized. Following the short Austro-Prussian war in 1866, which brought about an overwhelming Prussian victory, the German Confederation that had been in existence since 1815 ceased, and it was replaced by the North German Confederation which was the "anteroom" of the united German Empire, which was declared in 1871 after the Franco-Prussian War and also included Alsace-Lorraine.

verein), which included the northern and western states of the German Confederation, was established (Mátyás 2003). However, only in the last third of the century onwards can we talk of a modern German economic system that can be investigated in a systematic way.

Economists and politicians of the era came to the conclusion that the principles of the classical Anglo-Saxon economy should not necessarily be the model for the young German state's economic policy. While its productive capacity lagged behind, the country had to compete with other states in a more advanced phase of capitalist development. The contemporary German economy was characterized by the coexistence of a premodern system of semi-feudal large landownership, the world of the Prussian Junkers, and a few more developed "capitalistic islands." Representatives of early German economics, among them Friedrich List, who developed serious theoretical work, believed that in such circumstances, realizing Adam Smith's night-watchman state—that is, leaving the players of the economy at the mercy of the invisible hand of the market and dismantling the outer customs borders—would result in the suicidal retreat of Germany in the global competition over commerce, manufacturing, and colonization, which was becoming stiffer and stiffer (Fukuyama 1997).

In works such as the notable "The National System of Political Economy" published in 1841, List explains that the individualist approach (enterprises following their self-interest) does not necessarily create common good; rather, the state has to shepherd the market players to achieve the above (Mátyás 2003). The Bismarck era's economic policy is based on this early model of the *developmental state*. It was successful because it built on the targeted development of industry; the subordination of industrial production to national interest (pre-eminently increasing the capacity of the army); and it also generously subsidized scientific research. German economic thought and economic policy intended to give the state a significant role as the managing authority and—in some areas—also as owner. According to the concept supported by the governance of the Empire, instead of joining the increasingly fierce competition over colonies, Germany was to become the global leader in industries utilizing state-of-the-art scientific inventions: for example the chemical, electronics, machine, and heavy machinery industries.

Research and development, which was heavily emphasized, was mainly related to a few corporations led by iconic business people (e.g., Werner Siemens, Alfred Krupp, Wilhelm Cuno and Emil Kirdorf). Cartelization and the development of oligopoly structures could be viewed as one of the major characteristics of the era, and—especially after the Panic of 1873—they were regarded as beacons of stability against the "swings" of the market. Even corporate law was modified to provide greater protection to private investors via various state guarantees.

Increasing investment also provided an incentive for the development of the modern German banking system, since the improvement of new industries was characterized by an intense hunger for capital. Before the birth of the unified nation state, lending was mainly restricted to some shipping and mainland commercial centers (Hamburg, Frankfurt), but the financial institutions operating there could not and were not willing to participate in lending to and financing the emerging industries, which were risky for a number reasons (Ziegler 2000).

In the 1870s, however, new financial centers were also created as the hubs of economic activity (Cologne, Berlin) shifted, because capital markets were underdeveloped, and the purchase and sale of stocks and state bonds was performed via banks. In the very beginning of the 1870s, many privately owned large banks specializing in financing large scale investments were established; Commerz- und Disconto Bank and Deutsche Bank, established at the same time, were the first, and then came Dresdner Bank in 1872. The foundations of the banking system, which to date, had been operating in a three-pillar structure, were fixed at the time. Besides privately owned large banks, numerous savings banks (Sparkasse) operating under the ownership of federal states and federal state banks (Landesbank) also came into existence to serve smaller depositors. Additionally, a few so-called credit unions operated under state ownership (Genossenschaftsbank, Volksbank) (Ziegler 2000).

The predominance of state ownership (imperial or constituent territories) was visible in two main areas: in public service sectors—with the purpose of serving the needs of civilians and private investors in possibly the most effective and most predictable way; and in specific corporations utilizing natural resources and exploiting the country's mineral deposits.

The overwhelming majority of all large firms constructing and operating railroads and public roads and those related to mining and agriculture were state-owned in the period between 1871 and 1914. In 1906, a total of thirty-nine mines, among them all the coal mines, five salt mines, three quarries, and, in the Ruhr, twelve ironworks, operated under state-ownership (Henderson 1975). These corporations served the needs of the German economy. Furthermore, they had such a remarkable export capacity that by 1890, Germany became the second largest exporter of coal after Great Britain. Another sign of the success of Bismarckian state capitalism is that from 1871 onwards, the German Empire increased its national product by 21.6 percent every decade (the same indicator was 12.5 percent for Great Britain), and between 1879 and 1921 the gross annual income of German companies grew from 79 million marks to 712 million marks (Henderson 1975). The economic and subsequent military-political power of the country had become oppressive for rival Great Powers, and thus the European balance of power was reconfigured in new ways, which contributed to the outbreak of World War I.

The Consequences of World War I and the Economic Policy of the Third Reich

World War I brought about even more centralized industrial production and tighter state control in Germany. More than two hundred special war corporations, so-called *Kriegsgesellschaften,* were established, and in some industries—for example in aluminum production—a state monopoly was maintained. The huge devastation resulting from the lost war, combined with the consequences of the Versailles Peace Treaty (e.g., the payment of reparations, the annexation of a crucial area of industrial production, i.e., Alsace-Lorraine, to France) produced a dire recession in the country. As a result of strengthening socialist movements, the idea of a social economy (*Gemeinwirtschaft*) became popular towards the end of the war. It represented a kind of compromise between a market economy and a planned economy. This form of economy did actually work at the regional level in a few places though its success was not, however, long lasting (Peterson 2005).

From 1919 onwards, following the formation of the Weimar Republic, the consolidation of state-owned enterprises was finalized relatively quickly, while at the same time, the state urged the establishment of those private enterprises that had some benefit for society as a whole. This was because the obligation to pay reparations burdened only state-owned enterprises. After the shock caused by the Great Depression, which began in 1929, another wave of nationalization began: masses of enterprises were organized into groups where the state tried to effect consolidation as the majority owner. This process, however, did not prove permanent.

After their full takeover of power in 1933, the Nazi administration aimed to create a stable welfare state with a series of state investments (e.g., the construction industry and road construction), and it achieved significant success. Contrary to official propaganda and the NSDAP program, not only did the Nazi regime not commence expansive nationalization, but in the second half of the 1930s, a previously unseen wave of privatization began even in those areas where the dominance of state-ownership had been fundamental earlier. In 1934–35, the German state sold its block of shares in Deutsche Reichsbahn (the German Imperial Railway) for 224 million Reichsmarks, which secured strategic control over the Reichsbahn (Bel 2003). A major wave of privatization began in mining, the steel industry, shipbuilding, and in shipping as well. The proportion of state-owned shares in the second largest steel industry trust, the Vereinigte Stahlwerke AG, fell from 52 percent in 1932 to 25 percent in 1934. In 1936, private investors gained majority ownership of two major shipping and shipbuilding companies (namely, Deutsche Schiff- und Maschinenbau AG and Hamburg-Südamerika Dampfschiffarts Gesellschaft) and the four largest banks (Bel 2003).

There was a complex web of reasons motivating this massive privatization. To finance monumental investments, the state needed resources, which could be best raised this way. Additionally, Hitler's purpose was to create a loyal economic elite and gain the sympathy of the factory-owning stratum, which had been against the NSDAP earlier. Selling state-owned share blocks proved to be a good means for Hitler to achieve these goals. Several sources prove that Hitler did not regard nationalization to be a necessary condition for securing total control over the economy; rather, the peculiar repressive oligarchic structure he created was perfect for this.[2]

Going Different Ways after World War II: The Public Sector in the Economy of the FRG.

In the period following the collapse of the Third Reich and World War II, the western part of Germany (liberated by the western Allied powers) and the eastern part integrated into the Soviet sphere of influence went in radically different directions. In the German Democratic Republic (GDR), established in 1949, the complete nationalization of the means of production started simultaneously with the dismantling of important large industrial concerns and the movement of their remaining exploitable productive

---

[2] Some statements of Hitler regarding his views on this remained. "Why should I use halfway measures such as nationalization, when much more effective means are at hand? We don't nationalize corporations or banks, but people." My own translation. As quoted in Bel (2003, 17).

capacities to the Soviet Union in exchange for war reparations; and, finally, with the formation of the socialist planned economy.[3]

In the Federal Republic of Germany (FRG) that was formed contemporaneously, the direction of economic development was influenced by the following: the requirements of the Allied Control Council; the conditions of Marshall Plan aid; and also the obligation to consolidate and operate those factories and groups of factories "inherited" from the National Socialist era, which then came under the control of the West German state.

Although the FRG—based on a social market economy—produced economic development resulting in previously unseen prosperity, groups that had earlier constituted the engine of the German economy played a smaller role. This happened partially due to changes in global economic circumstances and the overhaul of the ownership structure of the above groups of factories. In the Federal Republic, one of the strictest competition laws of Europe during the period came into force in 1958 (which is still in effect today with minor modifications). The law forbade every form of cartelization.[4] The newly framed economic system favored the establishment and development of SMBs (Mittelstand), which became the engine of the FRG economy, especially in the fields of services, light industry, and agriculture. This did not mean, however, that decentralization became predominant in every field immediately.

Under strict state supervision, the reorganization of large enterprises showed considerable concentration, especially in the first half of the 1950s. Six of the older imperial large-scale enterprises deemed suitable for consolidation were reorganized in the form of joint-stock companies in the FRG, and they equated to two-thirds of the country's entire industrial property. The state (even with a gradually decreasing share) was a majority owner in

---

[3] The study does not aim to analyze the economic system of the German Democratic Republic, because as a socialist country, a comparative analysis of the role of the state and state-owned enterprises there would require a different framework of interpretation.

[4] The creation of this law has several roots. At the Potsdam Conference, leaders of the Allied Powers had already established that the main course of action in consolidation after the war would be the decentralization and division of the mammoth groups, which played key roles in the operation of the German war economy and secured the economic operability of the Third Reich. Accordingly, the British-American-French military control accepted the statute of decartelization in 1947 which, among others, was also the basis of the 1958 law. The law, its amendments, and modifications are available at http://www.gesetze-im-internet.de/gwb/BJNR252110998.html#BJNR252110998BJNG000103360.

these until the 1980s. These six companies were the following: Salzgitter AG[5] (earlier Hermann Göring Imperial Works), Vereinigte Industrieunternehmungen (VIAG), Vereinigte Elektrizitäts und Bergwerks AG (VEBA), Volkswagenwerke, Saarbergwerke, and Lufthansa (Toninelli 2000).

The proportion and form of state ownership varied according to sectors, and it was different among states, the federal government, and local governments. In the case of air navigation for example, the state owned 100 percent of Lufthansa, while some inland airports were operated by state-owned companies (Toninelli 2000). The central state had 100 percent ownership of four out of nine electricity groups, and in another four it had over 50 percent ownership, and in one, it held a 30 percent stake (namely Rheinisch-Westfalisches Elektrizitätswerk or RWE AG). Nevertheless, starting in the 1960s, a slow privatization process began in the electricity sector. Besides RWE AG, the two largest partially state-owned enterprises, VIAG-Bayernwerk and VEBA-Preusswerkelektra, were also gradually privatized (Toninelli 2000).

Coal mining and enterprises related to the Saar and Ruhr regions had a radically different path. These suffered heavily from the global transformation of the energy market (namely, the rapid surge of nuclear power). Contrary to decentralization, the federal government tried to consolidate firms individually sustaining losses and depleting coal mines under an umbrella enterprise (Ruhrkohle AG), of which it owned 25 percent of shares (Wengenroth 2000). Dependency on the state and its influence, however, remained strong even in companies with the most privately owned member shares, because the group continued suffering losses despite centralization, and therefore needed continuous state subsidies. Between 1949 and 1967, six out of seven billion marks invested in coal mining came in the form of budgetary state subsidies (Wengenroth 2000).

The financial sector was the third area (besides public services and heavy industries) in which state ownership and influence was important, since the modern form of the system of federal member state banks (Landesbanks) was constructed at that time. It formed the most important segment of enterprises owned regionally and by federal member states. The main purpose of Landesbanks was to credit the SMBs, the Mittelstand, which had an exceptional role in economic growth. Even though the principles of neutrality in competition and views of the state as a regulatory body rather than owner were priorities in the economic policy of the

---

[5] AG: *Aktiengesellschaft*, that is, a share company.

FRG, in case of the Landesbanks, these principles were disregarded. For example, when needed in the case of losses, the federal government was always ready to generously subsidize these unique "hybrid" banks, which stood on the border between the state and private economy.

Accelerating Privatization: The Kohl Era (1982–98)

Except for subsidies for the industrial centers of the Rhine region, which burned significant budgetary resources, in the economy of the FRG as a whole, it could be said that no such proportion of the excessive growth of state-ownership and state subsidies began that would markedly distort the competitiveness of the country, as in the example of Great Britain, where the above caused great tension by the 1970s. As for the desirable structure of the economy, there was a relatively stable consensus among successive governments and individual parties themselves with minor differences in emphasis. In this consensus, instead of having ideological foundations, both the right and the left had a rather practical approach to the proportion of state ownership and intervention. It could be briefly summed up by saying that the state remained present in certain fields either as a majority or sole owner. Such fields were primarily transport, public services, and the regional banking sector, which was related to federal member states. In the rest of the sectors of the economy, however, mixed forms of ownership were favored. (See the previous section.)

From the beginning of the 1980s onwards, the global transformation of the energy market and acute problems with competitiveness did not leave the FRG untouched. Therefore, reform and restructuring became inevitable.

In 1982, the coalition of Social Democrats and Liberals was succeeded by Helmut Kohl's Christian Democrat and Liberal coalition, and the new Chancellor made "returning to [a] real social market economy" his main aim. Besides introducing a series of reforms "traditionally" used to increase competitiveness (raising the retirement age, more flexible labor market regulation, etc.), the government initiated a serious wave of privatization. The goal was not to upset the status quo between the state and the private sector in the Thatcheresque way, but rather to boost modernization and structural change primarily in the centers of the coal and steel industry and a number of other fields of heavy industry. Another vital aspect was that the federal government generated substantial revenue for the budget by selling its share blocks. While the first wave of privatization

(1983–89) in the Kohl Era cannot be regarded as "shock therapy," it still caused numerous labor code conflicts with unions that were traditionally powerful in Germany. Such conflicts were caused by situations in which employment conditions were drastically transformed in companies that fell into the hands of private owners (Leaman 2009).

Between 1983 and 1989, as a first step two main groups (VEBA AG, VIAG) were partly or fully privatized, though state-owned shares for these groups had been partly sold by Germany earlier in the 1960s and 1970s. The proportion of share ownership by the state in VEBA AG, which specialized in supplying electricity and coal mining, dropped from 43.8 percent to 30 percent in 1984, and in 1985, it further decreased to 25.5 percent in another wave of privatization (Leaman, 2009). In the case of the holding company VIAG, which also brought together mining and energy firms, the changes were even more dramatic: state ownership first plummeted from 87.4 percent to 47.4 percent in 1986, followed by its full privatization in 1988. The remains of both companies, which had long histories, merged into the E-ON group later on (Leaman 2009).

At the end of the decade, the waves of privatization and restructuring also reached some fields of transport and the telecom industry. In 1988, Volkswagen was fully placed in the hands of private investors when the state sold its share block of 16 percent ownership. Next, in the same year, the ownership structure of Lufthansa was also transformed. In the case of the latter, state ownership fell from 65 percent to 51.6 percent, which could be seen as a bold move since the airline was regarded as a national champion in the FRG, and it was thought to be important that the state preserve its portion of ownership to secure strategic control. In 1989, the German Federal Post Office was broken up, and its shares were put on the market. Owned by KfW Bank (which, in turn, was partially owned by the state), three new joint-stock companies were set up: Deutsche Post AG, Postbank AG, and Deutsche Telekom AG (http://www.privatizationbarometer.com/database.php)

One peculiarity of the privatization process was that enterprises issued large volumes of so-called residential shares (Volksaktien) so as to make owners of the broader middle class. This, however, did not prove to be a popular form of investment, because the population was extremely suspicious of stock exchange transactions because they were regarded as too risky.

The volume of privatization did not decrease from the 1990s to the 2000s, and thus, the German state gave up all its shares in enterprises which became partially privately owned in the 1980s (e.g., Lufthansa,

Deutsche Post AG, and Postbank AG) (http://www.privatizationbarometer.com/database.php)

> ## From Imperial Symbol to Listed Group Undertaking: The Transformation of Deutsche Post
>
> Throughout its 150-year-long existence, changes in the operation of Deutsche Post—the symbol of modern German telecommunications—provide us with a good example of how technological development, consumer behavior and demand, and changes in the market can force large enterprises (enterprises that once started out as state monopolies) to adapt.
>
> In the second half of the nineteenth century, Reichspost (Imperial Mail) became one of the main symbols of national sovereignty and control, when in 1876 the telegraph service and the system of post offices were placed under unified state control, and even a separate ministry was established for this purpose. This significantly sped up communications and the news, which promoted swift economic development. Reichspost operated as an independent state-owned enterprise, and after World War II in 1950, it was reorganized under the name Deutsche Bundespost. Still state-owned, it expanded its range of services with savings-banking and tour operations to meet new demands. Its first step towards participating in global business life was its gradual fusion with the package service DHL, which was established in 1969. Since the 1970s, DHL has been present in the global market: Europe and the United States were followed by China, Singapore, and Latin America.
>
> Legislation reacted to the changing market environment in two steps. The first postal reform bill initiated by the Kohl government provided for the division of Deutsche Bundespost into three parts. Thus, besides Postdienst—the pillar providing traditional postal services—Deutsche Post Postbank and Deutsche Post Telekom were created. This way, the management of the different fields of activity became independent on both the professional and the business side of their respective divisions. Major policy and strategic decisions were brought about by the directory composed of the executives of the three companies. Parallel to these developments, the three companies' client contracts were transformed into private contracts.
>
> The second postal reform law in 1995 laid down the foundations for the privatization of the three enterprises by transforming them into

share companies: Deutsche Post AG, Deutsche Postbank AG, Deutsche Telekom AG. The law provided for a five-year transitional period, during which the shares had to remain in the ownership of the state. As a result of the first public offering of equity shares in November 2000, 29 percent of Deutsche Post shares went into private ownership, and 6 percent of private shareholders were employees of the enterprise. Fusion with DHL was completed in 2002; in the first step, 75 percent, and then the remaining 25 percent of its shares were bought up by Lufthansa Cargo. Cross ownership among the three enterprises was created at that time, as Deutsche Post DHL Group held 52 percent of Deutsche Postbank AG shares. Later, in 2009, Deutsche Post DHL Group sold this share block to Deutsche Bank, and thus it ceased to be an investor in the financial sector. According to data for 2015, the Federation has a remaining 21 percent indirect ownership in Deutsche Post DHL Group through KfW Bank. (https://www.dpdhl.com/en/about-us/history.html)

The other members of the group also remained crucial operators in the German economy. Deutsche Telekom, whose development was very similar to that of Deutsche Post, is a significant enterprise in the global telecom sector. After Eastern and Central Europe, it aimed to win new markets in the Far East, especially in China. The German state owns 31.7 percent of Deutsche Post shares either directly or indirectly. The remainder of it is owned by institutional and private investors (https://www.telekom.com/de/investor-relations/unternehmen/aktionaersstruktur) Even though the German state is not a majority shareholder in any of the three enterprises anymore, the influence and lobbying power of these in German (economic) diplomacy is probably the second largest after automotive enterprises. Deutsche Postbank, whose majority of shares was purchased by Deutsche Bank in 2009, has become a critical market operator in the German banking structure, and in 2003, it had the highest number of clients in Germany. Instead of becoming a global operator like its two siblings, it is still a local one, and as a subsidiary of Deutsche Bank, it remains primarily active in the insurance and private banking businesses. (Adapted from "The history of Deutsche Post DHL Group: 500 Years of Postal History from the Founding of the Modern Postal System to the Establishment of the World's Leading Logistics Group." https://www.dpdhl.com/en/about-us/history.html)

Changing the ownership structure of savings banks and banks owned by federal states, and partially or fully privatizing them was already on the agenda in the Kohl Era. But, in the end, the Chancellor himself dismissed these possibilities (Zopp 1999). The following two challenges to this plan were discussed at that time: state support for the Landesbanks, which went against the neutrality of competition; and, in times of crisis, increasing their capital, which devoured significant budgetary resources.

The risks of privatization were, however, deemed to be bigger than the potential benefits (increasing market competition for financial institutions; the improvement of services; and liberation from the burden of state financing). One challenge was transforming the contracts of depositors into private contracts without causing potentially years-long disputes, which might have ended up as costly litigations in the case of both private persons and businesses. Another important argument against privatization was that the shares offered might be bought up by a few well-capitalized big banks, which would gain a quasi-monopoly (Zopp 1999). However, this would have broken competition and anti-trust laws which were pivotal in the economic policy of the FRG.

The strongest reason, however, was probably that the banks owned by federal states had an especially important role in the economic growth of postwar West Germany. Lending to small and medium-sized enterprises, which had the most important role in the economy of the FRG, was almost exclusively done via Landesbanks. Additionally, the stability and predictability provided by Landesbanks was of utmost importance to their clients (Zopp 1999). Therefore, it was feared that some sectors that periodically performed weakly or ones that would likely fall into recession would have extremely limited growth opportunities if the operation of this unique group of banks was radically transformed. It also needs to be mentioned that the Landesbanks and the savings banks were strongly intertwined with politics—especially at the regional and federal state levels. Those who insisted on privatization were often accused of wanting to be beneficiaries of a possible privatization. In summary, it could be said that the privatization of Landesbanks would have signaled such a serious disregard for both the economic and the political status quo that the political elite was not willing to carry it out.

The Way to a Market Economy: The Challenges of Privatization and Economic Transition in the GDR

The introduction of a socialist planned economy essentially changed the development path of East German federal states, which belonged to the Soviet sphere of influence after the end of World War II. Gradually, the

German Democratic Republic separated from the western part of the country, and its economic and commercial relationships with the FRG were demolished.

The Soviet Union confiscated most of the remaining productive capacities as part of war reparations, dismantling and removing them from the territory of the GDR, which significantly thwarted economic recovery. At the same time, the process of total nationalization in the economy started under Soviet inspection, similarly to other states within the Eastern Bloc. Consequently, the country severely lagged behind its western neighbor regarding economic growth, innovation, and the optimal redistribution of the wealth produced there. It is important to note here that no considerable attempt at a "mixed economy" could be realized in the GDR—unlike in Hungary, for instance—due to the more radically oppressive nature of dictatorship, so there were no "capitalist islands" or subsistence agriculture.

In an economy built exclusively on state ownership and on central planning governed by the "Politbüro," the relationships between economic actors had very different features than their counterparts in the FRG system of "democratic corporatism" and social partnership. Instead of free cooperation between enterprises and employees, their trade unions, and the system of negotiations and agreements based on equal rank, in the GDR, a hierarchical relationship formed in which the system of production and the operation of enterprises were defined by political dictates (Koch 1998).

Consequently, the main challenges of the unification of the two countries included, on the one hand, privatization that terminated exclusive state ownership, and, on the other, the creation of optimal conditions for a social market economy. The difficulties of the economic transition and the burden of reaching economic cohesion for the eastern German federal states remained the primary challenges for Germany until the end of the 1990s. This also involved a decline in the country's economic performance. One of the first steps of economic unification was the establishment of the German Economic, Social and Monetary Union in 1990, and then the so-called Treuhandanstalt. The task of the latter authority was directing and monitoring the process of privatization. According to the principle of privatization, previously nationalized properties and companies "owned by the people" (*"Volkseigene Betriebe"*) had to be returned to their original owners if possible. Between 1990 and 1994, approximately 13,000 companies were returned to private owners, the process of which influenced about four million employees.

Basically, three types of companies could be distinguished during the economic transition of the former East German market. The first category included enterprises that were founded as pioneers right after the transition, mostly with significant financial support from the FRG or the European Community. Firms belonging to the second type tended to be small and medium-sized companies producing goods for the local market. Many of these were purchased by Western concerns because they had difficulties weathering the challenges of the transition. Finally, the third category contained firms operating in a specific "niche" sector, which enabled them to maintain their market positions (Tribe 1992). The number of companies radically increased between 1991 and 1995, growing from 178,000 to 353,000 in the industrial and service sector alone (Koch 1998).

The economic transition and especially privatization were, of course, accompanied by major difficulties and abuses regarding competitiveness, social issues, and productivity, which shed an unfavorable light on the managers of the process and the employees of Treuhandanstalt as well. In course of setting the agenda for the economic transition, the decision was made that a one-to-one rate of exchange between the Eastern and Western German Mark would be guaranteed, and a radical devaluation of the currency should be avoided. There were primarily political reasons for the decision: a substantial devaluation of the currency would have definitely meant a social crisis, mass dissatisfaction, and increasing unemployment in the short run, which could have easily turned citizens of the former GDR against reunification. Certainly, the productivity and development of the eastern federal states were far below the FRG's standards, and the over-valued currency seriously hindered the start of development.

The program for Building Up Eastern Germany (*Aufbau Ost*) remained in focus in German domestic politics, and it is not over yet as the transfers between the federal states and the reduction of inequalities among regions regarding development are still important objectives. According to the original plans, the system of cohesion transfers was to be maintained as long as the per capita GDP in the eastern federal states reached at least 70% of the Western average. The accomplishment of this was estimated to happen by the turn of the millennium. However, the fund established for this purpose (*Fonds Deutsche Einheit*) was already replaced in 1995 by different, more general monetary resources (*Solidarpakt*) aimed at the reduction of regional inequalities in every region.

The Structure of the German Economy in the New Millennium

Germany became a country fighting increasing economic challenges in the middle of the 1990s, and, as a result, was labeled the "Sick man of Europe" by journalists at the time. The reunification of the country entailed significant costs paid for by the former West German federal states, and reform of the welfare state was becoming increasingly urgent. There was pragmatism and foresight in many fields, which—through the use of continuous, gradual and flexible privatization from the 1960s onwards—prevented overgrowth and deficits in the state sector. For a long time, however, this attitude did not apply to the areas of social services and welfare expenditure. This considerably endangered the competitiveness of the country, its leading role within Europe, and the productivity of the corporate sector.

The central issue of economic policy debates was therefore not privatization, but rather the methods of accomplishing the reform of the welfare state. Eventually, the coalition of the Social Democrats and Greens led by Gerhard Schröder launched reforms by announcing the program *Agenda 2010*. It aimed to reestablish a pattern of growth through labor market liberalization and cuts to social expenditures.[6]

Naturally, in the meantime, privatization continued in many fields in accordance with the spirit of the age. By the millennium, the German state had practically given up its predominant ownership in every field of the economy. Furthermore, private investors appeared in such fields, where, for reasons of state interest or because of mercantile traditions, private investment had been avoided earlier. There were exceptions, of course, and one of them is rail transport: Deutsche Bahn AG is still exclusively state owned. Yet in 2015, the government established an expert committee to investigate whether partial privatization could further improve the efficiency of operations. No consensus has yet been reached regarding this question, thus privatization is not yet on the agenda. Even though the

---

[6] The most important part of the reform package, the so-called Hartz reforms, were carried out under the Schröder government between 2002 and 2003. The package was a series of actions carried out in four stages (Hartz I, II, III, and IV). It aimed to make the labor market more flexible. Part-time and alternative employment was encouraged in this framework, and unemployment benefits were lowered altogether by merging a number of former types of aid. However, the resources allocated for training and job placement were increased.

enterprise operates under state ownership, in 2001, three track sections (Düsseldorf, Bielefeld, Solingen) were operated jointly with private enterprises (https://www.deutschebahn.com/de/konzern/geschichte/sammlungen/unternehmenshistorisches_archiv-1187860)

The table below includes the most important German enterprises in which—based on data going up to 2007—the German state either directly or indirectly held shares.

Table 1
The twenty largest enterprises with partial state ownership (2015)

Enterprise	Proportion of ownership (%)
KfW Bankengruppe	80
Deutsche Telekom	31.7
Deutsche Post	21
Fraport AG	51.8
Volkswagen AG	11.8
Landesbank Berlin Holding AG	98.6
MVV Energie AG	66.2
IKB Deutsche Industriebank	37.9
RWE AG	16.09
Deutsche Energie-Agentur	76
Forschungszentrum Jülich	100
Flughafen München	26
Norddeutsche Landesbank Girozentrale	65.6
Helaba Landesbank Hessen-Thüringen Girozentrale	100
Salzgitter AG	26.5
Deutsche Bahn AG	100
GAG Immobilien AG	68.8
AG Bad Neuenahr	27
Bochum-Gelsenkirchener Strassenbahnen AG	3
Flughafen Köln/Bonn GmbH	30.9

Source: http://www.privatizationbarometer.com/database.php

Currently, 90 percent of the companies remaining in state ownership are local enterprises or local government enterprises, 8 percent of them are owned by federal states, and a mere 2 percent are owned by the federal government (OECD 2012). This ownership structure in itself implies that the areas of operation and the activities of the state-owned enterprises have changed. Large-scale industrial holding groups have been replaced by companies specifically serving local and regional needs. Forty-one percent of all state-owned enterprises operate in the fields of water and energy supply; 11.9 percent are related to inland transport operations; and virtually the same proportion, 11.8 percent, are state-owned enterprises providing social and health services. According to OECD data, in 2012, 15,127 enterprises were in some sort of public ownership, and this is 0.4 percent of all 3.6 million companies registered in Germany (OECD 2012). The federal government is a partial or full owner of 111 enterprises which are mostly linked to transportation, logistics and freight, and culture and science. Deutsche Bahn's 100 percent state ownership and Deutsche Telekom with 31.7 percent state ownership can be regarded as the two most significant and most serious consortiums with the most international lobbying power among those companies that are federally owned (OECD 2012).

It is important to emphasize that since the beginning of the 2000s, the greatest challenge has been posed by the operation and reform of federal state banks belonging to the regional pillar of the state sector. This challenge was further complicated by the economic crisis of 2008. Despite the fact that Landesbanks gained a reputation for conservatism and were the main financiers of small and medium-sized enterprises based on the experiences of the post-war decades, the number of anomalies had been increasing since the beginning of the new millennium. The crisis and the period leading up to it shed light on their serious weaknesses, and both individual federal member states and the federation as a whole had to confront conflicts because of them. Landesbanks had been receiving generous subsidies in various forms, and their management and owners were heavily intertwined with local political elites as well. Their profits were the result of subsidies rather than their competitiveness (*The Economist* 2014).

First, starting in 2001 and on a number of other occasions—because of concerns about the neutrality of competition—the European Committee criticized some of the Landesbanks' methods of raising capital and state guarantee programs aimed at preserving stability and remaining competitive with globally well performing big banks. In 2005 following one of the largest federal guarantee programs, many Landesbanks bought up a significant amount of toxic American securities from banks that crashed in 2008. Even though the German economy was not hit as hard by the crisis as its European neighbors (as a result of the above investments), the federal government had to allocate significant resources to save the Landesbanks. Crisis management cannot be viewed as a complete success in this field: five out of seven federal state banks were saved, and these five are still fighting for survival. A good example of this is HSH Nordbank, which is owned by the federal states of Hamburg and Schleswig-Holstein and could barely pass the ECB stress test (*The Economist*, 2014). Based on the above experiences, it is possible that the federal banking sector will be the next segment of the German economy in which the state will withdraw and enterprises will be restructured.

The focal point of political and scientific discourse from the 2000s onwards is no longer the comparison between the advantages and disadvantages of privatization and nationalization, but rather making the performance and transparence of state-owned enterprises more similar to those of market economy companies. The OECD among others has investigated how to make the competitiveness of state-owned enterprises and the quality of their services sustainable in the long term. Monitoring these enterprises, auditing their operations, and adjusting them to market standards could, in principle, improve the efficiency of the fight against corruption and the waste of state resources. Opponents of extensive state ownership mention this argument in favor of privatization.[7]

Germany, too, seeks to guarantee the effective and transparent operation of publicly- owned enterprises with a number of regulations, most of which came into effect after 2008. These regulations are collected in the *Public Corporate Governance Kodex*. The Federal Ministry of Finance is obliged to annually report on all state-owned enterprises whose direct or indirect state ownership is at least 25 percent and its nominal capital share is more than €50,000. Furthermore, the reports investigate whether these enterprises have complied with complex social, environmental, and sustainability rules explicated by the Code. A specific example would be the 2015 report, which focuses on equal opportunities for female executives. It details the number of female executives, their distribution in different sectors, and the steps taken to support promotion within their enterprises.[8]

---

[7] See, among others, OECD (2015) "Coherence for Development. State-owned Enterprises: Good Governance as a Facilitator for Development," available at https://www.oecd.org/pcd/State-owned%20enterprises_CfD_Ebook.pdf.

[8] See Beteiligungsberichte des Bundes 2015 Download: http://www.bundesfinanz ministerium.de/Content/DE/Standardartikel/Themen/Bundesvermoegen/ Privatisierungs_und_Beteiligungspolitik/Beteiligungspolitik/Beteiligungsberichte/ Beteiligungs.

Conclusions

Numerous fault lines cut through the history of the modern German economy, but the aptitude of the state for gaining economic property could not be viewed as a characteristic that could dominate eras. On the contrary, the influence of the state as owner was predominant in basically two areas: in public services and transportation (mostly for social reasons), and in the exploitation of natural resources, specifically in mining.

Although the continental and especially the German economic system is often labeled state centered in Anglo-American scholarship, it is important to note that there has not been a single era since the birth of the modern German state when the state aimed to guarantee its influence on the economy by amassing property, except for the GDR, which, however, was excluded from this study. Much more significant was the role of strict regulatory regimes, which were enacted as mercantile duties, commerce policies, and rigid rules of the stock exchange in the early Wilhelmine–Bismarckian era. Then came the payment of reparations related to the Peace Treaty of Versailles after World War II and the limitation of the operation of German conglomerations. After 1945, several characteristics of the West German economic regime were a result of the shock of World War II: the consequences felt by the new political elite; and the expectations of occupying powers. The cartel law, which sought to prevent the reorganization of group-holding monopolies (that used to be the economic basis of the nationalist war machine), might be regarded as especially relevant for the topic of this study.

The government of the Third Reich did not exercise total control of the economy through nationalization, but rather by a peculiar oligarchic system through which it intended, on the one hand, to bind the German economic elite loyal to the Reich in every possible way to itself, and on the other, to expel big businesses labeled as alien and against the Reich (mostly Jewish, naturally), and redeploy their resources to the above loyalists.

Due to the revival of strong Christian Democratic and revisionist Social Democratic traditions, massive nationalization was never really supported by the politics of the FRG after World War II. This would have been alien to the ordoliberal system regardless of the partisanship of the governing political elite. Several large industrial holdings and mining trusts came to be owned by the German federal state as part of the postwar consolidation in the 1950s. Privatization of these, however, was advocated in the 1960s: the first public offer of shares took place at this time.

Privatization gained impetus in the 1980s and 1990s, but it did not cause such a wavering of public trust and peace as in other European countries with more or less successful liberalization revolutions. The image change of the Social Democratic Party partially restructured the party, and its good relations with the unions deteriorated. The latter effect, however, was more likely a result of general labor market forces aimed at deregulation.

The economic crisis of 2008 did not greatly affect Germany, as it was and is relatively isolated from Anglo-American capital markets, and thus it did not result in a significant transformation of the relationship between the state and the private sectors. Federal state-owned banks are an exception to this, as many of them were pushed to the brink of bankruptcy as a consequence of the crisis, and they could survive only with substantial state subsidies. Because they still perform badly in stress tests, serious debates continue as to how their operation should be reformed.

On the whole, it could be ascertained that since important traditions of practical levels of market regulation were predominant earlier in the country, the discourse on the alleged failure of neoliberal capitalism never had a central role in Germany.

REFERENCES

Bel, Germá. 2006. "Against the Mainstream: Nazi Privatization in 1930s Germany." Universitat de Barcelona, Facultat d'Econòmiques. https://papers.ssrn.com/sol3/papers.cfm?abstract_id=895247

Beyer, Jürgen, and Martin Höpner. 2004. "The Disintegration of Organised Capitalism: German Corporate Governance in the 1990s." In *Germany: Beyond the Stable State*, edited by Herbert Kitschelt and Wolfgang Streeck, 179–98. London and Portland: Frank Krass.

The History of Deutsche Bahn: The Foundation of Deutsche Bahn AG. https://www.deutschebahn.com/en/group/history/topics/foundation-1210924

Dietrich, Irina, and Hans-Gerhard Strohe. 2011. "Statistik der öffentlichen Unternehmen in Deutschland: Die Datenbasis." Statistische Diskussionsbeitrage. University of Potsdam. https://ideas.repec.org/p/pot/statdp/44.html.

Economist. 2014. "State-owned Assets: Setting out the Store." January 11. https://www.economist.com/briefing/2014/01/11/setting-out-the-store.

Economist. 2015. "German Landesbanken: Lost a Fortune, Seeking a Role." January 8. http://www.economist.com/news/finance-and-economics/21638143-seven-german-landesbanken-survived-financial-crisis-are-still.

Fukuyama, Francis. 1995. *Trust: The Social Virtues and the Creation of Prosperity*. New York: The Free Press.

Gall, Lothar, Gerald D. Feldmann, Harold James, Carl-Ludwig Holtfrerich, and Hans E. Büschgen. 1995. *Die Deutsche Bank, 1870–1995*. Munich: C. H. Beck.

Gesetz gegen Wettbewerbsbeschränkungen (1998). Bundesministerium der Justiz und für Verbraucherschutz http://www.gesetze-im-internet.de/gwb/BJNR252110998. html#BJNR252110998BJNG000103360 (Retrieved 28. 03. 2016.)

Green, Simon and William E. Paterson, eds. 2005. *Governance in Contemporary Germany: The Semisovereign State Revisited*. Cambridge: Cambridge University Press.

Happ, Richard. 2016. "Why investors in Germany need investment protection. European Federation for Investment Law and Arbitration." European Federation for Investment Law and Arbitration, March 29. http://efilablog.org/2016/03/29/why-investors-in-germany-need-investment-protection/.

Heddenhausen, Matthias. 2007. "Privatisation in Europe's Liberalised Electricity Markets: The Case of the United Kingdom, Sweden, Germany and France." Understanding Privatization Policies: Political Economy and Welfare Effects. Stiftung Wissenschaft und Politik, Research Unit EU Integration, December. http://swpberlin.org/fileadmin/contents/products/projekt_papiere/Electricity_paper_KS_IIformatiert.pdf.

Henderson, William Otto. 1975. *The Rise of German Industrial Power (1834–1914)*. Berkley: University of California Press.

Koch, Karl. 1998. "The Impact of German Unification on the German Industrial Relations System." *German Politics* 7 (3): 52–68.

Leaman, Jeremy. 2009. *The Political Economy of Germany under Chancellors Kohl and Schröder. Decline of the German Model?* New York: Berghahn Books.

Link, Heike. 2009. "Public Transportation in Provincial Areas: Regional Rail Companies in Germany." *Japan Railway & Transport Review* 52: 38–45.

Mátyás, Antal. 2003. *A korai közgazdaságtan története* [History of premodern economics]. Budapest: Aula Kiadó.

North, Michael, ed. 2000. *Deutsche Wirtschaftsgeschichte. Ein Jahrtausend im Überblick*. Munich: C.H. Beck.

OECD. 2011. "State-Owned Governance Enterprise Reform: An Inventory of Recent Change." https://www.oecd.org/daf/ca/corporategovernanceofstate-ownedenterprises/48455108.pdf.

Kane, Korin and Hans Christiansen. 2015. "State-owned Enterprises: Good Governance as a Facilitator for Development." Coherence for Development 5. OECD. https://www.oecd.org/pcd/State-owned%20enterprises_CfD_Ebook.pdf.

The Local. 2012. "Rösler plans to sell off state owned firms." December 25. http://www.thelocal.de/20121225/46973.

Toninelli, Pierre Angelo. 2000. *The Rise and Fall of the State Owned Enterprise in the Western World*. Cambridge: Cambridge University Press.

Tribe, Keith. 2014. "Enterprise Formation and Market Structure in the Five New Bundesländer." KeithTribe.co.uk, November 8. http://keithtribe.co.uk/wp-content/uploads/2014/11/Unification.pdf

Welfens, Paul J. J. 1992. *Economic Aspects of German Unification: National and International Perspectives*. Berlin-Heidelberg: Springer-Verlag.

Werner-Sinn, Hans. 2015. "What can Europe learn from German Reunification?" *World Economic Forum*, November 5. https://www.weforum.org/agenda/2015/11/what-can-europe-learn-from-german-reunification/.

Zopp, Stephan. 1999. "Sparkassen und Landesbanken im Umbruch. Rechtsform hinterfragt, Geschäftsgebaren und Visionen auf dem Prüfstand." MA Thesis, University of Augsburg.

CHAPTER 4
The Relationship between State and Private Enterprise in the Austrian Economy

István Kőrösi

Introduction: An Overview of Macroeconomic Data

Austria is one of the countries in European Union that is growing in terms of its population, economic performance, job creation, and also its increasing standard of living. In 2018, the population of the country was 8,795,000, or 1.7 percent of the EU's total population. Between 1990 and 2018, the population grew by 1.1 million, mostly because of immigration. The country generated 2.4 percent of the EU's GDP, which it the tenth largest economy in the EU. Austria generates a GDP more than three times that of Hungary and twice as large as Czechia's. The Alpine country achieved a modest but internationally significant pace of growth: 1.7 percent adjusted annually between 2000 and 2005, and annually 1.4 percent adjusted between 2005 and 2010. The number stagnated in 2013, and thereafter, the yearly growth rate increased to 3 percent.[1]

Presently, Austria is the sixth wealthiest member country of the European Union with an annual per capita GDP of 42,020 Euros, which is about 30 percent higher than the EU average. It surpasses Sweden, Denmark and Finland. Austria is a net contributor to Brussels' budget, paying in 400 million Euros annually. Each year, every Austrian citizen pays 50 Euros for EU membership.

This is a very meager sum compared to the fact that the annual tax burden per person is 900 Euros in Austria. Being an EU member is obviously well worth the expense, as profits from foreign trade, capital connections, and cooperation are so much higher, and thus integration in fact yields financial profits for Austria.

---
[1] From the 2018 data of Eurostat Brussels.

The Characteristics of State Participation in the Austrian Economy

The state has a significant role in economic redistribution and improvement. The rate of public expenditure is 51.2 percent of GDP, which ranks Austria sixth in the EU. (We can find larger state budget expenditure rates in Denmark, France, Finland, Belgium, and Sweden.) Social expenditures are 30.4 percent of GDP, which equals the average of the Eurozone, but it is significantly higher than that of the EU 27. Between 2000 and 2010, the rate of social expenditures in relation to GDP has grown everywhere in the EU without exception. In Austria, it grew by more than 2 percentage points over ten years. All this required levying a significant earnings withholding rate: it reached 44.1 percent including taxes and contributions. In 2007, before the crisis, the rate of withholdings was 43.2 percent, so the growth of the burden resulting from the crisis is relatively low. (Austrians wish they had low Swiss taxes and contribution burdens. They do so for a reason: withholdings in Switzerland are a mere 28.6 percent altogether.) Tax burdens in Austria are consolidated in general, but they are higher than the average of the EU 27, and by far larger than those in Hungary.[2] Tax policies are highly balanced in this Alpine country, and even small changes are rarely and carefully made for the sake of predictability.

The Austrian state participates widely and significantly in the economy, applying a combination of direct and indirect financial instruments. The main forms of direct intervention are capital injections into state-owned enterprises (SOEs) (by raising share capital), public and infrastructural investments, and public commissions. In the past, direct intervention often went together with an inefficient use of assets. Several large projects proved to be failed designs (the AKH hospital investment, the Zwentendorf nuclear power plant), and for a long time direct intervention inadvertently resulted in the congelation of the production structure in much of the public sector; it also concealed the consequences on behalf of the loss-making management (especially in Voest-Alpine). The fact that public projects often dragged on and exceeded appropriations also signaled inefficiency.

An overall successful area of state intervention was public infrastructure development programs, which, having built up the regional operation

---

[2] Eurostat Brussels, 2015, and data from the Österreichische Nationalbank available at http://www.oenb.at.

framework of the economy, had a role in establishing and supporting significant and continuous growth. Regional infrastructure programs generated direct industrial improvements by establishing production infrastructure. The efforts of state commissions stimulated regional production and employment and prepared the ground for private investment.

Weighing the proportion of state intervention instruments, it can be safely said that between direct and indirect instruments, the latter unequivocally have a decisive role. Stimulating private investment is carried out with a comprehensive and extensive set of instruments. We must emphasize the role of the state and its subsidized institutions, providing information, assisting with organization, giving advice, stabilizing the credit guarantee and credit insurance system, and helping new investments overcome initial hardships.[3]

The central and intertwined areas of state intervention are regional policy, restructuring industries in crisis, and stimulating investment and employment. In the framework of regional policy, the federal government grants substantial funds as part of budgetary redistribution. The overwhelming majority of regional development programs are designed by the states themselves. Most of these include major infrastructural and communal investments. According to central directives, both the suppliers and the workforce needed for these projects should be recruited from with a 50 square km area (if they are available and competitive).

In restructuring industries in crisis, the focal point is maintaining the highest possible rate of employment, primarily within the framework of corporate employment plans as they relate to modernization, and in cases where this is not possible, comprehensive retraining programs are initiated. Furthermore, stimulating regional job creation is a priority. The comprehensive national credit and credit guarantee system of investment subsidies is complemented by subsidies granted by regional investment funds; building production infrastructure or taking over a portion of building costs; and, in specific cases, by direct subsidies related to employment (e.g., when employing long-term unemployed or disabled workers).

Heavy polarization is a distinctive dimension of the structure of Austrian industry: the very small, mostly family-owned businesses (under ten employees) make up 95 percent of all factories, while on the other end of the spectrum, less than 1 percent of all factories are large enterprises

---

[3] On state participation in the economy and instruments of intervention, see Gál (1984).

(employing more than one thousand persons), and these play a crucial part in industrial production and exports. The heavy subvention of small businesses is among the main elements of Austrian industrial, investment, and regional economic policies.[4]

Austria has had positive results in stabilizing small businesses. The main elements of this subvention policy are: professional support for establishing companies; clear and predictable subvention conditions, despite their complexity; and the long term validity of these conditions. Subventions are provided mostly in the form of credits and guarantees. Sufficient capital share is one of the main conditions for taking these subventions. Thus, private risk taking and capitalization are factors that improve stability. Credit subvention and guarantees granted to an individual small business are rather limited, which, on the one hand, enables the simultaneous subvention of many small businesses, while on the other hand, if some of fail, the losses are small.[5]

The state-owned large enterprise sector had been operating rigidly and often inefficiently for a long time, though it reliably supplied the processing industry with raw materials and energy. The downsides of the sector were maintaining the production of non-profitable products, the exacerbation organizational and management problems, flawed investment allocations, and subventions that paid for losses, which became the norm. Nevertheless, large enterprises have always played an important role in balancing out economic booms, employment stabilization and regional economic growth. However, restructuring the sector became necessary.[6]

Since its accession to the EU in 1995, major changes have taken place in economic policy and the management of the public sector. Loss financing schemes and market problems connected to "solutions" have been abolished. In order to regain competitiveness, there has been a managed, coordinated, and controlled transition and reorganization of companies (based on profit-centers); the strictly selective transformation of the product structure based on rentability; and the introduction of new enterprise resource systems selected through investments concerning modern-

---

[4] Key figures for Austrian companies by size of company https://news.wko.at/news/oesterreich/unternehmen-in-oesterreich-nach-groessenklassen.html

[5] An overview of the role and activities of small and medium-sized enterprises with current data and facts https://news.wko.at/news/oesterreich/wirtschaftskraft-kmu-summary.pdf

[6] On the Austrian structure of industry and the role of the state-owned large enterprise sector in the development of economic policy, see Kőrösi (2005).

ization. The main successes that resulted from these changes were investments based on preliminary rentability studies, the development of modern enterprises, production management systems, and complex packaging plans connected to customers' individual expectations.

The experiences of modernization, stabilization, and partial privatization in recent years, have led to a new pragmatism in Austrian economic policy. Consequently, the main negative aspects of previous state subsidies, that is the rigidity of production and product structures, have been largely eliminated, and the restructuring of employment has been accomplished with a much lower social and economic cost than in most other countries. Small companies, which are considered to be Austrian specialties, offer solutions that are a good mixture of regional, industrial, and employment policies. The refundable but preferential interest rates, guarantees, and credit insurance; the conditional rules and clearly oriented investment incentives (tax preferences, accelerated favorability descriptions); and the preference for savings combined with tax incentives for innovation effectively serve the Austrian regional and industrial policy objectives.

The above mentioned impacts have had comparatively positive results internationally regarding (i) the favorable economic conjuncture in recent years; (ii) the avoidance of potential conflicts surrounding the employment problem despite accelerated structural transformation; (iii) the observable decrease in regional differences; (iv) the halting of Austrian industrial space losses in several niche markets; and (v) the comparatively low socio-economic costs of restructuring the state-owned industry.

Historical Milestones of Austrian Nationalized Industry

The history of post-World War II nationalization in Austria began on July 26, 1946, when the National Council (*Nationalrat*) of the Parliament issued the first comprehensive nationalization act. This took place in order to prevent the Soviet Union from taking ownership of "German-owned" companies. German-owned companies were not just companies founded by German Nazi Party members—among them the Hermann Göring Works in Linz—but also former Austrian state-owned companies, such as the First Danube Steamship Company (Erste Donau Dampf-Schiffahrts-Gesellschaft).

Before 1983, the Austrian state-owned corporate sector was extensive. It represented one-fifth of Austrian GDP, which included the three largest banks, the entire coal mining industry, every significant factory involved in the production and refinement of crude oil, and every major factory involved in heavy industry. These renationalized industries came directly under the authority of the Austrian government and its ministries[7].

Regarding the management of Austrian state-owned industry, a major shift occurred at the end of 1966, following the adaptation of the ÖIG Act and the launch of the ÖIG (*Österreichische Industrieverwaltungs-Gesellschaft* [Austrian Industry Association]) by the Josef Klaus government in 1967. Following the amendment of the ÖIG Act of 1969, companies were transformed into Ltds. (GmbH) in 1970. In July 1970, the ÖIG became the ÖIAG (*Österreichische Industrieverwaltungs-Aktiengesellschaft* [Austrian Industrial Management Company]), and in 1972, the Viennese Electric Power Plants Ltd. (*Wiener Schwachstromwerke, GmbH*) was merged into the ÖIAG.

The next turning point occurred in 1989, when the Austrian Industries Conglomeration was founded, which was 100 percent owned by the ÖIAG. The conglomeration consisted of chemical, electrical, electronics, machinery, and equipment manufacturing companies, the ÖMV and VOEST-ALPINE were also members of the group. The partial privatization of the Austrian Industries Group was designed to retain the influential, controlling role of the state. This privatization did not take place, however, and in March 1994, the Austrian Industries Concern re-merged with the ÖIAG.[8]

After 1987, multiple privatization waves occurred in Austria. The first major period lasted from 1987 to 1999. In 2000, a new shift took place. With the passage of *Gesetzes 2000*, the ÖIAG was transformed into a privatization agency. Beyond the industrial ownership of the Austrian state, in May 2000, the Post und Telekombeteiligungsverwaltungs-Gesellschaft and Post und Telekom Austria Aktiengesellschaft also merged into the ÖIAG. An important feature of the ÖIAG 2000 law was that the management of the ÖIAG received significant independence from its owner, the Austrian state. An independent and continuously expanded Supervisory Board was also institutionalized with the co-option law. Two-thirds of the members of the Supervisory Board could have been elected by the state, but instead the members of the Supervisory Board could independently select new supervisory board members. However, the government delegated elected members of the board. Employees' representation authority elected the

---

[7] On the nature of the stated-owned sector in the Austrian economy and on the operation of the ÖIAG from World War II until the 1980s, see Richter and Székffy (1987).

[8] On the history of the operation and the multiple reorganizations of the company, see https://www.voestalpine.com/group/en/group/history/

remaining third of members. Insider operations remained fundamental to the supervisory board. Later on, the "self-service" method prevailed instead of "self-renewal" (*Selbstbedienung statt Selbsterneuerung*).

In 2000, the Schüssel government decided to launch a new major privatization wave. Telekom Austria AG, the Vienna Airport (Flughafen Wien AG), the Postal Savings Bank (Österreichische Postsparkasse AG), Austria Tabak, Print Media Austria, which is the printing house of the state (Österreichische Staatsdruckerei GmbH), and the Dorotheum Auction House were selected for privatization. According to the Privatization Act, the aim was to achieve the highest possible revenues while simultaneously enforcing the interests of companies and the Austrian state. The simultaneous implementation of the different interests of the companies and the state mentioned seldom occurred and had a limited effect during this wave of Austrian privatization. However, the outcome of the privatizations managed by the Schüssel government was positive overall, primarily due to the fact that after the sale of those large companies, they performed well on the stock exchange and saw some appreciation and an increase in their values. However, this process stopped in the mid-2000s. Several anomalies occurred concerning the privatization of Austrian Telekom, and in 2011, a major scandal broke out. Following the financial crisis in November 2008, the Austrian state founded a company to coordinate state capital injections to banks. This institution, the FIMBAG, was headed by Hannes Androsch, the former minister of finance.

In 2011, the Austrian Telekom scandal broke out. Several executives of Telekom Austria were acquitted in December 2014 for their roles in various shady economic transactions. Within the ÖIAG, serious debates occurred. The CEO of the ÖMV was dismissed soon after expanding his mandate. Many professional criticisms followed concerning the alleged unfavorable privatization conditions—from the standpoint of the state—of Austrian Airlines and the Dorotheum Auction House, as well as other companies.

The Reorganization of the ÖIAG in 2015 and the Birth of the ÖBIB

In February 2015, the National Council of the Austrian Parliament decided to reform the ÖIAG, and in March 2015, it was reorganized with ÖBIB Ltd. (Österreichische Bundes- und Industriebeteiligungen [Austrian State and Industrial Holding Limited]). The main motivation behind this action was to reaffirm the ownership and direct control of the state. The ÖIAG operated as a form of joint-stock company, so its management made decisions legally free from external instructions, while its successor, the ÖBIB, operates as a Ltd., which means that its management needs to directly follow its owners' instructions. At ÖBIB, the state's ownership's legal mandate was assigned to and executed by the Austrian finance minister. The ÖIAG Supervisory Board's previous co-option powers and individuals' decision-making powers were terminated. The ÖBIB Act made an important exception to the general rules of the Ltd. Act: the members of the Supervisory Board of the ÖBIB shall not be nominated by the Executive Directors of the ÖBIB, but shall be nominated by a separate nomination committee composed of two secretaries of state and two private company directors (currently Chairman of Andritz AG and Chairman of the Supervisory Board of the Vienna Insurance Group). Starting in July 2015, Martha Oberndorfer, the former head of the Bundesfinanzagentur (Federal Fiscal Agency), manages the ÖBIB. The creation and operation of the ÖBIB clearly shows that the Austrian State has, once again, succeeded in directly managing the companies under its full and partial ownership. (The Austrian state possess over 50 percent of shares in the ÖBIB). Following the 1985–6 crisis in the state-owned sector, the Austrian authorities tried to introduce some parts of the ÖAIG into the stock exchange and reorganize the concern into a composite group for a long time, but all this effort was later removed from the agenda. With the new status quo in 2015, it became clear that the Austrian state, because of its ownership rights and management, tends to define the roadmap and strategies of development and implement it via the state's development policy instruments.[9]

Special Austrian Characteristics of the Relationship between State-owned and Private Companies

The separation of state and private investments—as international standards describe—in the Austrian economy, especially in infrastructure, is practically impossible because they are so interconnected. Major private investments in infrastructure are implemented by fully and partially state-owned companies, but the private sector's share investment performance is not clearly defined. Austria never wanted to discard its public sector, and the state, provinces, and municipalities exert major influence on infrastructure investments. Private companies separated from the public sector still

---

[9] On the foundation and operation of ÖBIB, see http://www.obib.co.at/.

maintain a close relationship with the state and, in a functional sense, take part in public sector activity. Exclusive private property practically does not exist in the Austrian infrastructure sector. For example, although energy companies have spread ownership of stock, the state and provinces have majority ownership, usually at least 51 percent. The role of state-owned companies is dominant in water supply and wastewater treatment. Investments in transport companies, ICT infrastructure, education, and healthcare are funded mostly by the public sector.[10]

The transformation of the Austrian public sector is primarily focused on increasing performance. On the other hand, they want comply with the provisions of the Maastricht Treaty and the Stability and Growth Pact in order to improve the financial position of the public sector by outsourcing part of its finances.

According to the European System of National Accounts ("Europäisches System Volkswirtschaftlicher Gesamtrechnungen" or ESA 95) standards, the state may provide private companies with up to 50 percent of the total cost of production, while maintaining their classification in private sector ratings. The transformation of the electricity market has not led to genuine competition. However, in the telecommunications sector, there was a spectacular improvement in performance due to improved service quality, interconnectivity systems, and price decreases. Railroad development has not led to substantial productivity growth or specific cost savings, but the high quality of service has further improved through speed, comfort, and accessibility, which greatly contribute to the rise in living standards. The ESA 95 separates the market producer from the non-market producer by the following definition: if more than 50 percent of the cost of production comes from market sales (sales, subscription fees, etc.), it is considered to be a private company; in less than 50 percent, it is a non-market player.

There are several outsourced companies in the sector of Austrian infrastructure. Since its foundation in 1982, the Autobahnen und Schnellstrassen-Finanzierungs-Aktiengesellschaft (Autobahn and high way financing stock corporation; or ASFINAG) has been responsible for the construction and maintenance of motorways and expressways. Since 1997, it has been fundamentally financed by vignette revenues, and ASFINAG is classified as a private sector company.

---

[10] For key structural data on Austrian companies, see: Structural Business Statistics, https://www.statistik.at/web_en/statistics/Economy/enterprises/structural_business_statistics/index.html.

The Österreichische Bundesbahnen (Austrian Federal Railways or ÖBB) used to be a public (federal) property (Bundesbetrieb) and it was the part of the Austrian fiscal budget until 1993. Since 1993, ÖBB has been a concern, and its group members were reclassified as private sector companies according to the national accounts system.

The Communal Supply- and Waste Management Company (Kommunale Versorgung- und Entsorgungsbetriebe) was reclassified as a private sector company with its own legal identity in 1997.

In 1992, the Federal Property Management Company (Bundesimmobiliengesellschaft or BIG) was established as a public company to manage federally owned properties, and their maintenance, infrastructure-related public investments, and the merchandising of unused properties.

Since 1997, provincial hospitals—Hospital Operations of Federal Provinces (Krankenanstaltenbetriebsgesellschaften der Bundesländer)—have gradually been reclassified in the corporate sector because of the modality of financing (clearing system). Consequently, most hospital construction projects and equipment purchases do not appear as public gross fixed capital investments. (As a result, the balance of the latter is improved as the expenditure side decreases according to accounting principals).

From 2014 onwards, the calculation of national accounts (Volkswirtschaftliche Gesamtrechnungen) modify the public and private sector's classification criteria to provide a clearer and more transparent picture, which is required by law.

Holding companies usually are classified as NACE 64s in terms of their financial services and are, therefore, not included in the infrastructure group.

The Austrian state, provinces, and municipalities claim some ownership in approximately 3500 companies. Out of those, approximately 140 function explicitly in the public sector; the rest might be found in the private sector. Public ownership occurs in 100 state-owned companies and approximately 1850 private companies engaged in infrastructure. Private companies that regularly supply at least one public enterprise are considered to be state-related companies. In total, 91 percent of communal units (cities, municipalities) have shares in at least one private company and approximately 2200 private companies are considered to be state-related.[11]

The term "state-related" requires a proper definition, which is not easy given that the term is filled with different content from case to case.

---

[11] Regarding the public sector of the Austrian economy, see www.statistik.tuwien.ac.at/oezstat/ausg011/papers/franz.doc.

This concept often means a mixed property, and may mean a majority or minority state, or an indirect form of state ownership. State-relatedness often occurs when it gains access to public orders and a connection to state development strategies. Through the size, scale, and conditions of the development sources share, major public development policy objectives are realized. Cross-ownership is also a considerable measure, especially in state, provincial, and communal companies' networks.

The Austrian Steel Giant, voestalpine Plc.

Voestalpine Plc. (voestalpine is the correct spelling of the company since 2003) was founded in May 1938 as a subsidiary of Reichswerke Aktiengesellschaft für Erzbergbau und Eisenhütten "Hermann Göring" Berlin, which was founded in 1937 (its full name was Reichswerke Aktiengesellschaft für Erzbergbau und Eisenhütten Hermann Göring, Linz). The concern owned two large companies: Eisenwerke Oberdonau GmbH for military operations and Stahlbau GmbH (Engineering- und Montagebetrieb), which was in charge of the site's creation and maintenance. They were merged with the former Österreichisch-Alpine Montangesellschaft in 1939, then Alpine Montan AG continued to operate as Hermann Göring, Linz. By 1944, four giant forges had been constructed.[12]

After World War II, the United States seized the Hermann Göring Werke, which was renamed VOEST (Vereinigte Österreichische Eisen- und Stahlwerke [United Austrian Iron and Steel Works]) and then Alpine Montan AG was spun off from it. The Americans turned over VOEST to Austria in July 1946. That same month, VOEST became property of the Austrian state under the 1946 nationalization law. Large-scale reconstruction began in 1947. First the power plant and then the forges and steel processing plant were restored, and starting in 1947, a new Siemens-Martin oven produced the company's high-grade steel.

VOEST was the anchor of nationalized industry and one of the main pillars of the ÖIAG. VOEST steel had been increasingly utilized for ship production, so the company founded its own shipping company, the Ister-Reederei, which introduced Linzertorin Flensburg in 1958. VOEST also

---

[12] On the major eras defining Austrian economic history, see Eigner and Helige (1999).

built ships at the Schiffswerft Korneuburg ship factory, including more than one hundred passenger ships that were sold to the Soviet Union.

Alpine Montan AG, which was separated from VOEST in 1946, operated independently for decades, but in 1973, it was facing a deep crisis, and as a result, it remerged with VOEST following a political decision. Two other steel companies were also merged with the concern for the same reasons, Böhler and Schoeller-Bleckmann. This is how VOEST-Alpine AG (as it was spelled in 1973) was established via state planning, decision making, (re)organization, and financing. In the post-1973 years, the Austrian state tried to achieve progress in two areas of the concern. Investments were financed with state money. More and more investment support was needed for development. In the technological sense, high quality investments have been implemented, however these were not financially successful, especially with regard to profitability. This was largely because of the widespread European steel crisis of the 1970s, which led to the decline of the steel industry throughout Europe. However, the Austrians expected that via technological progress and the sale of high quality products they could effectively address the crisis.

The other significant area of state intervention was the extension and maintenance of employment in the steel industry. To avoid massive unemployment as much as possible, Austrian public policy and economic policy have always paid particular attention to the job creation. The maintenance of steel jobs required more and more public support. Since the beginning of the 1980s, VOEST-Alpine has been constantly growing on an annual basis. In 1985, VOEST faced another deficit of 25 billion Schillings due to their loss-producing business manufacturing petroleum products. For this reason, in 1985, the concern had to be reorganized and the number of employees was reduced in several phases. Ferdinand Lacina, who was minister of finance at the time, dismissed the entire management of VOEST. It was a major step in adopting a new law that ended, at least legally, the Proporz system, which had allowed the heads of public companies to be proportionate to the showing of two major parties, the ÖVP and the SPÖ, and thus appointed because of their political affiliation and not their suitable economic qualifications. As a result, when leadership positions were filled, the governing system and the influence of the governing parties continued to exist.

In September 1986, a large-scale sanitation concept was initiated, and 9,400 workers were dismissed while state provided more than 21.5 billion Schillings in subsidies up to 1990. In 1987, the Steel Foundation (Stahlstiftung) was introduced to support the reemployment of displaced workers. The ÖIAG Group was largely restructured in 1988–9 and created six large holding companies. Four out of the six took over VOEST-Alpine plants. VOEST-Alpine Stahl Holding assembled all the steel manufacturing and processing plants. In 1989, the ÖIAG's six divisions were merged into Industrie- und Beteiligungsverwaltungs GmbH, which was the ÖIAG's possessed subsidiary (100 percent owned), and then restructured into Austrian Industries AG. A "Going public" bond was issued to prepare for an initial public offering. In 1993, a new privatization act was adopted, which resulted in the consolidation of the concern into three companies, which were partially privatized in 1995. VOEST-Alpine Stahl AG was introduced on the Austrian Stock Exchange in 1995. The Swedish Uddeholm steel mill was merged with Austrian Böhler. In 1995, it was listed on the Austrian Stock Exchange under the name Uddeholm-Böhler. VOEST-Alpine Industrieanlagenbau was part of the newly founded VOEST-Alpine Technologie AG and was acquired by Siemens Industrial Solutions and Services in 2005.

VOEST-Alpine's partial privatization began in 1995. The company was restructured into four divisions in 2001: steel, railway systems, motion (from 2005, automotive). In 2003 the Austrian government decided on full privatization, and the last state share was sold on the stock exchange. In 2007, the company decided to acquire the Böhler-Uddeholm steel company. The deal took place in three stages, and by 2009, the Böhler-Uddeholm steel company was purchased by voestalpine.[13]

After the collapse of the Lehman Brothers on September 15, 2008, voestalpine's orders dropped radically due to the crisis, and its economic condition decreased gradually. The concern implemented a comprehensive crisis management strategy, group-wide cuts, and enhanced effectiveness programs were launched. According to the Forbes's so-called "The World's Biggest Public Companies" list, voestalpine generally ranks around 900. Voestalpine recently has intensively turned toward the U.S. and China, enlarging its production in both countries. In 2014, the company invested €50 million ($70 million) for an automotive body parts subsidiary company in Cartersville, Georgia. The company's largest foreign investment was the construction of its reduction facility in Corpus Christi, Texas, for which it spent €550 million ($740 million). They are still planning major projects in China and the U.S.

---

[13] On the history of voestalpine, see "The history of voestalpine" on their website, https://www.voestalpine.com/group/en/group/history/.

The share capital of voestalpine is currently €307.13 billion, which totals the price of 169.05 million shares. The main shareholders are the Oberösterreich Invest GmbH and Co. with 15 percent, voestalpine Mitarbeiterbeteiligung Privatstiftung with 13 percent, Oberbank AG with 5 percent, and the remaining 67 percent of shares belong to small shareholders. In 2015, voestalpine employed workers in fifty countries, in more than five hundred subsidiaries and locations, totaling more than fifty thousand people worldwide. Its revenue was €11.2 billion in 2014. Its main profile has changed from steel and raw materials metallurgy to more technologically-demanding and sophisticated metallurgy technology and industrial products.

The Austrian Banking Sector: The Transformation and Interconnectedness of Private and State Ownership

Austria has one of Europe's densest banking networks with more than eight hundred financial institutions operating approximately 4,460 branches. Baron Salomon Meyer von Rotschild funded a bank in Austria in 1820, which played a major role in the industrialization of the country, including the construction of Nordbahn and the extension of credit to Austro-Hungarian nobles. In 1855 under the auspices of the Rotschild bank, Meyer's son funded the so-called Kaiserliche-königliche privilegierte Österreichische Credit-Anstalt für Handel und Gewerbe bank, or the Creditandstalt, which was the largest bank during the Dualist period. Its biggest competitor was the Länderbank funded by French capital in 1880, which separated from its French parent bank to become independent.[14]

The Anglo-Österreichische Bank was funded in 1864 with English capital, which was acquired by the Creditanstalt in 1926. The Allgemeine Kaiserliche-königliche privilegierte Boden-Credit-Anstalt was funded in 1863 with French capital, which got into trouble and was absorbed by the Creditanstalt by government decree.

In 1946, the large Austrian banks were nationalized. The Creditanstalt and the Länderbank operated as state-owned banks, which meant that a further 15 to 20 percent of the Austrian economy was controlled

---

[14] A comprehensive picture of Austria banking history providees: Bank Austria Creditanstalt (2005): 150 Jahre österreichische Bankengeschichte im Zentrum Europas. (Bank Austria Creditanstalt (2005): 150 years of Austrian banking history in the center of Europe).

by the state. Thereafter, the state directly and indirectly—through actions made by the two large banks—controlled more than 40 percent of the Austrian economy as an owner. These two large banks were directly state-owned until the 1980's, when they privatized through offerings on the Austrian stock exchange. Their sale on the stock exchange was a major step because the two banks were capitalized, and due to strong performance on the stock exchange, they became more solvent and their profits increased.

The Creditanstalt-Bankverein, Girozentrale, and the Länderbank were Austria's three largest banks in 1990. Ten years later, in 2000 none of them remained as independent institutions. The 1990s was a period defined by mergers, acquisitions, major transformations, and privatization. The merger of Zentralsparkasse and Länderbank in 1990 resulted in the establishment of the Bank of Austria. Giro-Credit emerged from the merger of Girozentrale and the ÖCI (Österreichisches Credit-Institut) in 1882. In 1997, the Bank Austria obtained a majority share in the Creditanstalt. That same year, Erste Österreichische Spar-Casse-Bank acquired Giro-Credit, and this is how Erste Bank der Österreichischen Sparkassen, or Erste for short, was born. In 1998, the Bank Austria bought all remaining shares of the Creditanstalt, and since then, the bank is called Bank Austria Creditanstalt (BA-CA). The Hypo Vereinsbank (HVB) bought the majority of shares in this new bank. However, not much later, the HVB experienced a crisis, and it had to sell its shares in BA-CA to ease its burdens. Finally, the HVG was acquired by the Italian Unicredit Bank in 2005.

The Raiffeisen Group was originally funded and operated on a cooperative basis. In 1978, a new law on loan banks was adopted in Austria, which re-regulated the operations, management, and supervision/oversight of cooperatives. Due to this law, the number of Raiffeisen branches decreased by half. The Raiffeisen Zentralbank (RZB) played a major role in real estate financing. Under the Raiffeisen International (RI) name, a separate subsidiary that operates mostly in the Central and Eastern European region was funded. In 2010, parts of the RZB merged with RI and operates under the name Raiffeisen Bank International.

The Austrian Sparkassen (savings banks) also experienced major structural transformation. Erste obtained shares in several large Landessparkasse. Parallel with this, Erste built a large network of bank branches in Central and Eastern Europe. However, the number of Sparkasse branches managed by the Austrian provinces decreased to fifty-three. This happened through the acquisition of the former Gemeindesparkasse (community savings banks). An interesting and important detail is that "communities" were not the actual owners of the Gemeindesparkasse, owners guaranteed their operations through warrants and largely without financial collateral.

The legal successor of the Zentralsparkasse der Gemeinde Wien was also the Bank of Austria, but in 2004, it quit the savings bank business. Another large bank, the Bank für Arbeit und Wirtschaft (BAWAG), was owned by the ÖGB (Austrian Trade Union Federation) until 2006. It was transformed into a public limited liability company in 1997, and was partially privatized in 2000. BAWAG and ÖGB maintained their collaborative contract with the Austrian Post plc. and Post und Telekom Austria plc. The so-called BAWAF scandal, which involved the fraudulent misuse of funds, became known in 2005. The ÖGB was forced to sell BAWAG to cover its losses. The American fund management company Cerberus became the new majority owner. In 2007, Bayerische Landesbank (Bayern LB) obtained the majority of the Hypo Group Alpe-Adria shares.

During the financial crisis in 2008–9, banking in Austria took a new turn and nationalization began. In 2008, the Austrian state acquired Kommunalkredit. Due to a lack of will and/or financial reserves, Bayerische Landesbank was not able to provide capital to the Hypo Group Alpe-Adria, which consequently was fully nationalized by the state. In 2012, another major nationalization took place with the Volksbanken acquisition, when, after experiencing huge losses, the Austrian state purchased 43.3 percent. These developments illustrate the Austrian bank sector's frequent, obligatory, and ad-hoc changes. Austrian finances are stable, but the country's financial institutions change frequently; they are restructured in order to maintain and increase available capital. The normative tools of banking regulation and banking supervision are now used instead of ad hoc intervention. Waves of nationalization—privatization— re-nationalization have softened the effects of the constant and parallel reorganizations, survival struggles, and maneuvers. However, the above patter might actually sharpen those effects. (The expression *durchwursteln*, "to muddle through," illustrates this situation).

The Impact of the State, the State Sector, and the Economic Policy on Companies

To analyze the nature of the Austrian market economy, it is very important to keep in mind that among western European countries, the proportion of fully and partially state-owned or indirectly controlled companies in the economy is the largest in Austria. Even after the end of the Monarchy, the two largest Austrian banks, the Creditanstalt and the Länderbank operated under state ownership. After World War II and for much of the second half of the twentieth century, the situation largely remained the same. Those two banks represented a significant share of state ownership both in industry and infrastructure. The rate fluctuated around 20 percent. The state totally disposed of over two-fifths of Austrian capital stock through direct ownership and indirectly through the control of state-owned banks.[15]

The nationalization act passed in July 1946 and the nationalizations that followed signaled, on the one hand, the country's sovereignty. On the other hand, they showed the active role of the state in rebuilding the country. Nationalizations ensured the control and the direction of reconstruction, but in legal terms, according to the Potsdam Treaty, the majority of the seventy largest companies came under the direction of the Allied occupation powers, and only reverted to Austria after the Austrian State Treaty in 1955.

Austria pragmatically repurchased the Schwechat Oil Refinery from the Soviet Union, and Austria paid for chemical product shipments for many years. During the 1950s and 1960s, essentially all of the largest companies were owned by the state or were under state control in every major sector excluding hospitality and tourism.

The pillars of the banking sector were the nationalized Creditanstalt-Bankverein and the Länderbank; in the mining industry, the largest company was Alpine, in the chemical industry, it was the successor of the Österreichische Stickstoffwerke from Linz, Chemie Linz; in the steel industry, VOEST; in the oil industry, the Schwechat Oil Refinery; and all the key companies involved in energy production were state owned. The state's development and investment policy were implemented directly through the state-owned commercial banks' financing, and borrowing on investments was adjusted to the expectations of the state.

State ownership was dominant in the most capital intensive industries with slow return rates, but the evolution of the production chain and the direction in which it moved was formed according to the goals of the Austrian state's industrial policy. The dominance of state ownership in the second half of the twentieth century was decisive in the iron and steel industry, oil and gas drilling and refineries, and in the chemical industry. Austrian private equity was relatively widely distributed. Regarding levels

---

[15] For more information on the interconnectedness of the economic policy and policy with changes in the role of the state, see Sandgruber (1995).

of accumulated capital stock, fully or partially state-owned large companies dominated small and medium private companies.

By the 1970's, the Austrian state sector's roles and functions had been transformed. Activities like restructuring, widening product ranges, and modernizing technological investment took place in order to maintain the viability of Austrian iron, steel, and chemical industries, which were struggling. Besides structural and management changes, the state's economic policy focused on achieving and maintaining high levels of employment.

From the 1960s, major concentration and centralization were executed in the state sector. The "Re-concentration Act" was adopted in 1960, which in most cases led to the reunification of companies that had previously been part of a single giant company that had been broken apart. Due to the concentration process, the new companies were more capital intensive and moved closer to the sizes of other western European companies. State-owned companies' organizational systems and operational conditions had been gradually transformed during the 1960s and 1970s. The main goal of the changes was that state-owned companies should be as profitable as privately-owned businesses. However, a fundamental difference remained: in state-owned companies, economic policy was implemented more directly, and the investment decisions and financial supports influenced the operation of this sector and especially its investments.

A special Austrian-Keynesianism characterized Austrian economic policy in the decades after World War II, and after several modifications, it still does today. In effect, Austria implements the mechanisms and prescriptions of Keynesian economic policy in a certain, constantly adaptive way. State orders, financial supports/subsidies, investment stimulations, and fiscal policies play a special role in Austrian economic policy. Following government decisions, advantageous credits and investment supports are the key actors in credit policy. Contrary to the Keynesian model, regulation of the money supply had never been a top priority. In that sense, Austria substantially differs from Germany. Instead of the magical quadrangle, which is present in German economic policy, in Austria there is a magical pentagon. Austria tries to achieve its goals by adding a fifth element: the fair distribution of income, to the priorities of the quadrangle, that is: financial stability, economic growth, high levels of employment, and balanced foreign trade accounts. Maintaining high employment was a priority during the crisis of 1974–5, in the period of structural transformation, and also in the management of the 2008-9 crisis. In times of crises and recession threats, the Austrian antidote was an expansive fiscal policy, and until 2002, the state was also especially focused on the stability of the national currency. The Austrian Schilling rate was fixed to the Deutsch Mark, which was stable between 1973 and 2002 (1 DM = 7.04 ATS).[16]

An important characteristic of Austrian economic policy is its employment-oriented structural policy, which was announced in the 1970s. They simultaneously tried to save jobs and enforce the consequences of the structural alignment. Austrian-Keynesianism transformed over time, but since the 1980s it has waned in popularity. During consolidation, there were pressures to implement a "globally restrictive, but selectively expansive" economic policy. Companies could have expected state supports if they could accomplish any of or exceeded the state's goals regarding employment, structural policy, and foreign trade. Following accession to the European Union in 1995, FDI inflow increased because non-Austrian EU companies also applied for state supports if they, like Austrian companies, accomplished the above mentioned policy aims. Austrian economic policy and the state's grant system is quite sophisticated in terms of the conditions it places on companies.

The maintenance of the low-level inflation and unemployment at the same major restricting took place time remains undoubtedly the great success of the Austrian state's economic policy. It is also important to emphasize the well-functioning social partnership (Soziale Partnerschaft) and the effective parity committee system. I do not address macroeconomic questions concerning the social partnership, I only highlight that the social partnership's core is the price and wage issues parity committee, which by analyzing the evolution of the prices has also made a major contribution to companies' price policy implementation. Aligned with wage policy agreements, this system has provided firms with a higher level of security and stability for decades, including today. Regarding price implementation, the parity committee's influence decreased due to Austria's EU membership, because in the single internal market, there is a high level of balancing.

Austria's Relationship with the European Union

Austria has experienced a high level of economic integration and cooperation with the European Union and transnational large companies, and this has had a significant impact on Austrian economic policy. Established

---

[16] On the nature of the Austrian-Keynesianism economic policy, see Schulmeister (2005) and Richter and Székffy (1987).

ownership, production, and sales relationships have majorly influenced the nexus between the state and private companies, especially through Austria's close market connection with the German economy, the presence of German large corporations in Austria, and Germany's role in the Austrian economy. I will briefly summarize this relationship below.

For decades, Austria and Germany have maintained very close economic and trade cooperation. Since Austria became a member of the European Union in January 1995, this relationship has further strengthened over the past twenty-one years. Approximately 68 percent of its imports are from the EU and the 66 percent of its exports' are sold within the EU. (Only 7 percent of Austria's imports come from EFTA countries and 9 percent of its exports head to these states.) The country's largest foreign trade and cooperation partner is Germany. Around 40 percent of Austrian exports are delivered to Germany, and 43 percent of Austria's imports come from Germany. Approximately 70 percent of the economy depends heavily on German shipments and orders. Austria has traditionally carried a deficit in its foreign trade with its largest partner, Germany, and with the EU. The consolidated balance of Austrian foreign trade also regularly shows a deficit.[17]

Austria's economic concentration on the EU market is multifaceted. In addition to commercial and capital relations, research and development, technical imports, tourism, and transportation and transit-related shipments are also significant.

One-third of Austrian industry is foreign-owned. Germany is the main source of foreign capital holdings, technology, and also know-how. Of the former EFTA countries, Austria is the second largest foreign trading partner in the EU after Switzerland. Austrian working-capital exporters increasingly focus on the European Union.

The decisive economic factors that shaped Austria's EU accession were mergers in the real economy, its foreign trade and capital relations, its technical development impulses, tourism, transportation and shipping, and the transformation of its currency and banking. The political aspects of Austria's alignment with German currency and exchange rate policies, and later the EMU's monetary and interest rate policy, played a stimulating role. There were a number of important arguments in favor of accession. Joining the EU offered promising opportunities for Austria's political engagement on the continent, because its policy of neutrality has lost its

---

[17] On the Austrian foreign trade and inward and outward direct investments, see: https://www.oenb.at/Statistik/Standardisierte-Tabellen/auszenwirtschaft.

usefulness following the disappearance of the East-West conflict. Furthermore, economic growth and prosperity are much more secure within the EU than outside of it. A small, developed country can substantially benefit from one large integrated market, while staying out would have disadvantaged Austria by making them less competitive.[18]

Austria has high levels of economic openness, dependence on foreign trade, and concentration with respect to the German and other EU markets. Per capita export value in Austria is about $6,500, which is more than three times larger than that of Japan.

EU accession has provided a major stimulus to the modernization of Austria's economic structure and institutional system. The state's economic interventions have decreased due to the adoption of EU rules, and in many sectors of the economy, a number of state-public quasi-monopolistic positions have been eliminated.[19]

In agriculture, despite some adaptation burdens, overall, there have been positive effects. The prices of food products have fallen by about 14 percent as a whole due to accession. About 200,000 Austrian employees work in EU countries, and are treated as equals in their respective local workforces.

Austrian companies enjoy anti-discrimination protections when they apply for investments within the EU. However, around 90 percent of state-public investments in the EU go to domestic companies, and the market for state orders remains national even today.

Regarding transportation and environmental policy, it is clear that effective solutions are impossible within a national framework. However, EU-level coordination over the past twenty years has not led to the genuine internationalization of these challenges.

Economic Policy and the Adaptation of the Economic Structure

Staying within in the framework of this study of Austrian economic policy and its structural adjustments, I will explain the characteristics of the Austrian economic policy-making process and describe how the Austrian

---

[18] Breuss (2010) has analyzed the main effects of Austria's EU accession for the period from 1995 to 2010.

[19] Foreign affiliates of Austrian companies: main results by economic activity (2016) http://www.statistik.at/web_de/statistiken/wirtschaft/unternehmen_arbeitsstaetten/auslandsunternehmenseinheiten/index.html.

decision-making process differs from other EU member states. Then I will review the impact of Austrian industrial policy, and briefly summarize site-level development factors and the effects of the corporate sector's response. I will show that as companies adapt, some of them focus on marketing and sales cooperation, while in other cases, the formation of strategic packages (clusters) plays an important role.

Austrian economic policy is defined by a number of characteristics: the highest priority is achieving full employment, even if monetary stabilization policy (fiscal consolidation, a hard currency course) appears to occupy this primary position. Stabilization policy is only one tool for achieving employment targets. In order to ensure long-term competitiveness (and employment), all tasks are subordinated to urgent budgetary problems. In principle, the growth, stability, and cohesion targets are complementary. However, the preparations for an economic and financial union (EMU) have led to the prioritization of stabilization over full employment.[20]

The EU exercises the most significant influence on the Austrian budget. Unlike monetary and currency policy, fiscal policy is not linked to EMU, however, the Maastricht criteria must be met. Austria's budget deficit resulted from an economic recession and structural problems. Only through the pressure exerted by EU membership and the EMU did fiscal discipline increase to such an extent that fiscal consolidation could no longer be postponed.

Creating a long-term competitive advantage by employing a traditional (direct benefits to domestic companies) industrial policy is no longer possible. In order to strengthen the national economy, horizontal measures have been implemented over the past twenty years. This includes everything that improves human capital, promotes research and development, modernizes financial infrastructure, makes the commodity and labor market more flexible, and increases the attractiveness of the economic area through the deregulation of legal and administrative procedures. Favorable legal and fiscal environments and better material and intellectual infrastructure leads to an increasingly competitive site. In Austria in particular, this led to a necessary reevaluation of the various economic supports, organizational systems, legal pricing instruments, and the privatization goals and income policies at both the federal and provincial level. Despite its high level of development, EU accession put a great deal of pressure on

---

[20] Economic Policy in Austria: https://english.bmf.gv.at/budget-economic-policy.

Austria to adapt the country's economic policies, so substantial adjustments have been made over the past two decades.

The sector that experienced perhaps the most painful adjustment was agriculture. In Austria, the structure and extent of subsidization of this sector is much higher and different than in the European Union as a whole. The Austrian system of guaranteed purchase prices had to be changed, and the EU's common agricultural policy had to be implemented. The main result has been that the rate of income supports have increased, while the rate of the set-price purchases of products has decreased. The importation of cheaper EU agricultural products has increased competition on the market, and food prices have decreased. Small agricultural entities' position has deteriorated, while larger agricultural concerns have grown and expanded their exports to the EU.

The adaptation process in the industrial sector has also created several specific problems. In Austrian industry, raw material processing and production was strongly subsidized by the state. For decades, the Austrian state focused on strengthening the supply base of domestic manufacturing, but it was costly and challenging. Following EU accession, Austria was forced to give up its subsidization policy in mineral production and coal mining, as well as the traditional state monopoly of salt mining. Import restrictions on brown coal also had to be abolished. As a result, imports of raw materials have grown and their prices have decreased. Because of German capital, acquisitions, and restructuring, the Austrian mining industry is exposed to German interests.

The current Austrian energy system is regulated, and depends on the close relationship between suppliers and users. Large consumers (an annual consumption of 100 gigawatts or more) are free to choose their energy supplier partner. The state was forced to relinquish its sales monopoly on fuel, and the prohibition of nuclear power production remained in effect.

Before accession, the construction industry enjoyed strong, de facto national protections. Austrian and German cement factories were barely present in each other's markets. Over the past twenty years, this situation has changed significantly, and a mutual interconnection has evolved. Austrian building materials were more expensive than the EU average, but prices for construction were much lower. Austrian construction companies are effectively involved in the EU's public procurement market. Most Austrian bridge and road construction firms are internationally competitive. However, with the creation of the European Economic Area, the Austrian public procurement markets had to be opened up to foreign companies.

The Austrian automobile market is based on imports. Over the past twenty years, the market for cars manufactured in the EU has expanded, as prices for cars decreased. By adopting the EU's external customs duties, the price of Japanese cars has increased. Former general importers' rights have ceased to exist, and competition in the EU automobile market has become more intense. An important rule is that a car license issued in any EU country is valid everywhere. The Austrian state subsidization of foreign-owned sites in Austria is hotly debated. The Austrian state paid one-third of the investment costs of the American Chrysler site in Graz. The EU insisted on reducing the subsidy rate below 20 percent. The only solution was that U.S. and Austrian private investors (Steyr) raised their capital investments and reduced the state's share to the desired level.

There are two major effects in the electronics industry. In the EU, Austrian companies that produce electronic equipment can use external imports without authentication certificates (as well as producers in other industries), thus making it possible to include cheaper Southeast Asian inputs into export-oriented products. With the significant reduction of external tariffs on electronic products, the competition in the electronic products market has increased substantially.

Strengthening competitiveness requires national economic policy, regional development, and corporate strategic measures. Austrian economic policy is very successful in achieving required macroeconomic and financial indicators, but fails to provide the necessary framework for continuous structural change and a favorable economic climate.

Austria was forced dismantle its former direct subsidies of industry, individual project supports, and transport cost supports when it joined the EU. The role of the state in the creation of individual mega projects and in the case-by-case subsidization of foreign investors could not go unchanged. The main direction of the change was that individual and case-by-case subsidies had to be replaced by a regional development policy, and direct job-creation subsidies had to be replaced by normative systems of general labor market incentives.

A relatively strong intra-industrial division of labor characterizes Austrian foreign trade. The Grubel-Lloyd coefficient (the ratio of intra-industry foreign trade to total foreign trade) is 69 percent for the total foreign trade of Austria and 68 percent for its foreign trade with the EU. In comparison with other EU-15 countries, this proportion is higher in France (83 percent), Belgium, Great Britain, Germany and the Netherlands (76–77 percent). The value of other countries in the index is lower than that of Austria.[21]

The sectors that are highly exposed to external competition and are sensitive to competition have a major impact on the Austrian economy as a whole. Those sectors are: iron and steel production, the fine ceramics industry, chemical raw materials, fertilizer manufacturing, pharmaceuticals, other chemical products, automotive rubber manufacturing, most of the agriculture and food industry, the shoe industry, the textile and clothing industry, the paper and printing industry, office machines manufacturing, agricultural machinery manufacturing, shipbuilding, railway car manufacturing, the sports and toy industry, and the manufacture of electrical household appliances.

Companies in these sectors are forced to permanently adapt to recent market actions. The facilitation of this adaptation pressure might explain many major Austrian industrial policy interventions.

According to critics of the Austrian industrial policy strategy, between 2010 and 2020, a further major restructuring of subsidies is necessary. Former corporate supports should be replaced by site development. Competition policy will have a greater role in increasing competition. Competition pressures will be particularly strengthened in sensitive sectors. This trend is also enhanced by the wave of corporate mergers in the EU, which also significantly affects Austria.[22]

The improvement of site conditions will be a future key factor in the realization of structural transformation investments and in attracting capital and job creation. This requires a new concept and strategy in relevant sub-policies. At the core of those Austrian economic policies there will be infrastructure programs, communal investments to improve some regional sites, research and development subsidies, and state-sponsored public and infrastructure services. Although the direction of these strategies seems to correct, it might be criticized for the lack of concretization of the above-mentioned goals. Concretization and implementation of Austrian economic policy requires much effort over the next decades.

---

[21] Österreichs Wirtschaft im Überblick. Die österreichische Wirtschaft und ihre internationale Position 2014/2015, Statistik Austria, Wien.
[22] For details on Austrian start-ups and liquidations, see https://www.statistik.at/web_en/statistics/Economy/enterprises/business_demography_since_2015/index.html.

The success of Austrian adaptation, its external trade performance, and the improvement of its competitiveness depend mainly on the corporate sector's reaction to changes. Some companies seek to improve their position through marketing and sales cooperation. For example, some companies cooperate to sell their products and services because without this relationship, it would cost much more and would be less efficient to manage an individual sales strategy. However, these same companies can separately focus their corporate development strategies and capital investments on production.

Another group of Austrian companies form strategic packages (clusters) to streamline to production chain of products. The user prefers complex solutions to problems. For example, telecommunications equipment manufacturers cooperate with the manufacturers of control systems and measuring instruments, as well as investors and software engineers. This road promises to increase competitiveness in several areas. However, it should be noted that this is not recommended way for companies to operate, especially those that are deeply embedded in local markets and lack special competitive know-how.[23]

One segment of Austria's problematic industrial sectors produces solely for domestic markets with significant foreign capital. These include the electrical industry, the chemical industry, the textile industry, and the food industry. Subsidiaries operating in these sectors have already established their sales and purchasing relations with foreign partners, often with their EU counterparts, and consider their Austrian market position to be internationally significant. That Austrian subsidiaries often cannot meaningfully influence the development strategy of their foreign mother companies is a serious disadvantage. Regarding the electrical industry, the high foreign capital ratio limits the formulation and implementation of domestic industrial strategy.

This survey of Austrian economic policy as it has changed and adapted over time, has led us to further investigate Austria's status as a production site and the position of the country and Austrian companies on the EU market?

---

[23] Wissensfabrik—Unternehmen für Österreich https://www.wissensfabrik.at/DieWissensfabrik.

Austria as a Production Site: The Position(s) of the Austrian Economy in the European Union

Austria's economic policy regarding European politics assumes that without the EU, Austria would not be "the second Switzerland," but an economic dwarf. The country lagged far behind Switzerland in terms of development, export, and competitiveness indicators before EU accession in 1995, but since then, Austria has been steadily catching up. Since EU membership, the Austrian economy has grown by about 2 percent annually, which is a faster pace of growth than in Germany and Switzerland. This was largely due to EU integration. Nearly one-third (.06 percent) of Austria's 2 percent annual growth rate is due to EU membership. The financial impact of integration is also positive; every Austrian citizen gains €800 annually from EU participation, which is roughly the cost of a nice dinner out every month. In the long run, Austria has developed better than Switzerland, has achieved higher growth rates and greater increases in employment rates.[24]

Competition on the labor market has increased significantly over the past twenty years. Due to the concept of the free movement of persons, the number of foreign workers and foreign students has substantially increased in Austria. Labor costs did not increase as a result of integration, and in some professions, the competitiveness of East-Central European workers even intensified. Austrian job creation strategies, in large part, generated 12,600 new jobs annually due to integration. However, trends in the Austrian labor market are mainly influenced by the automation of industrial production and the rapid spread of imports from Asia. Better-educated Austrian workers, however, are in a better position in both the national and international labor markets. Austrian productivity levels are the fourth highest in the EU following Luxemburg, Ireland, and Belgium. The number of those self-employed is significant; in 2012, it was 483,000 people. Employment in Austria between 2009 and 2013 increased by 4 percent, while in the rest of the EU, it decreased on average. The profitability of employment is facilitated by the fact that unit labor costs in 2012 were below 2000 levels. Profitability is mainly achieved by increasing output through higher productivity. (With the exception of Luxemburg

---

[24] Kőrösi (2013 and 2015) analyzes the position of the Austrian economy in the European Union and the characteristics of Austrian development policy.

and the Scandinavian countries, this is exceptionally remarkable among EU countries.) Real wages constantly increased until 2009, but decreased in 2010 and 2011 by 0.6 and 1.2 percent respectively, which had not occurred in Austria for decades. Then, in 2012 and 2013, real wages per capita stagnated.[25]

As a production site Austria has become more competitive, and its regional development has accelerated. The share of fixed capital investments is 21 to 23 percent of the annual GDP. There is generally a higher investment rate in Austria than in the EU, and especially in the EU-27, where it is not more than 18 percent on average. The opening of the internal market has strengthened competition. At the same time, competitiveness was increased through the use of EU funds. Research and development expenditures from abroad have increased from €190 million in 1995 to €1.13 billion in 2012, mainly due to the country's participation in the research and development framework of EU programs and due to activities of large EU—mainly German—companies in Austria. The catching up process is the most remarkable in Burgenland and Lower Austria (Niederösterreich). Lower Austria received three times more money than it paid into the budget due EU supports for border regions. The introduction of the Euro also strengthened the Austrian economy. Having been a member of the European Monetary Union for sixteen years, Austria has not had to fear the exchange rate fluctuations of its competitors. The Austrian range of goods has continued to expand and price competition has also increased. A number of durable consumer goods have become cheaper over the past fifteen years in Austria, where the prices on washing machines, electronics, and computers have declined even in nominal terms. Without EU membership, the Austrian annual inflation rate would have been 1 percent higher annually.

The free movement of goods and persons has increased intra-EU trade and services. The opening of the Austrian border due to EU membership has saved costs and additional benefits of €4.2 billion annually. By 2012, the value of exported goods per capita increased to €15,400 and the value of imported goods increased to €16,500.[26] The Austrian commodities market opened more to foreigners and Austrians in foreign coun-

---

[25] Regarding the labor market data used here, see *Arbeitsmarkt*, http://www.statistik.at/web_de/statistiken/menschen_und_gesellschaft/arbeitsmarkt/index.html.

[26] For the source of Austrian foreign trade data, see Österreichische Nationalbank https://www.oenb.at/Statistik/Standardisierte-Tabellen/auszenwirtschaft/Auszenhandel/auszenhandel.html.

tries. Austrian FDI abroad increased to €153.56 billion in 2012, while FDI in Austria amounted to €118.30 billion, making the country a net-FDI exporter.[27] These processes led to a major internationalization of the Austrian economy. Austrian industry has benefitted significantly from the introduction of European norms and also from the full or partial standardization of those norms.

Austrian companies benefited from their competitive advantages in the domestic and EU markets. Currently, approximately 70 percent of Austrian exports go to other EU countries. Between 1995 and 2013, Austrian exports to the EU tripled. Most export growth has been the result of the positive effects of Central European systemic changes. Consequently, since 1989, the Austrian economy has been growing faster than the EU-15 average.

Austria did not play an important role in the origin of the European financial crisis. The European financial crisis would have occurred without the Euro due to financial imbalances. The introduction of the Euro meant much cheaper lending terms for Mediterranean countries, and these countries did take on some irresponsible debt. However, large Western European banks mismanaged lending (mainly French and German banks that provided credits to Greece). Austria went through the Eurozone crisis more smoothly; the external shock in the previous Schilling regime might had been more severe.[28]

Austrian capital investments grew considerably from 1995 until the crisis, primarily due to the activities of Austrian banks in Central and Eastern Europe. Until the crisis, more than €300 billion of capital investment was made in Central Europe, reaching more than 110 percent of Austrian GDP. At present (in 2019) the share of Austrian invested capital in foreign countries is higher than 140 percent of GDP. On the one hand, this demonstrates the strength and the capitalization of the Austrian financial sector, but on the other, it majorly exposes the country because of the risks associated with repayment.

Without EMU membership, international credit rating agencies might have downgraded Austria's creditworthiness due to the absence of cooperation. For Austria, the integrated capital market has a lower cost. Austrian financial policy and its professional role in EMU fit well in the country's European policy, and it has been relatively successful in the aftermath of

---

[27] For more information on the flow of Austrian foreign direct investment, see https://www.oenb.at/en/Statistics/Standardized-Tables/external-sector/foreign-direct-investment.html.
[28] Kőrösi (2009) has analyzed the impact of the 2008–2009 crisis on Austria.

the crisis. However, Austrian European policy's communications strategy is not very professional, particularly regarding financial policy, where the majority of media outlets provide tabloid and sensational press on economic problems. Most Austrian citizens are barely involved in financial matters, especially their deeper contexts. The Austrian state failed to adequately communicate the complexity and background of its strategy to the public.

Research and development and tourism are among the sectors in which the country has achieved significant benefits due to European integration. The share of research and development in the broader economy has doubled since 1995. Every year, more than 800,000 tourists travel to Austria from the Visegrád countries alone, and spend over € 250 million annually year, which support 70,000 jobs.

The full impact of the benefits of EU membership over the last 20 years can be found in the additional growth results, the potential growth-enhancement effect, increased research and development efficiency, and increased consumption, which is due to prosperity and increased tax revenue.[29]

Summary and Conclusions

In Austria, the state's role in ownership, economic development, and redistribution is very important. Public expenditures add up to more than 50 percent of GDP, which makes Austria sixth in the EU rankings. Already prior to 1938, a large public sector emerged, representing around one-fifth of the production value of the Austrian economy. The Nationalization Act of July 1946 focused on avoiding the expropriation of "German-owned" companies by the Allies. Ownership, control and supervision are key aspects of the steel industry, heavy industry, and oil production and refinery, and these are also crucial for maintaining the full or part state-ownership and strategic control of the banking system.

In this paper, I presented the historical milestones of the transformation of Austrian state property, state and private business relations, and the waves of privatization. In the spring of 2015, ÖBIB (Österreichische Bundes- und Industriebeteiligungen) was established as a limited trade company that controls Austrian federal and industrial shares. By estab-

---

[29] On the Austrian economic position and its European policy, see Kőrösi (2013) and Kőrösi (2015).

lishing the ÖBIB, the Austrian state once again put full and partially owned companies under direct state control. The Austrian state, provinces, and municipalities have ownership stakes in over approximately 3,500 companies, in particular in infrastructure and public services. Through developments in the operation, ownership, and management of voestalpine, an Austrian steel company, the transformation of motivations for state intervention is well illustrated. Based on the ownership and regulation of the Austrian banking sector, it is also clear that the goal was to ensure the state's strategic control role and to implement the state's strategy through investment and capital allocation.

Austrian economic policy is commonly characterized by an "employment-oriented structural policy," which has led to major industrial policy interventions. Significant transformations have occurred in the economic policy of Austria during the period between 2010 and 2015, and the main direction of those transformations was the replacement previous corporate subsidies with complex aspects of site development. By improving site conditions, comprehensive efforts were made in order to promote investment incentives, lending with favorable interest rates, and job creation all at once. The overall ownership share of the Austrian government is about 20 percent, but through the partly state-owned banking system, there is additional indirect state influence in the economy.

The waves of centralization-decentralization-recentralization show that the symbiosis of the state and the market was characterized by the special amalgamation and concentration of Austrian-Keynesianism and pragmatism. This concentration appears in complex ownership, part-ownership, investment relationships, and profit sharing, and this makes analysis of this symbiosis particularly difficult. Mainly through flexible conflict management in the Austrian economy, this symbiosis has proved to be efficient during constant transformations and adaptations over the past decades.

An important factor in Austrian economic stability is the exceptionally high proportion of family businesses. More than 95 percent of all Austrian private companies are family businesses. The majority of those companies operate in tourism, hospitality, and local services, which plays a vital role in the utilization of local factors and the stability of employment.

The economic operations of the large corporate and banking sectors under state and mixed ownership have long been associated with politics. For decades, the main characteristic of the Proporz system was the proportional division of appointees to boards of directors and supervisory boards between the two large parties, the Austrian People's Party (ÖVP) and the Austrian Socialist Party (SPÖ) on the basis of their performance in elections. The two parties' coalition ceased to exist in 2017 due to their fundamentally conflicting views. A new situation has evolved since the 2017 elections. The Austrian People's Party and the Austrian Freedom Party (FPÖ) organized a new government with Sebastian Kurz as Prime Minister. The Austrian Socialist Party went into opposition. The main emphasis of Kurz's government is on two basic issues, which he explicitly promotes as vital for the Austrian economy and society: tax reduction and the suppression of illegal immigration.

The Kurz government prepared a detailed, 182 page program for the 2017–2022 period based on the shared views of ÖVP and FPÖ. The Kurz program mirrors a definite shift in both parties' preferences and a policy trend that supports entrepreneurship prevailed. Specific preference is given to the reduction of the central state redistribution share. The total tax- and contribution rate should be reduced from 45–50 percent (the level between 2010 and 2017) to 40 percent in the long term. This reduction should be achieved mainly through corporate tax reductions. Currently, Austrian corporate tax rates are higher than in any of the neighboring countries except Italy. The tax reform plan intends to change this situation by altering the tax structure through the reduction of corporate taxes and wage-related contributions so as to improve the corporate sector's position. The goal is to enhance corporate competitiveness mainly through a reduction of the corporate income tax rate. Tourism is supported through lower taxes paid after accommodations are provided. The VAT (Mehrwertsteuer) is applied to all online purchases from extra-EU countries and is strictly controlled. Also, there will be stricter monitoring of multinational companies' taxes. All companies should pay taxes on activities carried out in Austria. Pre-tax income transfers abroad are to be curtailed. The applicability of this measure is questionable considering the EU principle of free capital movement and income transfers through multinational corporations' transfer pricing practices.

The government program also prioritizes support for investment activity, corporate financing, and the development of capital markets. This means increasing the influence of venture capital and investments that promote corporate expansion and the extension of credit guarantees for the corporate sector.

Bolstering Austrian firms' competitiveness is expected in three main areas: 1) an increase in large companies' exports based on improvements in productivity and labor market changes that favor companies over workers. Further, state support is provided for the establishment of new research-intensive jobs and job training programs. 2. Maintaining the stability of family businesses and the improvement of their income-generating potential. Income from tourism and hospitality, as well as sales of local products and services should increase. Related taxes will be reduced, and a higher share of promotional costs will be deductible from income generated through tourism while state-sponsored promotional costs will increase. 3. The development of a special knowledge-generating sector will be promoted mainly through SMEs in the ICT sector.

The main priorities of development policy in the state-owned sector are incorporated in environmental protections and climate and energy strategy. By 2030, all of the Austrian electrical energy supply is to be based on renewable energy. The achievement of this goal is realistic given that 70 percent of the electricity supply in Austria is already provided by renewable sources, mainly hydroelectric power stations. The share of renewable energy in the total energy supply was 33 percent in 2018. The development of traffic and transport infrastructure is also prioritized. Research and development in this sector will be carried out by the state. Maintenance and operation costs will be covered using current revenues. The associated services should, however, be provided by market-oriented agents. The development of railways is financed by the state, and losses from personal travel are covered through cross financing with cargo transport profits. Stations' shops are given to concessions through tenders oriented toward profit maximization.

As is seen in the program's targets, the state intends to strengthen business support policies. But at the same time, the government would like to maintain or increase its popularity by promoting its achievements in welfare. This maneuvering (*Durchwursteln*) is a lot more difficult today than it was previously.

Austria intends to simultaneously maintain the social welfare achievements of the social market economy and increase corporate competitiveness. The difficulties of this policy have become increasingly evident over the past few years (2013 to 2018). Compared to Germany, three main problems in the performance of the Austrian economy worth highlighting are: first, Austria's rate of economic growth did not reach that of Germany between 2013 and 2018, although it used to surpass it. Second, unemployment used to be traditionally lower than in Germany, but it rose in 2018 (5.5 percent in Austria and 3.6 percent in Germany in summer 2018 according to Eurostat data). Third, state debt surpassed 80 percent during the mid-2010s, and in 2018, it is still much higher than state debt in Hungary or Germany, which is a reversal of earlier patterns.

To conclude, Austria has a special position in the Varieties of Capitalism literature. Austro-Keynesianism was based on consolidation beginning in the early 1950s and was most effective from 1955 to the 1973 crisis. Austro-Keynesianism failed several times during crises, as shown in the analysis of crisis management. Therefore it cannot be treated as a panacea. However, pragmatic economic policy, the consensus-oriented cooperation of employers' chambers and unions, and the high number and significance of family businesses enhanced Austria's economic stability. Per capita GDP as well as average wages are still higher in Austria than in Germany. With the successful implementation of the Kurz program, Austro-Keynesianism may be replaced by a new policy paradigm, which would increase the role of the markets and strengthen the competition-related aspects of Austria's economic strategy.

REFERENCES

Rathkolb, Oliver, Theodor Venus, and Ulrike Zimmerl, eds. 2005. *150 Jahre österreichische Bankengeschichte im Zentrum Europas* [150 years of Austrian banking history in the center of Europe]. Vienna: Zolnay-Verlag.
Breuss, Fritz. 2010. "Österreich 15 Jahre EU-Mitglied" [15 years of Austria's membership in the European Union]. *WIFO Monatsberichte* (2): 117–136.
Eigner, Peter, and Andrea Helige. 1999. *Österreichische Wirtschafts- und Sozialgeschichte im 19. und 20. Jahrhundert* [Economic and social history of Austria in the 19th and 20th century]. Wien: Brandstätter.
Gál, Péter. 1984. "Ausztria" [Austria]. In *Korunk világgazdasága II* [World economy of our age II], edited by József Nyilas, 417–471. Budapest: Közgazdasági és Jogi Könyvkiadó.
Kőrösi István. 2005. "Ausztria új szerepe: közép-európai államként ismét az európai centrumban" [A new role for Austria: as a Central European state in the center of Europe]. In *A Huszonötök Európái* [The Europes of the Twenty-Five], edited by László J. Kiss, 550–588. Budapest: Osiris.
———. 2009. "Ausztria—a válság hullámai elérték a stabilitás szigetét" [Austria—the waves of the crisis have reached the island of stability]. In *A pénzügyi-gazdasági válság hatása és kezelése az EU fejlett kis tagállamaiban* [Impacts and management of the financial and economic crisis in EU small member states], edited by Krisztina Vida, 7–13. Budapest: MTA VKI.
———. 2013. "Ausztria Európa-politikája és gazdasági pozíciója az Európai Unióban" [Austria's European policy and economic position in the European Union]. *Külügyi Szemle* (2): 23–54.
———. 2015. "Ausztria" [Austria]. In *Európa-politológia: A tagállamok Európái* [Europe politology: The European member states], edited by Attila Marján, 257–297. Budapest: NKE.

Richter, Sándor, and Klára Székffy. 1987. *Ausztria gazdasága. Fejlődés—megtorpanás—válságjelenségek* [Austria's economy. Evolution—a pause—crisis phenomena]. Budapest: KJK.

Sandgruber, Roman. 1995. *Ökonomie und Politik. Österreichische Wirtschaftsgeschichte vom Mittelalter bis zur Gegenwart* [Economy and politics: Austrian economic history from the Middle Ages to the present]. Vienna: Ueberreuter.

Schulmeister, Stephan. 2005. "Anmerkungen zur Wirtschaftspolitik und Wirtschaftsdynamik in Österreich seit 1955" [Comments on economic policy and economic dynamics in Austria since 1955]. In *Physiognomie der 2. Republik Von Julius Raab bis Bruno Kreisky* [Physiognomy of the 2nd Republic from Julius Raab to Bruno Kreisky], edited by Gerbert Frodl, Paul Kruntorad, and Manfried Rauchensteiner, 333–365. Vienna: Czernin Verlag.

CHAPTER 5

Some Aspects of State Ownership in East-Central European Transition

Miklós Szanyi

Introduction

The topic of this chapter is deeply influenced by the complicated web of transition policies in Central and Eastern Europe. We focus on East Central Europe (ECE), but more precisely on the Visegrád countries (Poland, Czechia, Slovakia, Slovenia, and Hungary). However, occasionally we compare some aspects of transition with those of (western) Balkan countries or with patterns in countries that emerged from the former Soviet Union (fSU). Many scholars from the varieties of capitalism (VoC) literature state that Central European capitalist development is markedly different, especially from the model in the Commonwealth of Independent States (CIS) countries (Lane 2007; Csaba 2007; Szanyi 2012; Bohle and Greskovits 2007; Bohle and Greskovits 2013). Nölke and Vliegenhart (2009) began their work with a positive description of the Central European capitalist model and highlighted positive and negative features of multinational companies' strong influence, a kind of new dependence for these countries (the dependent market economies—DME—model). In an earlier paper, I suggested adding the role of the state to the list of features of the DME model, especially direct state intervention in the form of state-owned companies (Szanyi 2012). Further research on the East Central European capitalist model also highlighted corruption as a factor that is more dominant in ECE than in other European capitalist models (Szanyi 2012, 22–23). Corruption is also linked to the strong role of the state, which can be misused by politicians because of weak institutions (political, social, and market institutions alike).

This chapter is based on an earlier paper published in *Acta Oeconomica* (Szanyi 2016).

State property management of transition economies began with privatization. Once on the trail of transition, the post-communist countries of East Central Europe began to de-nationalize state property. It is important to see that the period (the 1980s and 1990s) was deeply influenced by neoliberal economic thought. This was expressed in the practice of international organizations participating in the transition process, but also in the solid conviction of many influential local personalities, "reformers" like Václav Klaus, Leszek Balcerowicz, and Yegor Gaidar. Nevertheless, the transition process evolved as a mix of conflicting economic principles. In most countries, the pro-market drivers of the neoliberal thought and local pressure groups' expectations simultaneously shaped transition policies, including the privatization process. In the case of Hungary, there has been a general consensus about the necessity of reducing the size of the state sector. However, there have always been interest groups lobbying against the privatization of certain firms or sectors. For example, the sale of Hungarian Electricity Works was discussed, and finally only some segments of the business (including fossil fuel power plants and local distribution networks) were privatized, but not the entire nationwide transmission system and the Paks nuclear power station (Mihályi and Sztankó 2015). In other cases, the privatization process was not blocked but rather influenced by stakeholders (Szanyi 1996). Clashes between multinational businesses and local interest groups' representative networks in Hungary have been described (Szanyi 2016) and, in the case of Poland, thoroughly analyzed (Kozarzewski and Baltowski 2015).

State and public ownership is present in every established market economies. Corrections for many types of market failures can be most easily achieved by the public provision of certain services. Furthermore, one of the main instruments of the developmental state is the SOE. If we look at the ownership structure of coordinated market economies like Austria or Germany, or mixed market economies (France and Italy), we find a large number SOEs in all of these countries. Although de-nationalization of the state-owned sector was on the agenda in several European countries (the UK and France) and in the Americas (Mexico and Chile), especially during the 1980s, these privatization deals concerned individual companies and not national economies. The former were not part of broader systemic changes unlike privatization in the transition economies.

Privatization in transition economies, on the other hand, was always regarded as a key element of the transition process. The usual tasks and properties of SOEs were largely replaced by the political and institutional goals of transition policies. They were determined by the mainstream neoliberal ideology, which was spread by international financial institutions and development agencies. Privatization was regarded as a tool for increasing the popularity of the transition process too (Appel 2004), either through the implementation of giveaway-style privatization methods, and/or by supporting ideological and political (anticommunist, nationalist) arguments. In Hungary, economic reform traditions provided very fertile soil for pro-market arguments. In Poland, the privatization process was based on stakeholder consensus rooted in the strong self-management desire of the Solidarity movement. Variations in the privatization policies of ECE countries were reflected in the well-known gradualism versus shock therapy debate,[1] which was mostly about the social acceptance of transition measures and the potential threat of reversal by a resistant "nomenclature" and incumbent communist political forces.

The strong political charge of privatization and the equally strong neo-liberal influence on the transition process resulted in a high emphasis on the speed and depth of privatization in ECE, regardless of the actual technical solutions (voucher schemes, insider buyout or sales methods). Not surprisingly, according to EBRD transition reports, over two-thirds of GDP production in all ECE countries was private by the end of the 1990s, regardless of the substantial differences in privatization policies (Schoenman 2014). Similarities continued, when after 2000 disappointment in the results of transition process swept over the ECE transition economies. Privatization was then a major area of debate, and public opinion in general regarded it as "organized theft" (Appel 2004). More serious, albeit not quite nuanced, were critics' characterizations of the 1990s transition process as a period when free market ideology had been aggressively pushed on post-communist governments (Stiglitz 1999). Appel (2004) argued that the role of ideology in post-communist economic policy making was much more nuanced than what is reflected in earlier debates and later critics. She called for the consideration of individual and group interests arguing, "the beliefs and preferences of actors on the ground deserve much more recognition than Stiglitz allows for" (6). Thus, while the overall attitude toward transition policies had a heavy ideological charge, local personnel and group interests always influenced the actual implementation of policies.[2]

---

[1] For a good summary see, among others, Roland (2000).
[2] Mihályi and Sztankó (2015) recalled the case of the privatization attempts of MVM, the Hungarian electric company, which was effectively opposed by the incumbent management regardless of the ideological orientation (liberal, nationalist) of various succeeding governments. In Poland, the Solidarity movement could never be neglected, and this led to a slower, but socially grounded, consensus-based privatization policy.

Based on Kopecky (2006), Schoenman (2014) stated that because political parties in ECE had weak ideological underpinnings, voters switched parties frequently. It seems that ideological values were barely transmitted to the general public. However, in the early phase of transition, the values of the "international adviser community," in cooperation with local political leaders, and officials were transmitted to the population. The political leaders' role was to gain public support from various groups. In doing so, they could use ideological argumentation to legitimize political decisions. But more frequently they used either coercive mechanisms (the threat or actual use of force) or remunerative measures (economic incentives). Naczyk (2014) interpreted the most recent (ideological) changes in Polish and Hungarian economic policy as simple shifts in the content of "economic patriotism." He argued that, during the 1990s, the most important national goal was the quick departure from communism and central planning, which was supported most enthusiastically by the neoliberal idea. During the late 2000s, when these earlier goals were effectively achieved, new content was added to economic patriotism: the strengthening of national businesses' presence and preventing further internationalization of ECE economies. Both the Hungarian and the Polish histories of transition provide many examples of similar changes in policy preferences.[3]

From the above discussion, an important conclusion can be drawn, which will be developed in this chapter. The relationship between ECE political parties to economic issues is less ideological and more pragmatic than in case of more established market economies. The actual implementation of economic policies is determined by several factors. First, there is the ideologically based, "mainstream" influence of the international adviser community (which was broadly supported during the 1990s but rejected in many cases after the 2008–9 crisis). Second, the implementation of policies was always strongly influenced by domestic pressure groups including business groups (local and international), individual entrepreneurs, and

---

[3] Naczyk (2014) mentioned, among others, Krzysztof Bielecki, who was Prime Minister in 1991 during the period of Polish shock therapy. Later, in 2014, he called himself a "pragmatic liberal," and as a member of the Council of Economic Advisers he supported the Tusk government's promotion of national champions and other steps reflecting increasing economic patriotism in Poland. In the case of Hungary, the political career of the current Prime Minister Viktor Orbán and his party reflects a similar flexibility in ideological underpinnings ranging from liberal ideas during the first half of the 1990s to economic patriotism and the vision of the illiberal state in contemporary Hungary.

social organizations like trade unions, and less by civil society. Third, policies were influenced by the (self) interests of political parties and even their strong leaders.

In this chapter, I will argue that changes in economic policies were increasingly initiated by this later factor, the polity, after the crisis, because the first two factors lost much of their influence. The international adviser community lost influence because the underlying mainstream economic ideas they represented were largely discredited during the crisis. Unions and other social groups were also weakened by the hardships of the crisis and had to comply with government policies. Finally, in the new member states of the EU, European controls were weakened largely because political attention shifted away from new members to the Euro crisis and the Mediterranean economies. In such cases, when the legitimation of governments does not come from ideologically supported and well tested principles (as was demonstrated previously), policies may fall victim to individual or group (party) interests.[4] Thus, one of the main messages of this chapter is that this type of "pragmatic" economic policy seriously undermines market economic institutions because of its arbitrary nature. The lack of or weakening normative policy measures threatens the rule of law.

Privatization and State Asset Management in ECE Transition Policy

The role of state ownership in established market economies is described mainly as a policy tool to correct market failures, and debate largely centers on the optimal size and efficiency of the state sector. In the case of transition economies, state property is usually regarded as a substantial part of the economic system of the previous political regime that should be reduced in order to make way for the institutions and players of the new market-based economic system. Therefore, the issue of state ownership is complex and involves not only business considerations and the usual aspects of correcting market failures, but also the larger challenge of systemic change.

---

[4] Of course party and individual interests always play a role in modern societies. As Drahokoupil (2008) described, the central European transition economies of the 1990s were characterized by the emergence of a new political elite, the "comprador service sector," which effectively supported and complemented the spread of multinational business in the region. Thus, the economic regime of neoliberal economic thought also served certain individual and party interests.

As Frydman and Rapaczinsky (1994) stated long ago, privatization was a significant issue from a political perspective, since it could contribute to eliminating the economic power of the previous political regime's elite. This specific effect of the systemic change together with the, by then, dominant neoliberal theory put considerable pressure on policy makers to privatize as much and as quickly as possible. The campaign-like expectations of international institutions were repeatedly and insistently articulated and expressed in formats such as the EBRD's *Transition Index*.

Privatization was treated not only as politically important but also as a tool of economic restructuring. In this sense, two main issues came to the fore. One was the improvement of corporate performance as the inherited state-owned companies suffered from a variety of serious weaknesses. The importance of privatization for strengthening corporate performance was highlighted mainly by scholars of the gradualist approach (Kornai, Roland, Portes, Aghion, and others). The other issue was the general support for institution building, which included strengthening capital markets and supporting plans to make various social strata the new owners of productive property. The desire to improve corporate efficiency dominated the Hungarian privatization process; capital market development and the maintenance of social consensus prevailed in Poland; and the creation of a strong new bourgeoisie was the aim of the Czech voucher privatization scheme. The fierce activity of various interest groups could be observed in the background of different privatization policies. They all wanted to shape the details of policies in ways that would benefit them.

The primary neoliberal logic of privatization purports to decrease state intervention in the economy. In particular, direct state involvement was regarded as avoidable. Privatization was treated as the primary method of strengthening private businesses. State property was to be distributed among private stakeholders in order to create a strong capital owner and entrepreneurial strata in ECE societies that was expected to support the new post-communist political elite. This consideration was the most important factor in the design of the Czechoslovak voucher privatization scheme. Privatization supported many of the newly established market economic institutions. For example, virtually all ECE countries introduced privatization methods that included the establishment of stock exchanges. Initial public offerings (IPO) of SOEs were among the first corporate shares traded. Here again we can see that initial high expectations became only partially effectual. It seems that only the Warsaw stock exchange gained momentum and became sizeable after the early years of transition (Ozsvald 2014). The growth of all of the other stock exchanges stopped;

no important new IPOs were launched; and moreover, the securities of former SOEs were largely withdrawn from the exchanges.

It was not only foreign advisers who stressed the importance of privatization in ECE. There were also numerous practical reasons for giving away SOEs. Pre-transition SOE's activity was organized with no respect for market economic principles according to the logic of the command economy, which was to be abolished completely. The typical SOE possessed outdated products (sold only for large discounts on Western markets, if at all), old-fashioned technologies, and limited engineering capacity that focused on the redesign of existing technical solutions. They did not possess managerial knowledge applicable in a competitive market environment, nor did they have marketing acumen, or capital for investments in new technologies or the development of new products and markets (firms had no right to withhold and accumulate reserves from their own sales revenue). Not all of these problems were foreseen at the beginning of the transition process.

Transformational recession occurred because of the huge drop in SOEs' sales revenue at the beginning of the 1990s (Kornai 1994), and privatization was seen as a major tool for making firms more efficient and competitive. The second rationale for privatization was the need for restructuring, the introduction of new products, technologies, markets, managerial know-how, and large-scale investments. This was the business rationale for privatization. A third rationale for privatization was formulated by the leading political forces behind the transition process. The new political elite urged de-nationalization in order to undermine the economic power of the previous regime's exponents. The total destruction of the hated communist party was only possible if the economic basis of SOEs was transferred to new owners (Frydman and Rapaczynski 1994). This argument was based on the fact that SOE managers had close ties with communist party leaders who acted as the chief executive officers of the command economy. The ambition to eliminate the economic power of communist party members was not successful in any of the ECE economies. The second tier communist party leaders and corporate managers became the new owners of former state assets in one or another way. The successor parties of the former communist parties also maintained political influence.

The interplay of the three main drivers of privatization changed over time in all ECE transition economies. The role of international advisers remained important throughout the period up to EU accession, but especially during the 1990s. Pressure stemming from business considerations was also rather strong, especially in the period of the transitional crisis. In fact, the interplay of liberalization (increased competition), effective bankruptcy regulation, and privatization through the sales method could be also used to cure the old behavioral problem of ECE economies: state paternalism. Under socialism, the bargaining process over available resources and expected output created fertile soil for rent seeking. The process itself was characterized by cozy relationships among company management, state officials, and party leaders. This kind of state paternalism repeatedly resulted in major bail out programs for inefficient SOEs. This type of paternalistic behavior by the state and the expectations it generated among SOE managers had to be eliminated in order to address SOEs' restructuring ambitions (Szanyi 2002).

Breaking these paternalistic ties was also important with regard to the third driver of privatization: politics. Since company managers could not be easily replaced (in the short run, there was a limited supply of economists and managers), privatization was an effective tool to control them. Certainly, some forms of privatization resulted in insider deals (on a mass scale in the post-Soviet region, but to a more limited extent in ECE). Insider privatization cannot be regarded as efficient from the business standpoint because SOE managers' capabilities did not improve. The emergence of oligarchs was financed by state loans obtained with the help of federal or local politicians, as was usual in the previous regime. The old style of paternalism survived in the form of the crony capitalism that spread quickly in the former Soviet Union during the Yeltsin era. Altered forms of state paternalism also survived in ECE economies. Privatization was used as a tool for transferring economic power to the new political elite. However, this did not mean the end of state paternalism or the elimination of the channels of crony capitalism, but rather the establishment of new forms and channels. The new political elite also strengthened its economic power and entered the arena of crony capitalism.

The political condition of privatization was therefore largely fulfilled, though not in the sense that former communist leaders were excluded from the economy. Rather privatization balanced the economic power of the old and new elites. Therefore, the threat of reversing the political transition was lifted. Old and new elites became equally integrated into the new market economic system. Thus, instead of reversing political transition, what emerged was a new type of paternalistic relationship between business and government, a form of crony capitalism, that may bring new threats to the efficient economic development of ECE.

Privatization tendencies in the ECE region are well known. Hungary effectively completed the process by the end of the 1990s using mainly the sales method with a preference for foreign direct investments (FDI) in the process. The Czech Republic and Slovakia maintained a higher share of state property during the 1990s, but continuous SOE management problems and slow restructuring forced the governments to sell companies by the turn of the millennium. The Polish privatization process was more sluggish, mainly because of the need for complex social negotiations with stakeholders and the effective blocking of many SOEs' privatization by their employees and the Solidarity movement. Hence, the volume of state assets remained relatively high in Poland, and government agencies together with SOE managers were forced to pursue effective adjustment policies. Polish governments repeatedly launched privatization programs to sell remaining assets until quite recently. The last such program launched in 2012–13, however, it was not completed.

The Political Economy of Privatization and State Asset Management

Many dimensions of the political context of privatization have been discussed, but below I will focus on two that may help us better understand the changing attitude of governments toward the status of publicly held assets. The first thread of scholarship deals with the impacts of political influence on corporate restructuring in public and private companies. The other highlights the role of privatization in strengthening private property and the rule of law in a broader sense. These two dimensions strongly determined the privatization process in ECE but also influenced the development of market economic institutions, thus contributing to the basic systemic elements of the capitalist model in ECE. The turn in state asset policy can also be explained by changes in these aspects of the privatization process.

The first politically motivated argument in favor of privatization, which was the typical approach during the 1990's, was described in a fairly sophisticated way in the seminal paper by Boycko et al. (1996). This paper collected empirical survey results on the inferior business performance of SOEs and provided a theoretical explanation of the phenomenon.[5] The starting point of the paper was the commonplace observation that public

---

[5] The survey of empirical results has been referred to in studies carried out in some developed market economies including the United States and many developing countries. No transition economies were included at that time.

enterprises are inefficient because they address the objectives of politicians rather than maximize efficiency. For example, one of politicians' key objectives is employment: they care about votes of the people whose jobs are in danger and, in many cases, unions have significant influence on political parties. The "average voter" argument in the explanation of various features of business-polity interplay is often used, albeit the conditions of its use are hardly controlled (this is outside the scope of modeling). Based on the discussion included earlier in this chapter, it is likely that excess employment was a strong determinant in the Polish and possibly also in the Czech and Slovak transition stories, but it was much less relevant in Hungary, especially in the privatization process. In Hungary, political influence was directed more toward various, more direct forms of political rent seeking.

The argument of Boycko et al. (1996) continues with the comparison of direct state ownership and private ownership in terms of their options for responding excess employment, and the cost of maintaining it. In the case of a SOE, excess employment deteriorates corporate efficiency and therefore limits profitability. The price of maintaining the level of employment for a firm is lost profits. Politicians can easily move SOE managers to give preference to employment over profitability. SOE managers remained executors of the political will just as before the transition. They were nominated and withdrawn by the same political formation that also directed them. In my view, this could have contributed to the survival of state paternalism. Politicians kept on trying to influence business to achieve their political goals. In the case of private (privatized) firms however, this proved to be more difficult and expensive: control over management often weakens or disappears; new shareholders' interests must also be respected, and this group is mainly interested in profits.[6] Thus, excessive employment can be financed through state subsidies from the treasury rather than by sacrificed profits. The main question of Boycko et al. (1996) is why a politician would fail to buy his way to high labor spending through subsidies? This is because subsidies are financed by excess taxes or inflation, both of which are extremely unpopular.

> The public and the reformers may not be aware of the potential profits that a state firm is wasting, but they are keenly aware of the alternative

---

[6] In cases where the new owners are independent. However, new owners may be clients of politicians, and firms may become partisan. In this case, the use of them for political rent seeking may be similar as in the case of SOEs.

uses of tax revenues, and would not wish to spend public money to subsidize private firms not to restructure. This difference between the political costs of foregone profits of state firms and of subsidies to private firms is the channel through which privatization works.... (Boycko et al. 1996, 311)

This paper's arguments and its conclusions strongly influenced how advisers and reformers from ECE thought about privatization, especially the elimination of the close ties between business and polity.[7] The paper also highlighted the difficulties of privatization especially in the presence of strong unions (Poland). The suggested solution of selling to strategic investors was the dominant privatization method in Hungary, where business rationale rather than political considerations drove privatization during the 1990s. Simultaneously, privatization to independent new owners also contributed to the withering away of paternalistic links to the state and to the hardening firms' budget constraints.

The second highlighted aspect of this section is the role of privatization in strengthening private property and the rule of law. Rapaczynski (1996) provided important comments on the changing attitude of governments toward state-owned assets. He directed attention to the fact that in ECE, the state itself might be the most significant threat to the security of property rights. "The role of the state in securing property rights from encroachments by third parties is probably much less significant than its ability to precommit credibility to respect these rights itself" (93). The first such encroachment possibility is outright confiscation by the state. Relatively speaking, this rarely happens, but the legislative guarantees against such expropriations "are usually quite fuzzy at the edges" and this is not accidental. The state routinely engages in economic regulation in cases that result in encroachments on property that are not considered compensable seizures. But general protection from the spread of such expropriations should be provided by the political system together with economic and social pressure groups "that ensure that the state does not go 'too far' in interfering with the owner's control over assets. This politically determined thin line may be understood as the real definition of property rights conferred by the state... In fact, without a significant historical record of state forbearance from excessive and redistributive regu-

---

[7] Or perhaps the paper reflected and conceptualized the mainstream way of thinking and practices.

lation, it is hard to make the state's commitment credible... The threat posed by the state to the security of broadly defined property rights is particularly severe when the state also happens to own a significant proportion of national assets" (93).

Rapaczynski's 1996 argument supported the efficient privatization policies of the time. But his statement on the dangers the state poses to the security of property rights, which intensify with significant state asset ownership is still valid. Achievements in establishing market institutions may be easily broken if the "politically determined thin line" of the definition of property rights changes. Governments may establish both positive and negative historical records over time that promote or weaken social trust in the enforcement of property rights. As was emphasized earlier, a solitary economic measure and its enforcement may have a bigger influence on the evolving soft social institutions in ECE than a series of new laws. If privatization is stopped or even reversed, if governments carry out unusually excessive expropriations as was the case with private pension funds' assets in both Hungary and Poland, such steps demolish much of the weak and nascent social institutions and undermine trust in the rule of law.

The complex role of privatization in the transition process increased the impact of the methods and also determined the outcome of current economic developments in the countries of East Central Europe. The three decades of ownership changes contributed to the establishment of a general business and investment climate and norms of government policy practice. In Hungary, for example, there were two influential systemic components: foreign company ownership and integration into multinational value chains on the one hand, and the crony capitalism of local politicians and capital owners on the other. The two components were not separated, but they existed as two poles of a dual economy. Successive Hungarian governments often pursued policies that favored one or the other poles. The activity of foreign companies was usually influenced by indirect legal measures (taxes, license conditions, and the like), which often contradicted the principle of equal treatment by favoring or punishing them. Local business was more often treated informally, creating a space for the emergence of crony capitalism.

In my understanding, crony capitalism means a legally uncontrolled (badly controlled) interaction between the polity and businesses that works against the principles of free enterprise and fair competition. Policy makers and influential business people cooperate to create preferential treatment for "friendly businesses" in exchange for the material support of parties, politicians, and election campaigns. This type of cooperation is not unknown in developed economies, though a more developed institutional background and strong civil society control may limit the harmful impacts of cronyism on market economic institutions. If party financing is transparent and lobbying for industry (corporate) interests is institutionalized, then cronyism is under control. Of course, this does not mean that markets are free of marginal interest enforcement. But in cases where cronyism is not transparent and not controlled, it may lead to very high social losses and even illegal transactions. A major difference between most of the established market and transition economies lies in the level of institutional and social control of polity-business interactions. Loose control in transition economies deteriorates investment and the business climate, which is expressed in low rankings in competitiveness reports and high finance costs.

Interaction between polity and business has been surveyed in the ECE region by many scholars. Well known contributions by Stark (1996), Stark and Bruszt (1998), McDermott (2002) have shown that privatization and the establishment of the new ownership structure in ECE was marred by cronyism and favoritism and established new interest groups. These groups incorporated representatives of the political sphere as well. Papers from the 1990s expressed fears about the reestablishment of the economic power of the "nomenclature." This argument is present in the mainstream literature (for example, Boycko et al. 1996). Nevertheless, as time passed, the fears of a reversion to pre-transition communist rule proved to be unfounded. However, instead of a political retreat to communism, increasing cronyism posed new threats to the development and efficiency of market economic institutions.

Schoenman (2014) has made a new contribution to the above scholarship on the role that networks and interest groups have gained in the post-transition decades. His book differentiated ECE economies according to the type and strength of their polity-business interactions. The intensity and main values of the relationship were determined by the levels of uncertainty in politics and business (political changes, regulatory environment, macroeconomic policies, etc.) and the structure of business networks. Broad networks link cross-sector coalitions and facilitate collective action. The role of networks is especially strong in societies with weak institutions. Instead of institutions, networks may become even more important channels for representing interests. Business networks tend to develop mutually beneficial political ties in cases where there is political competition and politicians and parties in need of (financial) support. Political and economic uncertainty accelerate the process. Referring to Kitschelt (2000), Schoenman also states that when there are strong business networks, state institutions are more likely to become "broadly distributive," providing for a larger group of businesses (i.e., independent from agents' political sympathies and support). In contrast, "selective advantage" institutions distribute benefits to targeted recipients who are among the supporters of the ruling political party.

Under high levels of uncertainty, collective action evolves in the presence of broad networks. This is because of efficient information flow, which increases the threat to corporate reputations in cases of selective agreements. High levels of uncertainty and small networks make cooperation between business and polity unlikely because the value of political promises is low due to the lack of support by businesses. Furthermore, cooperation does not spread due to inefficient information flows. Consequently, businesses lean directly on the state and not in a concerted manner. In cases of low uncertainty levels and small business networks, the polity is not afraid of political competition and can exploit atomized firms. Under low levels of uncertainty and broad networks, the state is likely to enter into collusive relations with firms. The four types of relationship are summarized as follows:

Table 1
The effect of networks and uncertainty on the state

		Uncertainty	
		Low	High
Network structure	Narrow	Patronage	Captured
	Broad	Embedded corporatist	Concertation

Source: Schoenman (2014, 50).

Different consequences result from the distinct settings of polity (state)–business relationships. In high uncertainty environments, broad business networks tend to establish regular cooperation with the polity and the state that broadly favor the business community. In exchange, the networks provide political parties with necessary financial support. The state develops mutually beneficial institutions for collusion in the long run. The state generally functions as a coordinating agent; it channels information and mediates conflicts of interest. When networks are small (business elites do not cooperate) and uncertainty is low, and the political structure is solid and monolithic and there is a solid economic environment, the state applies "selective advantage"-style institutional solutions and selects the winners. This setting is called patronage. Where there is both high uncertainty and small business networks, economic elites dominate political elites, which potentially leads to state capture. Finally, low uncertainty and broad networks describe the embedded corporatist state. In this case, well established political elites do not face uncertainty and cooperate with business networks. In Schoenman's opinion, this particular set up is unlikely to happen in competitive election systems.

Schoenman (2014) runs a factor analysis using various proxy measures of uncertainty and network densities for ECE economies. While the indicators and the actual relevance of the results may be of nominal interest, the typology is remarkable (*Table 2*). Patronage and captured states corroborate the concept of state and business capture (Yakovlev 2006). The typology he produces can also be used in the explanation of recent changes of polity-business relationships in Poland and Hungary.

Table 2
Networks, uncertainty, and state types

		Uncertainty	
		Low	High
Network structure	Narrow	Patronage states: Czech Rep., Latvia, Estonia, Slovakia, Slovenia, Romania	Captured states: Albania, Bulgaria
	Broad	Embedded corporatist	Concentration states: Hungary, Lithuania, Poland

Source: Schoenman (2014, 174).

The Imprint of Cronyism in Changing Ownership Patterns

Hungary was considered a highly successful transition economy during the 1990s with the successful implementation of the sales method of privatization. Not much state property remained, and the privatization process was supposed to be completed in 2008. This not only meant that a further reduction in state property was not foreseen, but that eventually an increase could be also proposed. And indeed this happened sporadically up to 2010 and on a larger scale since then under the right-wing governments of Viktor Orbán and Fidesz. In terms of asset volume, the amount of property re-nationalized after 2010 was smaller than that of privatized assets after 1990 (Mihályi 2015). The importance of state property policies thus did not decline. The state still has an important and complex role in enforcing property rights, including the need for occasional nationalizations. Such actions must not go too far in interfering with owners' control over assets. The "politically determined thin line" in this implicit definition of property rights (Rapaczynski, 1996) must be considered by governments, otherwise the historical record of state forbearance from excessive and redistributive regulation gets lost together with political credibility.

Voszka (2013) and Mihályi (2015) compiled a comprehensive list of re-nationalizations in Hungary after 2010. Based on this information, it is possible to describe the main reasons for the transactions and identify beneficiaries and political aims. The first major nationalization transaction took place in 2010, when the second pillar of the pension system was nationalized. Due mainly to demographics, financing the pension system became difficult. The problems were exacerbated by redirecting a considerable part of pension contributions from the pay-as-you-go system (first pillar) to the second pillar (privately held accounts), while actual payment obligations from the first pillar remained unchanged. The government, however, argued differently and called for the security of accumulated pension funds to be taken out of the hands of private pension funds that failed to bring the expected returns. The government also applied the "opting out" trick, which meant that those who wanted to keep their pensions untouched had to face the threat of losing their first pillar services. The size of this nationalization transaction was equivalent to 10 percent of Hungary's GDP. The transaction brought the valuable liquid assets of the state budget together with a rather substantial and diversified portfolio of various kinds of securities including corporate shares and bonds.

A second major, politically motivated series of transactions and regulatory changes were undertaken with the political aim of cutting utility costs. The promise of savings on utility costs was a major campaign promise during the 2010 and 2014 Hungarian election campaigns. The most efficient implementation method was the nationalization of the service providers. As a first step, the price regulations on services markets were changed. When private companies could not cover their costs with operational revenues, most of them sold their equity to the state. In most cases, the Hungarian government paid generously (e.g., to German multinationals in the electricity sector). A third major aim of re-nationalization transactions was the support of political clients or simple personal rent seeking. Favoritism can take place if market regulation is altered so as to favor some actors over others, or when re-nationalized assets are resold to clients (as in the case of the Hungarian banking sector). In some cases, the loss-producing companies of clients were bailed out by the state through the generous acquisition of assets. Clientism was labeled economic patriotism, because it supported loyal domestic businesses over selfish multinational corporations. Another form of clientism is filling the boards of SOEs with party officials who need positions and cash. The simplest form of rent seeking is thus bound to sizeable state-ownership.

In the case of Poland, state property management practices have not yet been reversed as of 2018. Privatization in Poland was always slower than in other ECE countries mainly due to the continuous search for social consensus and the necessary approval of stakeholders in every case. After the rather sluggish practice of the 1990s, 1999 and 2000 witnessed skyrocketing privatization activity in Poland. This was due to the direct sale method, which was favored at the time, and the denationalization of some large banks and service providers. However, this momentum stopped in 2001, when the previous sluggish insider-oriented methods continued. Privatization sales were revived under the Tusk government. After necessary preparations, privatization revenues began to grow in 2009, reached their zenith of $6 billion in 2010, and then fell to half that level in 2011. The net privatization income of the Tusk government between 2008 and 2012 reached $15.5 billion (*The Wall Street Journal* 2012). The same source also heralded a change approach: large firms regarded "strategic" were not to be privatized. This meant that the new, still rather ambitious privatization program of the years 2012–13 was not enforced with the enthusiasm of previous years. *The Economist* observed a peculiar halt in the sale of controlling shares of some "flagship companies" mainly in the financial sector,[8] which was already visible during the otherwise successful privatization campaign of the period from 2008 to 2011. The Polish government seemed to pull the privatization train's emergency break. In this context, maintaining state assets is quite similar to the conceptual changes of state asset policies in Hungary.

Instead of systemic dimensions, fiscal aspects gained importance in the Polish government's state property policy after 2011. While only minority shares were sold, which, in most cases, did not eliminate effective state control, the fiscal revenues of the central budget were increased by dividend payments from state-owned companies (Kozarzewski 2015; Blaszczyk and Patena 2015). The growing importance of budget revenues from the profits of running SOEs demonstrates an important departure from the systemic aspects of privatization and state property management

---

[8] "Privatization in Poland. Overcoming Miner Obstacles." *The Economist*, 6 July, 2011.

in Poland. Naczyk (2014) analyzed a series of steps taken by the different Polish governments toward strengthening state control over mixed ownership firms. The governance structures of these firms were transformed, and "poison pills" that gave the state extra veto rights even in the case of minority state ownership were incorporated into the statutes of the companies. This meant that the Polish government also put a long-term emphasis on maintaining and using SOEs for various policy purposes.

Reasons for Reversing the Privatization Logic

Boycko et al. (1996) calls excessive employment the most typical political pressure forced on companies that reduces their efficiency. At the same time, there is the potential for other forms of political opportunism and rent seeking. They mention an article that describes the perverse credit policy of the French state-owned bank Credit Lyonnais, which favored clients from the ruling party. Although this case was discussed as exceptional, in ECE, this type of rent seeking has always been more important than employment issues for voter appeal. When I talk about the reversal of the privatization logic, I mean that steps were taken in ECE countries to target political and personal interests rather than the interests of broader societies concerning state property policies. Privatization and the dominance of private property were once regarded as safeguards against this type of rent seeking. The increasing economic role of the state sector can be regarded as a deliberate attempt to create more potential for abuse.

I distinguish various types of actual cash transfers from the economy to politicians and their clients. One of them is outright corruption and bribing (i.e., moral hazard). In this case, bribes go from the business to the politician and the bureaucrats to buy preferential treatment or simply a business license. The corrupt politician and the bureaucrat may expand this activity to its extremes with business capture, as was conceptualized by Yakovlev (2006), and corporate raiding (Viktorov 2013). ECE's conditions are, of course, not nearly as bad as those in Russia, but corruption also exists in ECE. High level scandals that involved government officials and other high-ranked party politicians or their clients revealed that countries like Hungary, Poland, Slovenia, and the Czech Republic are not immune from these dangers (EU transfers to Bulgaria and Romania were effectively stopped due to high levels of corruption).

Corruption, especially of highly ranked officials, is punishable by law. But there are other, not necessarily illegal albeit seriously unethical opportunities for financial transfers from businesses to the polity. State ownership is the most relevant of these. The clients of politicians regularly fill top management and board positions in SOEs.⁹ This practice, on one hand, eliminates conflicts between the management and politicians. But this also creates an opportunity for milking SOEs for funds through various channels. SOEs are useful for this purpose regardless of their potential efficiency. The social cost of this practice is no longer just lost profits, but the continuous flow of cash from various state institutions (the state budget) transferred through the SOE to private persons or enterprises. SOEs may finance various social and cultural events, give politicians the red carpet treatment, donate to charity organizations, or sponsor any number of activities on behalf of the government and politicians. SOEs are also used to reward the clients of the politicians by paying them consulting fees, for example.

Of course, the usage of SOEs for these purposes is not new nor is it unique to the transition economies of ECE. However, current policies designed to maintain state ownership are aimed at widening the rent seeking activity of political parties and governments. The latter is made possible precisely because of the low levels of transparency and social control. Furthermore, this new rent seeking causes the same types of problems described in papers on privatization published in the 1990s, and is therefore very harmful for the future of market institutions in ECE. The reasons for intensive rent seeking in ECE are manifold. Apart from personal enrichment, the lack of regulated party financing is also important. Political parties' budgets are very meager, and parties spend far more on election campaigns and other advocacy work than what is legally allowed.

There have been some changes to methods of milking state assets during the thirty years of transition in ECE. Initially, the main source of cash revenue was privatization. Even more important than corruption was the support of clients in obtaining valuable state assets at rock bottom prices. The process was well documented in the case of Russia, and there is some anecdotal evidence for Slovakia as well. However, this practice was not unprecedented in other Visegrád countries either. In some recent Hungarian cases, the potential redistribution of assets re-emerged when the government declared it was ready to re-privatize some firms.¹⁰ Nevertheless, opportunities for privatization are quite rare today in Hungary. In the

---

⁹ Skuhrovec (2014) reported peeks of personnel changes in Czech SOEs' supervision bodies in national election years.

¹⁰ For example, MKB bank, once a German-owned large commercial bank, was purchased by the state in 2015. After several changes in ownership, including

case of Poland, rent seeking during the privatization process was perhaps less widespread due to more transparent privatization transactions.

Today, one reason for less privatization and more state ownership may be the changing structure of rent seeking activities by politicians. Of course, the decline of available state assets has also contributed to this: most of the remaining assets are notoriously loss-producing companies (like mines in Poland) and it is not financially worthwhile to own them. Another issue is that several large service providers cannot be easily transferred to rent seeking private hands but are SOEs well suited for exploitation on a mass scale. Another reason for maintaining state assets may be the changing domestic and international environment. International organizations are no longer as concerned about privatization as they were in the 1990s. Therefore, international pressure for privatization declined.

The same applies to the European Union and its role as a modernization anchor for CEE countries. In 2004, the Visegrád countries became members of the EU. Attention was directed rather to fiscal deficits and not to the condition of market institutions or levels of state ownership. The status of the state budget is also influenced by the performance of SOEs and their state subsidies, but this is an indirect link. The importance of the business rationale for privatization diminished in the meantime. On the one hand, the overall condition of all transition economies improved (probably not because of improving SOE performance but mainly due to the increased activity of multinational companies and de novo private firms), and the presence of a number of loss-producing SOEs could be more easily tolerated also by EU offices. Consequently, the third political rationale for the redistribution of assets, or more recently controls on cash flow, became the strongest factor in decisions about maintaining or selling state property.

The reversal of the privatization logic creates the danger of the increased obscurity and arbitrariness of economic policy. It also can lead to an overall decline in the effect of market institutions against politically determined influences. This may be expressed in the growing impact of "selective advantage" measures against "broadly distributive" institutions, or if using the categories of Schoenman (2014), the shift away from a cooperative relationship and effective institutions toward state patronage and less effective market institutions. Some government declarations expressed a deliberate shift in Hungary and the failure of the markets, calling for more

---

various offshore companies, the main owners at the time of writing this paper have become investors who are regarded as clients of the ruling political elite.

government intervention in the economy. This increased government intervention seems to have pushed the polity-business relationship toward the patronage state, and has already weakened established market institutions.

Changes in state property management in Hungary were complemented by a series of other steps exhibiting state favoritism ranging from public procurement to market regulation. Many of these steps seriously contradicted normative regulations and violated the principle of equal treatment and EU competition laws. Selective advantages have been provided to clients, and simultaneously, competitors of clients were frequently punished by unfavorable regulation. This is most clearly visible in the example of the punishment of multinational business with selective disadvantages (extra taxes, exclusive regulation), while other members of the same community were rewarded and included in the close circle of the Hungarian government's strategic partners. Simultaneous steps in the opposite direction can be interpreted as a deliberate policy aimed at breaking apart established business networks (those of foreign companies/multinational business). Using Schoenman's typology, this is a move toward narrow networks and the patronage state (business capture), since political uncertainty is perceived as very low by the government. This is understandable given that the ruling party won three successive elections with a two-thirds majority in Parliament.

These cases illustrate the withdrawal from the "competition state" (Drahokoupil 2008). The concept of the illiberal state attacks the free market system and democratic institutions. The above case, as well as the broader departure from Western values, have been conceptualized by the government as parts of a sovereign decision to establish a new economic system in Hungary. Populist followers of the Hungarian agenda can also be found in Poland. The Law and Justice Party (PiS) leader openly declared his appreciation for the concept, declaring that hopefully the actions taken in Budapest will spread to Warsaw. But the general opinion of Polish observers is that the concept of economic patriotism has already been introduced in Poland. This is reflected in the changes to state ownership policies, among other things.

Conclusions

What does this analysis contribute to the concept of the ECE model of capitalism? I argue that changes in political attitudes have an important role in the model. Increasing direct state intervention in the economy changes the rules of the game very quickly and in the ways described in this chapter. Weaker social institutions and deliberate government policies aimed at increasing discretional decisions and limiting transparency will also limit the rule of law. Uncertain and increasingly arbitrary business conditions will influence not only the domestic but also foreign owners of operations in ECE. Foreign firms' role as the anchors of the economy may decline as they either change their operations or leave the region if they are not willing to adjust to the new market and political conditions. Contrary to the assumption of the DME model, governments may also influence multinational firms' activities for good or ill, as was evidenced by the Hungarian case. Governments may try to use the uncertainty of conditions to rule in their favor, even at the risk of foreign corporations' withdrawal. This policy is easily sold to the broader population through populist statements made by the government.

The populist argument frequently refers to the fact that there are good examples of successful and efficient SOEs. The idea of incorporating SOEs into the economic system is, indeed, not ridiculous. I do not think, however, that SOEs' role in ECE models is identical with those in other European capitalist models. We should not forget the conditions for adequate SOE activity, which is effective social, political, and economic control. Moreover, state companies must support economic policies in deliberate ways. However, in ECE, politicians use SOEs for political and personal rent seeking. This threatens the social acceptance of basic market economic institutions and the rule of law. Strengthening control institutions over public policies in general is a precondition for maintaining democratic values and preventing the pendulum from swinging further toward autocracy. Controlled direct state intervention in the economy should serve public welfare and not private interests.

A further lesson for the ECE model is therefore the outstanding importance of social and political control institutions. ECE models implicitly assumed that foreign control has the capacity to prevent governments from flirting with illiberal political and economic solutions. It seems that this control lost all validity after 2004. The loosening of democratic controls tempted ambitious politicians to move the economic and political system away from traditional Western norms toward an authoritarian model more typical in the East. In fact, this type of shuttling between East and West and democracy and autocracy has always been characteristic of the countries of the region. The shuttling itself causes the most harm, because it is always bound to result in sizeable institutional changes that are always very costly. But even more damage is caused by the unreliable, permanently fluctuating environment that makes long-term business planning impossible. Consequently, from the business standpoint, the maintenance of some secure institutions (e.g., the security of property rights), even in autocracy, are still highly valued.

REFERENCES

Appel, Hilary. 2004. *A New Capitalist Order: Privatization and Ideology in Russia and Eastern Europe.* Pittsburgh: University of Pittsburgh Press.
Blaszczyk, Barbara, and Wiktor Patena. 2015. "Post-Privatization Corporate Performance in Poland. Evidence from Companies Privatized in 2008–11." Paper presented at the 1st World Congress of Comparative Economics at Tre University, Rome, June 26, 2015.
Bohle, Dorothee, and Béla Greskovits. 2007. "Neoliberalism, Embedded Neoliberalism and Neocorporatism: Towards Transnational Capitalism in Central-Eastern Europe." *West European Politics* 25 (3): 443–66.
Boycko, Maxim, Andrei Shleifer, and Robert W. Vishny. 1996. "A Theory of Privatization." *The Economic Journal* 106 (3): 309–19.
Csaba, László. 2007. "Átmenet vagy spontán rendetlenség?" [Transition or spontaneous disorder?] *Közgazdasági Szemle* 54 (9): 757–73.
Drahokoupil, Jan. 2008. "Who Won the Contest for a New Property Class? Structural Transformation of Elites in the Visegrád Four Region." *Journal for East European Management Studies* 13 (4): 360–77.
Frydman, Roman, and Andrzej Rapaczynski. 1994. *Privatization in Eastern Europe: Is the State Withering Away?* Budapest; New York: Central European University Press.
Hungarian Government. 2014. "J/8582. számú: Jelentés az ÁPV Zrt. és jogelődei—mint a privatizáció lebonyolítására létrehozott célszervezetek—tevékenységéről és a teljes privatizációs folyamatról (1990–2007)" [No. J/8582: Report on the activity of ÁPV Zrt and its predecessors—organizations that were established to conduct privatization—and the whole privatization process]. http://www.kozlonyok.hu/nkonline/MKPDF/hiteles/MK09036.pdf.
Kitschelt, Herbert. 2000. "Linkages between Citizens and Politicians in Democratic Polities." *Comparative Political Studies* 33 (6/7): 845–79.
Kopecky, Petr. 2006. "Political Parties and the State in Post-communist Europe: The Nature of Symbiosis." *Journal of Communist Studies and Transition Politics* 22 (3): 251–73.
Kornai, János. 1994. "Transformational Recession: The Main Causes." *Journal of Comparative Economics* 19 (1): 39–63.
Kozarzewski, Piotr. 2015. "Poland: Privatization in the Shade of Statism." Paper presented at the 1st World Congress of Comparative Economics at Tre University, Rome, June 26, 2015.
Kozarzewski, Piotr and Maciej Baltowski. 2015. "Change in Economic Policy Paradigm: Privatization and State Capture in Poland." Paper presented at the 2nd

Polish–Hungarian Roundtable Conference at the Institute of World Economics (KRTK MTA), Budapest, December 17, 2015.

Lane, David. 2007. "Post-state Socialism: A Diversity of Capitalism?" In *Varieties of Capitalism in Post-communist Countries*, edited by David Lane and Martin Myant, 13–39. New York: Palgrave MacMillan.

McDermott, Gerald A. 2002. *Embedded Politics: Industrial Networks and Institutional Change in Post-Communism*. Ann Arbor, MI: University of Michigan Press.

Mihályi, Péter. 2015. "A privatizált vagyon visszaállamosítása Magyarországon 2010–2014" [Re-nationalization of privatized property in Hungary 2010–2014]. Discussion Paper. Institute of Economics, Centre for Economic and Regional Studies, Hungarian Academy of Sciences.

Mihályi, Péter, and Éva Sztankó. 2015. "A tőzsdei bevezetés jelentősége két magyar óriásvállalat példáján—MOL és MVM" [The role of stock exchange public offering, the example of two large Hungarian firms, MOL and MVM]. Discussion Paper. Institute of Economics, Center for Economic and Regional Studies, Hungarian Academy of Sciences.

Naczyk, Marek. 2014. "Budapest in Warsaw: Central European Business Elites and the Rise of Economic Patriotism since the Crisis." *Sciences Po Paris*, July 15. http://papers.ssrn.com/sol3/papers.cfm?abstract_id=2550496.

Nölke, Andreas, and Arjan Vliegenthart. 2009. "Enlarging the Varieties of Capitalism: The Emergence of Dependent Market Economies in East Central Europe." *World Politics* 61 (4): 670–702.

Ozsvald, Éva. 2014. *Corporate Governance in Central Eastern Europe: A Comparative Political Economy Approach*. Unpublished manuscript.

Rapaczynski, Andrzej. 1996. "The Roles of State Property and the Market in Establishing Property Rights." *Journal of Economic Perspectives* 10 (2): 87–103.

Roland, Gérard. 2000. *Transition and Economics: Politics, Markets and Firms*. Cambridge, MA; London: MIT Press.

Schoenman, Roger. 2014. *Networks and Institutions in Europe's Emerging Markets*. Cambridge: Cambridge University Press.

Skuhrovec, Jiří. 2014. "The Unreasonable Lightness of Stuffing Czech Company Boards with Political Cronies." *Visegrad Revue*, March 17. http://visegradrevue.eu/the-unreasonable-lightness-of-stuffing-czech-company-boards-with-political-cronies/.

Stark, David. 1996. "Recombinant Property in East European Capitalism." *American Journal of Sociology* 101 (4): 492–504.

Stark, David, and László Bruszt. 1998. *Postsocialist Pathways: Transforming Politics and Property in East Central Europe*. Cambridge: Cambridge University Press.

Stiglitz, Joseph. 1999. *Whither Reform? Ten Years of Transition*. Washington, DC: The World Bank.

Szanyi, Miklós. 1996. "Adaptive Steps by Hungary's Industries during the Transition Crisis." *Eastern European Economics* 34 (5): 59–77.

———. 2000. "Bankruptcy, Liquidation and Full Settlement as Methods of Privatization." In *Privatization in Hungary*, edited by Ágota Erőss, 51–74. Budapest: Állami Privatizációs és Vagyonkezelő Rt.

———. 2002. "Bankruptcy Regulations, Policy Credibility and Asset Transfers in Hungary." IWE Working Papers 130. Institute for World Economics, Centre for

Economic and Regional Studies, Hungarian Academy of Sciences. https://ideas.repec.org/p/iwe/workpr/130.html.

———. 2012. "Varieties of Development in Post-Communist Countries with Special Regard to the Transition in Hungary." *Competitio* 11 (2): 5–25.

———. 2016. "The Emergence of Patronage State in Central Europe: The Case of FDI-related Policies in Hungary." Working Paper 222. Institute of World Economics, Centre for Economic and Regional Studies, Hungarian Academy of Sciences. https://ideas.repec.org/p/iwe/workpr/222.html.

Viktorov, Ilja. 2013. "Corporate Raiding in Post-Soviet Russia." *Baltic Worlds* 6 (2): 4–8.

Voszka, Éva. 2013. "Államosítás, privatizáció, államosítás" [Nationalization, privatization, nationalization]. *Közgazdasági Szemle* 60 (12): 1289–317.

Yakovlev, Andrei. 2006. "The Evolution of Business: State Interaction in Russia: From State Capture to Business Capture?" *Europe–Asia Studies* 58 (7): 1033–56.

CHAPTER 6
Listed Companies with State Ownership: The Case of Poland

ÉVA OZSVALD

Introduction: The State as Shareholder

State ownership of companies is a subject that can be approached from a variety of angles, as this volume of essays clearly demonstrates. This chapter focuses on an important though less frequently analyzed issue of state ownership: the activity of the state as a majority or minority shareholder in public companies. Poland was chosen as a case study since this country is the home of one of the largest groups of such companies in the OECD area.

The first decade of the new millennium brought about fascinating developments on global stock exchanges, including the significantly increased activity of numerous national states as majority shareholders. Today around one-fifth of the total value of the world's exchanges is accounted for by state-owned companies (SOEs); this amount has doubled since the early 2000s. The increase is heavily concentrated in a few large emerging economies, mostly those in the BRIC group, with China in the lead. The ownership structure of the Fortune Global 500 companies has also undergone a significant change between 2005 and 2014. The share of SOEs jumped from 9 percent to 23 percent in this period. Again, China accounts for the lion's share of this increase.

As far as the OECD countries are concerned, the state presence on most stock exchanges has remained rather modest. In the majority of the OECD member states, the number of public companies with state ownership is just a few or zero. There are, however, a few significant exceptions, including France, Italy, Norway, South Korea, and, prominently, Poland. The Polish state has a stake in twelve (seven majority and five minority) of its twenty-five largest companies. Among Central Eastern Europe's ten largest companies, seven are Polish (*Pekao, PGNIG, PKO, PKN Orlen,*

PZU, PGE),[1] and the Polish state has either majority or minority control over each of them.

Dozens of books and studies raise the question of how, to what extent and in which sectors it is useful or dysfunctional for fully state-owned companies to operate in normal markets. The privatization wave in developed western countries during the last two decades of the twentieth century and in Eastern Europe's economic transformation, demonstrated that market-based rationality won over arguments related to statist-paternalist-protectionist economic policies. Issues at this level of abstraction, however, are not the subject of this paper. Nor do we deal with closed state-owned companies. Our research focuses on the intriguing phenomenon of the joint functioning of public and private ownership in publicly traded companies.

The stock market is a quintessential institution of a market economy. Stock market players are basically private actors that are guided by the profit motive. From this perspective, the first question is why the state remains a player on the stock exchange and, in particular, what are its long-term goals there. The next question concerns whether and how state assets, if invested for purposes other than profit maximization, conflict with the business interests of the other shareholders of the company.

It is reasonable to assume that the state's business decisions are embedded in politics. When it comes to the question of whether state ownership in public companies is justified, many argue that the state's role includes solving and managing broader social issues beyond private corporate interests. Such tasks belong to the realm of the so-called national economic interest, strategic foresight, workplace protection, etc. In terms of public companies, however, the state's pursuit of these objectives must be carried out in such a way that it keeps a close eye on the company's attractiveness to private investors.

In order to switch from general considerations to the assessment of the real situation in Poland, we have rephrased these questions. We seek to find what advantages and disadvantages have arisen from the Polish state's sale of only a part of SOE assets to stock market investors during privatization, while maintaining a long-term position as either a majority or minority shareholder in various large corporations. One official justification for the enduring state ownership of public companies in Poland is that the dictates of national interest—the strategic importance of specific large

---

[1] Deloitte: Central Europe Top 500. https://www2.deloitte.com/ce/en/pages/about-deloitte/articles/central-europe-top500.html.

companies—necessitate long-term statist control through ownership stakes. Another explanation relates to the fiscal balance of the country, namely, that regular dividends coming from well-managed state assets are an important source of the central budget's revenue. One should add to these explanations the findings of some politico-sociological research indicating that various interests of politicians, bureaucrats, and influential groups also contributed to the deceleration the privatization process and the maintenance of state control through ownership.

The literature offers diverging approaches concerning the role of state-owned entrepreneurial assets. Based on experiences from the past as well as ideological grounds, liberal-minded scholars do not see the benefits deriving from the direct involvement of the state in business ownership. On the other hand, a growing number of experts point out that the business environment for the "new generation" of entrepreneurial SOEs has changed to such an extent that the differences in the market behavior of private and public owners have become smaller, especially when both are exposed to the transparency of the stock market and more stringent corporate governance rules.

The empirical literature is rather inconclusive on the question of whether the value of a given company is enhanced or reduced by the state having an ownership stake. Recent large studies, however, offer convincing results. For example, Beuselinck et al. (2016) analyzed the performance of 4,737 public companies from twenty-eight European countries for the period from 2005 to 2009. This research showed that during the 2008 financial crisis—in contrast with the previous period—state ownership had a positive effect on company values, but only in those countries with a good institutional environment. According to the indicators used in the study, institutional quality is strong when investor interests are well protected and corruption is perceived as low. Obviously, the implications of institutional quality pertain to the Polish context as well.

The Structure of the Study

In all Eastern European postcommunist countries, including Poland, the activation of the stock market and the emergence of various models of state ownership and control were closely linked to the privatization process during transition. This period is discussed in the second section of the present study. The third and fourth sections present the first years of the new millennium—the years marking the success of the Warsaw Stock Exchange on the one hand, and the slowing down of state withdrawal from the economy on the other. This is followed by a review of developments taking place between 2008 and 2015, a period characterized by a renewed dynamism in privatization and the more active management of state assets. Section six discusses the major corporate governance issues of listed mixed-ownership companies. The seventh section deals with the recent (2016–17) developments in Poland: the paradigmatic shift towards illiberalism and its short-term impact on partially state-owned public companies. The chapter concludes with a summary of its main findings.

Table 1
State ownership in companies on the stock exchange and their value according to market prices
(January 18, 2014)

Name of the company	Ownership of the state treasury (percentage)	Market value (million PLN)
PHN	75.00	882
PGNiG	72.40	21,400
PGE	61.88	19,200
JSW	55.16	3,240
Lotos	53.18	2,450
Enea	51.50	3,010
PKP Cargo	51.70	2,025
Energa	51.52	3,400
Ciech	38.72	610
PZU	35.18	13,000
GPW	34.99	574
Groupa Azoty	33.00	1900
KGHM	31.79	7,240
PKO BP	31.39	15,800
Tauron	30.06	2,220
PKN Orlen	27.52	4,960
BOS	56.62	577
RAFAMET	47.28	31
Polimex-Mostostal	22.48	39
Interferie	66.81	46
AB SA	5.50	28
EC Bedzin	14.88	10
Bogdanka	9.76	415
Paged	8.37	48
Total market value		103,106

Source: Patena (2014).

Privatization during Transition

To understand the unique features of the current ownership structure of Poland's biggest companies, we have to look back on the history of privatization in Poland during the transition period.

The privatization strategy was a cornerstone of the reform program of the first Polish government after transition. Privatization was primarily important for political-ideological reasons and for making the transition to a market economy irreversible. In thinking about economic rationality, the majority of experts took the axiomatic stance that state-owned large companies could not operate effectively in any political system. As for the implementation and the success of the privatization policy, it was understood that, in time, the whole process must start with the creation of a strong legal framework and the appropriate institutions of legal enforcement, regulation, and supervision. Polish economic policy makers also made the sound decision to create an economic environment conducive for the restructuring of large companies *before* privatization.

With the introduction of the Balcerowicz plan, which has been praised as a milestone in the early transition, the operational milieu of companies indeed changed dramatically. Suffice it to say, there were three dimensions to the plan: 1) liberalization that opened up markets and boosted competition 2) the robust reduction of subsidies; 3) the enhancement of bankruptcy proceedings against insolvent companies initiated by banks and supplier companies (Tamowicz and Dzierzanowski 2002).

At the beginning of transition, Poland faced serious economic problems, including the almost unmanageably high external debt and hyperinflation. However, the country has been surprisingly successful in stabilizing the economy within a relatively short time and establishing the fundamentals for rapid economic growth, the dynamism of which is still above the international average a quarter century later. Important factors is this success story were the fast adjustment of many state-owned companies to the market and the new regulatory environment and the resulting restructuring that had taken place before their official privatization. Brian Pinto (2014) provides a comprehensive account of the process. The author worked as a representative of the World Bank in Poland and described the rapid transformation of a major part of large former socialist companies using case studies and first-hand information.

With regard to the golden age of privatization, Pinto recalls that the majority of renowned economists emphasized the importance of the speed of the privatization. He referred to authors such as Roman Frydman, Stanislaw Wellisz, and others who, like most experts, had predicted that state-owned companies would become unviable if they were to pay a positive real interest rate on their bank loans or if they had to face competition induced by liberalized imports. The weaknesses of state-owned companies' corporate governance practices, together with the lack of incentives to accumulate corporate assets, were also used as arguments for fast-paced privatization. In reality, however, what happened was that numerous large SOEs were willing and able to adjust to the new rules of the evolving market economy. There were three main reasons why—contrary to expectations—this positive outcome occurred. The first reason was the hard budget constraints, which replaced the former "soft" operating conditions thanks to the uncompromising reform policy of the Ministry of Finance. The ministry tried to resist the bargaining attempts of many SOEs, blocked the flow of production subsidies, and placed limits on the bank loans granted to loss-making state-owned companies. The second reason was related to the beneficial effects of trade liberalization. By lifting import restrictions, a new competitive environment had been created, which pushed the previously protected actors of the domestic market toward more prudent and efficient management. The third reason was that the managers of state-owned companies strove to build up their own business reputations. Since they were aware of the forthcoming large-scale privatization program, they wanted to demonstrate their preparedness for the new business environment.

In the early transition period, 8,453 state-owned companies were designated for privatization. The chief methods of Polish privatization included: 1) direct privatization aimed at small and medium-sized companies, 2) liquidation privatization in the legal sense 3) indirect or capital privatization. From here we shall follow in detail the third method, since this was what was mostly applied to the privatization of large companies, including the nascent public mixed-ownership corporations, which are the focus of this chapter.

The indirect privatization process for state enterprises took place in two stages. In the first, so-called commercialization phase, SOEs were transformed into joint-stock (or limited liability) companies. In this stage, an administrative body representing the state—between 1966 and 2017 it was the Ministry of Treasury (MoT)—was the sole owner of the companies. The next step was to decide on the proportion of the company's shares to be transferred into private hands and the method of selling. Here, the applied techniques were public tender, negotiations undertaken by invitation, and public offerings. This last method was the one that linked the privatization process to the rebirth and development of the capital market.

The privatization process of small and medium-sized companies had already been completed swiftly during the first few years of transition. The privatization of large state-owned companies, however, happened gradually, often in successive waves, over decades. In particular, the privatization of companies of "strategic importance" has been slow. These included oil refineries, coal mines, power plants, utilities, railways, chemical companies, pharmaceutical companies, and the large institutions of the financial sector (Błaszczyk and Patena 2015). The sluggishness of privatization in Poland is partly explained by the prudence of preparations and the long procedure of consensus seeking between political and social partners. In addition, as time passed, the privatization of large state-owned companies encountered more and more political hurdles. Behind-the-scene deals and rampant corruption that came to light in political battles threw cold water on citizens' initial enthusiasm. There was an observable connection between the fluctuation in the pace of privatization of large state companies and political campaigns during general elections. Capitalizing on the changing public opinion on privatization, either the opposition or the governing party (with strong interest groups behind each) stepped up or blocked the privatization process from time to time (Błaszczyk et al. 2005).[2]

Linking Privatization and the Development of the Capital Market

Among the transition countries in Central and Eastern Europe, Poland was, by far, the most successful in linking privatization with the fostering of the capital market. The privatization of large state companies through the stock market had many benefits that offset the higher transaction costs when compared to other methods of privatization. Being listed on a stock exchange provided companies with new sources of funds and helped them

---

[2] An example of the variablity described here is the new right-wing government's 1998 plan, which put the privatization of the so-called strategic sectors on the agenda again. The plan was very ambitious in terms of both the sectors (infrastructure, large banks, telecommunications) and the deadlines for the completion of deals. The privatization boom was also reflected in the spectacular surge in budget revenues. Three years later, however, with the fall of the government coalition, privatization lost momentum, and a sluggish period of privatization followed.

enhance their good (business) reputations. A further benefit was that the transformation into a listed company automatically implied an upgrade in corporate governance standards as well. In the case of Poland, it was particularly important that the stock market provided a unique opportunity to combine state and private ownership. In such mixed setups, the state could preserve its influence on companies that it regarded as strategically significant while letting the market signals and disciplinary power of the market function.

Depending on whether the companies entered the equity market for the first time or went through second and third rounds of privatization, we distinguish between privatization-induced initial public offerings (PIPO), initial public offerings (IPO), and secondary public offerings (SPO). At the beginning of transition, PIPOs helped launch the Warsaw Stock Exchange (abbreviated GPW from the Polish name), which was established by the state treasury. In November 1990, five major state-owned companies were introduced to the GPW. In three of them, a minority stake (not more than 30 percent) was retained by the state. At the same time, the regulations on foreign investors limited their ownership shares to between 25 to 40 percent. As a result of the political weight of trade unions, the employees of the respective state companies were granted 15 percent of the company's shares for free.

The successful launch of the GPW and the effective monitoring applied by the Polish Securities Commission were widely acknowledged already in the 1990s. According to experts' opinion, the regulations and the rigorous supervision of the Warsaw Stock Exchange were well above the standards elsewhere in the region. A quarter of the 207 large-scale privatization projects earmarked for the first decade of transition were implemented through the capital market. One-third of the total privatization income in the period between 1990 and 1999 was obtained through these fifty-five privatization-induced initial public offerings. In most cases, share packages were sold in successive installments via the stock exchange. In the case of PIPOs, on the average two-thirds of the shares of a given company were sold.

In 1998, 165 companies were listed on the main GPW market and market capitalization reached $20 billion (15 percent of GDP in 1998). That year, the telecommunication industry with the IPOs of Telecomunikacija Polska (TPSA) was the driver of the GPW's dynamism. TPSA alone raised the capitalization of the Warsaw Stock Market by almost one-third. In terms of market shares, the financial sector came in second with one-fifth of the GPW's capitalization.

Preserving higher shares of state ownership was mainly decided on the basis of a company's character, in other words, whether they were considered of "strategic importance" or not. Enterprises in low priority sectors (such as the food industry) were privatized almost fully within a relatively short time. The privatization of companies in "sensitive" sectors (e.g., financial institutions), however, were frequently delayed, and, in many cases, the state remained a majority owner. Most of the companies in the heavy industry group were treated as strategic. Slow and only partial privatization was the rule in these industries, too, as illustrated by the fact that less than half of the twenty-five Polish steel companies were privatized by the beginning of the new century (Nachtigal 2014).

The first privatization wave of transition culminated in the 1999 pension reform, which gave a new impetus to the development of the Warsaw Stock Exchange. The new laws prescribed mandatory contributions to private pension funds, which, in turn, were obliged to invest up to 50 percent in stocks, 95 percent of which had to be invested in companies listed on the GPW.

Although the pace of privatization slowed down starting in the beginning of the 2000s, there still remained huge interest in IPOs on the Warsaw Stock Exchange. In 2004, PKO Bank (the largest domestic commercial bank) was partially privatized. The state followed the established strategy as it retained share ownership of 50 percent plus 1. Through various measures, it also encouraged domestic small investors to participate in the privatization process. In 2005, the main attraction for investors was the partial privatization of PGNiG, the largest domestic gas company. In this case, the need for ensuring the security of energy supply was the main justification for maintaining majority state ownership in the company. In the first round, only 15 percent of PGNiG was sold through the stock market. This could only partially satisfy the strong demand for the company's shares, which persisted in spite of the fact that the likely winner of the upcoming elections, the Law and Justice Party (PiS) led by Jarosław Kaczyński, pledged to suspend the privatization of PGNiG.

The Slowdown of Privatization

The incoming Kaczynski government blocked the sale of several large companies already designated for privatization (including companies that belonged to politically sensitive sectors such as shipbuilding and coal mining), and secondary public offerings on the stock market also came to a halt. (The privatization of the aforementioned PGNiG, nevertheless, continued). In 2005, there were still around one thousand state-owned enterprises on the registry of the Ministry of the Treasury. The government's negative stance towards privatization was partially ideological, but it was also connected to the scandals that had accompanied some earlier privatization deals. Since Poland ranked poorly on international corruption lists, the government was determined to fight corruption on all fronts, including all transactions related to SOEs.

The analyses of Bałtowski, Kozarzewski, and Senderski are useful for studying the fluctuations of privatization, including the mid-2000 slowdown. Bałtowski and Kozarzewski (2016) wrote about influential rent seekers who had an interest in maintaining a relatively large state sector and had the power to hinder market reforms on several fronts. Illustrating his work with concrete examples, Senderski (2015) came to a similar conclusion. Walecki (2007) analyzed party financing and political corruption and shed light on the channels through which money flowed from SOEs to party coffers. Bałtowski and Kozarzewski (2016) also drew attention to the controversial situation that stemmed from the Ministry of Treasury's dual role as a privatization agency on the one hand, and as an owner and manager of the state's assets on the other. The conflict arose from the fact that with the shrinkage of state ownership, the political weight of the ministry was obviously diminishing together with the potential benefits (e.g., supervisory board seats in SOEs) that could be drawn from state asset management.

Bałtowski and Kozarzewski (2016) examined the slowdown of privatization from the point of view of fiscal policy as well. They summarized changes that began in the mid-2000s with the switch from privatization revenues to dividend incomes. According to fiscal statistics, from 2005 onwards, earnings from state assets showed a steady upward trend. Between 2006 and 2009, each year dividend income exceeded privatization revenues in the state budget.

The New Wave of Market Reforms

After the parliamentary elections of October 2007, which were held two years ahead of schedule, the center-right Civic Platform (Platforma Obywatelska, PO) led by Donald Tusk, took power. The prime minister vowed to implement liberal economic policies coupled with solidaristic social policy. Following Polish liberal traditions, the government introduced several market-oriented reforms, including the reduction of the share of state ownership in SOEs. In the background of the commitment to reduce the state's influence on the economy, there were ideological presumptions as well as pragmatic considerations aimed at increasing national competitiveness.

In the second half of the 2000s, the Polish economy performed rather well. Nevertheless, some criticisms concerning the functioning of the economy arose primarily from international organizations (the World Bank, OECD, EBRD). One often repeated negative comment took aim at the persistent weight of the state in the Polish economy, pointing out that the private sector's share of GDP was lagging behind that of the other new EU member states. Thus, a new chapter in the Polish privatization program was drafted, but this time, it coincided with the beginning of the global financial crisis. One year later, when the impact of the crisis reached Poland, the pressing need to increase budget revenues appeared as an additional impetus for the acceleration of privatization.

Civic Platform's privatization policy prevailed for two election cycles. The eight-year-long privatization story can be divided into two, clearly distinguishable periods. Between 2008 and 2011 the goal to reduce the state's ownership role as much as possible was unambiguous. By emphasizing the importance of a free and private economy, Civic Platform politicians wanted to demonstrate their dedication to the completion of the transition, as well the final break with the "communist past." The prime minister also referred to the need to protect the economy from political influence when he said, "There is no better protection against politicians interfering in the management of companies than a real increase in the competitiveness of Polish companies and the Polish economy. This is achievable by wise, fast and dynamic privatisation" (Tusk 2007).

Mainly as a result of its successful economic policy, Civic Platform was reelected for a second term. From that time on, however, the enthusiasm for privatization started to wane. The influence of those who argued for maintaining state control—primarily, but not exclusively, in the energy sector—was strengthened. SPOs on the Warsaw Stock Exchange slowed down, which meant that the share of state ownership in public companies remained the same or only marginally decreased. In a number of listed companies, the maintenance of mixed ownership was re-considered as an optimal solution in the long term.

Next, we shall examine the privatization history of the Civic Platform-led government in detail. "'Everything is for sale,' this is what Polish newspapers advertise on their front pages," reported the June 2, 2008 issue of the Hungarian economic weekly *Figyelő* in its coverage on privatization in Poland. The article included a quote from a representative of the largest Polish opposition party, PiS, who called the adoption of the law which permitted the sale of 740 state-owned companies, "the darkest day of Polish legislation" and a primary example of squandering national wealth.

At the beginning of the new privatization wave, 1,237 companies belonged to the Ministry of Treasury and more than a quarter of them was under liquidation or close to bankruptcy as of March 2008. In the "actively operating" category, 887 public companies were registered, and among those, the 2008–2011 plan designated 740 for privatization. The eventual completion of the plan was heralded as the final act of transition privatization. As far as the revenue from the sale of state-owned companies is concerned, the treasury calculated it brought in an amount of five to seven billion złoty (€1.43 to 2.0 billion) on average per year. The privatization record of the Tusk Cabinet between 2008 and 2011 was considered successful by most professional measures. The Ministry of Treasury also made efforts to fulfill the promise of the ruling party's election campaign: the pledge that this round of privatization would be more transparent, honest, and less bureaucratic than ever before. The Ministry of Treasury published both privatization plans (2008–2011 and 2012–2013), as well as the details of their implementation on its website. In three years, approximately 80 percent of the privatization program was completed, both in terms of the number of companies and the revenue received by the treasury (Błaszczyk and Patena 2015). Further quantifiable results of the 2008-2011 privatization include the reduction of the public sector's ratio of GDP to below 20 percent and the lowering of the proportion of public sector employees in overall employment figures to about 16 percent.

The state's ownership activity and control, however, remained quite different across the sectors. Like other Eastern European countries, it was almost negligible in manufacturing industries but remained relatively strong in the extractive and infrastructure sectors. The state's presence also depended on the size of the given corporation: the larger a company was (is), the more likely it belonged (belongs) to a group in which the state had (has) majority ownership. The state remained present as an owner in twenty out of the one hundred largest Polish companies and in almost half (twelve) of the twenty-five largest companies. These twelve companies accounted for two-thirds of the group's sales and employed 68 percent of its employees.

In mid-2014, the Ministry of Treasury published a document ("Priorities in the management of the portfolio of entities supervised by the

Minister of Treasury up to 2015")[3], which included the principles of the privatization and asset management of the wholly or partly state-owned companies. The Polish Government presented the list of twenty-two companies regarded as strategically most crucial for the national economy:

> Industrial Development Agency, Bank Gospodarstwa Krajowego, Azoty Group, Lotos Group, KGHM, PGE, Polska Wytwornia Papierow Wartosciowych, Polska Grupa Zbrojeniowa, Orlen, PGNiG, Polskie Inwestycje Rozwojowe, Polish Radio, PKO BP, PZU, Przedsiebiorstwo Eksploatacji Rurociagow Naftowych Przyjazn, Przedsiebiorstwo Przeladunku Paliw Plynnych "Naftoport," Tauron, Telewizja Polska, Totalizator Sportowy, Szczecin and Swinoujscie Harbour, Gdansk Harbour and Gdynia Harbour.

As can be seen, the list is varied as it includes large seaports, public service media companies, the gambling industry, and also a few from the the twenty largest companies on the Warsaw Stock Exchange. In the "strategic" companies the Ministry of Treasury had full or majority ownership and was firm on maintaining its stake in the long run. The management of these companies is closely monitored by state authorities, and a number of them are key players in government-initiated programs such as "Poland's Energy Policy 2030" or "The Petroleum Sector Policy of the Government of the Republic of Poland." Financial institutions also featured heavily on the list, and they included Bank Gospodarstwa Krajowego (the bank responsible for—among other things—financing regional development and the management of EU funds) and Polskie Inwestycje Rozwojowe (PIR.S.A.), which mainly financed long-term infrastructure investments.

As discussed before, in the years of the global financial crisis, the Warsaw Stock Exchange performed very well, and it overtook most European exchanges in terms of the number of new listings. However, in 2014 only thirteen IPOs were registered on the GPW's main market, representing a 72 percent fall in the overall value as compared with 2013, which resulted in the GPW's fall to eleventh in the European rankings. The modest results of the Warsaw Stock Exchange in 2014 were closely related to the slowdown in the privatization of large companies, including SPOs. The dynamics of the stock market were also hampered by the nationaliza-

---

[3] Ministerstwo Skarbu Panstwa (2014), Warsaw.

tion of half of private pension fund assets in 2013, as Polish pension funds used to be the most important investors in the GPW.

Corporate Governance Regulation and Practice

To what extent the long-term state's ownership share affects the efficiency of listed companies? On the basis of the mixed results derived from various empirical papers no simple answer can be given to this question. The general opinion regarding the role of the state as an active owner—based on decades of experience and common knowledge—however, is mostly negative. In 2015, the renowned international consulting firm, PricewaterhouseCoopers (PwC) conducted a survey on state-owned enterprises. According to their results, 86 percent of top managers sampled opined that state ownership often entails politically motivated engagement in businesses, while 83 percent stated that it distorts competition. Moreover, the ratio of those with negative opinions rose by at least 10 percentage points compared to 2010. Focusing on the Polish case, several other studies point to the fact that depending on the strength of the given political party in power, state ownership frequently serves parties' or influential groups' interests at the expense of the company's and/or other shareholders' business interests (Kozarzewski and Bałtowski 2015; Senderski 2015).

Ideally, the state as shareholder, together with the other owners of the company, considers maximizing shareholder value as its main task. Moving away from this ideal primarily depends on the quality of corporate governance mechanisms. In assessing the corporate governance (CG) strengths and weaknesses of listed companies, the most commonly considered issues include the criteria and procedure of electing board members; the competence of senior management; leadership aptitude and integrity; compliance with legal obligations; transparency; availability and reliability of the data required for the decision-making process; and regulation and practices related to fair relations between majority and minority shareholders. In the case of joint public-private corporations, it is especially important to ensure high quality CG as a safeguard against the abuse of state power.

By the 2000s, the international best practices in corporate governance of state-owned companies were already established. The OECD was at the forefront of formulating these guiding norms. In 2005, the "Guidelines on Corporate Governance of State-Owned Enterprises" was published (OECD, 2005), with recommendations for an effective and transparent operation of state-owned companies in the member states. The acknowledged aims of the "Guidelines" were the following: a) the professionalization of the state as an owner; b) making SOEs operate with similar efficiency, transparency, and accountability as private enterprises following best practices; and c) guarantees that competition between SOEs and private enterprises is conducted on a level playing field[4]. According to the document, both government ownership passivity and excessive interference in businesses should be avoided.

Poland revised its corporate law in several phases following transition and after becoming a member of the OECD. These modernized laws, unlike their predecessors, make explicit references to the rules of corporate governance and make a sharper distinction between private and public companies. Poland has adopted corporate governance solutions based on the "best practices" principle proposed by the OECD and incorporated them into its corporate governance codes for stock exhange listing requirements and governance rules of public companies.

The evolution of CG characteristics showed a close correlation with the development of the Warsaw Stock Exchange. For the GPW to build its currently outstanding reputation, it was necessary to adopt formal rules corresponding to European standards, which Poland accomplished well. Laws and rules on the book, however, were just one part of the story. Research (Pistor, Raiser, and Gelfer 2000) has drawn attention to the fact that the harder tasks in the creation of an efficient business environment and capital markets in emerging economies, including Poland, lie in legal enforcement, the actual implementation of regulations.

The ownership structure of publicly traded companies is one of the most important internal corporate governance elements. For outside investors and stakeholders too, it matters whether a corporation is widely held or dominated by blockholders and which categories of owners prevail. Similar to most EU countries, the ownership structure of listed companies in Poland is typically concentrated. Quantifying the degree of concentration, relying on the average of data from 2004 to 2008, we find that the average share of the largest shareholder in GPW-listed companies was 41 percent, while the three largest shareholders accounted for 56.9 percent. In international comparison, these figures indicate that the ownership concentration of companies listed on the Warsaw Stock Exchange is high, but lower than those of on other Central and Eastern European stock exchanges.

---

[4] OECD. 2005. "Guidelines on Corporate Governance of State-Owned Enterprises."

Poland is even more different from its Eastern European neighbors if we compare the weight of various ownership categories. The most important difference is that in Poland many companies (30 percent of all listed corporations) were founded after the transition in the 1990s, and their main owner is a natural person and/or a single family. (Such ownership groups cannot be found, for example, on the Budapest or Prague stock exchanges). The share of foreign owners (investment funds and commercial banks), however, is relatively low at 21.9 percent. Another differentiating factor is the ownership role of the state which is only strong on the Warsaw Stock Exchange. Here the state is the largest shareholder in seven of the thirty largest companies.

The state as owner may appear in centralized or decentralized organizations. In most OECD countries, the centralized model is typical, and this applies to Poland too, where the Ministry of Treasury represents the state. The centralized model has many advantages. Probably this model offers the easiest way to separate the ownership role of the state from its other functions, first of all, regulation.

The change of government in 2008 brought not only the acceleration of privatization but also a new wave of corporate governance reforms. Increasing the transparency of the privatization process and the operation and management of existing SOEs was one of the goals emphasized in the reforms. The guidelines published on the website of the Ministry of Treasury show that in principle there cannot be a difference between the CG practices of state-owned companies and privately-owned entities. State-owned assets should be managed so that they generate profits and dividends and the state must refrain from non-business type of interventions in listed companies. In the case of the so-called strategic companies, however, the state is entitled for a broader scope of direct intervention.

One of the most important corporate governance mechanism is the composition and authority of supervisory committees. Shareholders of companies listed on the GPW are represented on the supervisory committees in proportion to their ownership share. The Ministry of Treasury as a shareholder delegates its representatives to supervisory boards, and these are responsible for appointing members of the executive board and monitoring the management. More than half (53 percent) of the supervisory board members of the eighteen mixed public-private companies are either employed by the Ministry of Treasury or are other state nominees. In addition to positions on the supervisory boards, mixed companies may employ two to three other people who "represent" the Ministry of Treasury. For some companies, the Ministry of Treasury has a special right to appoint the members of supervisory and of management boards. In such cases, the right of appointment is not proportional to the ownership ratio. For example, in the case of PKO PB, the largest commercial bank, it is up to the Ministry of Treasury to decide how many supervisory board members it wants to assign, and the Ministry also has the right to appoint the chairman and the deputy chairman of the board of directors.

In order to be a candidate for supervisory board membership, the Ministry of the Treasury's nominee has to demonstrate her or his comprehensive legal and business expertise in a preliminary examination. Those who successfully pass the examination will be listed as potential supervisory candidates in the database of the Ministry of Treasury.

During the last round of CG reforms, Poland made efforts to comply with OECD Guidelines when selecting members of the supervisory boards. As of 2012, in the case of companies of strategic importance, a nomination committee with ten independent members has to be formed, and members are appointed by the Prime Minister. This nomination body then makes its recommendations to the Ministry of Treasury for openings on supervisory committees. The representatives of the Ministry have stated on several occasions that a new approach to the supervision of state-owned companies is envisaged, which includes the selection of top executives on the basis of professional skills and a promise that political connections are given less consideration. As opposed to this optimistic rhetoric, Kozarzewski and Baltowski (2016), along with others, prove that political profiteering as a motivation in state property management has remained frequent, and political aspects still prevail during the selection of supervisory board members of both pure SOEs and mixed ownership corporations. In the next section, we shall demonstrate that these findings have been fully confirmed by events that have unfolded starting in late 2015.

The Illiberal Turn

After the elections in October 2015, a significant reversal occurred both in the economic role of the state and the prospects of wholly or partially state-owned companies. After eight years of governance based on liberal ideology and practice, Polish voters brought the rightist-conservative Law and Justice Party (PiS) to power. This conservative-nationalist party turned against a number of important economic policy issues promoted by the preceding government and launched the second illiberal turn in the region after Hungary's in 2010.

Analysis of the failure of the previous government and the emergence of right-wing populism in Poland is beyond the scope of this paper. One point, however, should be emphasized: the performance of the economy hardly features on the list of explanatory factors. The Polish economy achieved remarkably good results in the previous two decades and also performed well in international comparison during the global financial crisis. Between 2007 and 2014, Poland's GDP expanded by 4 percent. (According to Eurostat, the same figure was 0.3 for Hungary and 0.7 percent for the European Union as a whole). The indicators of income inequality have remained around the European average, and macroeconomic imbalances were not a matter of grave concern either. The uninterrupted flow of credits in the peak crisis years and the stability of the whole financial system have also won widespread appreciation. In the competitiveness rankings of the Institute for Management Development (IMD), Poland has moved from the 52nd place in 1997 to the 33rd in 2013, while UNCTAD's "World Investment Prospects Survey 2013–2015" regarded Poland as Europe's fourth, and globally the fourteenth, most attractive destination for foreign direct investment.

The first steps taken by the PiS administration included a series of high-level personnel changes based on political proximity and perceived loyalty. The Szydlo government had already started work on personnel changes in the top management of state-owned enterprises[5] in the first weeks after coming into power. In November 2015, the media[6] was awash with reports on the dismissals of members of the supervisory boards and boards of directors of the largest Polish companies and the appointment of loyal cadres (including well-known personalities from the previous PiS government). All the former chief executive officers of the thirty-two largest state-owned companies (with the exception of PKO BP) were removed

---

[5] "A bill authored by Poland's governing party Law and Justice (PiS) . . . opens the door to dismissing some 1,600 executives in various public offices. Candidates for the vacated posts will no longer be selected through competitions, but appointed. They will be allowed to be active party members and won't have to take part in the, so far mandatory, preparatory training. Assuming the bill is passed into law before Christmas, the governing party may have full control over key offices as soon as in February." Source: http://www.warsawvoice.pl/WVpage/pages/article.php/33993/news 02.12.2015.

[6] *The Warsaw Voice Newsletter*, an online news service, provided regular reports on such events in English.

and replaced by leaders who the ruling party considered trustworthy.[7] The political motives behind the purges were obvious. David Jackiewicz, the new government's Minister of Treasury, made a statement during a parliamentary debate that the support of and the commitment to the new political course was one of the main considerations to be taken into account when appointing the management of large companies. According to him, the leaders of these companies had to be unquestionable supporters of the government's new economic program and were expected to place the nation's interests higher than the "narrow" interest of the companies they helmed.

Basing top personnel changes on loyalty to the governing party was a common practice of former Polish governments too. With the new PiS regime, however, the extremely high number of posts involved and the speed of implementation was shocking for many observers. According to the Polish daily *Rzeczpospolita* (April 14, 2016), the tempo of cadre change during the first months of 2016 was the fastest since the year 2000.

In thirteen of the fourteen state-controlled companies of the WIG-30 group listed on the Warsaw Stock Exchange, new candidates were nominated and approved for chief executive posts by the Ministry of Treasury. The market reaction to the political appointments and to the possibility of an implied expansion of interventionist policies appeared quickly. The stock index already began to fall during the first month after the elections mainly due to the growing sense of uncertainty among investors. After a few months of the Szydlo cabinet, credit rating agencies downgraded their—then high-level—country ratings for Poland. Moody's was one of the credit agencies that drew attention to the increased risk concerning the prospects of the Polish economy. Analysts believed that changes in the legal and institutional environment were likely to result in a loss of business confidence that could lead to the decline in growth dynamics.

With the benefit of hindsight, however, it must be acknowledged that the gloomy predictions proved wrong. After a short, temporary setback, the Polish economy grew again by impressive rates, and the Warsaw Stock

---

[7] The following are two concrete examples from the largest companies: the chief executive officer position of PKN Orlen Oil company was given to W. Jasinski, a member of parliament as well as the inner circle of Jaroslaw Kaczynski. P. Wozniak, the Minister of Economy of the previous PiS government took over as the head of the largest gas industry. company. In early 2016, the positions of the president of the Warsaw Stock Exchange as well as several members of the supervisory board were also replaced.

Exchange moved up in the ranks of best performing exchanges. Investors' sentiments seemed to be no longer affected by political upheaval. The GPW saw a large increase in the capitalization of local companies and boasted the third largest number of IPOs of any European stock exchange in 2017.[8]

Let us return to the determination of the PiS government to overhaul the whole concept of privatization and establish a new attitude toward SOEs. The strategy included the push for investigating the allegedly corrupt privatization transactions of the previous government between 2007 and 2015, concentrating on the media and energy sectors. D. Jackiewicz, in his interview with *Dziennik Gazeta Prawna* (May 18, 2016), evaluated the privatization of several energy companies as a mistaken policy and envisaged their partial or full re-nationalization. The minister accused the previous government of initiating irresponsible sales transactions in order to increase privatization revenues at all costs. The Supreme Audit Office placed some of the suspected cases of corruption under investigation. According to the Office's report, during the previous government, the Ministry of Treasury privatized several large companies, including the Ciech Chemical Trust, in a non-transparent way and possibly for unjustifiably low prices.

The new government not only harshly criticized the previous governments' privatization practices but also emphasised the discontinuity in SOE policies and introduced a series of regulatory and institutional changes. It has publicly announced the end of privatization and liquidated the former main institution of state asset management, the Ministry of Treasury.

The new SOE governance law was implemented in 2017. After dismantling the MoT, one group of companies was directly subordinated to the Prime Minister's Office, while other SOEs were transferred to the control of the ministries corresponding to their sectoral classification. The Act on Rules of State Asset Management set forward provisions that concerned large companies of strategic importance. At present, there are thirty such companies, and they are placed under the special supervision of the Prime Minister. The Act also forbids the practice of direct privatization.[9] According to the former Minister of the Treasury, the original purpose of the reorganization was to

---

[8] https://www.gpw.pl/ri-press-releases?ph_main_01_start=show&cmn_id=106572&-title=GPW+Ranks+Third+by+Number+of+IPOs++on+European+Exchanges.
[9] https://warsawinstitute.org/wp-content/uploads/2017/10/NEW-APPROACH-TO-COMPANIES-WITH-STATE-TREASURY-SHAREHOLDING-POLAND-%C2%A9-Warsaw-Institute.pdf

strengthen the competitive power of companies by realizing synergy effects from cooperation among them. By contrast, opposition parties saw the liquidation of the Ministry of the Treasury and the new legislation on SOEs as more proof of the rising statist approach to managing the economy.

The state's more active involvement in the economy has become a de facto part of its development plans. In March 2016, the "Responsible Development Plan"[10] championed by the Minister of Development[11] and Deputy Prime Minister Mateusz Morawiecki (since December 2017, the prime minister of Poland) was published. According to the guidelines of the plan, state companies have a key role to play in the reindustrialization of Poland, in innovation-driven growth, as well as in breaking out of the middle-income trap. In the vision of the "new Poland," beyond strengthening public control, the next important pillar was the concept of "re-polonization." One slogan of the plan repeatedly announced by the former Prime Minister was: "more Polish economy in Poland's economy" (*więcej polskiej gospodarki w polskiej gospodarce*).

The Morawiecki plan pointed out that the development of the Polish economy was negatively affected by a lack of balance between foreign and domestic capital during the previous two decades. While, on a general level, the positive contributions of foreign direct investments were acknowledged, measures to reduce perceived over-dependence on foreign investment were planned. A Development Ministry official explained in an interview: "We need to become less dependent on foreign capital, especially in such crucial, strategic sectors like media, banks or energy. Therefore we need to support and mobilise national investments."[12]

---

[10] According to the goals of the plan, the government wants to achieve the following by 2020: a rise in investment to above 25 percent of GDP; spending on research and development to reach 2 percent of GDP; the number of Polish-owned medium and large companies to be increased to over 22,000; the outward Polish FDI to be increased by 70 percent; the growth rate of industrial production to exceed GDP growth; Poland's GDP per capita to reach 79 percent of the EU average.

[11] The Ministry of Development, responsible for developing economic development strategies, was established in November 2015 after the reorganization of the Ministry of Economy and the Ministry of Infrastructure and Development. To facilitate the more effective coordination between the agencies, the Economic Committee of the Prime Minister's Council was formed. The Council, which is also managed by Morawiecki, supervises all the economic ministries.

[12] Paulina Pacula, "Poland seeks to boost state control of economy," *EU Observer*, Feb. 24, 2016, https://euobserver.com/beyond-brussels/132421.

At the time when the PiS government started office 60 percent of bank capital was foreign owned which was indeed well above the OECD average. The negative evaluation of this fact, however, was not new: The high ratio of foreign banks was a concern for the previous administration, too. The first significant measure to raise the share of domestic ownership was taken already in the first half of 2015, when PZU S.A., Poland's largest insurer (a listed company under government control) purchased a substantial stake in Alior Bank.[13]

After the elections the PiS government continued the repolonization of the financial sector with increased vigour. The plan was to initiate and support buyouts so that the share of foreign lending institutions would fall below 50 percent. The applied strategy for strengthening Polish capital in the financial sector and simultaneously creating a strong state-controlled banking group was to continue the acquisition of controlling stakes in foreign-owned banks. In 2017 in a major buyout deal, Unicredit, the giant Italian bank sold its 33 percent stake in Bank Pekao (Poland second-largest bank) to PZU S.A. and the Polish Development Fund (PFR). Previously, the share of Unicredit in Pekao was the biggest equity stake held by an international lender in a Polish bank.[14]

The above-described transactions fulfilled the twin goals of the PiS government: In relatively short time the share of domestic ownership in the banking sector grew to 55 percent and one third of banking assets got directly and indirectly under state control. The two biggest Polish banks (in terms of assets), PKO Bank Polski and Bank Pekao are public companies yet both are under the strong ownership control by the state.

Opinions are divided concerning the expected benefits from the changes. The Polish Financial Supervision Authority e.g. considers the new structure of the banking sector to be optimal.[15] On the other hand, a number of experts warn of the inherent risk of the increased presence of the government in the financial industry. They talk about the danger of distorting competion, the tendency for and the concrete examples of directed lending based on political preferences and other negative effects of politicising business.[16]

---

[13] https://internationalbanker.com/finance/polands-top-insurer-buys-a-stake-in-alior-bank-with-more-of-the-same-to-follow/.
[14] https://www.ft.com/content/f7283548-5cd1-11e7-b553-e2df1b0c3220.
[15] https://thelawreviews.co.uk/edition/the-banking-regulation-review-edition-10/1190893/poland.
[16] https://euobserver.com/beyond-brussels/13.

The idea of repolonization is envisaged be applied to other sectors as well. This is justified by the fact that at present more than 60 percent of Polish exports are produced by companies financed by foreign capital. Here too, development plans promise changes in the balance between domestic and foreign interests. There is also determination to increase the number of Polish "national champions," whose number is still below ten. The Morawiecki plan requires $250 billion for development purposes over the next twenty-five years. As for the sources of these investments, half of the amount is calculated to come from European Union funds, while the other half is expected to be covered by domestic funding, including significant contributions from state-owned companies.

Summary

This study has been built on the observation that the state is permanently present as a minority or majority owner of Polish companies listed on the Warsaw Stock Exchange, Central Europe's largest exchange. From the beginning of Polish economic transition, the privatization of large SOEs was linked to the development of the domestic capital market. In sectors that were considered strategic or politically sensitive, stock market privatization was carried out in several phases, and the state still (as of summer 2018) maintains its majority or minority control in fourteen large public companies. Theoretically and occasionally, the mixed private and state ownership in public companies has the potential to be an efficient combination. The exposure to competition on the capital market helps increase efficiency and transparency, which, under optimal conditions, places limits on the enforcement of non-business, including political objectives arising from state ownership. In Poland, however, the interdependence of politics and the economy has remained strong, thus creating space for rent-seeking behaviors and various forms of corruption.

In Poland, the latest major wave of privatization began in 2008, when the center-right, market-oriented Civic Platform came to power. The Tusk government, with its large-scale privatization program, accomplished several goals simultaneously. It strengthened the commitment to market reforms by giving the green light to further reductions in the state's ownership stakes in strategically important large companies. Because the majority of shares were sold on the capital market, the Warsaw Stock Exchange became a European top performer in the field of IPOs, even during the worst years of the global financial crisis. The sale of hundreds of millions-of-dollars-worth share packages also added considerable revenue to the tight state budget. Meanwhile, however, various forms of state control (with concomitant examples of mismanagement) persisted, even in cases when the state was only in the position of a minority shareholder.

In October 2015, a significant reversal in the economic role of the state and in the prospects of wholly or partially state-owned companies took place after the anti-liberal Law and Justice Party (PiS) came to power. The Szydlo government started making changes to top personnel right after its inauguration, and this affected almost all mixed and state-owned companies. The goal was to put politically engaged and trustworthy cadres into key positions. As for the future of state-owned companies, the end of privatization was openly declared together with a commitment to the more active and responsible involvement of state agencies in the economy.

The main ideological pillars of the economic policy of the new political regime are patriotism (which includes the concept of "re-polonization") and the greater centralization of and control over state assets. The mobilization of state-owned companies' funds to achieve national development goals has also been taking place. Measures were applied to increase the domestic ownership ratio in the financial sector. The recent buyout transactions serve as a good example of how the structure of the financial sector has been changing in line with the new economic policy: the share of domestic ownership is increasing together with the stronger direct and indirect control of the state.

REFERENCES

Bałtowski, Maciej, and Piotr Kozarzewski. 2016. "Formal and Real Ownership Structure of the Polish Economy: State-owned Versus State-controlled Enterprises." *Post-Communist Economies* 28 (3): 405–19.

Beuselinck, Christof, Lihong Cao, Marc Deloof and Xinping Xia. 2017. "The Value of Government Ownership during the Global Financial Crisis." *Journal of Corporate Finance* 42(C): 481–93.

Błaszczyk Barbara, et al., 2005. „Koszty spowolnienia i zaniechania prywatyzacji jako argument w polityce przekształceń własnościowych" [The costs of delaying and relinquish privatization as a motive for privatization policy]. In *Kierunki niezbędnych zmian gospodarczych w Polsce* [The directions of necessary economic reforms in Poland], edited by Barbara Błaszczyk. Warsaw: Centrum Analiz Społeczno-Ekonomicznych.

Błaszczyk, Barbara, and Wiktor Patena. 2015. "Post-privatisation Corporate Performance in Poland. Evidence from Companies Privatized in 2008–2011."

CASE Working Papers 125. Centrum Analiz Społeczno-Ekonomicznych. https://papers.ssrn.com/sol3/papers.cfm?abstract_id=2693541.
Gliniecki, Bartlomiej, and Kaja Zaleska-Korziuk. 2017. "Report on Corporate Governance in State-owned Enterprises—the Polish Perspective." *Pro Publico Bono – Public Administration* (Special Edition 1): 98–115.
Kozarzewski, Piotr, and Maciej Bałtowski. 2016. "Change in Economic Policy Paradigm: Privatization and State Capture in Poland." CASE Working Papers 3 (127).Centrum Analiz Społeczno-Ekonomicznych. https://papers.ssrn.com/sol3/papers.cfm?abstract_id=2814116.
Nachtigal, Matjaz. 2004. *A Decade of Transition and Beyond: Institutional Transformation of the Countries in Central and Eastern Europe.* Ljubljana: Fakulteta za Družbene Vede.
OECD. 2016. "Broadening the Ownership of State-Owned Enterprises: A Comparison of Governance Practices." https://www.oecd.org/publications/broadening-the-ownership-of-state-owned-enterprises-9789264244603-en.htm.
Patena, Wiktor. 2014. "Analysis of the Privatisation Process in Poland in the Years 2008–2011. Outcomes and Prospects." *eFinanse* 10 (2): 57–70.
Pinto, Brian. 2014. *How Does My Country Grow? Economic Advice Through Story-Telling.* Oxford: Oxford University Press.
Pistor, Katharina and Martin Raiser, and Stanislaw Gelfer. 2000. "Law and Finance in Transition Economies." *Economics of Transition* 8: 325-368.
Senderski, Marcin. 2015. "Inhibited Privatization: A Hurdle Race over Vested Interests." *European Journal of Government and Economics* 4 (1): 44–66.
Tamowicz, Piotr and Meciej Dzierzanowski. 2002. "Ownership and Control of Polish Listed Corporations." Working Paper Series. Gdańsk Institute for Market Economics. http://ssrn.com/abstract=386822.
Tóth, Máté, Gergely Baksay, Péter Bilek, Veronika Czakó, Pál Gáspár, and Gábor Orbán, eds. 2003. "A privatizáció összehasonlító elemzése a csatlakozó és egyes átalakuló gazdaságokban" [A comparative analysis of privatization in acceding and transforming economies]. International Center for Economic Growth, European Center. http://www.icegec-memo.hu/hun/kutatasi_projektek/privatization.pdf.
Walecki, Marcin. 2007. "Political Finance in Poland." In *Political Finance and Corruption in Eastern Europe: The Transition Period*, edited by Jurij Toplak and Daniel Smilov, 123-142. Farnham: Ashgate.

CHAPTER 7

The Changing Role of the State in Slovenia: Privatization and Bank Consolidation

MIKLÓS SOMAI

Introduction

In the period between the end of World War II and its declaration of independence, Slovenia was part of the Socialist Federative Republic of Yugoslavia (SFRY). As part of the SFRY, the transformation of Slovenia's ownership structure had already begun during the war: 80 percent of banking and industrial properties were nationalized via confiscation (in the case of collaborators) or lockouts (for foreign owners) in 1945. In agriculture, the Law of August 23, 1945 called for the expropriation of holdings above 45 hectares and church lands in order to subdivide and redistribute small plots to the people, and also to establish state farms (Gulyás 2009, 159).

But the Soviet-style state-socialist economic model ended rather quickly. Central planning was replaced by the so-called self-management socialist economic system, introduced more as a byproduct of the conflict between Tito and Stalin than as a result of the conscious struggle of the workers' movement.[1] Workers' councils, which lasted for forty years and formed a core element of this unique Yugoslav experience, gradually gained importance, transforming from a consultative body into an organ of workers' management. However, even at the peak of their influence in the mid-1970s—they gained the right to elect firms' executives, enact economic policy, and determine income distribution—they remained in the shadow of management, 76 percent of which belonged to the League of Communists and retained authority over day-to-day affairs. Interestingly,

---

[1] In agriculture, from 1953 on, farm cooperatives turned into self-governing agricultural organizations, from which members were free to withdraw and start their own business (Gulyás 2009, 160).

although the 1965 reform, by further liberalizing and decentralizing the system, did in principle intend to develop self-management and enable workers' councils to become more independent, in practice benefited mainly the managers to grab some of the decision-making power back from the state. While strengthening the managers as the real decision-makers in enterprises, the introduction of elements of a market economy caused strong social differentiation, a rise in unemployment and regional inequalities, and contributed to a growing general perception that the whole model of self-management was unjust. As the system proved unable to persuade less developed republics not to regard themselves as exploited by the more developed, the legitimacy of workers' self-management gradually weakened, and allowed nationalism to take its place as the dominant ideology (Marković 2011).

Transformation and Stabilization

When it gained independence, Slovenia was in a much better position than almost all the other postcommunist countries in Central and Eastern Europe. Due to its favorable geographic location, only high or middle-income countries surrounded it, and its economy could draw on a skilled and qualified workforce and extant trade relations with the West. Slovenia was, at the time, the most developed republic of the former Yugoslavia, and, together with the future Czechia, it took the lead in terms of real GDP per capita among the would-be EU-member states of the region.[2]

The independent Slovenia faced a threefold transition: from socialism to a market economy; from a regional to a national economy; and, most importantly, from a republic of Yugoslavia to an independent state that became a full member of the European Union in 2004 (Mrak et al. 2004, ix).

Interestingly, just as the Yugoslav self-management system had been a sort of moderate version of a socialist planned economy—with the business sector enjoying ample freedom in their investment, production, and pricing decisions, independent Slovenia adopted the mildest possible version of capitalism. It opted for the region's least radical strategy of marketization based on legally enforced negotiated management-labor, so-called neocorporatist social partnership, coupled with a generous (transforma-

---

[2] Economic Research Service. 2015. "Real Per Capita GDP (2010 dollars) Historical."

tion cost) compensation policy and welfare state. This strategy, which was made possible through the high level of the state's administrative capacity, high quality governance, and especially trust in the capacity and credibility of the state, resulted in a high degree of social cohesion and low levels of income inequality. The country also became a top spender on pensions and education in East Central Europe. Its ability to build the region's most stable and efficient state institution made Slovenia the most Westernized postcommunist country. Early on in its transition, it exhibited all the attributes of Western European small states because of its economic openness, capitalist accumulation (namely high level outward FDI), "protective and efficiency-enhancing compensatory policies, macroeconomic stability, and governance by established democratic and neocorporatist institutions" (Böhle and Greskovits 2012, 182).

The success of this socio-economic model, which was built on consensus, gradualism, and pragmatism, not only enabled Slovenia to gain membership in the most important international institutions (EU, NATO, OECD), but also contributed to the transformation of this small country into one of the fastest growing economies in Europe, and the first new EU member from the former Eastern bloc to introduce the Euro.

Undoubtedly, the most important component of this transformation process, which was also the guarantee of its success, had been the gradual, decentralized, and distributive character of the so-called first wave of privatization, which lasted from the late 1980s until 1999.[3] The characteristics of the process constituted a compromise between the interests of new and old elites: a decentralized process enabled old elites to maintain control, and the free distribution of shares legitimated new elites.[4]

The Slovenian privatization concept, apart from transforming more than 1,300 self-managed enterprises into private companies, also included

---

[3] The process was gradual in the sense that initial privatization allowed not only full, but also partial ownership transfers; it was also decentralized as far as self-managed enterprises were given the right to initiate their own transformation into private companies; and finally, it was distributive, since there was the free distribution of shares to citizens (Mencinger 2006, 6–8).

[4] Squeezing the managers out of the privatization process could have had drastic consequences. Due to information asymmetry, managers might have found "a way of taking possession of the corporate liquidity flow" (Prašnikar et al. 1999, 3), unless decision makers took into account both their central role in initiating the transformation process, as well as their *de facto* economic ownership position within the companies. So it seemed to be wiser to strengthen their property rights rather than weaken or destroy them (Mencinger 2006, 5).

the sale of approximately 100,000 council dwellings to their occupants, the restitution of assets that had been nationalized between 1945 and 1958, and the assignment of 40 percent of shares in food processing companies to farmers' cooperatives. It was a mixture of free distribution, internal buy-outs at discount rates and the possibility of deferred payment to employees, and commercial privatization. Apart from large, unprofitable companies, which were set to be placed under the control of the so-called Development Fund and sold after refurbishment, and strategic firms (e.g., steel mills, utilities) to be maintained under state ownership, shares of the companies identified by the 1992 Privatization Law were to be distributed through the following scheme: 10 percent were to be transferred to the Pension Fund (KAD); another 10 percent to the Restitution Fund (SOD); a further 20 percent to the Development Fund; 20 percent of shares were sold to employees (in exchange for their vouchers); and the remaining 40 percent remained in the hands of companies to decide on their distribution. In profitable small and medium-sized labor-intensive firms (i.e., more than 60 percent of companies identified by the law), workers and managers acquired majority ownership. The second most popular method of privatization (in more than 10 percent of cases) was applied to profitable large firms—in fact, firms that were too large for insiders to acquire a majority stake—where managers tried to maintain their influence by combining the internal distribution of shares with public auctions, thus opting for a dispersed shareholder structure rather than strategic and/or institutional owners (Simoneti et al. 1998, 95; Mencinger 2006, 7–11).

The first wave of privatization was followed by a non-transparent domestic consolidation of ownership, as transactions were mostly made on informal markets with limited competition and transparency. At the end of the process, managers, domestic companies, as well as state and private funds had become the key economic players (Simoneti et al., 2001, 31–32). This model enabled the state to maintain significant ownership in privatized firms through the distribution of shares to quasi-governmental funds (KAD, SOD).[5] Foreign and/or strategic investors played

---

[5] There are several names for these two funds in the literature. They are called state-owned, state-controlled, and even quasi-governmental funds. The latter name comes from the Slovenian literature and relates to the fact that the proceeds from the sale of their assets were not transferred to the state but were dedicated to cover the claims of the former owners of national assets (SOD) and co-finance the obligatory pay-as-you-go pension system on an annual basis (KAD) (Simoneti, Marko. 2016. Consultation via email, 16 June 2016).

a much smaller role in the privatization process.[6] Nevertheless, the first wave of privatization was still an organic one, as managers, who played an important role in preparing the transition process in the communist era, remained heavily involved in the lives of corporations.

The Financial Sector

Prior to transition, commercial banks were organized on a regional basis and virtually owned by the self-governing firms they served. When these companies were converted into public limited liability companies, banks were not treated as separate entities, so they were automatically privatized together with their clients-companies (Mencinger 2006, 20). Consequently, like their clients, the ownership structure for most of these banks became highly fragmented. Additionally, many new banks were established and foreign capital was allowed to enter the banking sector—partly through acquisition, partly through the creation of new units (World Bank 1999, 63).

At the beginning of transition, due to the disintegration of Yugoslavia and the ensuing financial hardships in the corporate sector, banks retained 30 to 40 percent of non-performing loans and a significant amount of liabilities largely due to London Club creditors. By 1993, a huge bank consolidation and nationalization program became inevitable. Because 45 percent of their loans were classified as non-performing, the three largest banks: Ljubljanska Banka (LB), Kreditna Banka Maribor (KBM), and Kommercialna Banka Nova Gorica (KBNG), which together represented 53 percent of the Slovenian banking sector, had two-thirds of their toxic assets swapped for government bonds issued by the newly established Bank Rehabilitation Agency (BRÜ). The total consolidation amounted to approximately DEM 1.9 billion, an amount just under 5 percent of the country's 1993 GDP. Later, KBNG merged with KBM, and the two remaining banks were split into two: the old banks took over all claims and liabilities against the former SFR Yugoslavia, and the new ones—100 percent state owned Nova Ljubljanska Banka (NLB) and Nova Kreditna Banka Maribor (NKBM)—retaining the rest. As a result of this successful program, by early 1997, both banks satisfied the conditions set by the Bank

---

[6] At the end of 1999, strategic investors held less than half (10.92%), while foreign ones less than one-fifth (i.e., 1.2%) of shares compared to what was considered to be optimal for the ownership structure of privatized Slovenian firms (Simoneti and Gregoric 2004, 225).

of Slovenia and were excluded from the consolidation process by mid-1997. Paradoxically, during the country's transition to a market economy, public ownership did not decrease but rather significantly increased in the Slovenian financial sector and stood at least at 50 percent by the end of 1990s (World Bank 1999, 62–64).

This excessive state involvement coincided with the relatively weak presence of foreign capital in the Slovenian financial sector. In 2001, the penetration ratio of majority-owned foreign bank affiliates stood at 20.6 percent, a fraction of what it was in other countries in the region soon to become members of the EU (Figure 1).

Figure 1
Penetration ratio of majority-owned foreign bank affiliates in CEECs (2001)

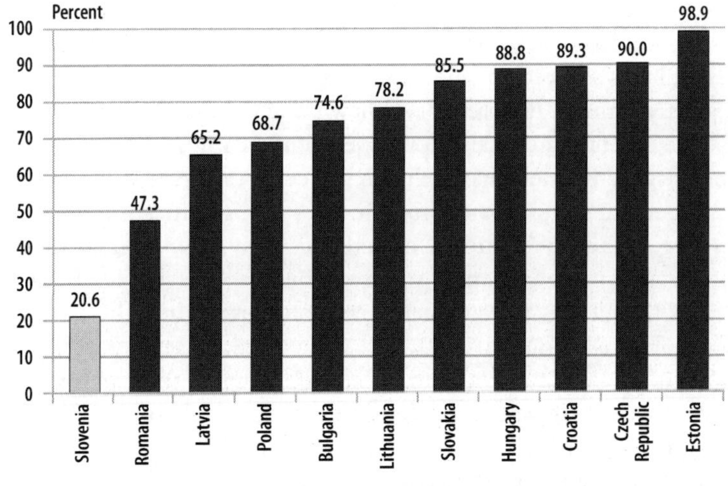

Country	Percent
Slovenia	20.6
Romania	47.3
Latvia	65.2
Poland	68.7
Bulgaria	74.6
Lithuania	78.2
Slovakia	85.5
Hungary	88.8
Croatia	89.3
Czech Republic	90.0
Estonia	98.9

Source: UNCTAD 2004. Penetration ratio: the ratios of assets of majority-owned foreign bank affiliates to host countries' total bank assets. CEECs: Central and East European countries.

The 2002 privatization program attempted to change this situation, when the government tried to include private capital in two of the largest state-owned banks: NLB and NKBM. While the privatization of the latter proved to be a total failure, that of the former was a temporary success. In 2002, the Belgian KBC bought 34 percent of NLB's capital with the goal of using it as a springboard to enter ex-Yugoslav markets, and the European Bank for Reconstruction and Development (hereafter EBRD) acquired another 5 percent. Nevertheless, the Belgians failed to reach an agreement with the main owner of the bank, the Slovenian government, about their plans for NLB and their future role in it. Disappointed, they divested their ownership share in two steps; in 2006, they reduced it to 22 percent and in 2012 to 0 percent (Smith and Norman 2012).

Overheating the Economy

Despite its unprecedented prosperity since 1993,[7] Slovenia has been increasingly under pressure to move closer to Western standards and reduce the public sector's stake in corporate ownership. This pressure paralleled the deepening of Slovenia's integration into the European and world economy.

In line with both Western expectations and the objectives of the Lisbon Strategy, which was renewed in spring 2005, gradualism was put to a halt. A so-called *Reform Strategy* was put into action by the new center-right government that returned to power after twelve years in the opposition. With a goal to boost the efficiency of public administration—and thereby economic competitiveness—the Reform Strategy outlined sixty-seven economic policy measures in a wide range of areas (e.g., health care, education, the tax and pension systems, labor market, social transfers, public utilities, infrastructure, research and development, the use of EU funds, etc.), covering practically every aspect of life in which the state had a say. Measures 19–23 were designed to deal with privatization and the development of the financial system.[8]

The second wave of privatization, which began in 2005, was received in diverse ways. On one hand, the government thought it was a transparent process that was open to foreign investors, and which provided opportunity for the domestic financial market to develop further, and therefore reconciled both big and small shareholders' interests, resulting in the gradual withdrawal of the state (represented by KAD and SOD) from the econ-

---

[7] If we compare the performance in the years between 2001 and 2005 with the five-year pre-transition period (1986–1990), we can see that Slovenia came the closest to the EU15 average in the region. Out of the CEECs, only three countries were able to reduce the gap with old member states in terms of real GDP per capita: Estonia by 0.4 percentage points, Poland by 4.0 percentage points, and Slovenia by 7.4 percentage points (*ERS* 2015).

[8] Slovenian Government. 2005. "The Framework of Economic and Social Reforms for Increasing the Welfare in Slovenia, adopted by Slovenia's Government on 3 November 2005." (pp. 66-75) http://www.slovenijajutri.gov.si/fileadmin/urednik/dokumenti/The_Framework_of_Economic_and_Social_Reforms_for_Increasing_the_Welfare_in_Slovenia.pdf.

omy.⁹ On the other hand, the opposition thought it to be a non-transparent process in which the government embraced the strategy of Spanish conquistadors (Damijan 2012). Their criticism focused on appointments of the government's men to board positions in both state-owned banks and companies and that the state-owned banks were then forced to finance management buy-outs (hereafter MBOs) in those state-owned companies. By doing so, the government exposed both the banks and companies to extreme risks and overheated the economy in cyclically sensitive sectors like real estate, construction, and financial mediation. Neutral experts called the process insider privatization (Ivers 2014, 29), and even the OECD drew attention to the fact that the weak framework of governance in state-owned banks was likely to have contributed to poor credit standards, excessive risk taking, and the misallocation of credits (OECD 2013, 9).

Apart from a handful of widely publicized success stories—the sale of 55.3 percent of SIJ (Slovenian steel group) to Russian KOKS and 48.1 percent of the second largest bank (NKBM) via an initial public offering (IPO)—counterbalanced by some notable failures (like the aborted privatization of Triglav or Telekom Slovenije), the aims of the second wave of privatization: to consolidate ownership interests and increase the role of strategic investors, have not been met. Although between 2004 and 2007, the number of companies owned by the state through KAD and SOD declined from 492 to 198 (Slovenian Government 2008, 13), in reality, the risk of potential political interference in the economy did not diminish. By 2007, the two funds, initially designed to become portfolio investors through various swaps of shares, managed to concentrate their control over Slovenian blue chips: they acquired at least a blocking minority (a 25 percent +1 voting share) in ten out of the twenty-eight most important companies listed on the Ljubljana Stock Exchange.¹⁰ Thus their role went beyond what had been initially projected, and they established the capacity

---

[9] The two state-controlled funds (KAD and SOD), which disposed of dispersed holdings in a large number of companies, were to be transformed into regular portfolio investors with an obligation to reduce their combined ownership in every single company under a threshold of 10 percent within two years in the case of listed companies or two and a half years in non-listed ones. No time limit had been set for eighteen investments of strategic importance and four companies of special national interest—i.e., the two major banks (NLB and NBKM), the biggest insurance company (Triglav), and Telekom Slovenije (Slovenian Government 2007, 12).

[10] Gorenje (home appliances), Krka (pharmaceutical), Petrol, Mercator (the leading food retailer), Luka Koper (the only seaport), Aerodrom Ljubjana (the main airport), *Delo* (the leading newspaper), etc. (Mencinger 2006, 27).

to formulate corporate strategies. Given the predominance of internal owners and state-controlled funds in the process, just as in the first wave, the second wave of privatization failed to attract enough strategic or foreign investors—a scenario that could have led to some restructuring in undercapitalized Slovenian companies (Georgieva and Riquelme 2013, 7).

The Roots of Trouble

In order to understand the motivations of the third wave of privatization that took place from the last quarter of 2013 onwards, it is necessary to consider the circumstances that led to the Slovenian crisis, which primarily manifested as a banking crisis.

When businessmen from the old elite realized they were being systematically squeezed out of leading positions in companies, they took up the struggle and began to buy state assets on the stock market. In the increasingly divided political atmosphere, the banks financed both sides of the conflict, that is, both the new and old elites (Damijan 2012). The growing demand pushed up prices, but because the country was on the threshold of Eurozone membership,[11] the gradually decreasing real interest rates created good conditions for privatization to continue throughout the 2004 to 2008 period.

Another factor in the Slovenian banking crisis was the introduction of International Financial Reporting Standards (IFRS) in early 2005, which, by replacing the previous conservative regulations with more permissive ones, had an impact on banks' business behavior and encouraged them to further expand their lending activity.[12]

Credit expansion was further bolstered by growing competition among the banks in Slovenia, reflected in a reduction of both effective interest rates and loan standards (e.g., through lower collateral requirements). Majority foreign-owned banks in particular proved to be very aggressive in their efforts to expand their market share; on the basis of their financially sound

---

[11] Slovenia joined the European Exchange Rate Mechanism (ERM-II) at the end of June 2004, whereby restrictions on movements of capital were lifted and the Bank of Slovenia lost control of the amount of money in circulation (Bank of Slovenia 2015, 7).

[12] Bank lending is by its very nature pro-cyclical, and this change in accounting standards entailed a reduction in the need for provisioning. So the banks obtained a part of the capital they needed for the intensive growth of lending indirectly (Bank of Slovenia 2015, 18; 41–44).

parent banks, they offered highly favorable terms and raised their loan to deposit (LTD) ratio to much riskier heights than did domestic banks.[13]

Among factors on the supply side, that is, those that enabled the high growth in lending, undoubtedly the most important was the large supply of assets on international financial markets. In the period from 2004 to 2008, Slovenian banks borrowed massively from the interbank market and provided domestic companies with cheap loans. And it is here, at the intersection of the supply side (more financing) and demand side (more investment) that the circumstances referred to in the title of this chapter, the "roots of trouble," come into the picture:

- Slovenian banks faced increasing exposure to risks arising from a maturity mismatch (i.e., short-term liabilities outweighing short-term assets), as interbank credit had historically been, and, with the crisis looming, was becoming even more short-term, whereas loans issued to the private sector were typically "generous" (Bertelsman Stiftung 2014, 19) and long-term (Arnesen 2014, 81);
- a substantial part of the above-mentioned loans financed corrupt insider privatisations—i.e., consisted of soft funding for buy-outs by politically connected managers (Ivers 2014, 30) and the often irresponsible expansion policy of the new owners. Thus the banks complied with the latter's desire to "obtain ownership influence over as much of the economy as possible" (Bank of Slovenia 2015, 20);
- probably the most dangerous aspect of the credit expansion was the very way in which banks provided loans for this "conquest" (i.e., totally inconsistent with the principle of risk minimization). As companies actively invested beyond their core business, thereby creating a real estate boom, the banks allowed an exceptionally high proportion of loans to be tied to the value of properties pledged as collateral, and therefore exposed themselves to excessive risks. Moreover, they committed similar errors by financing companies carrying out leveraged buy-outs (LBOs[14]).

In the period from 2004 to 2008, Slovenian banks' exposure to international financial markets (i.e., their liabilities to foreign banks) increased by

---

[13] As a result of their aggressive market strategy, foreign banks managed to increase their market share in Slovenia from 20.6 percent in 2001 to 29.74 percent in 2012 (UNCTAD 2004, 321).

[14] An LBO is the acquisition, with borrowed money, of another company, the assets of which are used as collateral.

almost four times, from €4.25 billion to €16.1 billion. At the same time, loans to corporations grew twice as fast as non-banking sector deposits, at a rate of around 20 percent versus 10 percent annually, which raised the LTD ratio for banks from less than 100 percent (in 2004) to more than 160 percent by the onset of the financial crisis. The fast-growing indebtedness based on foreign borrowing increased the vulnerability of the Slovenian economy to financial shocks abroad, which became apparent after the fall of Lehman Brothers in 2008 (Bank of Slovenia 2015, 14–15).

Almost Bailed Out

With the onset of the global crisis in September 2008 and the drying up of the interbank market (*credit crunch*), the banks found themselves in an entirely new situation. The loans they had borrowed from the wholesale market were not renewed, so they had to pass the pressure on to their clients. The latter, excessively indebted companies, were unable to withstand this pressure and meet their liabilities to the banks, and the number of those defaulting on their commitments began to grow. Hence, the fundamental problem for banks—especially state-owned institutions involved in the finances of the MBOs of the new elite—came from the rapidly rising proportion of non-performing loans, implying a deterioration of their asset quality and a limitation of the volume of credit they could extend to new clients (Arnesen 2014, 81–82).

The simultaneous effects of insider privatization, the denial of the severity of the crisis for a while (Kickert et al. 2015, 18) by the center-left government, which returned to power at the end of 2008 to early 2012, and some other factors like the W-shaped growth path of the country's main export markets (like Italy and Croatia, but also to a lesser extent Germany, Austria, and France) made the crisis in Slovenia one of the deepest and the most long-lasting in both the region and the Eurozone.[15]

---

[15] Indeed, it took time for the center-left government to realize the magnitude and the long-lasting nature of the crisis and take effective measures to overcome it. First, they favored mild measures, such as pay freezes, instead of painful cuts and mass layoffs, and they did not substantially reduce welfare spending or increase taxes other than excise duties (Pevcin 2014, 86). The same hesitation prevailed in regard to supporting banks through the mobilization of only half the money (in terms of GDP) that the EU did on average up to the end of 2010, when such support could still be exempted from EU state aid rules (Bank of Slovenia 2015, 33).

Partly having learned from the negative experiences of the outgoing government, and partly due to growing external pressure (from international financial markets and institutions) to implement real structural reforms that would restore the sustainability of public finances, the new center-right government, having returned to power in February 2012, followed the six directions set forth by the Commission in their 2011 recommendations almost step-by-step.[16] It had a much more holistic approach to reform than did their predecessor and, already in March 2012, took radical austerity measures. Practically the whole of 2012 was entirely devoted to fiscal consolidation.[17]

The center-right government first prioritized the consolidation of public finances in the coalition agreement (i.e., shored themselves against the desertion of their political allies), and ensured the involvement and consultation of social partners to the fullest possible extent. The country's economic situation began to significantly deteriorate in the last quarter of 2012, when the negative impact of austerity policy on the economy had already been fully felt—with the worst year-on-year GDP growth data (-3.5 percent). The government was nearing an announcement of further cuts in public sector wages together with additional austerity measures for 2013 and 2014.[18]

---

[16] Slovenia was advised to contain public expenditure to achieve the deficit target; ensure the sustainability of the pension system; help clear balance sheets across the banking sector; tackle labor market problems (the difference between permanent and temporary contracts, parallelism resulting from student work); enhance matching between skills and jobs; and boost the business environment and attract investment (Commission 2011, 6).

[17] The main measures were introduced in an omnibus act named the Balancing of Public Finances Act passed in May 2012. It applied to all areas, but especially to the remuneration of civil servants (cuts and freezes), welfare benefits (cuts), pension system (an increase of retirement age, end of indexation, incentives for prolonged employment), the labor market (flexicurity), and the tax system (increase/introduction of taxes with no direct impact on competitiveness) (Cankar and Petkovšek 2014, 100–102; Pevcin 2014, 86).

[18] Moreover, the government failed to forge national unity behind two important issues: the stabilization of the banking sector by way of the establishment of a bad bank, named Bank Assets Management Company (BAMC)— designed to help banks in their efforts to clean up their balance sheets and start lending to businesses again—and the stabilization of public finances through a centralized system for managing state-owned assets under the auspices of the renewed Slovenia Sovereign Holding (SSH). Opponents to the BAMC warned that it would create serious a moral hazard by transferring—through an exchange of banks' bad assets and non-performing loans against state guaranteed bonds—the misguided past decisions of bank managers and supervisors onto taxpayers (*Slovenia*

While speculations had been wild regarding the would-be anti-crisis measures, the situation became even worse due to a corruption scandal in Maribor on November 2, 2012. It spread over the whole country in just a few weeks, provoking a storm of street protests calling for the resignation and/or prosecution of the politicians, other political functionaries, and businessmen accused of corruption. Although it started peacefully, the movement soon turned violent and led to clashes between the police and protesters. There was wide coverage of the "Slovenian uprising" in the global media, so everyone could see that the country ceased to be what it used to be: the relatively stable democracy of the Balkans (Kirn 2014, 12–13).

By the time the "Slovenian uprising" came to a definitive halt in March 2013, it had already succeeded in destabilizing and breaking apart the ruling coalition, as well as ousting several prominent elite figures from their leadership positions. What first seemed to be a historic victory, however, soon proved to be rather pyrrhic, as the newly constituted (once again center-left) government was exclusively made up of old parties (Kirn 2014).

Although austerity remained at the fore of economic policy discussions, both financial markets and international institutions surely had some reason to think they could start worrying about whether reforms (i.e., austerity policy) and privatization in Slovenia would continue.[19] The three biggest credit rating agencies downgraded the ratings for all main state-owned banks as well as the country's sovereign debt in several waves. Slovenia, which had already been under the excessive deficit procedure since 2009—a deficit to be corrected by the end of 2013, but with no real chance targets to be met—found itself, in April 2013, in a situation where its macroeconomic imbalances were considered excessive.[20]

Times 2012). As for the SSH, there was a fear the government would sell state property without parliamentary approval (Majnardi 2012).

[19] First, because the new cabinet thought the Slovenian welfare model could survive and a more inclusive policy would even help mitigate the crisis (Haček et al. 2014, 4); and second, because delays and sluggishness characterized the privatization process. Although BAMC was formally set up in March 2013, the act establishing SSH was not yet implemented, as political parties could not agree on asset qualifications consisting of the definition and categorization of public assets, the determination of targets for their efficiency/profitability, and working out of methods for how to sell them (Bank of Slovenia 2015, 102). Moreover, the new coalition agreement, also signed in March, was "silent on bank privatization," a fact that did not escape the attention of EU rapporteurs (Commission 2013a, 38).

[20] In extremis, at the end of an "Excessive Imbalance Procedure," the country in question could even face sanctions (an interest-bearing deposit or fine) of up to 0.1 percent of GDP (EU Regulation No 1176/2011 on the prevention and correction of macroeconomic imbalances).

In the spring of 2013, open speculation about Slovenia as the next to be bailed out, that is, after Greece, Portugal, and others, became even stronger. European institutions (the European Commission and European Central Bank), together with international ones (IMF, OECD), and credit rating agencies, especially Moody's (Figure 2), pushed Slovenia towards advancing privatization and further opening its domestic market to foreign investors. Finally, in the early days of May 2013, the Slovenian government, unable to withstand the growing pressure, relented and fulfilled the requirements of both markets and institutions.

Figure 2
Government debt credit rating for Slovenia

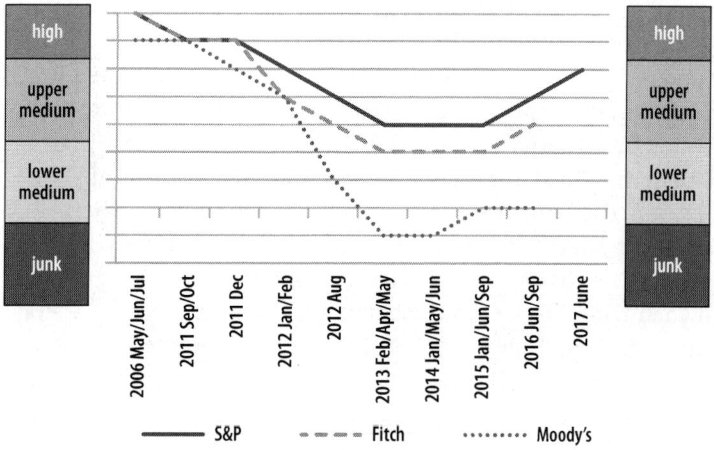

Source: Slovenia Credit Rating: http://www.tradingeconomics.com/slovenia/rating.

Capitulation

On May 9, 2013, a new austerity program of approximately €1.4 billion was announced. On the revenue side, it consisted of tax hikes (in court fees, VAT, and CIT rates) and several new taxes (e.g., on the lottery and non-alcoholic beverages) annually worth €650 million, while on the expenditure side, spending cuts (to public sector wages and investments, social transfers, and health insurance) amounting to a yearly €716.5 million were introduced (*Slovenia Times* 2013a).

On the very same day, Slovenia pledged to sell fifteen SOEs—including the second largest bank, the largest telecom operator, and its national airlines—and submitted its National Reform Program and its Stability Program to the Commission. In the latter, the government reported on the strengthening of the institutional and regulatory framework of the bad bank (BAMC) and presented a detailed plan for the transfer of the three largest banks' non-performing claims to it (Bank of Slovenia 2015, 70–71). Moreover, the Commission stuck to the view that the entire Slovenian banking system should be reassessed through a new, third-party, system-wide asset quality review (AQR) and new comprehensive stress tests[21] (Commission 2013b, 37).

In exchange for all of these "concessions," Slovenia was granted a two-year extension of the deadline (i.e., until the end of 2015) to bring its budget deficit under 3 percent of GDP and shore up fiscal consolidation with comprehensive structural reforms—including the further adjustment of the pension and social security systems to contain age-related expenditure growth (Council of EU 2013, 12–13).

The AQRs were performed in the second half of 2013, and their results, as well as those of the stress tests, were published on December 12, 2013. The stress tests identified, under the adverse scenario, a potential shortfall of €4.8 billion in the capital of the Slovenian banking system, but also proved that the country had the ability to recover from the crisis without being bailed out by European funds.[22] Furthermore, banks were allowed to write off €505 million of subordinated debt in a move that has been debated by those who lost ever since. Commitments were made to the European Commission that banks receiving state aid were to be privatized. Finally, it is important to mention that a couple days earlier, on December 7, 2013, the coalition partners came to an agreement on the

---

[21] An AQR consists of an assessment of data quality, the adequacy of the classification of a bank's claims (non-performing exposures included), collateral valuation and provisions, i.e., considers the key attributes of the bank's different asset portfolios in order to evaluate the quality of the assets. Based on the results of an AQR, stress tests are performed to reveal future losses in baseline and adverse macroeconomic scenarios, the latter serving to quantify the need for recapitalization (Bank of Slovenia 2015, 72–73).

[22] Apart from the recapitalization of state-owned banks to cover the losses due to NPL's provisions—amounting to €3.6 billion and causing, as a one-off impact, an approximate 11 percent increase (in GDP terms) in both the general deficit (from -4.0 percent to -14.7 percent) and general government spending (up from 48.5 percent to 59.5 percent) in 2013—the government decided on the transfer of the majority of the banks' lowest quality claims to BAMC in exchange for the latter's bonds and cash. The transfer of NPLs was conducted at their fair market value (~ €1.53 billion), equal to 30 percent of their nominal value (Commission 2016, 1–2).

guiding principles of the Slovenian Sovereign Holding (SSH) which, by the related act (ZSDH-1)[23] entering into force in April 2014, opened the way for both the concentrated management of state-owned assets and their regulated, gradual privatization (*The Slovenia Times* 2013b; Bank of Slovenia 2015, 102).

The Third Wave of Privatization

With a slight exaggeration, we can say that in Slovenia, the third wave of privatization started with large-scale nationalizations in the financial sector. As a result of the recapitalization/cleaning up (of banks' balance sheets) process, three major institutions (NLB, NKBM, Abanka) passed into full state ownership. Of course, already when the results of the stress tests were announced, it was clearly stated that full state ownership would not last long. NKBM and Abanka were to be completely sold, while in the case of NLB, the government was to reduce its participating interest to no more than 25 percent plus one share.[24]

Already by April 2016, NKBM was sold to the U.S. equity funds Apollo Management (80 percent) and EBRD (20 percent) for a price of €250 million (*SSH online* 2016).[25] The privatization of NLB had initially been planned to be completed by August 2017,[26] but it was postponed

---

[23] The law provided for the establishment of an institution (SSH) focused on the management of state assets and the orderly disengagement of the state from business. By virtue of the law, the SOD was to be transformed into the SSH, the latter of which would become not only the owner and manager of its own assets (formerly SOD assets), but also the manager (but not the owner) of the capital assets directly and indirectly owned by the Republic of Slovenia. Other funds (e.g., DSU and PDP) were to gradually merge into the SSH, the only exception being KAD (the pension fund), which remained an independent entity within the framework of the holding (Slovenian Sovereign Holding Act (ZSDH-1) https://www.zdruzenje-ns.si/db/doc/upl/ssha_1.pdf).

[24] Ministry of Finance and Bank of Slovenia. 2013. "Bank of Slovenia and Slovenian government announce results of stress tests." Press Release. December 12, 2013.

[25] At the beginning of December 2015, Apollo continued to expand into the Slovenian market, taking over Raiffeisen's local branches. According to media reports, Apollo is interested in creating the largest bank in the country through the acquisitions of both private and state-owned banks (*Slovenia Times* 2015).

[26] Ministry of Finance, Slovenia. 2015. "Ordinance on State Assets Management Strategy," July 13, 2015, 70. https://www.sdh.si/Data/Documents/asset-management/State%20Assets%20Management%20Strategy.pdf.

several times.[27] Finally, at the end of 2018, 65 percent of its shares have been sold in an initial public offering (IPO) process on Ljubljana Stock Exchange and on London Stock Exchange for a price of €670 million—to be compared to €1.56bn state aid for the bank in late 2013. The remaining proportion of shares of up to 75% minus one share will be sold by the end of 2019.[28] As for Abanka, the 3rd largest banking group in Slovenia, BNP Paribas has, at the end of 2018, been appointed to act as sole financial advisor to conduct a multi-stage sale process of 100 percent of its shares by end 2019.[29]

As NLB, Abanka and NKBM combined share accounts for around 45% of total banking system assets, the above privatization steps will substantially reduce the level of state ownership in the Slovenian banking sector and, in general, significantly reduce the book value of enterprises owned by the state. The partial privatization of NLB in 2018 and the ongoing privatization of Abanka are necessary steps to remove uncertainty related to a possible demand from the European Commission that the state aid provided in 2013 be repaid. Naturally, all this could have been avoided had the bail-outs occurred up to the end of 2010, when such support could still be exempted from EU state aid rules (see footnote 13).

As for the list of the fifteen SOEs to be privatized—decided upon during the most difficult period in mid-2013, and constantly updated with other SOEs since then—successful sales, as well as processes in progress or with no transactions, can be followed and checked on at the SSH website. As far as details are concerned, what immediately strikes the observer is that all the companies that have been sold passed into foreign hands. The Ljubljana Airport was taken over by German Fraport; Adria Airways

---

[27] To clarify the reasons, let us quote two resources dating from 2015 and 2018 respectively. "The main reason for the slow reduction of the state ownership share in businesses and financial institutions continues to be the lack of political consensus on the withdrawal of the state from ownership of companies" (*IMAD* 2015, 51). "The privatization of NLB has long been a polarizing issue, with the right calling for a prompt sale of the bank and the left insisting the government should do everything it can to delay or suspend the sale" (*Slovenia Times* 2018).

[28] See "First phase of NLB privatisation successfully closed by SSH." SSH website, News, Nov. 14, 2018. https://www.sdh.si/en-gb/news/1708/first-phase-of-nlb-privatization-successfully-closed-by-ssh.

[29] See "Public invitation to submit an expression of interest for the acquisition of 100 percent of the share capital of Abanka." SSH webiste, News, Oct. 11, 2018. https://www.sdh.si/en-gb/news/1687/slovenian-sovereign-holding-acting-on-behalf-of-the-republic-of-slovenia-the-seller-hereby-issues-a-

was purchased by the Luxemburg investment fund 4K Invest through its Munich-based subsidiary (AA International Aviation Holding GmbH); and the airline maintenance company (Adria Airways Tehnika) was bought up by the Polish Linetech. The paint manufacturer Helios was bought by the Austrian company Remho Beteiligungs, (owned, in turn, by Viennese Ring International Holding), Elan sporting goods manufacturer was purchased by the Cyprus-based Wiltan Enterprises Ltd. (owned by Russian VR Global Partners) and American Merrill Lynch International, while the laser systems developer Fotona was purchased by American Gores Laser Holdings. In the car parts industry, Cimos was sold to TCH (part of Italy's investment firm Palladio Holding Group), while Letrika was purchased by Mahle Holding Austria GmbH (directly owned by Mahle GmbH Germany). Finally, food processor Žito became part of Croatian Podravka (known for its internationally famous condiment Vegeta), and hygienic paper products manufacturer Paloma was taken over by Czech Eco-Investment and its Slovakian subsidiary (Eco Invest SVK).

Size, Structure, and National Strategy for the Public Sector

It is not easy to evaluate the role of the state in the Slovenian economy, as this role is in permanent motion. As a consequence of the compulsory settlements and bankruptcies during the crisis, which forced banks to swap loans for equity, the share of SOEs' equity capital vis-à-vis Slovenia's total corporate sector capital increased from 16.4 percent in 2008 to 23.2 percent in 2012.[30] These figures include shares that were bound to rise even further after the aforementioned bank bailouts in 2013–2014 (IMAD 2015, 51).

At the end of 2014, 642 SOEs/SCEs, representing about 1 percent of the total number of companies in Slovenia, were linked to the state via a complex cross-ownership structure (*Figure 3*). Excluding banks, financial services, insurance companies, insolvent and newly (in 2014) established firms, the remaining 561 NFCs[31] accounted for 24.8 percent of net sales, 34.2 percent of assets, 41.8 percent of equity, and 18.8 percent of employees. Based on sectoral value added, state involvement was particu-

---

[30] 30.0 percent if SCEs—state-controlled enterprises in which the state has at least a controlling minority ownership of 25 percent plus one vote—are also taken into account.
[31] Non-financial corporations.

larly strong (i.e., above 50 percent) in transport, energy, public utilities, postal services and ICT, tourism, chemicals, and pharmaceuticals, as well as in some manufacturing and repair. The state appeared as the largest corporate debt holder, as we already mentioned, due to its ownership in the financial sector, and was also the manager of 88 percent of pension assets and 60 percent of all insurance liabilities (Commission 2015, 24–25).

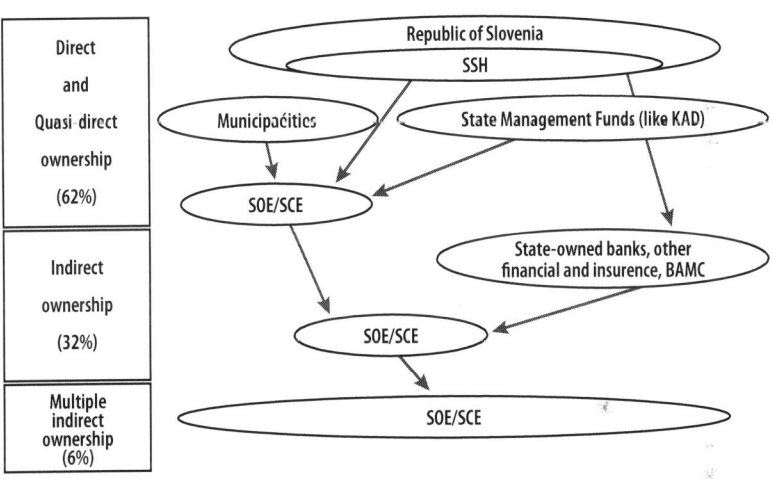

Figure 3
State ownership network in Slovenia
(percent in terms of book value of assets)

Source: Commission 2015, 23-4.

As a final step in the process forcing Slovenia to harmonize itself with OECD standards on state involvement in the economy, the adoption of the State Assets Management Strategy (hereinafter Strategy) in July 2015 provided a legal and institutional framework for the withdrawal of the state from company ownership. It also filled a gap: although ZSDH-1 created categories (strategic, important, or portfolio) for the classification of state assets, it did not assign companies to categories or define performance-related expectations (like the return on equity or assets, EBITDA margin, NPL, or combined ratio) to individual companies (*Slovenian Government* 2015, 51). The Strategy considered twenty-four companies to be strategic (allowing the maintenance of majority state ownership) as they were carrying out key infrastructural duties (e.g., network utilities in energy, transport, and communication), or running natural monopolies (like ports).

Twenty-one companies were classified as important (i.e., with controlling state ownership to be maintained), as they were vital for Slovenia's broader economic development or played an important role in the integration of companies into supply chains, or the internalization of the economy. Finally, forty-six companies were categorized as portfolio assets (i.e., serving only economic objectives).[32]

Final Remarks

In Slovenia, the first wave of privatization ensured a certain degree of continuity and resulted in balanced macroeconomic development, which allowed the old elite to remain involved in the lives of their respective companies. The situation began to go wrong when, during the second wave of privatization, the new elite tried to "complete" their political power with economic strength. This "conquest" came to a head and played a crucial role in causing the Slovenian economy to suffer the deepest slump in the Eurozone since the outbreak of the global crisis. The prolonged, W-shaped recession coupled with political instability strengthened the pressure placed on the Slovenian government by international (including European) institutions to bail-out the largest state-owned banks and undertake the third wave of privatization. The latter process is still ongoing, and—particularly for some banks and the telecom company—the "plans for privatization have been implemented slowly" (Council of the EU 2018, 10). During 2014–15, new laws and ordinances regarding the status and operations of the Slovenian Sovereign Holding company and the adoption of the State Assets Management Strategy were implemented. They can be considered fundamental to a clear and consistent ownership policy that ensures the governance of SOEs in a transparent and accountable manner (i.e., upgraded to OECD standards). They also serve as a legal and institutional framework for the withdrawal of the state from the economy.

---

[32] In the strategy, there was an additional ban on ownership concentration for five "important" companies (NLB, Petrol, Krka, Pozavarovalnica Sava, and Sava),which prohibited private owners from acquiring a stake in a company in excess to that of the state (Ordinance on State Assets Management Strategy (OdSUKND) 2015).

REFERENCES

Arnesen, Leif. 2014. "Rehabilitation of the Slovenian Banking System: Seeking Strength in the Aftermath of a Crisis." *Perspectives on Business and Economics* 32: 78–88.
Bank of Slovenia. 2015. "Report of the Bank of Slovenia on Causes of the Capital Shortfalls of Banks and the Role of the Bank of Slovenia as the Banking Regulator." https://www.bsi.si/en/publications/recovery-of-banks-201314/report-of-the-bank-of-slovenia-for-the-national-assembly-march-2015.
Bertelsmann Stiftung. 2014. "BTI 2014—Slovenia Country Report." https://www.bti-project.org/en/reports/country-reports/detail/itc/svn/ity/2014/itr/ecse/.
Bohle, Dorothee, and Béla Greskovits. 2012. *Capitalist Diversity on Europe's Periphery*. Cornell Studies in Political Economy. Ithaca: Cornell University Press.
Cankar, Stanka Setnikar, and Veronika Petkovšek. 2014. "Fiscal Instability in Slovenia during the Economic Crisis." *Zagreb International Review of Economics and Business* 17 (1): 95–105.
Council of the European Union. 2018. "Council recommendation of... on the 2018 National Reform Programme of Slovenia and delivering a Council opinion on the 2018 Stability Programme of Slovenia." http://data.consilium.europa.eu/doc/document/ST-9450-2018-INIT/en/pdf.
Damijan, Jože P. 2012. "Sloweniens Krise, ein Erbe unbewältigter Geschichte." *Die Presse*, September 8. http://diepresse.com/home/meinung/debatte/1288096/Sloweniens-Krise-ein-Erbe-unbewaeltigter-Geschichte.
European Commission. 2011. "Recommendation for a Council Recommendation on the National Reform Program 2011 of Slovenia." Brussels, 7 June 2011 SEC(2011) 816 Final
———. 2013a. "Commission staff working document, In-depth review for Slovenia." Brussels, 10.4.2013 SWD (2013) 122 final
———. 2013b. "Commission concludes in-depth reviews of macroeconomic imbalances in 13 Member States." Press Release Database, Brussels, 10 April 2013 http://europa.eu/rapid/press-release_IP-13-313_en.htm
———. 2015. "Country Report Slovenia 2015." Commission Staff Working Document. Brussels, (18 March 2015).
———. 2016. "The Bank Assets Management Company (BAMC) and its operations." Directorate D. Government Finance Statistics (GFS) and quality." (3 May 2016)
———. 2017. "Country Report Slovenia 2017 Including an In-Depth Review on the prevention and correction of macroeconomic imbalances." (Brussels, 22 February 2017)
European Council of the EU. 2013. Council recommendation with a view to bringing an end to the situation of an excessive government deficit in Slovenia. http://ec.europa.eu/economy_finance/economic_governance/sgp/pdf/30_edps/126-07_council/2013-06-21_si_126-7_council_en.pdf
Georgieva, Svetoslava, and David Marco Riquelme. 2013. "Slovenia: State-Owned and State-Controlled Enterprises." *ECFIN Country Focus* 10 (3): 1–8. http://ec.europa.eu/economy_finance/publications/country_focus/2013/pdf/cf_vol10_issue3_en.pdf.

Gulyás, László. 2009. "Regionalizáció, regionalizmus és a nemzeti kérdés a titói Jugoszláviában, 1945–1980" [Regionalization, regionalism and the national question in Tito's Yugoslavia 1945–1980]. *Tér és Társadalom* 22 (2): 155–69.
Haček, Miro, Susanne Pickel, and Frank Bönker. 2015. "Sustainable Governance Indicators: 2015 Slovenia Report." Bertelsmann Stiftung. https://www.sgi-network.org/docs/2015/country/SGI2015_Slovenia.pdf.
Ivers, Nicholas. 2014. "State Ownership in the Slovenian Economy: Progress from Catastrophe?" *Perspectives on Business and Economics* 32: 27–35. https://martindale.cc.lehigh.edu/content/slovenia.
Kickert, Walter J. M., Tiina Randma-Liiv, and Riin Savi. 2015. "Politics of Fiscal Consolidation in Europe: A Comparative Analysis." *International Review of Administrative Sciences* 81, (3): 562–84.
Kirn, Gal. 2014. "Slovenia's Social Uprising in the European Crisis: Maribor as Periphery from 1988 to 2012." *Stasis* 2 (1): 106–29. www.stasisjournal.net/index.php/journal/article/download/66/106.
Majnardi, Tilen. 2012. "Mental Bailout." *Slovenia Times*, October 28. Editorial. http://www.sloveniatimes.com/mental-bailout/2.
Marković, Goran. 2011. "Workers' Councils in Yugoslavia: Successes and Failures." *Socialism and Democracy* 25 (3): 107–29.
Mencinger, J. 2006. "Privatization in Slovenia." *Slovenian Law Review* 3 (65): 1–32. http://www.pf.uni-lj.si/media/mencinger.privatization.pdf.
Mrak, Mojmir, Matija Rojec, and Carlos Silva-Jáuregui, eds. 2004. *Slovenia: From Yugoslavia to the European Union*. Washington D.C.: World Bank.
NEOnline. 2017. "Slovenia to Sell its Biggest State Banks." *NewEurope*. December 22 https://www.neweurope.eu/article/slovenia-sell-biggest-state-banks/.
OECD. 2013. "OECD Economic Surveys: Slovenia." April. http://www.oecd.org/eco/surveys/Overview_Slovenia.pdf.
Pevcin, Primož. 2014. "Austerity and Cutback Management in the Public Sector: A Case Study for Slovenia." *Administrative Culture* 15 (1): 80–99. https://www.researchgate.net/publication/286117029_Austerity_and_cutback_management_in_the_public_sector_A_case_study_for_Slovenia.
Prašnikar, J., A. Ferligoj, A. Cirman, A. Valentinčič. 1999. "Risk Taking and Managerial Incentives during the Transition to a Market Economy: A Case of Slovenia." *Management* 4 (1–2): 1–26.
Simoneti, Marko, Matija Rojec, and Marco Rems. 1998. "Slovenia Enterprise Sector: Restructuring and EU Accession." Paper presented at the NATO Colloquium on Economic Developments and Reforms in Cooperation Partner Countries: The Role of the State with Particular Focus on Security and Defence Issues, Ljubljana, Slovenia, June 17–19, 1998. http://www.nato.int/docu/colloq/1998/10-simoneti.pdf.
Simoneti, Marko, Andreja Böhm, Marko Rems, Matija Rojec, Jože P. Damijan, and Boris Majcen. 2001. "Secondary Privatization in Slovenia: Evolution of Ownership Structure and Company Performance Following Mass Privatization." CASE Reports 46. Center for Social and Economic Research. http://pdc.ceu.hu/archive/00004865/01/RC46.pdf.
Simoneti, Marko, and Gregoric, Aleksandra. 2004. "Managerial Ownership and Corporate Performance in Slovenian Post-Privatisation Period." *European Journal of Comparative Economics* 1 (2): 217–41.

Republic of Slovenia. 2007. "Reform Programme for Achieving the Lisbon Strategy Goals: Implementation Report 2007." October. http://ec.europa.eu/social/BlobServlet?docId=6278&langId=en.

Republic of Slovenia. 2008. "Reform Programme for Achieving the Lisbon Strategy Goals: 2008." October. http://ec.europa.eu/social/BlobServlet?docId=6279&langId=en

The Slovenia Times. 2012. "Veto on Bad Bank." October 10. http://www.sloveniatimes.com/veto-on-bad-bank.

———. 2013a. "Stability Programme to Bring in EUR 650M and Cut Expenditure by EUR 716.5M." *The Slovenia Times*, May 11. http://www.sloveniatimes.com/stability-programme-to-bring-in-eur-650m-and-cut-expenditure-by-eur-716-5m.

———. 2013b. "Deal Finally Reached on Sovereign Holding." December 7. http://www.sloveniatimes.com/deal-finally-reached-on-sovereign-holding.

———. 2015. "Slovenian Branch of Raiffeisen Bank Sold." December 10 http://www.sloveniatimes.com/slovenian-branch-of-raiffeisen-bank-sold.

———. 2017. "Govt Suspends NLB Sale Procedure." June 9. http://www.sloveniatimes.com/govt-suspends-nlb-sale-procedure.

———. 2018. "Ball back in Govt Court as Parliament Declines Guidance on NLB." *The Slovenia Times*, July 12. http://www.sloveniatimes.com/ball-back-in-govt-court-as-parliament-declines-guidance-on-nlb.

Smith, Geoffrey T., and Laurence Norman. 2012. "KBC Sells Its Stake in Slovenia's NLB." *The Wall Street Journal*. December 28. https://www.wsj.com/articles/SB10001424127887324669104578206793947429894.

United Nations Conference on Trade and Development. 2004. *World Investment Report 2004: The Shift Towards Services*. Geneva and New York: United Nations. http://unctad.org/en/docs/wir2004_en.pdf.

Vučkovič, Lidija Apohal, et al. 2014. "Development Report 2014." Republic of Slovenia, Institute of Macroeconomic Analysis and Development, July. http://www.umar.gov.si/fileadmin/user_upload/publikacije/pr/2014/Apor_2014.pdf.

World Bank. 1999. "Slovenia, Economic Transformation and EU Accession, Volume II: Main Report." World Bank Country Study. http://documents.worldbank.org/curated/en/724651468301130844/Main-report.

CHAPTER 8

The Role of State Ownership in and after Hungary's Transition to a Market Economy

MIKLÓS SZANYI

Introduction: The Historical Background of State Economic Intervention in Hungary

The discussion of direct state engagement in the Hungarian economy should begin with the classic industrialization policies of the Hungarian state after gaining independence from Austrian dominance in terms of its economic development policies after 1867. Prior to 1867, within the Habsburg Empire, Hungary's role was reduced to supplying food and raw material to the industrialized Austrian and Czech lands. This involuntary division of labor was reinforced by Habsburg monarchs and supported by administrative regulations like the double customs decree enacted in 1754, which practically banned deliveries of Hungarian industrial goods to other regions of the empire outside of this historic Hungarian Kingdom and supported food supplies instead. Prohibitions were lifted only in 1850. In 1867 also, when the political structure of the Habsburg empire changed, and the "Dualist" system was established. Political and economic repressions of the Hungarian parts of the empire were eliminated.

Soon after the transformation of the previous centralization efforts of the Habsburgs, Hungarian industrial development gained momentum. Of course the period was characterized by strong economic growth; nevertheless, the elimination of prohibitions enabled the owners of Hungarian capital to participate in economic development and progress. Parallel with the techno-economic paradigm of the time, major development was underway in railway construction, the production of railway equipment, mining and metallurgy, as well as in agriculture and the production of agricultural machinery. Industrial development was coupled with progress in banking and reforms in education and public administration. The Hungarian part of the Dual Monarchy converged with the traditionally industrialized western provinces. The "golden age" of Hungarian economic development came to an end with its defeat in World War I.[1]

State intervention supporting economic progress was substantial, but it was mainly in the realm of public procurements. Due to dynamic institutional developments, huge construction projects were launched on both the national and local levels, including canalization and river control, railway construction, and the establishment of schools and other public institutions. Many of these large-scale developments were financed by tax revenues from booming agribusiness. But by the end of the nineteenth century, the state intervened more directly through fiscal incentives (tax holidays for industrial investments) and public enterprises, for example railway services and local public services. Over time, the number of state-owned companies increased and their activities expanded to various services and support industries like railway equipment maintenance (Berend and Szuhay 1978).

In the interwar period, the importance of state intervention increased further. This was partly reinforced by the 1920 peace treaty, which required Hungary to cede two-thirds of its historic territory; these lands had been important markets for Hungarian foodstuffs and these territories had also been the center of Hungary's prewar mining and metallurgy industry. A fundamental restructuring as well as the re-creation of vital capacities that had been lost to the Habsburg successor states had to be carried out with significant direct state support, especially in heavy industry and engineering. Huge industrial complexes were constructed in some industrial hot spots. Besides Budapest, Győr and Miskolc became important centers of heavy industry. The process was accelerated after the Bled treaty (1938), which lifted restrictions on the number of Hungarian armed forces and military equipment production. In the process of war preparations, the Hungarian state invested heavily in military equipment production in state-owned firms (e.g., MÁVAG in Győr for airplane and truck production; Diósgyőr Steelworks for guns), but private firms' involvement in military production efforts was also promoted (e.g., the Weiss Manfred Works in Budapest for aircraft, armored vehicles, and

---

[1] Tomka (2011) used more recent GDP figures from the Maddison data base and concluded that the period of the Dual Monarchy was less remarkable, especially in comparison with the interwar period. The relative level of economic development measured by per capita GDP was the highest around 1910 reaching 60 percent of developed nations' average. This was achieved again in 1939 despite the huge economic shocks of loosing World War I and the Great Depression.

ammunition). During World War II, like all belligerents, state control over private firms increased to efficiently support the Hungarian war effort.

State intervention was aimed at promoting the development of the high-tech industries of the time. It is difficult to measure the success of this activity. Since the interwar period was defined by strong protectionism and isolationism, comparing the technological sophistication of products has generally only been possible through the study of armed conflict. During World War I, the technological equipment of the Austro-Hungarian Monarchy was not inferior to its rivals; in some areas, it was a "market leader" (river gunboats, heavy howitzers), although the mass production of innovative products like airplanes and armored vehicles (tanks) was not well developed, and, in some cases was missing altogether. In the aftermath of World War I, Hungarian military equipment production as a whole was vastly inferior to most countries, including smaller states like Romania and Czechoslovakia. Nevertheless, Hungarian industry was capable of applying for German licenses that were readily available only after Allied bombing forced the relocation of production from Germany to Hungary in 1944. For example, the leading German fighter aircraft models were produced in Győr and Budapest according to a bilateral agreement signed in 1942. Thus, the technological competence of specific sectors of Hungarian industry developed significantly, albeit firms had no time to successfully design their own products (Berend and Szuhay 1978).

Given the main focus of this analysis, an important turning point was the end of World War II, when Hungary once again found itself on the losing side. Moreover, Hungary was occupied by Soviet military forces and was transformed into a communist regime by 1948. Between 1945 and 1948, the country paid substantial compensation to the Soviet Union partly in form of deployed manufacturing equipment; after 1948, equipment delivered by the Soviets was used to respond to the losses of equipment and the massive damage caused by the war. In other words, the reconstruction of Hungarian industry was based on Soviet technology. This reconstruction took place in a country that already nationalized all of its major industries, and thus new equipment was delivered through bilateral state agreements to companies owned by the Hungarian state, which was, by then, fully controlled by the communist party.

During the first half of the socialist era, that is from 1948 till the 1960s, Hungarian economic development was relatively similar to that of other Central and Eastern European countries in the Soviet bloc. Economic growth was relatively fast, and new industries based on Soviet technology were also created in the countryside. Development was rather extensive and based on the massive reallocation of the labor force from agriculture to heavy industry. The development of consumer-oriented production and services was neglected. Consequently, the economic structure of Hungary reflected political needs, specifically the production of military supplies in the political conditions of the Cold War. The development of heavy industry was reinforced at the expense of higher living standards and because meeting consumer demand was placed on the back burner. Central planning also preferred large production units; hence another structural feature was the high share of large companies and lack of small and medium-sized ones.

Both structural and systemic problems emerged due to the drive for extensive economic growth. Firm managers and central planners were isolated from market information. They continued to use technologies and prices that had been typical when the system was introduced in 1948. Changes in relative prices on the global markets were not considered at all. The drive for autarchy and the embargo on imports of modern technology from the capitalist world (COCOM) limited the ability of the country to follow changes in technology. In fact, the rigidity of the system of central planning was highlighted in systemic critiques as early as the 1930s (von Mises, Hayek). Also the practice of planning was regarded as necessarily inefficient given the limited computing capacity and lack of detailed overviews of economic processes by bureaucrats. This leads us to the next systemic problem: the lack of proper incentives that resulted in low levels of productivity and waste, as well as low rates of utilization of all production inputs.

Hungarian economists and party and state leaders discovered the shortcomings of the system and made efforts to reform it. Starting in 1968, several waves of reform were introduced under the "New Economic Mechanism." The most important and successful steps were those involving the reintroduction of functioning incentive systems in the economy. On the one hand, firms were allowed to initiate their own production activities provided they had fulfilled their planned deliveries. Revenues from this extra activity were not collected by the state but could be used by firms for a variety of things, including financing additional wages for workers. On the other hand, small-scale private business was permitted again, first for families, but later for an increasing number of regular employees. The independent activity of firms and Hungarian entrepreneurs supported the accumulation of business experience, which proved useful at the start of the economic transition process after 1990.

Another set of measures attempted to deliver market signals in form of global economic prices. Thus, central planners created pricing mechanisms that reflected (with substantial limits) changing price relationships. The period was earmarked by high inflation globally, but central planners did not want to import inflation. However, Hungary did not avoid the oil price shock, and consequently, the authority responsible for setting prices had the difficult task of creating prices that delivered market signals but ignored inflation. In fact, this attempt was largely unsuccessful. The enhanced decision-making freedom of firms included more direct links to foreign markets. As a result, foreign (Western) partners' influence and information delivered market signals on the level of products.

There were also other areas of economic reform that nevertheless could not fundamentally improve the efficiency of the system. This was partly because the measures were always taken half-heartedly, and partly because big businesses were largely exempt from the impact of reforms.[2] Belatedly, during the second half of the 1980s, even a partial introduction of market economic institutions began in Hungary. A new Company Law that envisioned the transformation of state owned enterprises (SOEs) into corporations was enacted. A new, comprehensive tax system was introduced in 1988, which included a VAT, personal income tax, and a corporate tax. Branches of the Hungarian National Bank (the bank fully responsible for maintaining company accounts) were separated and transformed into (state-owned) commercial banks, and a two-tier banking system was created. These later measures formed the legal background of the comprehensive market economic transition that began in 1990 along with the first freely elected Hungarian government after communist rule.

State Ownership and Privatization in the Transition Process: The 1990s

One of the most important postulates of economic transition was privatization along with stabilization, liberalization, and institution building (SLIP). The existence of widespread state ownership was regarded as an essential

---

[2] Tomka (2011) found, based on the Maddison database, that there was no real convergence between Hungary and the developed world even in the 1950s: West European postwar reconstruction produced higher growth than forced industrialization. When the problems of central planning prevailed and the sources of extensive growth were exhausted, economic decline started even in absolute terms. Therefore, by the eve of the political and economic transition, Hungary's relative development level was less than 40 percent of the developed world (measured by per capita GDP figures).

element of the command economy that was to be replaced with a market economy. The simple logic in the political discourse of the time regarded private ownership as the opposite of state ownership just as a market economy was the antithesis of central planning. The political content of privatization was further increased by the strong political and personal relationships between company managers (especially directors) and political/ party leaders. The elimination of the Communist Party's political power was to be accompanied by the destruction of its economic basis, and this was carried out through the privatization of state-owned companies (Frydman and Rapaczynski 1994).

The reform legacy of the Hungarian economy concentrating on efficiency improvements as well as institution building also shaped privatization policies. The need for "real, responsible owners" required privatization options that produced new active and competent owners and concentrated ownership. The need to reorganize and modernize company activity (which proved to be inefficient due to serious structural problems) required new owners who possessed enough capital to be invested. As was shown by some empirical surveys, quick and substantial reorganization and modernization were key elements of the plans to make Hungarian businesses more competitive (Szanyi 1996). SOEs could not afford this due to the lack of capital. They did not accumulate sufficient capital during the years of central planning, and their state owner battled large state debts and could not afford financial supports. Although like most other Central European transition countries, in Hungary several alternative methods of privatization were used, the most important SOEs were sold to foreign investors through open tenders. Privatization was the most important avenue of foreign direct investments (FDI) in the early phase of transition.

Asset transfers started well before the privatization policy took shape in Hungary mainly after 1992. Before that, "spontaneous privatization," or "tunneling," took place, especially between 1989 and 1991. The 1988 Company Law and Company Transformation Law obliged SOEs to transform their legal form into modern corporate forms, and also creating the necessary internal organizational structure. However, the legal form they adopted was not filled with properly functioning actors: the separation of ownership and control rights took place without the nomination or effective presence of the state owner, and controlling managers worked without the effective supervision of the state owner. Ownership rights were spread among various state organs, ministries, and local councils, which could not organize themselves effectively. Until the establishment of the State Privatization Agency in 1992, the state's ownership rights had been hardly represented in SOEs.

Using the lack of supervision, many companies' management took action to strip companies of their valuable assets. Due to the loose and unclear regulations, this practice could not be prevented. According to Laki (2002), many important Hungarian entrepreneurs began their careers as SOE managers and gathered assets through the "spontaneous privatization" process. Others obtained permissions from the foreign trade authority to import necessary goods for the Hungarian market. These entrepreneurs held a quasi-monopolistic position. Laki and Szalai (2013) showed that most of the enterprises that were established on the basis of tunneled assets or monopoly licenses did not survive 1990s. They served market niches and created windows of opportunity that closed after the liberalization of trade and economic activities in Hungary during the 1990's. The owners of these firms possessed special skills for finding loopholes in regulation or had enjoyed useful networking capital to obtain licenses. These skills lost their value during the 1990s with the establishment of the "competition state." As a result, the most viable parts of state assets proved to be those items that were sold to foreign investors through open tenders.

Spontaneous privatization and the early emergence of quasi entrepreneurs during the late 1980s and early 1990s could potentially open up avenues for incumbent managers and party leaders to transform their pre-transition political positions into business opportunities. This could threaten the political goals of privatization (the completion of political transition). However, empirical surveys of Hungarian large-scale entrepreneurs revealed that this did not happen (Laki 2002; Kolosi and Szelényi 2010). The new Hungarian entrepreneurial class and the new business elite that emerged was recruited from the younger generation. Those who used the transition environment to establish themselves in large businesses usually could not maintain their positions after the consolidation of the Hungarian economy (Laki and Szalay 2013). This was not a very surprising outcome in a transition environment in which "capitalism should be created without capitalists" (Kolosi and Szelényi 2010, 10). However, the younger generation's new business elite consisted of various strata. Two of them stood out: genuine entrepreneurs, new business owners, and a new managerial class serving in multinational business. The managerial class can be also treated as a new elite due to its significant influence in business and in politics. Drahokoupil (2008) called it the "comprador service sector," which meant that local elites served interests of multinational corporations. Later, these multinational elites clashed with the local business elite in the Hungarian political arena.

The results of the privatization process can be seen in the data featured in Figure 1. As is clear, the privatization process directly affected a large number of companies. However, due to organizational changes (mainly the splitting up of large conglomerates into smaller firms with more homogenous activity structures or service providers with defined regional markets), the number of firms and their asset value can only be estimated. The valuation of state assets is problematic even today (see Voszka 2013), let alone in the 1990s when the asset value of firms was influenced by uncertainty. SOE's asset value heavily depended on the actual (financial) performance of the company and its relationship to transition policies that largely determined their future market potential and financial position. Typically an SOE accumulated some debt in the period between 1990 and 1992, i.e., the transitional crisis, due to the survival of soft budget constraints inherited from the communist period (Kornai 1993). Despite of the collapse of traditional markets (the trade organization of the Soviet block was dissolved in 1992; trade was liberalized in many commodity groups and international competition grew; public procurements declined due to the debt problems of the Hungarian government), SOEs usually continued production in order to maintain activity and employment (Laki 1994). Sales figures did not improve quickly, product sales could not be transferred to Western markets, and adjustment and modernization efforts were slow due to the lack of a developmental paradigm and a lack of capital to be invested. As a consequence, huge deficits appeared in the economy. Without sales revenues at the top of the value chain, SOEs could not pay for their supplies, and the payment of taxes and social security contributions was also on hold. Debts mounted, and by early 1992, they were as high as 21–22 percent of the GDP (Szanyi 2002). This amount was considered dangerously high (Kornai 1993).

Under such circumstances, the collapse of the Hungarian banking sector was looming, and cash payments were preferred over bank transfers because of the garnishment measures placed on business accounts. In 1992, a harsh bankruptcy regulation was introduced in Hungary. According to this regulation, unlike in traditional bankruptcy regulations where creditors initiate the procedure debtors had to file for bankruptcy (either reorganization or liquidation). Managers of debtor firms had to do this under the threat of legal punishment on their person provided they had any payment obligation overdue by more than 90 days against anybody. Individual CEOs were personally responsible for reporting. The

Figure 1
Privatization and nationalization (revenues and expenditure as per cent of GDP)

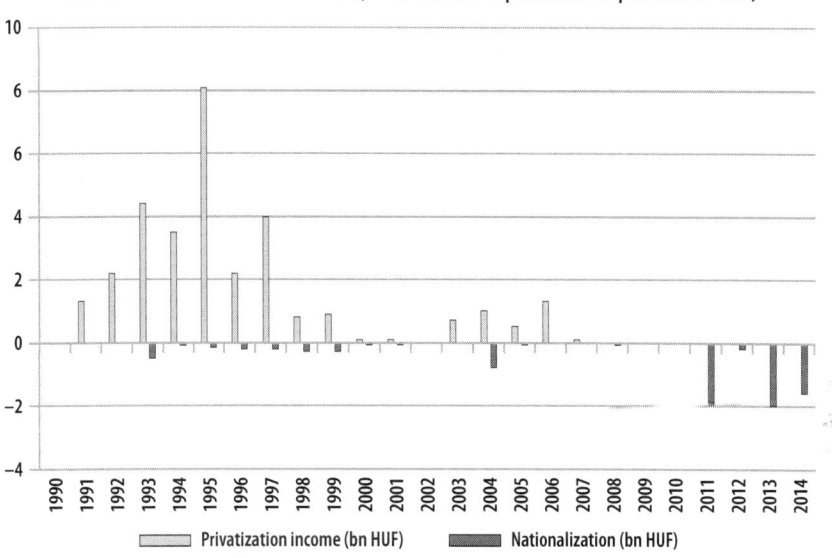

Source: Mihályi (2015, 65)

automatic trigger was in use until 1993, and during the twenty-one months it was in use, over 20,000 bankruptcy cases were filed, among them filings by more than 500 SOEs.[3] There were rather heated debates over the utility of the automatic trigger.

Critics of the automatic trigger argued that defaults on debt were not dangerously high (Bonin and Schaffer 1995; Schaffer 1997) and could have been addressed with other, less radical means. In fact, other analyses proved that the level of intercompany debt was indeed high and was still increasing in 1992. In the following months, the further accumulation of debt was successfully stopped, and the non-performing assets of commercial banks were liquidated and purged. Many claimed that with more patience, many bankrupted firms could have avoided liquidation. Yet the reorganization option was still present, and this procedure could provide

---

[3] The total number of SOEs in 1993 increased from the original 2200 due to the practice of splitting larger entities to more homogenous and easily transferred units (mainly factories). Therefore, we can only roughly estimate that approximately 30 percent of SOEs and state assets underwent either reorganization or, more typically, liquidation procedures.

necessary leeway with the consent of creditors.[4] Therefore, I can conclude that the bankruptcy episode of the state-owned sector during the first half of the 1990s eliminated approximately 15 to 20 percent of SOEs and state assets. Still, the overwhelming majority of this "loss" was due to the inherited structural and systemic problems of firms that could not be repaired due to the lack of market demand. The assets sold through liquidation sales were mainly real estate and were repurposed as other companies' assets. For this reason, the liquidation of SOEs can be regarded as a special form of privatization (Szanyi 2000).

Intertwined policies of the transition process created the specific transition pattern of Central European countries. During the transition crisis in the first half of the 1990s, macroeconomic imbalances, microeconomic adjustment and modernization, the establishment of market economic institutions, and the change in company behavior (hardening firms' budget constraints) were all urgent economic policy targets that also influenced each other. Debates about the sequence and speed of reform was fierce at the time (Roland 2000). Based on the institutional legacy of the reform communist period, the Hungarian government decided to tackle all these issues at once. Some of them were addressed quickly and others more gradually.

The hardening of corporate and also budgetary institutions' financial constraints was an important task that was rapidly addressed because of the rather serious internal and external indebtedness of the government and the country. Unlike Poland, Hungary did not ask international creditors to reschedule debt, hoping that the credibility of the country and government could best be sustained in this way. Income from privatization as well as the temporary introduction of an import surcharge in 1995 would reduce the debt burden. Concern for the credibility of the country paid off with increased foreign direct investments mainly through the privatization process. The massive inflow of FDI effectively helped reduce debt and also relieved the balance of payments. Unlike the Czech Republic, Hungary did not devalue its currency and did not accommodate the transition shocks of exporting firms. The powerful effects of bankruptcy procedures soon separated viable from non-viable parts of the economy, leaving the latter

---

[4] In fact, creditor passivity decreased first on the side of fiscal institutions, the tax authority, and social security institutions several years after the introduction of the automatic trigger.

behind with huge accumulated deficits, although further increases in debt was stopped, and budget constraints were hardened.

The harsh bankruptcy regulation was coupled with the tightening of regulations on commercial banks which would separate liquid assets from non-performing ones and create adequate risk reserves. At this time, most major commercial banks were state owned, and their business policy still reflected some inherited clumsiness and paternalism. Therefore, tighter banking regulations also served the goal of business development on financial markets: the development of banks' market-conforming behavior, especially in their lending policy. The main policy elements of the consolidation of Hungary's economy after transition got underway were bankruptcy, changing the lending policies of banks (less rolling over of overdue debt), as well as a firm commitment from the Hungarian government not to accommodate shocks by financial instruments (in part because of the high level of state debt). The government eventually made exceptions in a limited number of cases. Fourteen large companies were restructured with government assistance with mixed results: half of the bailed-out companies could be at least partially saved and half later went bankrupt. The Hungarian case also proved that shock accommodations mainly served to postpone the SOE exit in most cases. The limited leeway time of companies usually did not trigger effective restructuring efforts in the early transition period, which was still strongly affected by inherited paternalistic relationships and expectations of state bailouts (Szanyi 2002).

During the treatment of both sound and ailing parts of the economy, the Hungarian government's direct economic involvement increased. The State Privatization Agency (later State Property Management Plc.) began to work actively as the representative of the state as owner. The agency necessarily dealt with privatization issues and also controlled the strategic decisions of companies' management, but selling off SOEs to the highest bidders through public auctions remained the chief aim. In order to achieve this, however, the state's asset portfolio had to be improved. Because of the government's firm commitment to hardening budget constraints and preventing the re-emergence of paternalism, only a few SOEs received state support for restructuring.

As a consequence of these complex institutional and policy developments, by the mid-1990s, roughly one-third of SOEs and state assets were bankrupt. Accumulated bad debt was consolidated together with private debts in three steps. First, large parts of the accumulated intercompany debt were transferred to a newly established state owned-bank, the Hungarian Development Bank (MFB) for further management (debt consolidation). MFB took over the debt and the role of creditors in the bankruptcy process and started reorganization in a large number of bankruptcy cases (debtor consolidation). Second, the portfolio of the largest commercial banks was purged of remaining non-performing loans: government bonds helped with their recapitalization (bank consolidation). These loans were basically written off, and not much of these debts could be recovered through bankruptcy procedures. These untainted state-owned commercial banks were then sold to foreign financial institutions through the privatization process. It is difficult to estimate the total cost of the various consolidation programs due to their long-term effects and the involvement of many different agents and practices. Nevertheless, the total amount of consolidated non-performing loans in the banking sector (including private sector debt) is estimated at 350 billion Hungarian Forint (HUF) or 7 per cent of GDP in 1995. State authorities (the tax and customs offices and social security system) recorded a similarly high rate of unpaid obligations that was largely written off (Szanyi 2002). According to the report of the Hungarian State Audit Office, the consolidation of the most troubled institution, Postabank, alone cost 174.5 billion HUF.[5] Therefore, the total cost of debt accumulation during the transition crisis period was very high. However, some of this cost was not the real social cost. The avalanche of bankruptcies created good opportunities for rent seeking SOE managers and cooperating bailiffs to engage in a new form of asset tunneling, which took advantage of the limited control of bankruptcy courts (the shortage of judges) and creditor passivity (Szanyi 1996). Bankrupted state assets were de facto "privatized" in this way, that is transferred to private owners through uncontrolled channels.

Parallel with the privatization campaign of financial institutions, in the second half of the 1990s, many public service providers were also privatized and basically sold to foreign investors. Privatizations in this field were especially complex transactions. These companies operated in regulated markets where active state policies determined many important elements of the activity ranging from technical standards, through the regulation of cooperation contracts, to setting price controls. Selling service providers had to serve the specific interests of several stakeholders: the public (service users), the government (revenues), and investors (adequate profits

---

[5] "174,5 milliárd forintba került a Postabank konszolidációja" [Postabank's consolidation cost 174, 5 bn. HUF]. 17 May 2003. http://www.ma.hu/tart/rcikk/c/0/37058/1.

after modernization investments). Due to the complex nature of the transactions, their success can be measured only with due consideration of the various goals. These transactions later provided ample fodder for criticism concentrating only on specific dimensions of the deals (e.g., the relatively high and guaranteed profits for investors).

State Property Management after 2000

In 2008, the Hungarian government reported that the privatization process was complete (Hungarian Government 2009). Indeed, the frequency and magnitude of changes in state-owned property declined substantially (see data in Figure 1). Privatization as a systemic part of the transition process (the creation of market economy fundamentals) was over. This did not mean, however, that SOEs disappeared completely. Their role changed and was subordinated to the more stable policies of established market economies like competition policy, employment, and in some specific cases, fiscal policy. Some companies were regarded as firms of strategic importance. Active state property management policy was evident in the largest firms with mixed ownership (joint-stock companies), which often became subject to government intervention. For example, the Hungarian government repeatedly blocked attempts by various (mainly foreign) owners to increase or use their ownership rights in large, partly state-owned companies (e.g., MOL, the national oil company, and MVM, the national electric power supplier). Ownership changes in these firms was strongly influenced by the government during the 2000s. A law was modified in order to block the ownership rights of some block share owners who were regarded as unfriendly to Hungarian state interests in other cases, ownership transfers were prevented with claims that they attempted at a hostile takeover. Clearly, the state made efforts to maintain not only its interests, but also its control over these firms. In some cases, assets were sold (eighteen cases reported between 2003 and 2005), but frequently, government control was maintained or even strengthened. The emphasis of state property management shifted from privatization and revenue generation (typical for the 1990s) to asset management (typical after 2000). In this period, both privatization and, in some cases, also nationalization occurred. In some failed privatization deals, the Hungarian state bought back a few companies' shares (e.g., the Hungarian airline company MALÉV) already during the 1990s. Nevertheless, the decline of privatization actions automatically shifted the focus of State Asset Holding plc's (later the Treasury's) activity to active asset management (Voszka 2013).

The shift in focus away from transition-related policies (mainly privatization) to more regular tasks took place gradually during the 2000s. After 2010, the Hungarian government changed its attitude toward foreign-owned businesses and the role of the state was also reconsidered. In some cases, these changes interacted. For example, the government declared the political goal of reducing excessive foreign ownership in the Hungarian banking sector. This goal was achieved by massive renationalization in the sector mainly through government buy-outs of foreign owners in major commercial banks. Some of these assets were then reprivatized to Hungarian capital owners, but in other cases, the state retained these assets (Szanyi 2016). In order to understand the new policies, the main drivers of renationalization and asset management practices must first be analyzed.

The first driver was the traditional argument claiming market failures: important services are either not provided by private firms due to market imperfections or are only in limited scope due to high costs. These vital services (railway transport, public utilities) could be provided by both private and state companies, and during the 1980s and 1990s, the worldwide tendency in this regard was a clear shift from public companies toward private firms. This shift created the most important asset volume for privatization in some of the more developed market economies (e.g., in France and Britain). Also, in transition economies, the prevailing attitude favored the privatization of SOEs in these sectors. Hungary was pioneering in this regard with large-scale sales of various service companies mainly to foreign owners during the 1990s. Nevertheless, the privatization of utility services has never taken place without contradictions. The impact of privatization on the quality or cost of services was not always positive. In Hungary, the situation was also very complex, since privatization and market regulation was carried out simultaneously. Utility firms were sold in packages together with market regulation solutions that had to take into account the conflicting interests of various stakeholders. The modernization of infrastructure required large-scale investments that could be carried out with long-term guarantees of adequate levels of return on investment. This meant relatively high service prices, especially if we consider the middle-income status of Hungary. Thus, the complex issues related to public utility services and financial services could become politically important.

Efficient and cheap public services were also important issues from the economic and social development standpoint. Efficient transport networks were already crucial for increasing mobility during the industrial revolutions of the eighteenth and nineteenth centuries. The creation of adequate infrastructure for economic development was considered a primary interest of the state. As such, this ambition can also be regarded as the first appearance of the developmental state. State ambitions to establish new, high-tech industries appeared on the scene almost simultaneously in the global peripheries. The state played a significant role in the establishment of the railway network and the organization of railway services. It also supported high-tech industries like iron and steel, and railway machinery, construction, and maintenance. Through public procurements, shipbuilding, aviation, and military equipment were also promoted. The state played an important direct economic role in shaping economic structures and increasing the technological sophistication of production. Thus, a second motivation for establishing state control in the economy (mainly in industry) was the ambition of the developmental state. In this regard, the post-transition Hungarian governments did not heavily interfere in market processes. Technological development has not been a strong priority, which is also reflected in the fact that no technology ministry or equivalent organization has existed in Hungary between 1996 and 2018. State ownership could secure some research and development capacity in very few cases.

A selected list of asset management transactions further highlights some of the other political goals and preferences that influenced government decisions. Voszka (2013) and Mihályi (2015) compiled a comprehensive list of renationalizations in Hungary after 2010. Using this information, we would like to describe the primary and typical reasons for, the potential beneficiaries of, and possible political aims of these transactions. Each transaction was explained in some kind of government communication. The explanations shed light on the core elements of state property management policy, which has not been described conceptually up to now. It seems that various, sometimes only loosely connected reasons and considerations supported the most important nationalizations. They fit together only on a very high level of abstraction of the government's general (rather populist) attitudes toward its economic clients, multinational firms and associated businesses—government relationships, the overall desire for ad-hoc, arbitrary decisions instead of normative accountable regulation. Instead of a general policy concept, we can rely on the statements of politicians. Hungarian government officials repeatedly stated that the new economic policy required that at least 50 percent of the Hungarian banking sector to be under national (not necessarily state) ownership, and public utility firms must operate on a non-profit basis. The repeated antiglobalization attacks mainly targeted the largest multinational companies in various service industries. A reduction of Hungary's dependence on the globalized world economy is needed to place financial institutions in national hands (if public, all the better).

When looking over a list of renationalizations (Mihályi 2015, 17), the overall picture shows that between 2010 and 2014, 209 companies were affected, and the total value of transactions was slightly over 1573 billion HUF (approximately €5 billion). This amount included the sales prices paid to previous owners, the increase of share capital, and other commitments as well. The numbers and amounts seem to be very high, especially if we consider that successive Hungarian governments had already accumulated public debt in excess of the Maastricht criteria prior to the 2008–9 crisis. However, as Mihályi (2015) explains, these transactions did not increase state gross debt since they represented a simple change in the asset structure, a kind of securities swap of more liquid assets. However, if we look at the list of transactions, we can discover that the overwhelming majority of the financial commitments stemmed from transactions in the energy and banking sectors (1366 billion HUF). Moreover, the number of affected companies was boosted by a large number of small saving banks (137 financial institutions altogether).

Among the reasons for renationalization, various political aims can be detected. The first outstanding transaction was the nationalization of the second pillar of the pension system at the turn of 2010–11. The official explanation called for accumulated pension funds to be taken out of the hands of private pension funds, which failed to yield the expected returns ("played with hazardous securities"). Account holders of private pension funds were called to withdraw and channel their savings to the state pension system at the risk of losing their pension rights in the pay-as-you-go state pension system. The government applied the "opting out" trick, meaning that those who wanted to keep their pensions untouched had to face the threat, and furthermore, they were required to go through a complicated administrative procedure. Those who accepted the government policies did not have to do anything. Consequently, in the end, 2.8 million account holders channeled their savings back into the state pension system at a value of approximately 3 trillion HUF (€10 billion), which was equivalent to 10 percent of GDP. Most observers believe that the "voluntary" nationalization of private pension funds aimed at using the new assets for debt relief (debt that was partially accumulated by the social security system). The transaction brought in valuable liquid assets to the state budget together with a rather substantial and diversified portfolio of various kinds of securities including corporate shares and bonds. This campaign was the first major, albeit unintended, step toward increasing state ownership in a significant number of commercial companies.

In 2013, the method of regulatory capture was applied in the case of mutual savings banks. First, the state increased the level of required funding capital. Since these small banks could not meet the new obligations overnight, the state itself provided them with the necessary capital and connected this transaction to the acquisition of a controlling ownership share. Owners of the small banks were not asked beforehand but were given an ultimatum in case they rejected the initial generous offer. In 2014, the Hungarian state acquired MKB Bank from its German owners. The German parent bank was unwilling to run its Hungarian child at a loss and sold it to the only serious buyer: the Hungarian state. The losses were, however, caused by various negative changes in the business environment initiated by the Hungarian government (extra taxes on banks' profits, taxes on financial transactions), and losses due to the government-initiated debt relief program offered for the accommodation of increased debt burdens on the foreign currency loans of Hungarian citizens. The achievement of 50 percent national ownership in the banking sector was announced soon after. GE-owned Budapest Bank was purchased by the Hungarian state in 2015, when the American owner decided to abandon this line of business altogether. Later that year, a 15 percent stake in Erste Bank was purchased, increasing the national ownership share in the financial sector to over 60 percent of bank assets. MKB and Takarékbank were soon reprivatized to partisan financial investors (Király 2016). The strong partisan presence in the banking sector may enhance the selective distribution of credits and development aid (e.g., money from EU structural funds).

A larger number of transactions and regulatory changes over a longer period of time were undertaken under the umbrella of cutting utility costs. The promise of savings on utility costs was a major campaign tool of the 2010 and 2014 election campaigns. The government soon prohibited price increases of the public utilities. Later on, prices were set by government agencies at significantly lower levels than before, thereby eliminating profits from this sector. This was the first measure that directly affected the profitability of private businesses. Later, new taxes were implemented on financial transactions, mobile telephone calls, ATM cash withdrawals, advertisement revenues of the media (over certain threshold[6]), among

---

[6] The advertisement tax targeted the large revenues of the German media group RTL. Government communication explained the measure as a reaction to the

others. Limiting utility costs through price decreases resulted in companies moving into the red. Owners soon felt encouraged to sell their loss-producing assets. This process can be called regulatory seizure: company revenues dry up because of unfavorable changes in market regulations or excessive taxes. As a result, many utility firms were sold to national or local public bodies. Some of them received generous compensation (for example German RWE). The purchase of utility firms can be explained by the utility cost reduction policy of the government.[7]

Nationalized utility firms were under foreign ownership, and the regulatory capture and their resulting encroachment by the state indicated a third consideration: unfriendly relationships to selected foreign companies. The Hungarian governments repeatedly enacted market regulations and changed the tax system to capture more of the cash revenues of large multinational firms in order to create more favorable conditions for domestic capital owners. Nevertheless, this sentiment was targeted toward certain types of companies: financial institutions, media firms, large retail chains, and telecom companies. Governmental communications argued that their negative treatment was the result of their failure to contribute to the material (real economic) production platform of the Hungarian economy. This kind of populist confrontation of various economic branches has not been asserted since the beginning of the transition process.

A further important consideration behind renationalization is supporting clients or personal rent seeking. This can take place if market regulations change in favor of the domestic market players. Another possibility is selling (privatizing) acquired assets to clients. In some cases, loss-making companies of clients were bailed out by the state through generous asset acquisitions. The most striking example of this type of transaction was the redistribution of tobacco sales licenses. Tobacco sales were limited to special shops (normal retail stores were deprived of the right to sell tobacco products), and local authorities distributed the new sales concessionary licenses. In several cases, there was evidence that the tenders were not competitive. The political importance of supporting loyal domestic busi-

---

suspected tax evasion of the company. Yet, it was never explained why, if there was something illegal about RTL's taxation, was this not repaired by the responsible state institution or the tax office?

[7] It is, of course, another question if today's sales revenues are sufficiently high for the necessary investments? Observers state that public utility companies are still in extremely bad financial conditions and they do not make further investments, which may threaten the quality of their basic services.

ness people was emphasized several times by the Prime Minister (Mihályi 2015, 19). In addition to loyal capital owners, a wider range of state and party officials who need positions and revenues from the boards of companies are supported. This is the simplest way to reward clients. The right to appoint loyal persons to positions is not necessarily bound to dominant state ownership, but this makes it easier. Rewarding clients is perhaps the most commonly used, secondary (rent seeking) aim of nationalization.

SOEs as Sources of Cash for Political Elites

Material rents stemming from positions of political power occur in all political systems. The extent of rents as well as the number of channels for rent seeking depends on the efficiency of political and social control and democratic institutions. Nevertheless, we should not forget about the major driving force behind the establishment of modern political democracy: curtailing prevailing private (or closed group) interests over the needs of society as a whole. Strong regulatory institutions are important because they limit opportunities for rent seeking; political competition increases the risk of rent seeking. However, this does not mean the elimination of the drivers of corruption. The transition process in CEE could be also interpreted as a competition over the redistribution of economic power. In the case of privatization, this meant the redistribution of existing valuable assets, a process which was, of course, designed and executed by state institutions. The privatization process was the first main field of competition for personal wealth generated by state agencies in transition economies.

There were various political goals to be achieved through privatization including eliminating the business background of communist party members (Frydman and Rapaczynski 1994); the establishment of basic market institutions like the stock exchange; and strengthening the enforcement of property rights (Rapaczynski 1996). Contributions to this thread of literature were influenced much by the activity of the World Bank and the "global advising community" (Appel 2004). They usually took on the position of neutral observer or reformist politician, both of which were characterized by theory-based principles in the process of policy making (in this case, the neoliberal paradigm). Two decades on, we may conclude that this was a rather naïve approach: self-interest has always played a significant role, especially in those areas, like privatization policy, that were directly attached to the acquisition of property.

In this "competition state," the "comprador elite's" material well-being and enrichment was based on the existence and strong influence of multinational companies in the V4 countries. Salaried positions on boards and in the management of firms and advisory institutions as well as banks were filled by ruling party members and their clients. Business and administrative positions were frequently passed around and there was regular personal exchange between administrative and business positions (Drahokoupil 2008). The main beneficiaries of this setting were segments of the elite who supported multinational businesses in order to gain influence in the V4 countries. From the ideological perspective, mainly liberal parties took on this role, but they were frequently the allies of other larger parties that also supported liberal policies. The other main party group, the conservative-nationalist and Christian democratic parties, preferred strengthening a national bourgeoisie and typically did not enter the "comprador elite." "Business firm" parties of the V4 countries usually supported the nationalist agenda.

There is some empirical evidence showing the occupation of corporate boards and advisory committees by politicians and clients in various countries. Of course it is much easier to take up controlling positions in state-owned companies. It can be regarded as a general practice to change not only the supervision but the complete management of SOEs after changes in the government. Most of the empirical evidence is based on this group of companies. Skuhrovec (2014), for example, reported peaks of personnel changes in Czech SOE supervisory boards after election years. This practice eliminates conflicts between the management and the politician, but this also creates the opportunity for milking the SOE in various ways. SOEs can be used for this purpose regardless of their financial position. They are able to provide a continuous cash flow to private hands even from the state budget (in form of subsidies covering SOE financial losses). More typical benefits are bound to various positions in management. SOEs can transfer public revenues to private hands also through payments such as "expert" fees covered by fabricated agency contracts.

Unlike during the heyday of privatization during the 1990s, the main areas of rent seeking shifted from property acquisition, tunneling, and entrance into the sphere of interest of multinational business toward controlling and running enterprises. As was shown by Szanyi (2016), the privatization logic was reversed during the 2000s. Slowing privatization in Poland and nationalizations in Hungary aimed the maintenance and expansion of party-controlled state influence and rent seeking by SOEs. In this period, state ownership served to enrich elites that previously had not joined the "comprador elite group." Of course the decline of available state assets to be privatized also contributed to this. By the 2000s, remaining state property consisted of either notoriously loss-generating companies (the state railways or the Hungarian Post) that were not worth possessing, or they were large service providers that could not be easily transferred to rent seeking private hands but were instead used directly by the state for large-scale rent seeking.

An interesting and detailed empirical study intended to elaborate party-dominated companies' external networks in Hungary (Stark and Vedres 2012). In earlier papers, Stark called attention to the possibility of previous SOEs' incumbent managements' survival and the transfer of their economic power into new business forms using informal networks (Stark 1996; Stark and Bruszt 1998). This conceptualization changed in light of new empirical findings: the dominant networks of the 2000s did not threaten a systemic reversal. The new networks, even if they are controlled by former SOE's managers or Communist Party members, effectively work in the new economic environment. What is new, however, is the spread of partisan firms, in which politicians and their clients control very significant parts of private business beyond SOEs that are also used for rent seeking.

According to Stark and Vedres' (2012) survey, which was conducted with the data on 1,696 large and medium sized companies in Hungary for the period 1987–2001, party members and clients took controlling positions in less than 10 percent of firms on the eve of systemic transformation (1989), but this number steadily grew to almost 20 percent by 2001. Moreover, in terms of capitalization, the share of politicized firms grew from less than 10 percent in 1989 to over 40 percent in 2001. The authors differentiated between the political influence of the two competing main coalitions (right and left) and found that after elections, winning parties' influence accelerated and losers' declined. However, the magnitude of the fluctuation declined and influence became less dependent on government changes. In my interpretation, this meant a marked shift from control over SOEs toward privately owned companies, the management of which remained largely immune to political change.

Summary and Conclusions

Economic development and modernization of Hungary has been historically bound to the presence of foreign capital and the active role of the developmental state. The intensity of the impact of these two driving forces changed over time with the dominance of state policies during the two world wars and under state socialism. The systemic changes of the 1990s put significant emphasis on the creation of market economic institutions and the establishment of tangible private property rights through the process of privatization. The reduction of state property was seen as essential from economic, institutional and also political standpoint. The process overlapped with the overall neoliberal-minded current of the time and favored private property over state ownership even in cases like public service provision, where ownership patterns have always been the subject of discussions. By the end of the 1990s, the overwhelming majority of state assets were privatized; to large extent they had been sold to foreign capital owners. Besides privatization, various types of asset tunneling also played a role in transforming state property into private property. Loose owner control in the initial phase of the transition process created space for this. Later, it was mainly in connection to the liquidation of bankrupted state assets that concerns about fraud were articulated by some experts.

During the 2000s, the emphasis of state property policies shifted from privatization to asset management. State assets were treated as valuable tools to achieve certain political goals that could increase the reputation of incumbent governments, most importantly, cutting utility costs through state-owned service providers. But governments also used SOEs to increase fiscal revenues, increase employment, and limit dependence on multinational businesses. This later ambition was reinforced through rather populist, anti-globalization arguments and was coupled with other administrative measures intended to curtail the activity of foreign companies in Hungary.

A further component of increased interest in state asset management was personal and party-based rent seeking. Rents coming from the operation of SOEs is not uncommon in any market economy. The most obvious forms are filling companies' leadership ranks with party members or loyal personnel to be rewarded. SOEs are also suitable tools for channeling budgetary resources to politically determined private uses through outsourcing contracts or sponsorship activities. Empirical evidence indicates that this role and politically controlled businesses in general increased in size starting in the 1990s thereby creating the economic foundations of political parties. During the 2000s, SOEs' role in this did not increase because political parties successfully developed partisan businesses that could directly access public monies mainly through public procurement tenders.

REFERENCES

Appel, Hilary. 2004. *A New Capitalist Order: Privatization and Ideology in Russia and Eastern Europe.* Pittsburgh: University of Pittsburgh Press.
Berend, T. Iván, and Miklós Szuhay. 1978. *A tőkés gazdaság története Magyarországon 1848–1944* [Capitalist economic history in Hungary 1848–1944]. Budapest: Kossuth.
Bonin, John P., and Mark Schaffer. 1995. "Banks, Firms, Bad Debts and Bankruptcy in Hungary 1991–94." CEP Working Paper 657. Centre for Economic Performance, London School of Economics and Political Science.
Drahokoupil, Jan. 2008. "Who Won the Contest for a New Property Class? Structural Transformation of Elites in the Visegrád Four Region." *Journal for East European Management Studies* 13 (4): 360–77.
Frydman, Roman, and Andrzej Rapaczynski. 1994. *Privatization in Eastern Europe: Is the State Withering Away?* Budapest–New York: CEU Press.
Hungarian Government. 2009. J/8582. "Jelentés az ÁPV Zrt. és jogelődei mint a privatizáció lebonyolítására létrehozott célszervezetek—tevékenységéről és a teljes privatizációs folyamatról (1990–2007)" [Report about the activity of ÁPV RT and its predecessors: Organizations established for the conduct of privatization- and the entire privatization process (1990–2007)] http://www.kozlonyok.hu/nkonline/MKPDF/hiteles/MK09036.pdf.
Király, Júlia. 2016. "A magyar bankrendszer tulajdonosi struktúrájának átalakulása" [The transformation of the ownership structure of the Hungarian banking sector]. *Közgazdasági Szemle* 63 (7–8): 725–61.
Kolosi, Tamás, and Iván Szelényi. 2010. *Hogyan legyünk milliárdosok? A neoliberális etika és a posztkommunista kapitalizmus szelleme* [How to become billionaires? Neoliberal ethics and the spirit of post-communist capitalism]. Budapest: Corvina.
Kornai, János. 1993. "The Evolution of Financial Discipline under the Post-Socialist System." *Kyklos* 46 (3): 315–36.
Laki, Mihály. 1994. "Firm behavior during a long transitional recession." *Acta Oeconomica* 46 (3–4): 347–70
———. 2002. "A nagyvállalkozók tulajdonszerzési esélyeiről a szocializmus után" [About the chances of obtaining property by entrepreneurs after socialism] *Közgazdasági Szemle* 49 (1): 45–58.
Laki, Mihály, and Júlia Szalai. 2013. *Tíz évvel később—a magyar nagyvállalkozók európai környezetben* [Ten years later: Hungarian entrepreneurs in the European environment]. Budapest: Közgazdasági Szemle Alapítvány.
Mihályi, Péter. 2015. "A privatizált vagyon visszaállamosítása Magyarországon 2010–2014" [Renationalization of privatized assets in Hungary 2010–2014]. IE Discussion Paper. MT-DP-2015/7 Institute of Economics, HAS, Budapest.
Rapaczynski, Andrzej. 1996. "The Roles of State Property and the Market in Establishing Property Rights." *Journal of Economic Perspectives* 10 (2): 87–103.
Roland, Gérard. 2000. *Transition and Economics, Politics, Markets and Firms.* Cambridge, MA; London: MIT Press.
Schaffer, Mark E. 1997. "Do Firms in Transition have Soft Budget Constraints? A Reconsideration of Concepts and Evidence." *Journal of Comparative Economics* 26 (1): 80–103

Skuhrovec, Jiří. 2014. "The Unreasonable Lightness of Stuffing Czech Company Boards with Political Cronies." *Visegrad Revue*, March 17. http://visegradrevue.eu/the-unreasonable-lightness-of-stuffing-czech-company-boards-with-political-cronies/.

Stark, David. 1996. "Recombinant Property in East European Capitalism." *American Journal of Sociology* 101 (4): 492–504.

Stark, David, and László Bruszt. 1998. *Postsocialist Pathways: Transforming Politics and Property in East Central Europe*. Cambridge: Cambridge University Press.

Stark, David, and Balázs Vedres. 2012. "Political Holes in the Economy: The Business Network of Partisan Firms in Hungary." *American Sociological Review* 77 (5): 700–22.

Szanyi, Miklós. 1996. "Adaptive Steps by Hungary's Industries during the Transition Crisis." *Eastern European Economics* 34 (5): 59–77.

———. 2000. "Bankruptcy, Liquidation and Full Settlement as Methods of Privatization." In *Privatisation in Hungary*, edited by Ágota Erőss, 51–74. Budapest: Állami Privatizációs és Vagyonkezelő Rt.

———. 2002. "Bankruptcy Regulations, Policy Credibility and Asset Transfers in Hungary." IWE Working Paper 130. Institute of World Economics, HAS, Budapest.

———. 2016. "The Reversal of the Privatization Logic in Central European Transition Economies." *Acta Oeconomica* 66 (1): 33–55.

Tomka, Béla. 2011. *Gazdasági növekedés, fogyasztás és életminőség: Magyarország nemzetközi összehasonlításban az első világháborútól napjainkig* [Economic growth, consumption, and quality of life: Hungary in international comparison from World War I to today]. Budapest: Akadémiai Kiadó.

Voszka, Éva. 2013. "Államosítás, privatizáció, államosítás" [Nationalization, privatization, nationalization]. *Közgazdasági Szemle* 60 (12): 1289–317.

CHAPTER 9

The Changing Role of the State in Development in Emerging Economies: The Developmental State Perspective

JUDIT RICZ

Introduction

Fifteen years have passed since the seminal work of Hall and Soskice (2001) on Varieties of Capitalism (VoC), and extensive literature has emerged since then, which can be structured into possibly four generations. The first, the classical school of VoC, mostly relates to Hall and Soskice's work (see also Amable 2003) and the differentiation of liberal market economies (LME) (e.g., the U.S., U.K., Canada, Australia, New Zealand, Ireland) and coordinated market economies (CME) (e.g., Germany, Japan, Sweden, Austria). The second generation is generally labeled post-VoC literature and aims at developing further types of capitalist models, mainly related to different regions or groups of countries. In this regard, the dependent market economy model (Nölke and Vliegenthart 2009) can be highlighted, but also the work of the Hungarian scholar Beáta Farkas (2011 and 2017), who analyzed Central and Eastern European (CEE) countries in this framework. The third generation of VoC literature is called critical comparative capitalism (CC), and it mainly deals with more critical, global approaches and most current issues such as international economic integration (e.g., the Eurozone crisis) and tries to incorporate the demand side of analysis (see e.g., Ebenau et al. 2015; Farkas 2016). A fourth generation of VoC research is currently emerging, although this differentiation is made on a rather speculative basis. There are some works and signs indicating that VoC analysis has recently (during the last two to three years) moved toward intertemporal (instead of international) comparisons attempting to define and characterize historical phases rather than simply building valid models for certain countries or world regions.[1]

---

[1] Andreas Nölke drew attention to recent developments in VoC research in his presentation at the international conference on "The Role of State in Varieties

According to this theoretical structure, we see two entry points for our essay: first, emerging countries, even while gaining weight in the world economy and politics, have been generally left out by traditional VoC analysis (with some exceptions, such as Schneider 2009 and 2013; Nölke et al. 2015). Second, intertemporal comparisons are also often missing. Thus, we argue that studying historical development success stories and defining historical role models and lessons are valid research objectives.

The following chapter in this volume focuses on emerging economies and analyzes some of their success stories and divergent paths of development. Emerging countries have increased their share in the world economy substantially over the last decades. After the first[2] and second[3] generation of newly industrialized countries (NICs), more recently, we have witnessed the rise of large emerging economies, such as China, India and Brazil.[4] Despite annual fluctuations and some rather negative tendencies more recently (the crisis in Brazil starting in 2014, or the deceleration of economic growth in China since 2010), there is no well-grounded reason to assume that the long-term rise of these large emerging economies will be reversed and their weight in the global economy will substantially diminish (May and Nölke 2014).

Looking at both historical and contemporary development success stories it is conspicuous that these have been rather neglected by VoC analysis until recently. Some more recent works have attempted to fill this gap, however, these are exceptional and do not follow the mainstream currents

---

of Capitalism (SVOC): Achievements and challenges for Central and Eastern Europe and the emerging markets," organized by the Institute of World Economics (IWE), Center for Economic and Regional Studies (Hungarian Academy of Sciences) and the Center for EU Enlargement Studies (CENS, Central European University) on November 26–27, 2015 in Budapest.

[2] Besides Japan, South Korea, Taiwan, Hong Kong and Singapore are generally referred to as the first generation of NICs.

[3] Mainly referring to Southeast Asian countries, such as Malaysia, Thailand, the Philippines, and Indonesia.

[4] In line with the rise of economic power, geopolitical ambitions and institutional efforts have also appeared, as the large emerging economies of the Global South have begun to organize themselves and institutionalize their cooperation more recently. Examples are numerous: the IBSA Dialogue Forum (India, Brazil, and South Africa), the BASIC alliance (also including China), or the BRICS grouping (including Russia). Regarding the VoC approach and especially the role of state in development, we argue that South Africa and Russia are outliers, and the state-permeated variety of capitalism (state capitalism 3.0) is valid for China, India, and Brazil (see Nölke 2014).

of political economy analysis. Nölke (2014) and his co-authors have analyzed large emerging economies, the BICS group (Brazil, India, China and South Africa), and constructed the model of state-permeated capitalism. Kurlantzick (2016) and Wylde (2017) speak about the rise of state capitalism and developmental regimes (respectively) in the twenty-first century's emerging markets, while Schneider (2013) focused on Latin America and proposed the hierarchical market economy model to describe the *latino* variety of capitalism.

However, we start our theoretical introduction a few decades earlier. As we will argue throughout this chapter, there is a distinct thread in development economics, which can be regarded as the antecedent to VoC literature. Dating back to the 1980s and 1990s, the *developmental state school* has intensively analyzed a special variety of capitalism.

The first milestone in this line of inquiry was Chalmers Johnson's (1982) book on the Japanese miracle, in which the Japanese model of development was described as a capitalist plan-rational developmental state (DS). With this distinction, Johnson's main aim was to go beyond the contemporary dichotomous thinking shaped by the confrontation of the American and Soviet economies, i.e., capitalist versus socialist development. Johnson basically wanted to draw attention to the differences between the capitalist systems of the United States and Britain on the one hand, and Japan and its East Asian disciples on the other hand (Johnson 1999, 32). In this vein we argue that Johnson's work and that of his disciples in the revisionist school (developmental state literature) can be considered a quasi-forerunner of the Variety of Capitalism school.

There is also another argument to more thoroughly analyze the developmental state perspective, namely, the early VoC works have more often than not neglected to consider the role of state in development. Therefore, we are convinced that in order to better understand how state intervention may influence capitalist models currently, it is worth starting our theoretical introduction by looking at the historical model of the Japanese developmental state and the analytical framework of the developmental state literature. Moreover, the economic and developmental role of the state has been moved back to the center of economic debate. Following the financial and economic crisis of 2008–9 and in light of the prolonged economic recovery afterwards, we can observe different types of active state interventions and growing state involvement to reduce the effects of the crisis and to revive economic growth and development throughout the world. Simultaneous with this shift in the practice of economic policy-making, we can witness the renaissance of developmental state literature in economics. By the end of this chapter, we will argue that this new scholarly current is not the revival of the old or classical paradigm of developmental states (Woo-Cumings 1999), but the emergence of a new developmental state concept (though the breakthrough of a new paradigm has not yet occurred).

The chapter is divided into five sections: following the introduction, in the second part we define developmental states and then sum up main elements of the classical developmental state paradigm (DSP) based on Northeast Asian experiences, while embedding it in its global and regional context. In the third part, we argue that, due to substantial changes in the context, the classical DSP had run its course by the 1997–99 Asian Financial Crisis at the latest, and thus the theoretical concept has also collapsed. In the fourth part, we turn toward more recent changes: we provide an overview of the new challenges emerging (or intensifying) since the millennium, and based on most recent developmental state literature, we highlight the main elements of the new DS concept, which is still developing. Finally, we will present our conclusions.

Developmental States: A Special Variety of Capitalism

In the introduction we argued that the developmental state school should be considered a forerunner of VoC literature, with a special emphasis on emerging economies. We have also addressed the problems associated with the delineation of "emerging countries," and the controversies concerning BRICS and other acronyms. In reality, we can see that there is only a handful of countries that have managed to historically catch up with more developed countries. Examining per capita real incomes and defining catching up as the move from the low to middle, or middle to high income category (as defined by the World Bank) the following figure shows that out of 101 middle-income economies in 1960, only 13 became high income by 2008. Among those countries catching up, we can find a number of countries often dubbed as developmental states: Hong Kong, Ireland, Israel, Japan, Mauritius, the Republic of Korea (South Korea), Singapore, Taiwan and China.[5]

---

[5] We do not address the cases of the South European countries (Spain, Portugal, and Greece) here, and, for the rather obvious reason of resource (oil and gas-) dependency, we also leave out Equatorial Guinea.

Figure 1
Per Capita Incomes Relative to the United States, 1960 and 2008

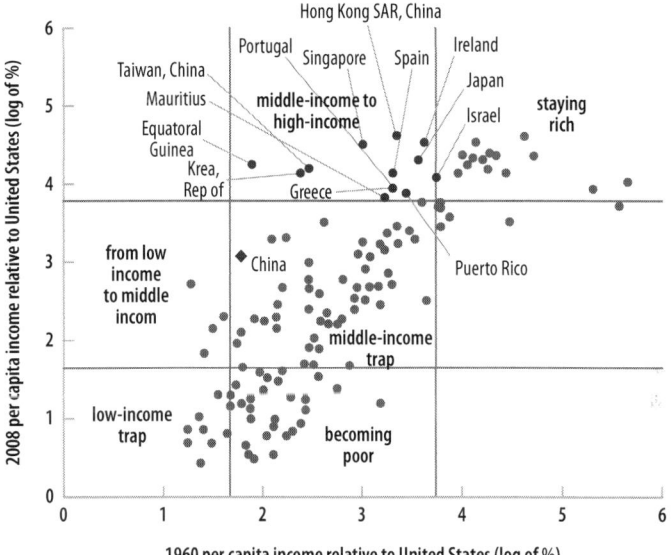

Source: Reprinted from the World Bank (2012, 2)

Even though in the following sections we will argue that the developmental successes (miracle) of the classic developmental states of Northeast Asia went well beyond mere economic terms and GDP growth, this figure is indicative not only for those reaching outstanding performance, but also for those (countries of Latin America and Middle East) that remained trapped in the middle after initial success (World Bank 2012), such as Brazil or Turkey.

In the following, however, we concentrate on the success stories of the attractive emerging countries that became known in development economics as developmental states. The classical paradigm of developmental states was based mainly on the experiences of North- (and later on also South-) east Asian countries. Therefore, our focus will be on the distinctive features of their state-led market economy models.

Defining Developmental States

At the latest, by the millennium the term "developmental state" became a buzzword (Fine et al, 2013, 3; Routley 2014, 159), as it has become "a generic term to describe governments that try to actively "intervene" in economic processes and direct the course of development rather than relying only on market forces" (Beeson 2007, 141). We are convinced, however, that in light of revived debates on the role of the state in development, the concept of developmental states is still a useful tool to promote clear and reasonable academic debate. It is necessary to stick to a clear definition,[6] and for this reason the original formulation of Johnson is a good starting point.

Accordingly, the term developmental state refers to: 1. a capitalist model: private property dominates the economy (no ideological commitment to state ownership); 2. a state-led development model: bureaucratic coordination replaces market coordination, and the active (even pro-active) interventions of state reach all parts of economic life, while discretional and selective interventions dominate; 3. the central role of economic (development) planning: medium and long term economic plans are formulated and implemented (though often in a pragmatic, rather flexible manner); 4. a long term commitment to a development-oriented approach (not US-style regulation or a Soviet-style socialist approach); 5. wide social consensus regarding both the central role of the state in promoting development and the most important social and economic priorities (with high-speed economic growth and catching up as the most important ones) (Johnson 1982, 19–23).

The archetype of classic developmental states was the Japanese model as described in Johnson's (1982) famous book, even though he was not the first[7] or the last attempt to describe and analyze developmental states.

---

[6] We have argued elsewhere (Ricz 2017a) that it is not justifiable to call any active, interventionist state (that relies on selective industrial policy measures) a developmental state—as they often are by the media, in policy discourse, and even in some scholarship—as it is a much more complex institutional solution and policy concept.

[7] Developmental states, of course, existed already well before Johnson wrote his seminal work and also in other regions of the world. Chibber (2005) and Bagchi (2004) consider, for example, the developmentalist experiments of Turkey, Brazil, and India as the first (less successful) attempts to build developmental states. In Latin America, Cardoso and Faletto (1979, 143–48) made the first reference to "developmentalist states" in their very influential book, *Dependency and Development in Latin America*.

During the following decades, this concept has been applied and expanded to several other countries: first, to Northeast Asian countries such as South Korea, Taiwan, Hong Kong, and as the only Southeast Asian country in this group, Singapore,[8] (the first generation of newly industrializing countries—NICs), and then to other Southeast Asian countries, including Malaysia, Thailand, the Philippines, and Indonesia (second-generation NICs). Later it became common to characterize the state-led developmental approach of some European (such as France, Finland, Ireland) and emerging countries (such as Brazil—see Chapter Twelve in this volume—India, Turkey—see Chapter Eleven in this volume—and Egypt) in this way, while more recently, it is also often associated with the Chinese case and to some fast-growing African economies (such as Rwanda, Ethiopia, or even South Africa).[9]

The Classical Paradigm of Developmental States

Vast literature on developmental states has emerged since the conceptualization of the original idea of Chalmers Johnson's (1982) plan-rational capitalist developmental state, the Japanese model. In this section, we aim to summarize the most important features of the classical model of developmental states based on the experiences of Northeast Asian countries (Japan, South-Korea, Taiwan, Hong Kong, and Singapore).[10] The most important elements of the model are relevant and applicable to the development experiences of Southeast Asian countries, such as Malaysia, Thailand, the Philippines, and Indonesia.[11]

To establish the foundations of the classical model of DS, we rely on core DS literature, such as Johnson (1982), Amsden (1989), Wade (1990),

---

[8] See Chapter Ten in this volume.
[9] For a breakdown of states considered to be developmental in both historical and contemporary scholarship, see Routley (2012, 11–12).
[10] The Japanese case is, in several aspects, unique, and the two city-states (Hong Kong and Singapore) deviate from the structuralist point of view. Yet it is still argued in literature that these Northeast Asian countries have relied on such a similar economic policy mix, that it makes them a unique group that is different from most other regimes" (Pempel 1999, 160).
[11] The main differences of North and Southeast Asian countries are highlighted by Booth (1999). For the specificities of Southeast Asian development models, see Raquiza (2012).

Evans (1995), Leftwich (1995), and the synthetic works of Onis (1991) and Woo-Cumings (1999).

Below are the most important dimensions of the classical paradigm of developmental states, based on the experiences of Northeast Asian developmental states between 1965 and 1990, the so-called economic miracle period.[12] This will serve as a reference point for the case studies presented in the following chapters.

The classical model of the developmental state contains the following elements:

1. Economic nationalism and social mobilization.
2. A strong, centralized and authoritarian state:
    i. Relative autonomy from influence of social groups.
    ii. A small and determined elite.
    iii. The state's power to discipline business.
    iv. A developmental dictatorship.
3. Wide-ranging interventionism and the central role of industrial policy (selective and discretionary measures and the practice of picking winners).
4. The central (economic, political, and social) role of large diversified business groups.
5. A meritocratic bureaucracy with embedded autonomy.
6. The primary role of the agricultural sector and land reform.
7. Export-oriented economic development strategy with state guidance and market-conforming methods.
8. Financial repression
    i. Based on high domestic savings, and fiscal and other incentives by the state, and state moves toward subsidized, strategic industries.
    ii. Implicit and explicit state guarantees.
    iii. Bailout policies (and practices) toward financial institutions as well as the business sector.
    iv. Limited entrance into financial markets.
    v. The closed and subordinated role of capital markets.
9. Macroeconomic stability and good macroeconomic management.
10. Shared and equitable growth.

---

[12] The high-performing Asian economies (Japan, Hong Kong, the Republic of Korea, Singapore, Taiwan, Indonesia, Malaysia, and Thailand) reached outstanding growth performance between 1965 and 1990, with a yearly average of 5.5 percent growth rates in GDP per capita, outperforming any other region in the world (World Bank 1993, 2).

Due to space constraints and the main focus of the current volume, one aspect of the above list will be highlighted, namely the pivotal role of the state versus large diversified business groups in economic catching up. Even though we have labeled Japan, South Korea, Taiwan, and Singapore as developmental states, there were significant differences in both their economic structures and strategies. While in Japan, private corporate groups, *keiretsus*, revolved around a central financial institution, in the case of the Korean *chaebols*, there was no such financial hub. At the same time, the industrial structure of Taiwan was more dominated by smaller companies, while in Singapore, a large state-owned enterprise sector has evolved. Financial sectors have also differed in their structure: in Japan, most banks were privately owned (and strongly linked to business conglomerates), but the Bank of Japan and the public postal saving system were key components of the financial hierarchy. In South Korea, almost the entire banking sector was private; however, the role of government in directing capital toward selected sectors (and companies) has been crucial. In Taiwan, mainlander control dominated the banking sector, while the financial and industrial spheres were kept relatively separate (Pempel 1999, 150). The role of foreign investment has also been different, and, in general, played a much more important role in the South Korea and Singapore, while it was largely excluded in Japan.

All in all, although state influence was present and has been a dominant feature of classic development states, their economies were mainly dominated by private companies, and state influence was exerted often via indirect means (not by ownership, but in terms of close state and big business relations, or via financial repression). However the power of the state to discipline big businesses was strong (at least initially) in all classic DS, and in exchange for generous state support, international competitiveness was expected as "each regime has operated with an eye toward world market" (Pempel 1999, 173). Thus state interventions have reinforced market principles, at least in their international dimensions (the domestic marketplace was dominated by entry barriers and oligopolistic structures).

According to Johnson (1998, 653), the classical model of developmental states, based on Northeast Asian experiences, consists of "...Asian values on subjects such as the nature of government, priority given to the community over the individual, and government guidance of a nonetheless privately owned and managed market economy, with economic growth tied above all to exports." Thus, it refers to a state-led market economy, and a capitalist model with substantial economic growth and increasing wellbeing intended to serve the whole society (a growth-with-equity approach).

The Context of Economic Success in Northeast Asian Developmental States

To fully understand the success and failure of the classical model of DS, we have to put it in its historical and institutional context, as these unique conditions contributed to these countries' overwhelming economic success, while at the same time, they made the model non-transferable and unrepeatable in other times and places (Pempel 1999, 180).

The historical interplay of (political, economic, ideological, social, regional, and security) forces has contributed to the East Asian economic miracle.[13] Some of these were temporal related, while others were geographically determined and region specific.

We distinguish three elements of the general environment: 1. The global political context of the postwar period (the national capitalist development concept, economic nationalism). 2. The global economic context of the post-war period (the neo-mercantilist approach, growing protectionism, relatively closed economic systems and models). 3. The context of late-development (national-based Fordist capitalism, the promotion of strategic national industries, and, in the context of underdevelopment, mass poverty and infrastructural deficiencies caused by the destruction of war and economic catching up as the first priority supported by wide social consensus). These permissive global conditions meant that national economic performance depended, to a large degree, on the competitiveness of large national firms, and created the basis for national dirigist state-led development policies.

In addition, three region-specific conditions have also substantially contributed to the unique context of the Northeast Asian developmental experience. First is Japan's outstanding role within the region: 1. as a former colonial ruler (which created the important institutional setting); 2. as an important economic donor, providing development aid, and, later on, capital; 3. in more general terms, as the regional economic leader (providing markets and serving as an economic partner); and 4. as a role model

---

[13] See also Doner, Ritchie, and Slater's (2005) arguments on the interactive conditions of systemic vulnerability present in the case of Northeast Asian DS. But the lack of these led to much less ambitious state-building efforts and, thus, much less outstanding development outcomes in Southeast Asian countries.

for economic development. Second, the complex role of the United States in security and economic policy, whereby it provide: 1. development and military aid based on geopolitical considerations; 2. foreign direct investments; 3. preferential market access; and 4. in more general terms, the commitment of the U.S. to ensure the stability of the region by all means (to stop the spread of socialism-communism, and to secure the border between the two poles in the Cold War). All of these have produced substantial implicit and explicit benefits for the development of the Northeast Asian region. As a third special condition, we highlight historical and cultural factors: most countries in this region have relatively homogenous societies (with small ethnic, religious, racial, linguistic, or other differences); have inherited extensive and high quality institutional systems from the colonial period (for example strong and well-performing core administrative systems, extensive, high quality educational systems). Asian cultural values have also played pivotal role by placing the community and its priorities above individual interests, which has had wide ranging economic consequences. Two examples of this are: the very strong individual commitment and maximizing efforts to contribute to the implementation of community priorities (resulting, for example, in extremely long working hours compared to European standards); and second, the provision of social security and welfare primarily through the family, community, and business enterprises has freed up important state resources.

We have summed up the most important characteristics of Northeast Asian developmental states, which is also called the classical paradigm of the developmental state. We have embedded Northeast Asian experiences, namely the region's economic miracle, in its proper historical and geographic context. During the 1990s (with some processes starting even before then), these general and specific conditions have substantially changed and fragmented the internal and external coherence of the model, which has led to the decline of the classical model of the developmental state (Benczes 2000 and 2002; Woo-Cumings 1999; Ricz 2017a).

The Fall of the Classical Developmental State Paradigm (DSP)

During the 1980s and 1990s, substantial changes took place in the external and internal environments of classic developmental states and have led to changes in individual states' room to maneuver. However, these changes have also altered expectations and perceptions as well as the decisions of economic actors and individuals. Altogether, this meant that the specific context that enabled the success of traditional developmental states (as discussed in the previous section) has changed significantly and led to the demise of the classical model.

The Asian financial crisis of 1997–99 (AFC) was a milestone signaling the end of an era (and the beginning of a new one). However, changes in the specific context of the classic DS already started years and decades earlier and accrued, culminating in the AFC.

The classical DS model emerged in a closed economic system in which trade flows dominated interactions between national states. The structural transformation of the global economy started already by the end of 1960s, leading to an open global economy dominated by capital flows and transnational corporations transcending national borders.

Another dimension of the structural transformation of the global economy has been the rise of the service sector's weight and the emergence of the bit-based knowledge economy. This led to the appreciation of human capital investments, access to information and innovation, and networking activities. Technological changes have not only affected sectors of the new economy, but have altered the organizational forms of traditional economic activities as well as modes of corporate governance.

Changes in the global financial system have been even more striking than changes in the economic production system described above. Financial globalization led by the private sector has intensified since the 1970s. Several interconnected elements can be highlighted: the deregulation of financial systems, the separation of the flow of goods and financial flows, the growing weight of speculative transactions, the intensification of capital flows, the appreciating role of stock exchanges, and the virtualization of financial transactions. All these processes taken together have significantly altered the options available to finance a nation-based development model.

Today's economic environment and structures substantially differ from those that reflected the specific context of late developing states during the 1970s. Changes were even more pronounced in the financial sector. Financial liberalization, globalization, and open capital accounts have placed efficient resource allocation at the heart of any current development strategy. Gone are the days of financial repression and selective industrial policies directed by the state and its bureaucracy as was common in the case of the classic DS. In light of ever more complex economic activities, the state or any other actor is less and less able to collect sufficient information to directly and successfully intervene in the shaping of industrial structures or select leading industrial sectors or enterprises.

In line with changes in economic structures and the transformation of the financial system, global governance and the regulatory environment has also significantly changed (see e.g., the World Trade Organization, Basel Accords, International Accounting Standards, etc.). This new institutional and regulatory setting significantly constrains developmental states' room to maneuver and their ability to apply classic tools of economic stimulation and deploy repressive financial practices.

International political and ideological settings have also changed. The end of the Cold War and the effects of postcommunist countries' transition have all contributed to significant changes in the specific context of the classic DS. It is enough to recall that the end of China's forty years of sequestration from the global economy has had an unprecedented effect on the international competitiveness of East Asian (and especially Southeast Asian) countries.

Ideational changes have also taken place, and according to Amartya Sen (1999), an outward orientation has been elevated over any nation-based economic strategy, and a capability-based interpretation of development, which has meant a significant departure from the former growth-maximizing approach. Besides the economic dimension of development, social, political, and environmental dimensions came to fore, and spatial, generational and gender issues lie at the heart of current understandings and interpretations of development.

Intensifying globalization has also led to changes in people's daily lives. Demonstration effects via the spread of new ICT and new mass communication tools and social media platforms have altered people's preferences and expectations in the quest for democratic systems and "good governance" (such as non-corrupt, rules-based, participatory, transparent, and accountable policy-making).

The above described processes have resulted in significant changes in the special context of the classic DS, which has enabled these states to directly guide the market and stimulate the economy with "traditional tools and measures" during the mid-twentieth century.

One of the most important implications is that, starting in the 1980s, the liberalization process has undermined the internal coherence of the classical DS model, which was not able to adapt itself to either the new external conditions or to the changed internal settings (shaped by weakening state capacities and the ever stronger private sector). Accordingly, the decline of the classical DS model has to be regarded as a systemic phenomenon, and the AFC only brought these internal controversies to the fore.

We sum up our preceding arguments in the following six points, which highlight the underlying mechanisms leading to the decline of the classical DS model:[14]

1. The structural transformation of the economy: global, transnational organization of economic production and growing complexity of economic activities undermine direct state guidance and "picking winners" strategies in the industrial sector, whereas domestic subsidies in a globalized production line do not necessarily increase domestic investments and production.
2. Significant societal changes: a more urbanized and "enlightened" society is probably less accepting of authoritarian and repressive regimes; the quest for democratization and good governance rises, while at the same time, altering preferences might lead to increasing consumerism (as in the case of Latin America).
3. Changes in the global financial system and capital market leave no or very limited room for development models based on state-led and repressive national financial systems, in which resource allocation is subordinated to long-term industrial goals rather than any efficiency measures (let alone price signals). Successful integration into the globalized financial system and capital market is, however, predicated on institutional reforms, as relational banking and cozy relations between the state and business sector are not compatible with the new global rules of the game.
4. Changes in corporate governance are inevitable consequences of the above-described trends, as above certain development levels, an increase in investment levels has to be accompanied by better management practices, efficient resource allocation (and well-functioning capital markets), and foreign ownership (to acquire new knowledge and technology).
5. Changes in state-business relations were also forged by the changes in the economic and social context. In the short run, Northeast Asian states could discipline the business sector. However, in the longer run, as intensifying integration into the world economy and efficiency criteria came to the fore, the capabilities of

---

[14] This argumentation builds on László Csaba's presentation on developmental states and the discussion that followed, held at Central European University during the course "New Political Economy of Development" held on February 19, 2015.

the state have weakened and crony capitalism emerged (with rent-seeking and corruption becoming the rule and not the exception).
6. The legitimacy of the mostly authoritarian, strong developmental states was provided on the one hand by US security considerations during the Cold War, and on the other hand, by exceptional growth performance that equally benefitted different classes of society. Both internal and external legitimacy based on the classical DS model broke down by the 1990s, which exposed the fragility of this very specific development model.

All in all, the classical model of DS reached its limits at the latest by the end of 1990s, as inherently signaled by the AFC. However, in the following section we will argue that this is not the end of the story. Although significant changes took place in East Asian developmental states as well as in other emerging countries, after years and decades of market-oriented and structural reforms, the state continues to play a significant, albeit mostly altered and transformed, role in most emerging economies, and certain continuities with the past prevail (see the national case studies in the following chapters).

The Quest for a New DS Concept in the Twenty-first Century

The need for re-thinking the analytical concepts for developmental states can be verified with the aforementioned fall of the classical DS paradigm and by the new challenges that emerged (or intensified) in the twenty-first century and created new circumstances (both possibilities and limits) for governments to formulate and realize their main socio-economic developmental objectives.

At this stage it is premature to speak about a new DS concept, and this is not the aim of this essay. However, there are some preliminary pillars around which consensus has formed in economic literature (Fosu 2013a and 2013b; Williams 2014), and these will be outlined in the following section. It is worth noting, however, the most important insights up to now: both economic and political sustainability requires an inclusive, Senian approach to development; transformative social and economic (structural) policies are needed, which place special emphasis on the enhancement of human capabilities and the new, service-based economy; and last but not least, for promoting these new developmental changes, building domestic institutional capabilities is a *sine qua non* condition, which is all too often disregarded by policy-makers, decision-makers, and even academic circles.

There are two straightforward ways to move toward a new DS concept: first, relying on the synthesis of the most recent theoretical results, and second, "streamlining" the latest experiences of states or groups of states as revealed by their development success and their economic policy practices. The theoretical starting point shall be the new paradigm of development (Sen 1999) embedded in modern theories of development economics, modern growth theories, as well as in new political economics and the new institutional economic school (Evans 2014). For more concrete theoretical underpinnings, see also the new developmentalist approach shaped by the work of Bresser-Pereira (2011, 2015, 2016) or the excellent book by Jan Winiecki (2016) on economic development strategies, structural change, and potential "shortcut strategies" for catching up in the less developed countries of the Global South. Related to the other methods of constructing a new concept, the most recent experiences of new DS, the most recent experiences of East Asian countries—not only in the Northeast, but also, or even more so, in Southeast Asian countries (Raquiza 2012), and, according to some analysts, also the particular development paths of China and India (Hua and Hu 2015; Hsu 2018; Székely-Doby 2017) have to be taken into account. In a broader sense, however, the experiences of the latest Latin American developmentalist experiments (Schneider 2015; Wylde 2012; Ricz 2017b) and those of some quickly growing African economies (Booth 2015; Routley 2014; Biedermann 2016) might offer some useful lessons.

We are convinced that approaches based on theoretical results and practical experiences move in the same direction, and combining both might prove useful for constructing a new DS concept. In this section, however, we have a much less ambitious objective: after some definitional issues, we aim to sum up the new challenges of the twenty-first century, which legitimize the quest for a new developmental state concept. Then, by synthetizing the most recent academic literature on developmental states, we aim to present a common analytical structure for developmental states in the twenty-first century. For a more practical approach and an overview of emerging economies' most recent experiences of reform and the transformation of the role of the state in development, see the following chapters and case studies.

The New Challenges of the Twenty-First Century

In the previous section we have argued that at the latest, by the end of the twentieth century, changes in the external and internal context of classic (East Asian-style) developmental states has led to the fall of the classical

DS paradigm. At the beginning of the twenty-first century, all the "to-be-developmental states" face new challenges that significantly differ from the circumstances and conditions prevalent when the classic developmental states emerged during the mid-twentieth century. The first four challenges are based on the work of Michelle Williams (2014, 8–20). Additionally, a further aspect is included (in line with Fine and Pollen 2016).

The first challenge is new economic re-structuring, which refers to the shift from manufacturing to the knowledge and service sectors, the so-called bit-driven or new economy based on knowledge and innovation. In this "new economic" setting, beyond physical capital accumulation, expanding human capabilities and the spread of information (through, e.g., investments in education, health, and legal infrastructure) play an ever larger role. The modern economy is increasingly driven by knowledge, innovation, as well as by business and financial services, and this stands in stark contrast to the twentieth century, which was defined by manufacturing. Along with this shift, different types of activities from both the state and the private sector (the entrepreneurial sector) are required to actively promote development. The state remains important in its traditional activities, but these have to be complemented with new activities supporting the creation and spread of knowledge and innovation, and those related to the state's new entrepreneurial roles, such as risk-taking and market-creation functions. At the same time, traditional networks between the state and the business sector have to be revised as well, in order to create a symbiotic rather than a parasitic relationship (Mazzucato 2013, 23).

The second challenge relates to changes in the political context of the twenty-first century's developmental states. Changes in domestic politics, namely the move from authoritarian regimes toward more democratic ones is moving hand in hand with the spread of new information and communication technologies. The emergence of a new bit-driven economy also has direct and indirect consequences for society and politics. Given the increased appreciation for knowledge and human capabilities, a new "enlightenment" is taking place, provoking changes in social needs, norms, and values. As long as the specific context of classic DS was determined by late development, mobilization for war, the external threat of the Cold War, and economic nationalism (and due to all these factors the societies of the classic DS were willing to make some sacrifices, such accepting repressive authoritarian regimes), today any "to-be-developmental state" must create and build up a new basis for legitimacy according to the new circumstances of the twenty-first century. Within this new political context, community priorities and a developmental agenda have to be set up based on a new alliance between state and society. In most cases, these changes imply the move from authoritarian regimes toward more democratic ones defined by the embeddedness of the political subsystem in society, political freedom, participation, the involvement of civil society, and the collective determination of the main priorities of the community. According to Amartya Sen (1999), a democratic political system based on representative, deliberative political participation is not just a means for achieving widely defined development but is a goal in itself.

The third challenge in Williams's list (2014, 18) is related to epistemic changes in the meaning of development and its interpretation. The expansion of the meaning of development is an unequivocal move away from the "economic growth-centered" thinking of the last century, toward a "development as freedom" interpretation according to Sen (1999); the latter is also called a human-capabilities approach. Thus, the promotion of development does not equate with a "technical problematic" of economic growth that merely requires economic knowledge; a development-oriented approach has to be increasingly considered a political problematic, as social welfare is a function of different non-economic factors (besides, of course, economic growth), such as social justice, poverty, inequality, or social participation and perception.

The last challenge mentioned by Williams (2014, 20) is ecological: environmental limits, including the new challenges posed by climate change and different aspects of environmental justice. By now, it is beyond any doubt that the resource-intensive development path of the last century, which was based predominantly on fossil fuels, cannot be sustained globally in the twenty-first century. This inherently leads to changes in existing consumption and production patterns and habits, while existing structures and infrastructures also have to be revised and altered. In light of market failures and externalities, the state has to play a central role in the realization of a green developmental path. At the same time, according to Mazzucato (2013), environmental limits also offer governments the opportunity to revise their development strategies and consider green technology developments as engines for economic growth, employment, and innovation in the long run (and to realize an environmentally sustainable development trajectory). Furthermore, we would like to add that given the past experiences of developmental states, in addition to the environmental aspects, greater attention must be paid to the spatial dimensions of development, and consequently there needs to be a greater focus on rural areas and the role of agrarian development.

The four challenges mentioned above could be further expanded by including the pressures that twenty-first-century developmental states face, which significantly alter their options and their room to maneuver: financial globalization and the experiences and effects of recent financial and economic crises. Due to these, the significance of efficient resource allocation has increased, while the financial viability of nation-based development interventions is deteriorating. In order to understand the logic of development-oriented interventions in light of financial globalization, one has to distinguish between productive (real) and speculative (financial) investments. While in the former case, it might be a stated and accepted objective to support employment growth or the expansion of human capabilities, for the latter, state regulation might be needed to decrease financial vulnerability. Fine and Pollen (2016) refer to this challenge as *financialization* ("the extraordinary growth of finance"), and highlight its wide-ranging consequences, such as the influence of finance on investments, value judgments, and more broadly, extending over economic and social policy issues, which, as a result, constrains (or at least transforms and conditions) prospects for development or even the emergence of developmental states.

Toward a New DS Concept

In economic historical terms, we can date the most recent generation of developmental state literature back to the start of the millennium. However, following the global financial crisis in 2008-9, we can observe a so-called renaissance of the developmental state approach (Fine et al. 2013; Mazzucato 2013; Wade 2014; Williams 2014). The most recent works on DS tend to build on the intellectual traditions of classic DS literature but also deviate from it in several key ways, such as its geographical focus, or by mixing institutional and economic policy approaches.

The core elements of the new, twenty-first-century DS concept are mostly compared with those of the classical DS paradigm, which serves as point of reference, to reveal the most important continuities and changes while drawing up the main tenets of the new DS concept. The starting points remain the new paradigm in development economics, the development-as-freedom approach, and the most recent structural changes in the economy (the increased weight of the knowledge economy), the result of which has been that the expansion of human choice and capacity becomes a primary goal and means of development.

According to the new paradigm of development (and because of economic and political changes—as presented in the previous section, which have resulted in the need to revisit socio-economic alliances and formulate a new social contract), new developmental states have to prioritize a socially (sustainable) equitable and inclusive development path. Successful "to-be-developmental states" have to dispose of a concrete (well-determined) developmental vision that, according to Mazzucato (2013), goes beyond a commitment to the development-oriented approach and consists of given (even sectoral) priorities. This developmental agenda is, however, in an ideal case defined by the inclusion and wide-ranging consensus of diverse social classes, economic actors, and other interest groups.

It is beyond the scope of this paper to go into the details of the latest DS literature (for a more in-depth discussion, see Fine et al. 2013; Mazzucato 2013; Routley 2014; Wade 2014; Williams 2014). Instead, we aim to sketch a new analytical framework that can be used to structure thinking and related academic debates on developmental states in the twenty-first century. To identify the main levels of this new structure, we rely on the development regime theory originally elaborated by T.J. Pempel (1998, 1999), and then applied by Christopher Wylde (2012) to Latin America, and on David Booth's (2015) somewhat modified version applied to contemporary African developmental experiments. The new developmental regime approach can be structured into three analytical levels: 1. socio-economic alliances or political settlements; 2. political and economic institutions, and the process of policy making; and 3. the public policy mix: developmentalist bias in relevant public policies.

On the first level, Mushtaq Khan[15] emphasizes how a development-oriented political settlement decreases political pressure on acting governments to patronize certain interest groups and to apply a short-term perspective to development.[16] . One of the main specificities of developmental states is that by building up balanced socio-economic alliances, these can lessen the role and share of discretionally distributed rents for buying the support and/or loyalty of certain elites or interest groups. At the same time, these makes it possible for governments to apply a long-term development-

---

[15] Khan, Mushtaq H. 2010. "Political Settlements and the Governance of Growth-Enhancing Institutions." Unpublished research material. Downloaded: https://eprints.soas.ac.uk/9968/1/Political_Settlements_internet.pdf

[16] For a more detailed explanation see Booth paper on "Political Settlements and Developmental Regimes: Issues from Comparative Research. A Paper for the Roundtable Seminar, The Ethiopian Developmental State and Political Settlement, Hosted by the Ethiopian International Institute for Peace and Development and the Royal Netherlands Embassy in Ethiopia, Hilton Hotel Addis Ababa, February 25–26, 2015.

oriented approach and implement their long-term developmental vision (beyond short-term changes in political leadership).

Pempel (1999, 158) argues that all (post-)modern developmental regimes must consist of the following key characteristics if they wish to actively and successfully promote economic and social development: 1. it has to support the creation of a socio-economic coalition that is stronger (in terms of disposing or owning more politically relevant resources) than any other coalition of opposition parties; 2. it has to be able to set main priorities in politics and thus put forward a national development agenda; 3. it has to be able to articulate a legitimate ideology that implicitly represents the interest of its supporters as the nation's common interests; 4. it must be able to reward its supporters with sufficient benefits in order to secure the sustainability of their support and the regime itself.

Mazzucato (2013) even goes further when she argues that only a developmental (entrepreneurial) state with a clear and well-determined (and well-articulated) developmental vision can be an equal partner with the private sector, and, thus, only such a self-confident state can avoid capture by certain interest groups. Such an entrepreneurial state can play a leading, and even a guiding role in the economy, and build up a symbiotic relationship with the business sphere, while focusing on such activities that are not taken up by the private sector because the latter is too risk-averse and dominated by short-term thinking).

In the new DS approach, the main difference to the classical paradigm is the inclusion of wider sectors of society (such as new relations with labor, which were repressed by the old DS). It explicitly aims to build new networks of state and society that are based on social participation, deliberation, and consensus building, while, at the same time, include wider segments of society (resulting in a new—inclusive—social contract).

Wylde (2012, 81) emphasizes that this new DR approach differs significantly from the classical DS theories, as the latter mainly focused on relations between the state and the industrial capitalist class (see also Evans's [1995] embedded autonomy theory). To build up the legitimacy of the twenty-first century's developmental regimes, much wider segments of society must be included. This is a much more complicated task for the new development-oriented governments; however, most groups in society share a common interest in expanding human choice and capacity, and the only task is to raise the public awareness of these issues and build up support for related investment decisions (Evans 2014, 234).

On the second level we look at the policy-making process. In the most recent developmental state literature (such as Booth 2015; Fosu 2013a and

2013b), there seems to be a consensus that the only lesson to be drawn from successful development-oriented experiments regarding the process of policy making is the primacy of pragmatic, problem-driven approaches.

By pragmatism we mean that successful East Asian countries did not aim to implement any grand(iose) plan, but political leaders and technocrats in the bureaucracy searched for the best answers to the most pressing problems, relying on the principle of trial-and-error and the learning-by-doing process (Routley 2014).

Building on experiences of developing and emerging countries Andrews et al. (2013) also highlights the problem-driven and iterative learning process as the key factor behind good policy choices and adequate institutional architecture. In this vein, they argue that the general lesson of the policy-making process for "to-be-developmental states" is the problem-driven iterative adaptation (PDIA) approach. Consequently, in the area of policy making, the one-size-fits-all approach is not applicable, and one has to search for its own solutions in light of its pressing problems and the prevalent context, while also learning from others' development successes and failures.

Similar insights are highlighted by Fosu (2013b, 7), which builds on the experiences of eighteen developing countries and argues that both orthodox and heterodox policies might be successful, depending on the specific circumstances. Accordingly, the main differences between successful and less successful countries can be linked to the application of a pragmatic approach to economic reforms, the specific nature of reforms, and the ability of countries to take advantage of market forces. At the same time, there is a main difference when choosing between orthodox or heterodox policies; the latter builds on a much broader set of active state interventions and requires a much more capable government with a much higher quality of public bureaucracy (see, for example, the classic East Asian developmental states).

In the capability approach to development, the only way to determine social and economic development objectives is through the democratic reconciliation process. Like human capabilities, one of the most important state capabilities is making choices, and the process of participation is not only the means, but also the end of development in itself (Sen 1999, 291). At the same time, according to the arguments of Rodrik (2000) and Evans (2014, 234), participatory political institutions have to be regarded as intermediary institutions that help elicit and aggregate local knowledge and, thus, result in an institutional learning process through which it might become more effective to build and operate better institutions of other types as well.

Finally, the third level consists of the analysis of development-oriented bias in public policies. Even though we admit that development strategies are context specific, and are valid within time and space constraints, and thus, as a rule, these cannot be emulated without adaptation under different circumstances. Still, we argue in line with Fosu (2013a and 2013b) that on the level of economic policies, there are sufficient commonalities across countries that are successful regarding the ability of some components of development to articulate guiding principles for other, less successful countries that have similar characteristics. Looking at a wider range of the scholarly literature, there emerges a certain package of economic policies that can be considered a general compass if applied flexibly enough, and if adapted to local conditions and circumstances. It is out of the scope of this introductory chapter to go into details on the specific characteristics and elements of a development-oriented public policy mix, but we can still summarize some important programmatic insights (see also Evans 2014; Fosu 2013a and 2013b).

First of all, both the capability approach to development and the newest restructuring of the economy (toward a bit-driven and service-based "new economy") result in the appreciation of the role of human capabilities, as these become the main driving forces behind development in the twenty-first century. With this, investments in upgrading human resources and in legal (and physical) infrastructure providing access to information and promoting the spread of knowledge gain central importance in development policies and strategies.

Investments in expanding human capabilities tend to remain below socially optimal levels due to the market logic (the difference between social and private returns, higher risk, and longer return periods). In the words of Evans's (2014, 230), "Public investment is the only plausible route to optimal levels of investment in human capabilities."

The provision of services aimed at expanding human capabilities (such as education and health) are traditionally considered the central tasks of any (not only development-oriented) state, and according to the new approach, the effective delivery of capability-expanding services and investments has to be carried out aggressively by entrepreneurial public institutions, and placed at the top of the growth (development) strategy (Evans 2014; Mazzucato 2013). At the same time, public awareness of its immediate distributional and welfare effects has to be raised significantly (Evans 2014, 231).

Socially, the only sustainable development path in the twenty-first century is the accomplishment of an equitable, inclusive, and long-term development agenda, not least to effectively mobilize the majority of a society in favor of these development objectives and to build up the legitimacy of the development-oriented approach. At the same time, according to a wide definition of social policies and the productive inclusion approach (or as Thandika Mkandawire [2007] calls it, transformative social policies), special emphasis should be placed on economic incentives that enable poor households to leave the self-sufficiency sector and productively get involved in the market-based economic sector.[17]

A second area of development-oriented state interventions is the active promotion of economic growth, namely infrastructural investments and industrial policy. Previously, we highlighted the central role of investments in the expansion of human capabilities. However, in developing countries, in addition to the need for human capital development, other infrastructural bottlenecks often pose important constraints on development. At the same time, private actors can often capture the returns of public investment, and the best example of this is the case of relatively mobile human capital.[18] To avoid this risk, a solution might be to improve (through increased public investments) the complementary business environment, which in turn might increase the derived demands on human capital). According to this logic, Fosu (2013b) highlights the importance of balance between human and other, more traditional (such as physical, economic, and legal) forms of infrastructural investment in order to improve the complementary business environment and to provide incentives for the better-equipped labor force to stay. An appropriate balance[19] of different (human, economic, institutional, and physical) infrastructural investments might not just decrease the exit-incentives for human capital, but often also acts as magnet to attract or maintain foreign direct investment (FDI), and in an ideal case, this might lead to the diversification of economic activities and technological development.

---

[17] See, for example, the works of Banerjee and Duflo (2011) on the economic lives of the poor, or the most recent magnum opus of Martin Ravallion (2016) entitled, *The Economics of Poverty*.

[18] To illustrate this case, we refer to the classic work of Hirschman (1970) on the "exit options" of human capital.

[19] See, for example, Kimura's (2013) new interpretation of the success of Japanese development. He argues that although social infrastructural investments played an important role, their share remained below 30 percent of total infrastructural expenditures, and economic infrastructural investments played a comparatively larger role.

In twentieth-century developmental states (at least in their classic iteration), industrial policy played a central role. In the most recent developmentalist approach, industrial policy has reappeared on the development agenda. However, according to the scholarship (Fine et al. 2013; Mazzucato 2013; Szalavetz 2015; Wade 2014) discussed above, it is easy to see that this renaissance of industrial policy should rather be called a science, technology, and innovation (STI) policy. At the same time, in most cases, the classic DS not only financed investments in location and equipment (physical infrastructure), they also facilitated the access of local companies to information, knowledge, technologies, and the creation of networks, and simultaneously encouraged companies to move toward economic activities that create new knowledge (and, thus, gradually move up the value chain).[20]

Regarding their industrial structure, developing countries in today's technology-induced global economy cannot flourish without a knowledge-based development strategy, though certainly different focal points are necessary for predominantly agrarian economies versus industrialized middle-income countries. An important consequence of new technologies and the most recent economic structural change is that today, certain stages of industrial modernization can be leapfrogged.[21] At the same time, according to Wade (2014, 781), price changes on the market facilitate gradual, step-by-step development, and these might impede larger changes, for example in innovation and economic diversification. To make these changes possible, active state interventions are needed in the twenty-first century.

This "old-new"[22] industrial policy role of governments is still subject to heavy academic debate in economics, although scholars of modern DS mostly argue for a proactive, entrepreneurial state and mostly oppose the conventional mainstream view, which has a much more sector-neutral position and stands for the improvement of the general business environment and institutional infrastructure so as to attract productive private capital

---

[20] Evans (2014, 232) mentions China as a typical example of how the state resisted overprotecting monopolized (mainly northern and more developed) corporations and thus "supported" access to the productive ideas of its citizens and companies.

[21] Thus, in this regard, Balassa's (1981) classical stages approach is outdated.

[22] Mazzucato (2013, 21) argues that these are not new industrial policy interventions and describes how the U.S. played a central role in developing new technologies, supporting new industries, but did this in a *hidden* way. Similarly, Szalavetz (2015) writes that industrial policies after the 2008–9 crisis are not new, but old industrial policy practices that have been revived.

and decrease the risk of out-migration of (state-financed) human capital. In contrast to this mainstream view, Mazzucato (2013) and Wade (2014) argue that, in our innovation-led economy, the state has to undertake risky innovative activities that are not performed by the private sector (including venture capital). For them, the state must go beyond (long-term, committed, and "patient") financing basic and applied research and development activities (which are even admitted and highlighted by mainstream economists).

Another rather contested area relates to the role of state ownership or state-owned enterprises (SOEs) as an important channel of state influence in the economy. State ownership has long historical precedents in all parts of the world, and has evolved cyclically in different waves (for more details, see Szanyi [2016] and the introduction of this volume; chapter one by Voszka; and Nölke 2014, 2–5), and most of the theoretical and empirical literature covers the efficiency considerations of SOEs as compared to their private counterparts. Different schools emphasize different underlying causes of efficiency losses, such as agency and social and political views (for more details, see Musacchio and Lazzarini 2014, 4–5). We, however, emphasize the industrial policy view, according to which in the early phases of development, the state should step in and offer a "guiding hand" (reducing capital controls or the costs of research and development, or by coordinating resources) to firms so they can develop new capabilities (see also Gerschenkron 1962; Amsden 1989; Wade 1990; Evans 1995; Rodrik 2007).

Moving beyond these debates is the role that SOEs play in large emerging economies and how this has evolved over time. In general, it can be claimed that SOEs have traditionally played a much more dominant role in late-comer economies, and in partially different forms. But even after waves of privatization (and in some cases of re-nationalization), SOEs continue to deeply penetrate into emerging economies' everyday life. Musacchio and Lazzarini (2014) describe alternative models of the organization of state influence and explore the spectrum of state interventions between the two extremes of full state ownership (Leviathan as entrepreneur) and the full private ownership. For in-between cases, the authors describe the Leviathan as the majority investor, where state retains majority control over partially privatized firms; and the Leviathan as minority investor, where the state has a residual, minority stake, or where firms receive loans and equity from state-owned development banks or investments from sovereign wealth funds (SWF) or other state-controlled funds.

While in more developed parts of the world, the recent rise of new forms of state ownership or influence has been related to crisis management after the 2008–2009 global financial crisis (GFC), in less developed, emerging economies, the rise of "state capitalism" dates back to the early 1990s and is not considered a temporary fix but constitutes a much more central dimension of long-term government policy and the key to economic success (Kurlantzick 2016, 11).

We could cite the Chinese case as a prominent example of the revival and (re)emergence of new forms of state ownership and influence over the economy. However, the following chapters that examine Singapore, Brazil, and Turkey (respectively) show that the story goes beyond China.

A third important issue is the financing of development, as it used to be a point of obsession in classical DS scholarship. Like the classic DS, Northeast Asian DS' very specific context (financial development aid from the U.S. and Japan, traditionally high domestic saving rates, relatively closed economic systems, and repressed domestic financial markets) contributed to the financial viability of its unique national development model. Conversely, the financial difficulties (not least signaled by the debt crisis in the 1980s) of the developmentalist experiments of their Latin American counterparts in the twentieth century serve as the antithesis.

Taking into account the current stage of financial globalization and the most recent experiences of global financial (and economic) crises, it is clear that developmental states in the twenty-first century have much narrower room to maneuver to finance their broader economic growth (development) agenda, as did their antecedents during the mid-twentieth century.

In a financially globalized world economy, securing macroeconomic stability becomes central, as a stable macroeconomic position is necessary to build up business confidence, encourage investors, and attract FDI. Though in the short run and only temporarily today's developing countries might also rely on external sources (in addition to FDI, foreign aid and credits) during the implementation period of their development strategies, in the longer run, a more balanced development budget is needed, and the role of domestic resources cannot be overrated. Incentives for domestic savings and the rationalization of government expenditures, the system of national taxes, as well as the government's abilities to collect those taxes become core development issues.

Fourth, by the twenty-first century, it became clearly evident that outward-oriented development strategies are superior to any other nationalistic and dissociative economic strategies. The experiences of the classic (Northeast Asian) developmental states have also confirmed the benefits of an outward-oriented development strategy for long-term economic growth and development. In the classic cases, export-orientation implicitly presumed that bureaucratic guidelines are in line with international market forces (Amsden 1989; Johnson 1982; Wade 1990). Therefore, taking into account and relying on international market incentives was at the heart of the classical DS model.

In the twenty-first century, however, we have to go beyond the articulation of an outward-oriented economic strategy, and in order to achieve export-driven economic growth, the enhancement of the role of domestic institutions and their improvement is inevitable. Following Fosu (2013a, 11), outward orientation has to go hand in hand with increasing competition in the domestic market and with building domestic institutional capabilities (the improvement of macroeconomic stability and the strengthening of institutional and human infrastructure). The most recent global financial and economic crisis has shown that economic diversification (not only in terms of export products but also export markets) is not only crucial for long-term economic growth; it also plays an important role in securing economic stability (or in other words, in decreasing economic vulnerability). Outward orientation (and economic diversification) plays a complementary role (and does not substitute for) in the development of the domestic market. The most recent experiences of successful large emerging markets (such as China) underline the need for this complementary approach, while some less successful cases (such as Brazil) serve as cautionary tales.

Finally, social change during the twentieth century, globalization and the following changes in domestic politics have led to an appreciation of the role of the capabilities and capacities of political institutions to effectively define developmental goals. This presumes a new type of bottom-up relationship between the state and society; it also highlights the role of spreading, collecting, and processing information, and shows an appreciation for the capabilities and capacities of the public sector to fulfill these new tasks (Evans 2014, 222). A meritocratic, well-educated, competent, well-paid, and—from the perspective of political power—relatively insulated (but still embedded) bureaucracy forms the core of the classical DSP. In the new DS approach, however, not just technocratic qualities are needed, but also other, more political qualities are necessary to collect, screen, and process information in the knowledge economy and society; to define collective objectives in a participatory and consultative manner; and to reorganize relations with the business and civil sector.

Mazzucato (2013, 5–6) goes even further and argues that the public sector should not be regarded as the social version or imitator of the private sector[23]; rather, its tasks and role in development should be totally reconsidered. The socio-economic challenges of the twenty-first century require a proactive, development-oriented state with entrepreneurial qualities.

This argument emphasizes the need for aggressive, effective, and entrepreneurial public institutions in order to secure the optimal level of investments for human capability expansion and to disseminate information and knowledge. At the same time, a capable and coherent bureaucracy is necessary but not sufficient for building successful developmental states in the twenty-first century. On the contrary, we argue that a special economic policy mix for constructing a new DS concept in the twenty-first century must be outlined, and at the very least it must contain investments in the expansion of human capabilities, broadly defined transformative social policies (including investments in education, health services, and labor market reforms), public sector reforms, as well as macroeconomic and industrial (or STI) policies, in addition to trade and tax policies.

These elements of a development-oriented public policy mix have to be taken together as a package, because they are mutually reinforcing with spillover effects that strengthen (or reduce) other areas. All of this underscores the argument that, by now, is almost a cliché in modern economics: it is not so much the volume of the state expenditures that matters, but rather its structure. Furthermore, long-term economic growth and development presumes a long-term commitment to socio-economic goals and the consistency of development-oriented public policies (not only on the rhetorical level, but also on the level of implementation).

The new DS approach we have outlined above is, however, much less a practical reality, and much more an opportunity that is too often overlooked or ignored by contemporary governments (Mazzucato 2013, 12). A government that aspires to be a developmental state in the twenty-first century shall be characterized by the following: a flexible and pragmatic approach; good networking and bureaucratic capabilities; the ability to coordinate the diverse interests of different social classes; and, more often than not, the ability to promote, implement, and realize incubation- and innovation-related activities. This new approach not only presumes tech-

---

[23] Mazzucato (2013) also highlights that this does not only alter cooperative relations between the public and private sector, but also changes the expected returns to the state and the scale of the reward justified by the state interventions, which is a central issue for all "to-be-developmental states" in the globalized world economy seeking to finance their development-oriented activities.

nical capacities and proficiency (as was the case with the old DS), but also requires new methods to define normative and political objectives. Consequently, the proactive promotion of development in the twenty-first century becomes more than the "simple" technical problem of economic growth; it becomes a central issue in domestic politics.

Conclusions

We have presented the classical developmental state paradigm based on Northeast Asian experiences, and argued that changes in its unique context during the last decades of the twentieth century have inherently and systematically led to its demise. However, more recently, with the onset of the global financial crisis in 2008–2009, we have witnessed the renaissance of the developmental state approach in economic scholarship. We have argued that this is not the revival of the old developmental state paradigm, but a new one in the making, at least in theoretical terms (economic policy practices are still rather eclectic and diverse as will be shown in the following chapters). The desire to revise the role of state in development and to construct a new concept for developmental states was based, on the one hand, on the fall of the classical developmental state paradigm, and, on the other hand, challenges that emerged and intensified at the dawn of the twenty-first century.

To conclude, we want to highlight some of the major changes that have surfaced when trying to conceptualize the "ideal" of a twenty-first-century developmental state. First, the classical developmental state paradigm has been focused on the special case of latecomers to development, and has made economic transformation and catching up its top priorities. More precisely, it focused on maximizing economic growth. Due to the specific and unique Northeast Asian context, development was achieved in such a way that economic growth served the wellbeing of a wider social base, but this *shared character* of economic growth was rather an unintended by-product and less the result of deliberate economic policies or political intentions. Any developmental state theory in the twenty-first century has to go beyond this old approach's focus on economic growth, and instead embrace the concept of broadly defined development and the so-called human-capabilities approach (Sen 1999) alongside the economic dimension of development. New DS models also have to focus on the inclusive character of development. We have to go even further because the economic and social dimensions, the political and environmental aspects, and the spatial, gender, and generational dimensions of development must be taken into account.

Second, the classical DS concept analyzed the structural transformation of backward, mainly agrarian economies within the specific context of late-development; so it mainly focused on the process of industrialization. The new economic transformation dating back to the end of the twentieth century has resulted in a shift toward the knowledge and service sector as the main driving forces behind economic growth. The new, bifurcated service sector (Evans 2014, 229) consists of a well-paid business and financial subsector providing employment opportunities for a small minority of service-sector workers, and a low paid—underestimated and under-rewarded—subsector of interpersonal services. This results in fundamentally different distributional and welfare implications just like twentieth-century industrialization did. One of the most visible consequences is the unprecedented rise of social inequalities. Against this background today we have to go beyond the special cases of late-development and industrialization, and analyze the structural transformation of economies at different stages of development in more general terms.

Third, this broader approach also implies that the geographical focus, which originally concentrated on (North-)East Asia, will not be exchanged for a new focus on Africa. But the new developmental state concept should also be extended geographically in order to shift focus to emerging economies worldwide.

Fourth, the immaturity of the new developmental state concept is well illustrated by the diversity of economic literature published in recent years. This scholarship often uses different labels for developmental states, emphasizing its catalysts, enabling role, or describing it as a facilitator. Mariana Mazzucato (2013, 21) even goes further in her book on entrepreneurial states, which she based on the experiences of more developed economies, mainly the United States. In it, she argues that a so-called "hidden developmental state"[24] has played an important and active role in the historical economic successes of highly developed economies. According to her analysis, the state (of the United States) has moved far beyond Keynesian-style macroeconomic interventions or even the passive financing of research and development activities, and has performed entre-

---

[24] For a longer discussion on the hidden developmental state, see Block's (2008) original article or the review article by Szalavetz (2015).

preneurial activities in the Schumpeterian vein, such as actively overtaking market risks or creating new markets.

To summarize, it might be helpful to compare the main characteristics of the new DS approach to the classical paradigm along the dichotomies of the state and society, the state and the market, and the state and the rest of the world. We argue in line with Pempel (1999) and Wylde (2012) that there is a need to go beyond the tripod alliance of the nation state, domestic and international capital that has characterized classic developmental states.

Regarding the state and the market dichotomy, the active and positive role of the state in development represents the main continuity between the old and new DS concepts. This is manifested, for example, in the significance of macroeconomic stability and stable investment environment, or in the reliance on active industrial policy. Behind these major guiding principles, however, there are numerous changes and differences partly related to the types of interventions. However, even deeper discontinuities can be highlighted; due to advancements in financial globalization and the liberalization of capital flows, efficient resource allocation became a *sine qua non* for "to-be-developmental states," while the need to decrease financial and economic vulnerability and the transformation of traditional industrial policy interventions also represent main discontinuities.

The relationship between the state and society has been undoubtedly and fundamentally changed. While the old, classic developmental states have achieved economic success despite the repression and political exclusion of wide segments (the majority) of their societies, in the case of the twenty-first century's DS, state-society relations are much more inclusive (to incorporate the working class) and will be based on more equitable, inclusive, and participatory processes. The new approach builds on the inclusion of the needs and interests of diverse social groups in domestic politics and prefers policy responsiveness and a balanced approach to these very diverse social needs. The formation of new socio-economic alliances is, however, shaped by the political institutional architecture, the distribution of political power, and bargaining mechanisms. These differ from the classic solutions of the old DS during the last century; further, most recent successful experiments also demonstrate the wide-ranging possibilities and diverse patterns of cooptation of different interest groups (see following case studies).

Regarding the relations between the state and the rest of the world in the era of advanced economic (and financial) globalization, outward orientation (based on export diversification both in products and markets) has to be placed on a new footing and backed by a stable domestic institutional setting. In the golden age of DS in the mid-twentieth century, when nationalistic and nation-based development strategies were viable and most successful, East Asian DS were connected to the world economy mainly through the trade of goods (and their export-oriented economic strategies); today outward-oriented strategies are far more complex. Taking into account international processes and changes in the twenty-first century is unavoidable, as these shape the (changing) development opportunities and constraints that determine the political and economic terrain of modern states with developmentalist aspirations. We must add, however, that although we have focused our analysis on the level of the nation state, the new DS approach must also be applied on the subnational (regional and local) level, as these arenas play an ever more important role in providing human capability expansion services (such as education and healthcare), and deepening democratic participatory mechanisms.

Finally, we have shown that the new DS approach, which reflects the new challenges of the twenty-first century, is fundamentally a market-friendly approach,[25] in which the state has an active but—compared to classical theories—re-defined and recurrent role in promoting widely defined development.

Through our presentation of the main pillars of the new DS concept, we have argued that, on the level of public policies and their developmental bias, a consensus seems to have emerged in the scholarly literature, and a development-oriented public policy mix in the twenty-first century at minimum contains the following elements: cautious and sound fiscal and monetary policies supporting effective macroeconomic management and macroeconomic stability; transformative social policies intended to decrease poverty and inequality (including education and health policies aimed at the expansion of human capabilities); physical, institutional, and human infrastructural investments (in a mutually complementary manner, and in a balanced way); new industrial (STI) policies that support technological learning and innovative activities; entrepreneurial public institutions; a strong technocratic and meritocratic central administration; and last but not least, innovative forms of financing development broadly defined.

The goal of the following chapters is to present a special set of Varieties of Development-oriented experiments in emerging markets. The case

---

[25] We can also call it developmental capitalism in the words of Bresser Pereira (2016).

studies do not seek to present the developmentalist experiments of countries in their totality, across every dimensions of state intervention, but rather concentrate on certain defining characteristics that represent distinctive features of the given case and/or are illustrative of recent trends and changes. These case studies can be regarded as illustrations of the ongoing changes to the role of state in development, and they contribute to a better understanding of continuities with and/or changes to the classical developmental state approach.

At the same time, we have argued that neither the classical developmental state paradigm, nor the newly emerging revised DS concept serve as role models to emulate. The main message from the classic success stories is that a pragmatic approach, along with trial and error, and homegrown (innovative and creative) solutions might succeed.

REFERENCES

Agénor, Pierre-Richard, Otaviano Canuto, and Michael Jelenic. 2012. "Avoiding Middle-Income Growth Traps." Economic Premise 98." The World Bank, Poverty Reduction and Economic Management Network (PREM). http://documents.worldbank.org/curated/en/422121468155111398/Avoiding-middle-income-growth-traps.

Amable, Bruno. 2003. *The Diversity of Modern Capitalism*. Oxford: Oxford University Press.

Amsden, Alice. 1989. *Asia's Next Giant: South Korea and Late Industrialization*. New York: Oxford University Press.

Andrews, Matt, Lant Pritchett, and Michael Woolcock. 2013. "Escaping Capability Traps through Problem Driven Iterative Adaptation (PDIA)." *World Development* 51 (C): 234–44.

Bagchi, Amiya Kumar. 2004. *The Developmental State in History and in the Twentieth Century*. New Delhi: Regency Publications.

Balassa, Béla. 1981. *The Newly Industrializing Countries in the World Economy*. New York: Pergamon.

Banerjee, Abhijit V. and Esther Duflo. 2011. *Poor Economics: Rethinking Poverty and How to End it*. New York: Public Affairs Books.

Beeson, Mark. 2007. *Regionalism and Globalization in East Asia: Politics, Security and Economic Development*. New York: Palgrave Macmillan.

Benczes, István. 2000. Válság és átalakulás a Távol-Keleten" [Crisis and transformation in the Far East]. *Külgazdaság* 44 (3): 56–75.

———. 2002. "A fejlesztő állam válsága Ázsiában" [The crisis of the developing state in Asia]. *Külgazdaság* 46 (5): 23–40.

Biedermann, Zsuzsanna. 2016. "The Case of Rwanda as a Developmental State." In *Entrepreneurship and SME Management across Africa: Context, Challenges, Changes*, edited by Leona Achtenhagen, and Ethel Brundin, 139–57. Singapore: Springer.

Block, Fred. 2008. "Swimming against the Current: The Rise of a Hidden Developmental State in the United States." *Politics and Society* 36 (2): 169–206.
Booth, Anne. 1999. "Initial Conditions and Miraculous Growth: Why is South East Asia Different From Taiwan and South Korea?" *World Development* 27 (2): 301–21.
Booth, David. 2015. "Toward a Relevant Concept of Development Regime." In *Developmental Regimes in Africa: Initiating and Sustaining Developmental Regimes in Africa*, edited by David Booth. Synthesis Report. London: Overseas Development Institute.
Bresser-Pereira, Luiz Carlos. 2011. "From Old to New Developmentalism in Latin America." In *The Oxford Handbook of Latin American Economics*, edited by José Antonio Ocampo and Jaime Ross, 108–29. Oxford: Oxford University Press.
———. 2015. "Reflecting on New Developmentalism and Classical Developmentalism." Working Paper EESP/FGV 395, June. www.bresserpereira.org.br.
———. 2016. "Models of Developmental State." FGV Working Papers 426. Sao Paulo School of Economics. http://www.bresserpereira.org.br/papers/2016/350-Models-developmental-state-TD-426.pdf.
Cardoso, Fernando Henrique and Enzo Faletto. 1979. *Dependency and Development in Latin America*. Berkeley: University of California Press.
Chibber, Vivek. 2005. "Reviving the Developmental State? The Myth of the National Bourgeoisie." In "The Empire Reloaded," edited by Panitch, Leo and Colin Leys. Special issue. *The Socialist Register* 41: 144–45.
Doner, Richard F., Bryan K. Ritchie, and Dan Slater. 2005. "Systemic Vulnerability and the Origins of Developmental States: Northeast and Southeast Asia in Comparative Perspective." *International Organization* 59 (2): 327–61.
Ebenau, Matthias, Ian Bruff, and Christian May, eds. 2015. *New Directions in Comparative Capitalisms Research: Critical and Global Perspectives*. International Political Economy Series. Basingstoke: Palgrave Macmillan.
Evans, Peter B. 1995. *Embedded Autonomy: States and Industrial Transformation*. Princeton, NJ: Princeton University Press.
———. 2014. "The Developmental State: Divergent Responses to Modern Economic Theory and the Twenty-First Century Economy." In Williams 2014, 220–40.
Farkas, Beáta. 2011. "A közép-kelet-európai piacgazdaságok fejlődési lehetőségei az Európai Unióban" [The developmental possibilities of Middle East-European market economics in the European Union]. *Közgazdasági Szemle* 58 (5): 412–29.
———. 2016. *Models of Capitalism in the European Union: Post-crisis Perspectives*. Basingstoke: Palgrave Macmillan.
Fine, B. and Pollen, G. 2018. "The Developmental State Paradigm in the Age of Financialization." In *Handbook of Development and Social Change*, edited by Fagan, Honor, G. and Ronaldo Munck, 211–27. Cheltenham: Edward Elgar Publisher.
Fine, Ben, Jyoti Saraswati, and Daniela Tavasci, eds. 2013. *Beyond the Developmental State: Industrial Policy into the Twenty-first Century*. IIPPE Series. London: Pluto.
Fosu, Augustin K., ed. 2013a. *Development Success: Historical Accounts from More Advanced Countries*. Oxford: Oxford University Press.

———, ed. 2013b. *Achieving Development Success: Strategies and Lessons from Developing World*. Oxford: Oxford University Press.
Hall, Peter A., and David Soskice, eds. 2001. *Varieties of Capitalism. The Institutional Foundations of Comparative Advantage*. New York: Oxford University Press.
Hirschman, Albert O. 1970. *Exit, Voice, and Loyalty: Responses to Decline in Firms, Organizations, and States*. Cambridge, MA: Harvard University Press.
Hua, Shiping, and Die Hu, eds. 2015. *East Asian Development Model: Twenty-First Century Perspectives*. New York: Routledge.
Hsu, Jennifer. 2018. "The Developmental State of the Twenty-First Century: Accounting for State and Society." *Third World Quarterly* 39 (6): 1098–114.
Johnson, Chalmers. 1982. *MITI and the Japanese Miracle. The Growth of Industrial Policy, 1925–1975*. Stanford, CA: Stanford University Press.
———. 1999. "The Developmental State: Odyssey of a Concept." In Woo-Cumings 1999, 32–60.
Kimura, Fukunari. 2013. "Japan's Model of Economic Development. Relevant and Non-relevant Elements for Developing Economies." In Fosu 2013a, 149–70.
Kurlantzick, Joshua. 2016. *State Capitalism: How the Return of Statism is Transforming the World*. New York: Oxford University Press.
Leftwich, A. 1995. "Bringing Politics Back In: Toward a Model of the Developmental State." *Journal of Development Studies* 31 (3): 400–27.
May, Christian, and Andreas Nölke. 2014. "Capitalism in Large Emerging Economies and the New Global Trade Order." In *Handbook of International Political Economy of Trade*, edited by David A. Deese, 450–70. Northampton, Mass.: Edward Elgar.
Mazzucato, Mariana. 2013. *The Entrepreneurial State. Debunking Public vs. Private Sector Myths*. London: Anthem Press.
Mkandawire, Thandika. 2007. "Transformative Social Policy and Innovation in Developing Countries." *The European Journal of Development Research* 19 (1): 13–29.
Nölke, Andreas, and Arjan Vliegenthart. 2009. "Enlarging the Varieties of Capitalism. The Emergence of Dependent Market Economies in East Central Europe." *World Politics* 61 (4): 670–702.
Nölke, Andreas. 2015. "Domestic Structures, Foreign Economic Policies and Global Economic Order: Implications from the Rise of Large Emerging Economies." *European Journal of International Relations* 21 (3): 538–67.
———, ed. 2014. *Multinational Corporations from Emerging Markets. State Capitalism 3.0*. Basingstoke: Palgrave MacMillan.
Onis, Z. 1991. "The Logic of the Developmental State." *Comparative Politics* 24 (1): 109–26.
Pempel, T. J. 1998. *Regime Shift: Comparative Dynamics of the Japanese Political Economy*. Ithaca, NY: Cornell University Press.
———. 1999. "The Developmental Regime in a Changing World Economy." In Woo-Cumings 1999, 137–81.
Raquiza, Antoinette R. 2012. *State Structure and Economic Development in Southeast Asia structuring Development: The Political Economy of Thailand and the Philippines*. New York: Routledge.
Ravallion, Martin. 2016. *The Economics of Poverty: History, Measurement, and Policy*. New York: Oxford University Press.

Ricz, Judit. 2017a. "A klasszikus fejlesztő állam megközelítés: egy letűnt világ nyomában" [The classical developmental state approach: In the footsteps of a lost world]. *Köz-Gazdaság* 12 (2): 65–91.

———. 2017b. "The Rise and Fall (?) of a New Developmental State in Brazil." *Society and Economy of Central and Eastern Europe* 39 (1): 85–108.

Rodrik, Dani. 2000. "Institutions for High-Quality Growth: What They are and How to Acquire Them." *Studies in Comparative International Development* 35 (3): 3–31.

Rodrik, Dani. 2007. *One Economics, Many Recipes: Globalization, Institutions and Economic Growth.* Princeton, NJ: Princeton University Press.

Routley, Laura. 2012. "Developmental States: A Review of the Literature." Global Development Institute Working Paper 03, February. Global Development Institute. https://ssrn.com/abstract=2141837.

———. 2014. "Developmental States in Africa? A Review of Ongoing Debates and Buzzwords." *Development Policy Review* 32 (2): 159–77.

Schneider, Ben R. 2009. "Hierarchical Market Economies and Varieties of Capitalism in Latin America." *Journal of Latin American Studies* 41 (3): 553–75.

———. 2013. *Hierarchical Capitalism in Latin America: Business, Labor, and the Challenges of Equitable Development.* New York: Cambridge University Press.

Schneider, Ben R. 2015. "The Developmental State in Brazil: Comparative and Historical Perspectives." *Revista de Economia Política* 35 (1): 114–32.

Sen, Amartya. 1999. *Development as Freedom: Human Capability and Global Need.* New York: Anchor Books.

Szalavetz, Andrea. 2015. "Post-Crisis Approaches to State Intervention: New Developmentalism or Industrial Policy as Usual?" *Competition & Change* 19 (1): 70–83.

Szanyi, Miklós. 2016. "The Reversal of the Privatisation Logic in Central European Transition Economies: An Essay." *Acta Oeconomica* 66 (1): 33–55.

Székely-Doby, András. 2017. "A kínai fejlesztő állam kihívásai" [The challenges of the Chinese developmental state]. *Közgazdasági Szemle* 64 (6): 630–49.

Wade, Robert H. 1990. *Governing the Market: Economic Theory and the Role of Government in East Asian Industrialization.* Princeton, NJ: Princeton University Press.

Wade, Robert H. 2014. "'Market versus State' or 'Market with State': How to Impart Directional Thrust." *Development and Change* 45 (4): 777–98.

Williams, Michelle, ed. 2014. *The End of the Developmental State?* New York: Routledge.

Winiecki, Jan. 2016. *Shortcut or Piecemeal: Economic Development Strategies and Structural Change.* Budapest–New York: CEU Press.

Woo-Cumings, Meredith, ed. 1999. *The Developmental State.* Ithaca, NY: Cornell University Press.

World Bank. 1993. *The East Asian Miracle: Economic Growth and Public Policy.* Oxford: The World Bank–Oxford University Press.

Wylde, Christopher. 2012. *Latin America after Neoliberalism: Developmental Regimes in Post-Crisis States.* Basingstoke: Palgrave Macmillan.

———. 2017. *Emerging Markets and the State Developmentalism in the 21st Century.* Basingstoke: Palgrave Macmillan.

CHAPTER 10
A Successful Model of State Capitalism: Singapore

Katalin Völgyi

Introduction

During the four decades after independence (1965), Singapore rapidly caught up with the developed West in both economic and social terms. By 1994, Singapore's per capita GDP surpassed that of Australia, Canada, and the United Kingdom (Menon 2007, 1). In 2014, Singapore placed third in the IMF's list of countries by their per capita GDP (PPP). In 2013, Singapore was ranked ninth on the *Human Development Index* list of UNDP (UNDP 2014, 159). It came before every other Asian country. In 2015, according to the *IMD World Competitiveness Yearbook* and the *Global Competitiveness Report* of the World Economic Forum, Singapore was the world's third and second most competitive economy, respectively.

Singapore represents a successful model of the developmental state and state capitalism (Rodan 2004; Sim 2011, 59; Hayashi 2010, 50). In Singapore, a state-led economy has evolved, or we might also say that Singapore is one of the archetypes of developmental states. An active governmental role describes the main character of developmental states, the aim of which is to promote national well-being. Developmental states intervene in the market economy to make it more productive, to increase private profit as well as public revenue, and to work toward citizens' prosperity. Developmental states are governed by goal-oriented and determined elites whose principal commitment is to the national well-being. According to the state-centric approach of the developmental state concept, successful economic and social changes require an interventionist government (Bellows 2006, 231).

The People's Action Party (PAP) came into power in Singapore in 1959, and took on an important role in the nation-building process and the development of the national economy. In order to achieve social and economic goals, it has created a corruption free, merit-based, well-paid, and effective public service. Since the very beginning (especially since 1965), the PAP government has been characterized by high interventionism. An extensive state-owned enterprise sector has evolved in Singapore, although the government has never pursued a radical program of nationalization. Extreme swings between nationalization and privatization have also been absent from Singapore. The Singaporean government has remained committed to a market economy (Chua 1995, 271). Unlike northeast Asian developmental states (Japan, Taiwan, South Korea), the Singaporean government did not rely on the local capital class, but largely on foreign transnational corporations and the state capitalist sector during the development of the economy. (The latter two have continued to propel economic growth of Singapore [Tan 1991, 201; Chua 2015, 3]). The state in Singapore acts as an entrepreneur. It undertakes market risks when it establishes a company. State-owned enterprises operate profitably. Loss-making companies (which are rare) are not saved, but closed. Similar to private companies, the operation of state-owned enterprises is regulated by the Companies Act (Tan 1975, 62; Ang and Ding 2006, 67). State-owned enterprises are run by a professional management team, which is paid a salary competitive with the private sector.

Singapore can be considered a rare example of successful state capitalism. The profitable and effective operation of the state capitalist sector offers several benefits to Singaporean citizens: low unemployment and crime rates, and little social unrest; world-class infrastructure; affordable housing, education, and health care, etc. The profits of the state capitalist sector are reinvested to maximize economic growth (Sim 2011, 59–60).

Historical Antecedents

The history of modern Singapore goes back to 1819 when Sir Thomas Stamford Raffles, employed by the British East India Company, established a commercial base on the island. In the following decades, Singapore became an important center of entrepot trade due to its strategic location and free-port status. Entrepot trade consisted of imports of Western manufacturing goods and Indian opium as well as the export of raw materials from Southeast Asian countries (e.g., rubber, tin). The British primarily regarded Singapore as an important entrepot, and they did not start to introduce manufacturing industries on the island, although some factories and workshops were established to serve raw material processing in the hinterlands. In contrast to the manufacturing industry, trade-related industries such as insurance, shipping, and banking services developed rapidly. After World War I, the British established a military base on the island. Parallel to Singapore's growing economic role, the population increased continuously.[1] Beside British merchants (and the staff of the colonial administration), other European traders (German, Dutch, French) as well as Chinese, Indian, and Arabic merchants began to settle on the island. Among the newcomers, the share of southern Chinese, Indian, and Malay immigrants who came to undertake physical labor in Singapore was much higher compared to that of the commercial and administrative personnel.

During World War II, and especially between 1942 and 1945, Singapore came under Japanese occupation. After the war, the returning British revived the entrepot trade and military base in Singapore. Throughout the 1950s, the raw material exports of Singapore grew continuously. Its economic growth was generated by trade with Malaysia and Indonesia, and the entrepot trade began to concentrate in the hands of Chinese merchants (Lee 1989, 11). Meanwhile, the population of the island grew from 938,200 to 1,445,900 between 1947 and 1957 (Li 2002, 24).

In 1959, the British granted Singapore the right to self-government. At that time, its social, economic, and political environment was not vastly different from that of other former colonial countries. As an underdeveloped "Third World" country, it was characterized by widespread poverty, low levels of education, high unemployment, and inadequate housing and health facilities. The primary aim of PAP, which won the general election in 1959 (and is still in power today), was to launch an industrialization program to create jobs (by breaking away from the limited growth opportunities of the entrepot system) and provide decent housing, basic medical care, and better educational opportunities for the broader society (Soon and Tan 1993, 8).

Because of the small size of domestic market, the Singaporean government decided to form an economic and political union with Malaysia to achieve its aims in the field of industrialization. Like most developing countries, Singapore accepted an initial economic development strategy focused on import-substitution industrialization. To reduce unemployment, the government first sought to attract labor-intensive industries. But the anticipated benefits of the merger with Malaysia in 1963 did not mate-

---

[1] Malays are the indigenous people of Singapore.

rialize (Soon and Tan 1993, 8–9). Because of political and ideological differences, Singapore left the Federation of Malaysia in 1965.

After leaving the Federation, the island faced a severe macroeconomic shock for two main reasons. First, the entrepot system fell into decline (because of Indonesia's Konfrontasi policy, bilateral trade stopped; Malaysia attempted to conduct foreign trade by explicitly avoiding Singapore [Lee 2000, 7]). Second, the complete downsizing of the British military base between 1968 and 1971 resulted in Singapore's loss of 20 percent of its GDP due to the diminishing expenditures of the British army. The withdrawal of the British army also caused the loss of 30,000 jobs directly, and 40,000 jobs indirectly (Lee 2000, 52). The British withdrawal caused economic challenges and security uncertainty, which undermined the future viability of Singapore. The government also faced the challenge of building a nation from a multiethnic population constituted mainly of descendants of immigrants (Chinese: 76.6 percent; Indian: 6.4 percent; Malay: 14.7 percent; other: 2.3 percent [Quah and Quah 1989, 106]), among whom there were often ethnically-based riots during the 1950s and 1960s.

Considering Singapore's status as a nascent small island state with a lack of natural resources; an underdeveloped economy without industrial capital; a multiethnic population and the concomitant social unrest; and a missing defense force while facing external security uncertainities, it is not surprising that, during the time of economic development and nation-building, significant state intervention evolved in both the economic and social life of Singapore, which still exists today. Singapore adopted a state capitalist approach to economic development and nation-building, which, in short, means that the government enters into business to create employment and generate profits. Unlike the state capitalist sector created by other newly independent decolonized states (e.g., Indonesia) or post-revolutionary communist regimes (e.g., China), Singapore established state-owned enterprises that are run by wage-earning professional managers and disciplined by market forces, and they stay in business only if they are profitable (Chua 2016, 500).

This study investigates the birth and evolution of state-owned companies as one of the most important tools of state intervention. On the one hand, this chapter explores the economic policy aims that have motivated their creation, and how successful state-owned companies help achieve these aims. On the other hand, it reveals the most important changes concerning state-owned enterprises in the different phases of Singapore's economic development.

The Development of the State Capitalist Sector in Singapore

THE EVOLVING STATE CAPITALIST SECTOR IN THE 1960S AND 1970S

In 1961, the PAP government put emphasis on industrialization in its economic development plans. The initial import-substitution industrialization became irrelevant after Singapore's separation from Malaysia. To replace it, the government chose export-oriented industrialization and free trade. In the absence of a domestic industrial entrepreneurial class,[2] the government primarily relied on foreign companies and the evolving state capitalist sector to achieve its economic development aims.[3]

The state appeared as an entrepreneur in several economic sectors. It established wholly or partially state-owned enterprises. In the latter case, the state entered into partnerships with foreign or domestic private companies. Like governments in most developed capitalist countries (except the United States), the Singaporean government became the exclusive provider of infrastructure and social services. State monopolies (in the framework of so-called statutory boards) were established in the fields of utilities, telecommunications, postal services, port and airport services, industrial estates, and media (e.g., radio, television) (Lim 1983, 755). Statutory boards were also created for financial/banking services, trade, health care, education, tourism, and housing. What differentiates these state activities in Singapore from those in other countries is that—with the exception of health, education, and low-income public housing—they all at least broke even, and most were profitable. They were not subsidized by tax dollars. State-owned enterprises worked for profit. The government did not hesitate to close down loss-making companies (Lim 1983, 755). This still holds true today.

---

[2] Domestic Chinese entrepreneurs were mainly engaged in trading, banking and financial services, real estate, and construction (Tan 1991, 201). Chinese merchants were accustomed to short-term risks and the rapid attainment of profits. They did not possess industrial know-how and were reluctant to get involved in long-term projects (Cheng 1991, 190).

[3] This decision by the government was briefly explained by Lee Kuan Yew, the Prime Minister of Singapore from 1959 to 1990, in the following way: "Had we waited for our traders to learn to be industrialists we would have starved" (Lee 2000, 66). Moreover, we must mention that the PAP government was suspicious of domestic capitalists for fear of their pro-communist and pro-China attitudes (Yeung 2004, 45).

Statutory boards are autonomous semi-government organizations established to perform specific functions laid down by special legislation passed by parliament. They are organizations that are separate from the civil service and government bureaucratic system but still remain within the portfolio of relevant ministries (Tan 1983, 255). Statutory boards are solely owned by the state. They are managed by a board of directors with representation from government ministries, the private sector, and professional and other interest groups (Tan 1975, 62). Like private companies, the operation of state-owned enterprises is regulated by the Companies Act. The government owns most of these enterprises through holding companies. Statutory boards can also possess companies.

Some of the state-owned enterprises and statutory boards were set up under British rule. Later, during the era of independence, they were reorganized and still function. Others were newly established. In the case of enterprises, establishment was often realized with the involvement of private (domestic or foreign) capital. Later on, some of the statutory boards were also transformed into state-owned enterprises.

In relation to Singapore, the literature often uses the term "corporate-state." Members of the first generation of political leadership, such as Lee Kuan Yew, Goh Keng Swee, and S. Rajaratnam, played a significant role in the creation of the corporate-state and its economic success. The corporate-state covers a large number of state-owned enterprises and statutory boards in addition to the civil service (Li 2002, 84).

STATUTORY BOARDS

First, it is worth addressing the role of the Economic Development Board (EDB) and Housing and Development Board (HDB) since the activity of these two statutory boards aimed to solve two of the most pressing economic and social problems facing Singapore post-independence, namely unemployment and the lack of housing.

The EDB was founded with the support of international organizations (UNDP, ILO) in 1961, and it is still the most important state organization for planning and managing the economic development of Singapore.[4] It launched the industrial development of Singapore and played a key

---

[4] The Industrial Promotion Board, which was established by the colonial government in 1957, was the predecessor of EDB, but its size was modest, which made it unable to effectively promote industrialization and economic growth.

role in transforming the small island state into one of the most attractive investment destinations for transnational corporations during the last six decades. This transformation was also supported by the network of EDB branches covering several continents. The fundamental tasks of the EDB have not changed over time, and they include: the development of new industries; support for different industries' economic growth; professional advocacy for companies; corporate financing through loans or equity participation; managing the supply of a skilled labor force; development of industrial estates, etc. The EDB has played a significant role in restructuring the Singaporean economy and sustaining the economic growth from time to time. It promoted import substitution and labor-intensive industries during the initial phase of industrialization as well as the export orientation and capital later on, together with the knowledge and technology-intensive industrial restructuring. In the 1970s, the development of the service sector also came to the fore, which became the second pillar of economic growth besides manufacturing in the 1980s. The EDB has proved to be successful not only in attracting foreign companies to Singapore, but also at promoting the international expansion of Singaporean (particularly state-owned) companies since the 1980s.

The Housing and Development Board was established in 1960. It replaced the Singapore Improvement Trust founded by the British in 1927, which failed to fulfill the growing demands for housing. Initially, the HDB provided housing only to low-income families, but later, the income ceiling for eligibility rose gradually. In 1960, 9 percent of the population lived in public housing. This share reached 84 percent by 1985. In other words, 75 percent of the population obtained public housing over 25 years. The performance of the HDB proved to be a success story that has not been repeated elsewhere in the world.

Relatively early on, in 1968, the PAP government introduced legislation to allow citizens to use their Central Provident Fund (CPF) contributions to purchase HDB flats (Quah and Quah 1989, 112). The operation of the CPF is also controlled by a statutory board. The CPF was established by the British colonial government in 1955 and it is the compulsory pension fund of Singapore. Every employer and employee has to pay a certain amount into the fund, but citizens can use their CPF savings for financing their needs in the fields of education, healthcare, and housing. The government also used CPF savings to finance the construction of infrastructure (e.g., harbors, airports, water, sewer systems, telecommunications, and electricity systems, industrial estates, schools, and universities) deemed essential to economic development (Soon and Tan 1993, 36).

Beside the CPF, the Post Office Saving Bank had a significant role in channeling residential savings into economic development. The Post Office Saving Bank was founded by the British colonial government in 1877. It became a statutory board in 1972 and it used residential savings to purchase government securities, provide loans to state-owned enterprises and statutory boards, and create deposits at the Development Bank of Singapore (DBS).

While the state program of industrialization was advancing, the activity of the EDB was becoming more and more complex. The government decided to streamline the EDB in 1968: the basic task, namely, investment promotion remained under the purview of the EDB, but several other tasks were detached from it, for example,[5] the Jurong Town Corporation (JTC) took over the management and development of industrial estates. The Development Bank of Singapore (DBS) as a state-owned company took over the financing of industrialization.[6] The International Trading Company (INTRACO) incorporated the export promotion department of the EDB. INTRACO was tasked with two objectives: first, developing overseas markets for Singaporean products and sourcing cheaper raw materials for local industries; and second, handling trade with other centrally planned economies (OECD 2015, 49).

In 1983, the Singapore Trade Development Board took over export promotion activity from INTRACO. It introduced an international network of branches to increase the merchandise and service exports of Singaporean companies and worked on renewing Singapore's role as an international trading center.

Besides the detachment of the EDB from its partner institutions, it is necessary to mention the role of Monetary Authority of Singapore (MAS) in the country's economic development. It started to operate as a de facto central bank in 1971. Its major functions were to promote monetary, credit, and foreign exchange policies conducive to economic growth. In the 1970s, it helped Singapore become an international financial center (Tan 1975, 67).

Several statutory boards were created to take charge of the development and management of infrastructure indispensable for economic

---

[5] For further examples of detached tasks, see Soon-Tan (1993, 26).
[6] Further tasks of DBS were the following: 1) financing urban development, tourist promotion projects, and the conversion of British military bases to commercial use; 2) providing loans to enterprises or participating in their equity capital; 3) conducting commercial bank operations; 4) developing Singapore as an international financial center, etc. (Tan 1975, 70-1).

development: 1) The Singapore Harbour Board was replaced by the Port Authority of Singapore in 1964. 2) The Singapore Telephone Board was transformed into the Telecommunication Authority of Singapore. 3) The Public Utilities Board was established in 1963. It took over the activities of the former City Council (water, gas, and electricity services). 4) In the 1980s, the Singaporean government founded the Civil Aviation Authority of Singapore, which became, among others, the operator of the Changi International Airport, which opened in 1981. It took on a key role in transforming Singapore into an international air hub. 5) Metro lines were built in Singapore during the 1980s, and these were operated by a newly established statutory board, the Mass Rapid Transit Corporation.

As mentioned above, several statutory boards were established in different fields of the economy and social life. There were also statutory boards related to tourism, the media, and education should also be mentioned. Those included the Singapore Tourism Promotion Board, Sentosa Development Corporation, Singapore Broadcasting Corporation, the National University of Singapore, Nanyang Technical University etc.

STATE-OWNED ENTERPRISES

The statutory boards mentioned above and the state-owned enterprises together constitute the state capitalist sector of Singapore. In a complementary way, they participated in industrialization and the construction of Singapore's national economy.

According to the data published by Tan (1975, 78–84), in 1973, the Singaporean state had thirty-three partially and twenty-six wholly state-owned enterprises. Through holding companies like DBS and INTRACO, it indirectly owned fifty-seven and sixteen enterprises, respectively.[7] The first important investment of the government was made in the iron and steel industry in 1961.[8] Later, in 1963, seven state-owned enterprises were established in different industries: the food industry/retail, real estate development, plastics, the textile industry, shipbuilding, and the construction materials industry.[9] The state's first investments in the industrial sector were made through the EDB. During the restructuring of 1968, the EDB's equity

---

[7] Data do not cover the number of subsidiaries.
[8] National Iron and Steel Mills Ltd (NatSteel).
[9] Sugar Industry of Singapore Ltd., National Grain Elevator Ltd., United Industrial Corporation Ltd., Singapore Polymer Corporation Pte Ltd., Singapore Textile Industries Ltd., Jurong Shipyard Ltd., Ceramics (M) Pte Ltd.

participation in companies was transferred to the Ministry of Finance, and later to Temasek Holdings (see later). In the 1960s and 1970s, more and more state-owned companies were established in the industries above as well as across the entire economy (e.g., automotives, aircraft, electronics, metals, petroleum, timber, footwear, transportation/logistics, finance, insurance, tourism, etc.). At the beginning of the 1970s, the share of state-owned enterprises in gross output was 26.3 percent in food, 20.4 percent in timber, 16.5 percent in chemicals, 85 percent in iron and steel, and 67.8 percent in the shipbuilding and repair industry (Tan 1983, 259).

At the beginning of the 1970s, the government's paid-up capital in partially-owned companies mainly concentrated in four companies: 1) Jurong Shipyard Ltd., which was started as a shipbuilding company through cooperation between the Singaporean government and a Japanese company (Ishikawajima Harima Heavy Industries); 2) Sembawang Shipyard Ltd., which was formed in 1968 as a result of converting the British Royal Naval Dockyard for commercial use; 3) Singapore Airlines Ltd., which was separated from Malaysia Singapore Airlines in 1972 and became the state-owned carrier of Singapore; and 4) the DBS, which took over the development financing functions of the EDB.

In case of wholly-owned state enterprises, the capital of the government was significantly concentrated in three companies: Keppel Shipyard Ltd., which took over the dockyard division of the Port of Singapore Authority in 1968; Neptune Orient Lines, which began to operate the national merchant fleet in 1968; and Chartered Industries of Singapore Pte Ltd., which launched activities such as the minting of coins for the Singaporean government and the manufacture of military equipment and supplies (Tan 1975, 69–73).

After the foundation of Chartered Industries in 1967, several other factories were opened in the military industry[10] as a result of the withdrawal of the British army. Singapore set up its own armed forces and sought to ensure it could be supplied through domestic production.

To control and co-ordinate the activities of a growing number of state-owned companies, the Singaporean government established Temasek

---

[10] E.g., Singapore Shipbuilding and Engineering Pte Ltd. (1968), Singapore Electronic and Engineering Pte Ltd. (1969), Singapore Automotive Engineering Pte Ltd. (1971), Ordnance Development and Engineering Pte Ltd. (1973), Allied Ordnance Company Pte Ltd. (1973), Singapore Aerospace Maintenance Company Pte Ltd. (1975), Singapore Aero-Engine Overhaul Pte Ltd. (1977), Unicorn International Pte Ltd. (1978)

Holdings (100 percent owned by the Ministry of Finance) and Sheng-Li Holdings (100 percent owned by the Ministry of Defense between 1974 and 1990, by Singapore Technologies Holdings between 1990 and 1994, and by Temasek Holdings since 1994) in 1974. Thirty-five state-owned companies were transferred to Temasek Holdings. State-owned companies operating in the military industry were transferred to Sheng-Li Holdings. To manage the state's investments, further holding companies were founded which fell under the oversight of the Ministry of National Development (MND Holdings), the Ministry of Health (Health Corporation of Singapore was established in 1987, and it late became MOH Holdings), and the Ministry of Education (Helicon Holdings). Information about these holding companies is limited. Currently, MND Holdings and MOH Holdings are wholly owned by the Ministry of Finance. MND Holdings owns certain remnant, but mainly dormant company shares, while MOH Holdings owns hospitals (Sim 2011, 64).

The initial tasks of the most important holding company, Temasek Holdings, were to oversee the activities of state-owned companies and report on the status of the government's investments and the operation of state-owned companies to the Ministry of Finance. By 1979, Temasek Holdings adopted a more active approach to provide focus and direction to its companies, to foster closer co-operation among companies, to seek out new investments, and to consider mergers with profitable companies. The "visible hand" of the state became more apparent in steering Temasek Holdings and the companies it controlled toward national development objectives (Yeung 2011, 631).

In 1981, the establishment of the Government of Singapore Investment Corporation (GIC) also served national economic interests, as GIC was created to invest the budgetary surpluses and foreign reserves of the rapidly developing and growing Singaporean economy. In addition to serving national economic interests, the two SWFs, Temasek and GIC, also contributed to the long-term political legitimacy of the PAP-led government (Yeung 2011, 629).

In 1986, the state directly owned eighty-seven companies and through them—partially or wholly—418 other companies (Ng 1989, 297).[11] Since then, some of these state-owned companies have significantly grown and become leading conglomerates in Singapore (Yeung 2004, 46).

---

[11] Most of the state-owned companies were under the control of Temasek Holdings. In addition, the state owned other companies through other holding companies, statutory boards, and ministries.

Privatization and Regionalization in the 1980s and 1990s

At the end of the 1970s, to overcome economic stagnation and unemployment, developed capitalist countries started to downsize the role of the state and expand market forces. Following the example of developed countries, highly indebted developing countries, influenced by the prescriptions of international agencies (the World Bank and IMF), began to launch privatization, deregulation, trade and investment liberalization, and reforms in the public sector. The Singaporean government also introduced such market reforms, although it had an efficient and well-managed public sector, which was virtually free of external debts and, thus, able to enact these reforms without direct external pressure (Haque 2004, 227–28). That is why it is worth investigating the reform motivations of Singapore and especially the measures and changes related to statutory boards and state-owned enterprises.

In 1987, the Singaporean government launched privatization in the state sector according to the recommendations of the Public Sector Divestment Committee.[12] The Committee planned not only the transfer of ownership—through sales of assets or shares— to the private sector, but also the introduction of liberalization and deregulation measures, the privatization of the state's production of goods and services, and the shifting financing to different state services (Ng 1989, 301). It opened a number of those sectors in which the state had had a monopoly as a statutory board (e.g., telecommunications, finance and insurance, public utilities, health care, etc.) to private companies. First, the state abandoned different dimensions of a defined sector to the private sector. Later, several companies that had been detached from statutory boards were incorporated and then were partially privatized or remained wholly under state ownership (more on this later).

The Singaporean government's motivations for launching privatization were the following: 1) The government wanted to withdraw from commercial activities that no longer needed to be performed by the public sector. 2) The government sought to add breadth and depth to Singapore's

---

[12] Disinvestment of some public enterprises started earlier. The Singapore government privatized the International Construction Corporation in 1976 and the Ming Court Hotel in 1981. Only partial disinvestment took place in the case of Jurong Shipyard, Keppel Shipyard, Neptune Orient Lines, and the Development Bank of Singapore (Ng 1989, 299).

stock market[13] through the flotation of state-owned enterprises and companies split from statutory boards. 3) The government wanted to avoid or reduce competition with the private sector (Feng et al. 2004, 2465). 4) It also wished to increase the role of the private sector in Singapore's economic development.

However, compared to the more substantial changes in favor of market forces in many countries, the policy shift in Singapore was rather slow and piecemeal. In Singapore, the government did not engage in wholesale, but limited privatization (Haque 2004, 232). Privatization instead revealed the restructuring of state ownership. The government divested itself in whole or in part of state-owned companies,[14] but concomitantly invested in newly evolving economic sectors[15] in which there was a lack of private initiative to achieve its economic development aims, namely high value-added, technological and knowledge-intensive manufacturing and services industries.[16] So the entrepreneurial role of the state continued in Singapore (Savage and Pow 2007, 33; Ng and Wagner 1989, 216). State-owned enterprises often bought shares of other state-owned enterprises in sales that highlight the narrowness of privatization in Singapore. Several statutory boards were reorganized too, and companies were spun off from them. For example, Singtel was separated from the Telecommunications Authority of Singapore in 1992. The Public Utilities Board's electricity and gas sector services were spun off to create Singapore Power in 1995. In 1996, the PSA Corporation was separated from the Port Authority of Singapore. These newly established state-owned companies obtained an official listing on stock exchange and were partially privatized (e.g., Singtel) or remained under full state ownership (e.g., Singapore Power and PSA Corporation). In the healthcare sector, hospitals were sequentially incorporated and placed under the Health Corporation of Singapore, which was established in 1987. The state maintained full owner-

---

[13] The development of the stock market had a significant role in the plan to transform Singapore into an international financial center.

[14] For further information about the changes (up to 1999) related to the divestments and shareholdings of Temasek Holdings, see Table 2 of Yeung (2011, 633–34).

[15] E.g., biomedical sciences, interactive and digital media, environmental protection, and water technology, etc.

[16] The Economic Development Board repeatedly played a significant role in developing new sectors. In 1991, it established a special company called EDB Investments, through which it invested in new economic sectors in order to support their initial development.

ship of hospitals, but they were given greater managerial autonomy (Phua 1997, 251). The private sector's (citizens, employers) share of national health care expenditures increased as the government's share correspondingly fell (Lim 1998, 19).[17]

In the 1990s, like privatization, the regionalization of the Singaporean economy, launched by the government in 1993, brought changes to state-owned enterprises. On the one hand, the government supported the restructuring of the Singaporean economy (to high value-added, technological and knowledge-intensive manufacturing and service industries). On the other hand, after the recession of 1985–86, it promoted regional investments of state-owned enterprises and domestic private companies in order to benefit from the rapid economic development and industrialization of the Asia-Pacific region and thereby diversify sources of economic growth in Singapore.[18]

According to the first state initiative for regionalization, the so-called Singapore–Malaysia–Indonesia growth triangle was established in 1989 and was based on the division of labor among these three countries with different comparative advantages. Cooperation encouraged the relocation of low value-added and labor-intensive production processes from Singapore to Johor (Malaysia) and Riau (Indonesia) (Yeung 1998, 403). In 1993, the Singaporean government announced the Regionalization 2000 plan in order to build up the external wing of the Singaporean economy with the involvement of domestic private companies and state-owned enterprises and statutory boards. It conducted negotiations with the leaders of different Asian states to prepare the environment for foreign investments by Singaporean companies. State-owned companies worked together with domestic private companies (in the form of a consortium or joint venture) when they invested abroad. State-owned companies usually managed large-scale infrastructural projects, and the industrial parks[19] established

---

[17] This type of privatization (privatization of financing) also appeared in the education sector.

[18] After the recession of 1985–86, there was a short period when the government promoted the globalization of Singaporean companies. To access new technologies and foreign markets, it encouraged Singaporean companies to form joint ventures with overseas companies in North America and Western Europe. But most of these investments proved unsuccessful, and the government put emphasis on regionalization instead of globalization (Yeoh et al. 2004, 4).

[19] China: China-Singapore Suzhou Industrial Park, Wuxi-Singapore Industrial Park; Indonesia: Batamindo Industrial Park, Bintan Industrial Estate; India: Bangalore IT Park, Sentosa City; Vietnam: Vietnam-Singapore Industrial Park etc.

in China, India, Indonesia, and Vietnam constituted key elements of the state's regionalization plan according to which Singaporean companies began their foreign operations.

The Asian financial crisis of 1997–8 also resulted in some changes to the state capitalist sector of Singapore. During the crisis, several experts cast doubt on the future of Asian developmental states, but the measures taken by the Singaporean government provided evidence to the contrary. The Singaporean government strengthened national companies with various state assistance programs and the restructuring of state-owned companies.[20] It turned the geographical focus of Singaporean companies' external expansion from regionalization to globalization. To ride out the Asian economic crisis, it became imperative for Singaporean companies to expand into growth regions in Europe, North America, South Asia, the Middle East, etc. (Yeung 2000, 136), and this was encouraged by several business and political missions organized by the Singapore Trade Development Board.[21]

The Singaporean State Capitalist Sector in the Past Fifteen Years

Since 2000, privatization has remained limited and gradual,[22] the state has continued to look for newly evolving economic sectors to invest in, and the global expansion of state-owned enterprises has not stopped. Several state-owned companies have become significant global actors in different industries, among others: Singtel (telecommunications), Keppel Corporation and Sembcorp Industries (shipping), CapitaLand (real estate develop-

---

[20] For example, in 1998, the DBS acquired the Post Office Savings Bank. The Sembawang Corporation (formerly Sembawang Shipyard) incorporated several state-owned companies and was renamed Sembcorp. In 2000, CapitaLand was created by the fusion of two real estate developers, DBS Land and Pidemco Land owned by DBS and Singapore Technologies. In 2003, the PSA Corporation was reorganized and the PSA International holding company was established. But before that, real estate (except harbors) of the PSA Corporation had been placed under the control of a newly established company, Mapletree Investments.

[21] In 2002, the Singapore Trade Development Board was reorganized and renamed International Enterprise Singapore according to its new primary function. Priority shifted more and more from export promotion to the support of the foreign expansion of Singaporean companies.

[22] At the beginning of the 2000s, Temasek Holdings sold its total shares in INTRACO, NatSteel, and the Insurance Corporation of Singapore. These companies had been in the portfolio of Temasek since 1974.

ment), DBS Group Holdings (finance), Singapore Airlines (air passenger transport), Neptun Orient Lines (shipping), etc.

The portfolio and the role of Temasek Holdings, which was created to handle most of the state's shares in companies, has changed significantly. It now helps Singaporean companies expand regionally and globally and has invested in private local companies with international growth potential as well as in foreign global enterprises (Chua 2015, 14). Besides promoting the economic development of Singapore, Temasek Holdings' task of attaining long-term, stable profits and increasing national wealth has also been determined by the government.

Table 1 shows the most important Singapore-based companies, which the state has partially or wholly owned through Temasek Holdings for a long time.[23] These companies also have additional subsidiaries that own more subsidiaries in a pyramid structure.[24] The state has indirect ownership in these companies.[25] We can also find globally significant foreign transnational corporations (e.g., Standard Chartered, AIA Group, China Construction Bank Corporation, Intouch Holdings, Bharti Airtel, Evonik Industries, Olam International etc.) in the portfolio of Temasek Holdings.

Table 1
The biggest Singaporean companies in Temasek's portfolio as of March 2015

Sector/Companies	Temasek shareholding (%)
Financial services	
DBS Group Holdings	29
Telecommunications, Media, & Technology	
Singapore Technologies Telemedia	100
STATS ChipPAC	84
MediaCorp	100
Singtel	51
Transportation & Industrials	
Keppel Corporation	20
Neptune Orient Lines	65

---

[23] Mapletree Investments, Pavilion Energy, and CapitaLand are not very old. They were established after 2000.
[24] Twelve out of the initial thirty-five companies (in 1974) have remained in the portfolio of Temasek Holdings.
[25] Each company owns somewhere between ten and more than one hundred subsidiaries.

Sector/Companies	Temasek shareholding (%)
PSA International	100
Sembcorp Industries	49
Singapore Technologies Engineering	51
Singapore Airlines	56
Singapore Power	100
SMRT Corporation	54
Retail, Tourism, & Real Estate	
CapitaLand	39
Mapletree Investments	100
SATS	43
Wildlife Reserves Singapore	88
Energy & Resources	
Pavilion Energy	100

Source: Temasek Review 2015

In 2015, the sectoral distribution of Temasek Holdings' portfolio was the following: financial services: 28 percent; telecommunications, media, and technology: 24 percent; transportation and related industries: 17 percent; retails, tourism, and real estate: 15 percent; energy and related resources: 5 percent; life sciences and agriculture: 3 percent; other: 8 percent. In the last decade, the geographical distribution of the portfolio changed: Singapore's share decreased from 49 percent to 28 percent, while at the same time, the share of Asia (excluding Singapore) increased from 20 percent to 42 percent. In 2015, 70 percent of Temasek's portfolio was concentrated in Asia. The remaining 30 percent was mainly distributed among North America and Europe (17 percent) and Australia and New Zealand (9 percent). The share of Africa, Central Asia, and the Middle East together was 2 percent as was that of Latin America (Temasek 2015, 3). Temasek Holdings primarily invests in Asian equities, so it is one of the least diversified sovereign wealth funds globally (Cummine 2015).

Since 1974, the net value of Temasek's portfolio has increased from 354 million Singapore dollars to 266 billion Singapore dollars. The dotcom crash of 2000–2001 and the global economic crisis of 2008–9 caused only a temporary decrease in the value of the portfolio. Due to the global economic and financial crisis, the net value of Temasek portfolio decreased by 55 billion Singapore dollars (from 185 billion dollars to 130 billion Singapore dollars) as of March 2009, in annual terms. During the year, Temasek Holdings made disinvestments in value of 16 billion Singapore dollars and investments in value of 9 billion Singapore dollars (Temasek 2009, 6-7). The exposure of American and British banks to the global financial crisis explains why Temasek Holdings divested out of Bank of America and Barclays. Regarding the old state-owned enterprises of Singapore, the Chief Executive Officer of Temasek Holdings, Ho Ching declared in 2009 that they would retain „family jewels",[26] and so it happened (see Table 1). In 2009, regardless of the global crisis, Temasek Holdings completed the long-planned disinvestment of three (profitable) power generating companies. Besides, it divested two of its companies founded in 1973, namely, SNP Corporation (printing company), Singapore Food Industries (Temasek 2009, 9-10), and Singapore Computer Systems. The Singapore Food Industries and the Singapore Computer Systems were bought by SATS and Singtel, respectively, which are owned by Temasek. Since 2009, there have not been any significant changes in relation to the „family jewels". However, the impact of the global economic crisis has not left intact these companies. This is confirmed by the fact that in the summer of 2015, Temasek Holding announced the sale of Neptune Orient Lines plagued with overcapacity and losses. (Carew and Venkat 2015).

In 2015, according to the ranking of SWF Institute, Temasek Holdings (with an asset value of 193.6 billion U.S. dollars) was the world's eleventh largest sovereign wealth fund. The other sovereign wealth fund of Singapore, GIC, was ranked eighth with an asset value of 344 billion U.S. dollars.[27] According to Shih (2009, 331), the performance of Singapore's SWFs is legendary, making them models for their peers around the world. In the last twenty years, the GIC portfolio generated an average annual real return of 4.9 percent.[28] In the last ten (twenty) years, the Temasek portfolio had a 9 percent (7 percent) total shareholder return (Temasek 2015, 2). Although there are differences in the function and geographical distribution of their portfolios,[29] Temasek and GIC have a common purpose:

---

[26] Retrieved from http://www.theonlinecitizen.com/2009/07/breaking-news-40-billion-losses-by-temasek-holdings/.

[27] Retrieved from http://www.swfinstitute.org/sovereign-wealth-fund-rankings/.

[28] Retrieved from http://www.gic.com.sg/report/report-2014-2015/investment_report.html.

[29] On the one hand, the Singaporean government created the GIC with a portion of surplus foreign exchange reserves and it receives an annual transfer (discretionary) from the government to help grow its principal. Temasek, on the other hand, has become entirely self-financing with five primary sources of funding: company dividends, divestment proceeds, distribution of fund investment earnings, and long- and short-term debt issuances (Cummine 2015). Contrary to

to supplement the domestic revenues of state budget with returns on their investments, which are then used by the government to support Singapore's social and economic aims. The two sovereign wealth funds have an important role in sustaining and protecting the long-term financial stability of the domestic economy. Clark and Monk (2010, 431) emphasized this in their study on the GIC's role as an investor of foreign reserves, which is very important in order to protect the Singaporean economy from financial crises, and, at the same time, impede the intervention of multilateral institutions in Singapore's economy, like the IMF did in neighboring countries during the Asian financial crisis of 1997–98, which resulted in decreased national sovereignty.

The philanthropic activities of Temasek Holdings are also worth mentioning. The Singaporean government established the Temasek Trust in 2007, and this organ coordinates and controls the philanthropic activities of Temasek Holdings such as disaster prevention, education, medical research, etc.

Summary

After gaining independence, the city-state of Singapore created an extensive state capitalist sector (statutory boards, state-owned enterprises), which still exists and operates today. The Singaporean government inherited some parts of this sector from the British colonial era, but other parts were built up by the government itself—in absence of a domestic industrial entrepreneurial class—to jump start (export-oriented) industrial development, make the society more prosperous, and preserve the independence of Singapore.

Together, the state capitalist sector and foreign transnational corporations are the two main pillars of economic growth and development in Singapore. They have had an indisputable role in transforming Singapore, over decades, into one of the world's wealthiest and most competitive countries.

Temasek, the geographical distribution of GIC's portfolio does not have an Asian focus; the U.S. and Europe have a considerable share in the portfolio of GIC. By law GIC is not allowed to invest in Singapore. In 2015, the geographical distribution of GIC's portfolio was the following: Americas—43% (United States—34%), Europe—25%, Asia—30% and Australasia 2%. Retrieved from http://www.gic.com.sg/images/pdf/GIC_Report_2015.pdf.

In Singapore, the state acts as an entrepreneur. The management of state-owned enterprises is based on the principles of the market and effectiveness. Loss-making enterprises are not saved but closed. Since its creation in the 1960s and 1970s, the Singaporean state capitalist sector has been continuously changing. On the one hand, the state has withdrawn from some economic sectors, while on the other hand, it has expanded into others according to the economic development aims of Singapore. As a result, the Singaporean state capitalist sector is always restructuring. The government decided to partially or wholly privatize companies not only because they were loss-making entities, but also if the participation of the state was no longer needed in a specific sector. Since the 1980s, many of Singapore's professionally managed, profitable state-owned enterprises operating in a competitive market environment have begun to expand regionally and globally beyond the borders of the city-state, and have become important actors in their respective sectors of the global economy.

The returns generated by the portfolio of Temasek Holdings and GIC, which are internationally successful SWFs, are reinvested through the state budget to support the economic and social aims of the city-state.

REFERENCES

Ang, James S. and David K. Ding. 2006. "Government Ownership and the Performance of Government-linked Companies: The Case of Singapore." *Journal of Multinational Financial Management* 16 (1): 64–88.

Bellows, Thomas J. 2006. "Economic Challenges and Political Innovation: The Case of Singapore." *Asian Affairs: An American Review* 32 (4): 231–255.

Carew, Rick and P. R. Venkat. 2015. "Temasek Puts Neptune Orient Lines Up for Sale." *The Wall Street Journal*, July 16. http://www.wsj.com/articles/temasek-puts-neptune-orient-lines-up-for-sale-1437038311.

Cheng, Siok H. 1991. "Economic change and industrialization." In *A History of Singapore*, edited by Ernest C. T. Chew and Edwin Lee, 182–215. Singapore: Oxford University Press.

Chua, Amy L. 1995. "The Privatization–Nationalization Cycle: The Link between Markets and Ethnicity in Developing Countries." *Columbia Law Review* 95 (2): 223–303.

Chua, Beng H. 2015. "State-owned Enterprises, State Capitalism and Social Distribution in Singapore." *The Pacific Review* 29 (4): 499–521.

Clark, Gordon L. and Ashby Monk. 2010. "Government of Singapore Investment Corporation (GIC): Insurer of Last Resort and Bulwark of Nation-State Legitimacy." *The Pacific Review* 23 (4): 429–451.

Cummine, Angela. 2015. "How Temasek Has Driven Singapore's Development." *East Asia Forum*, February 17. http://www.eastasiaforum.org/2015/02/17/how-temasek-has-driven-singapores-development/.
Feng, Fang, Qian Sun, and Wilson H. S. Tong. 2004. "Do Government-Linked Companies Underperform?" *Journal of Banking & Finance* 28 (10): 2461–492.
Haque, M. Shamsul. 2004. "Governance and Bureaucracy in Singapore: Contemporary Reforms and Implications." *International Political Science Review* 25 (2): 227–240.
Hayashi, Shigeko. 2010. "The Developmental State in the Era of Globalization: Beyond the Northeast Asian Model of Political Economy." *The Pacific Review* 23 (1): 45–69.
Lee, Edwin. 1989. "The Colonial Legacy." In *Management of Success: The Moulding of Modern Singapore*, edited by K. Singh Sandhu and Paul Wheatley, 3–50. Singapore: Institute of Southeast Asian Studies.
Lee, K. Yew. 2000. *From Third World to First: The Singapore Story, 1965–2000*. New York: HarperCollins.
Li, Kui-Wai. 2002. *Capitalist Development and Economism in East Asia: The Rise of Hong Kong, Singapore, Taiwan, and South Korea*. London; New York: Routledge.
Lim, Linda Y. C. 1983. "Singapore's Success: The Myth of the Free Market Economy." *Asian Survey* 23 (6): 752–64.
Lim, Meng-Kin. 1998. "An Overview of Health Care Systems in Singapore." *Journal of Public Health Medicine* 20 (1): 16–22.
Menon, Sudha V. 2007. "Governance, leadership and economic growth in Singapore." MPRA Paper 4741. Munich Personal RePEc Archive. https://mpra.ub.uni-muenchen.de/4741/.
Ng, Chee Yuen. 1989. "Privatization in Singapore: Divestment with Control." *The ASEAN Economic Bulletin* 5 (3): 290–318.
Ng, Chee Yuen and Norbert Wagner. 1989. "Privatization and Deregulation in ASEAN: An Overview." *The ASEAN Economic Bulletin* 5 (3): 209–23.
OECD. 2015. *State-owned Enterprises in the Development Process*. Paris: OECD Publishing.
Quah, Jon S. T. and Stella R. Quah. 1989. "The Limits of Government Intervention." In *Management of Success: The Moulding of Modern Singapore*, edited by K. Singh Sandhu and Paul Wheatley, 102–27. Singapore: Institute of Southeast Asian Studies.
Rodan, Garry. 2004. "The Coming Challenge to Singapore Inc." *Far Eastern Economic Review* 168 (1): 51–4.
Savage, Victor R. and Choon-Piew Pow. 2007. "Urban Planning during the Globalization." In *City, Society and Planning*, edited by Bhaleshwar Thakur, George Pomeroy, Chris Cusack, and Sudhir K. Thakur, 19–45. New Delhi: Ashok Kumar Mittal.
Shih, Victor. 2009. "Tools of Survival: Sovereign Wealth Funds in China and Singapore." *Geopolitics* 14 (2): 328–344.
Phua, Kai Hong. 1997. "Medical Savings Accounts and Health Care Financing in Singapore." In *Innovations in Health Care Financing: Proceedings of a World Bank Conference, March 10–11, 1997*, edited by George Schieber, 247–55. Washington DC: World Bank.

Soon, Teck-Wong and C. Suan Tan. 1993. *Singapore: Public Policy and Economic Development.* Washington, DC: World Bank.

Siddiqui, Kalim. 2010. "The Political Economy of Development in Singapore." *Research in Applied Economics* 2 (2). http://eprints.hud.ac.uk/id/eprint/9187/.

Sim, Isabel J. L. 2011. "Does State Capitalism Work in Singapore? A Study on Ownership, Performance and Corporate Governance of Singapore's Government-linked Companies." PhD dissertation. University of Western Australia, Business School.

Tan, Hock. 1991. "State Capitalism, Multi-National Corporations and Chinese Entrepreneurship in Singapore." In *Business Networks and Economic Development in East and Southeast Asia,* edited by Gary Hamilton, 201–16. Hong Kong: Centre of Asian Studies, University of Hong Kong.

Tan, Chwee Huat. 1975. "The Public Enterprise as a Development Strategy: The Case of Singapore." *Annals of Public & Co-operative Economy* 46 (1): 61–85.

———. 1983. "Public Enterprise and the Government in Singapore." In *Government and Public Enterprise: Essays in Honour of Professor V. V. Ramanadham,* edited by G. Ram Reddy, 249–63. London: Frank Cass and Company Ltd.

Temasek. 2009. "Shaping Our Journey: Temasek Review 2009." https://www.temasek.com.sg/content/dam/temasek-corporate/our-financials/investor-library/annual-review/en-tr-thumbnail-and-pdf/TR09%20English.pdf.

———. 2015. "Temasek Review 2015: Embracing the Future." http://tr15.temasekreview.com.sg/downloads/Temasek_Review_Highlights_2015_en.pdf.

United Nations Development Programme. 2014. *Human Development Report 2014: Sustaining Human Progress; Reducing Vulnerabilities and Building Resilience.* New York: UNDP.

Yeoh, Caroline, Chee Sin Koh, and Charmaine Cai. 2004. "Singapore's Regionalization Blueprint: A Case of Strategic Management, State Enterprise Network, and Selective Intervention." *Research Collection of Lee Kong Chian School of Business* 9 (4): 13–16. http://ink.library.smu.edu.sg/lkcsb_research/2365/.

Yeung, Henry W. 1998. "The Political Economy of Transnational Corporations: A Study of the Regionalization of Singaporean Firms." *Political Geography* 17 (4): 389–416.

———. 2000. "State Intervention and Neoliberalism in the Globalizing World Economy: Lessons from Singapore's Regionalization Programme." *The Pacific Review* 13 (1): 133–62.

———. 2004. "Strategic Governance and Economic Diplomacy in China: The Political Economy of Government-linked Companies in Singapore." *East Asia* 21 (1): 40–64.

———. 2011. "From National Development to Economic Diplomacy? Governing Singapore's Sovereign Wealth Funds." *The Pacific Review* 24 (5): 625–52.

CHAPTER 11

The changing role of the state in the Turkish economy

TAMÁS SZIGETVÁRI

Introduction

When modern Turkey was created in 1923, one of its top priorities was the modernization and realignment of the economically underdeveloped country. The process of modernization originated from above, on the initiative and according to the plans of the state, and it experienced uneven success. In the beginning of the 2000s, things took an unexpected turn. In the country with a secular state organization that had been created by Kemal Atatürk eight decades ago, a party with Islamic roots won the 2002 elections, a party that began its fifth term in office in 2018. This, however, has only made the latent process that began several decades ago obvious: the Kemalist project for modernization was less and less able to legitimate itself, and in a country inhabited mostly by Muslims, a moderate but clearly Islamic-based approach has become more and more popular. At the same time, starting in the early 2000s, Turkey has become one of the emerging economies that has been successful in joining global economic production and trade flows, and thereby has experienced fast economic growth. The combination of these two factors makes Turkey an interesting case study for observing changes in the state's role in the economy.

This study focuses precisely on the changing economic role of the state in Turkey and examines the following: whether the presence of Islam is a special feature and how it affects Turkish economic policy; what answers the government finds for the challenges of globalization, and what special features define the Turkish model of economic policy.

Economy and State in Turkey: A Historical Overview

Capitalism reached the Ottoman Empire relatively late. Despite the fact that it had been more or less integrated into the capitalist world system since the end of the eighteenth century, in the multinational (and multi-religious) empire, it took until the beginning of the twentieth century to develop a "national bourgeoisie" that could be the basis of an internal capitalist system. More specifically, it began to develop, but did so largely among non-Muslim populations (Greeks, Armenians, Jews, and Levantines, i.e., Arab Christians). The state powers did not represent their interests, and, in fact, these groups themselves were also interested in a weak central power that acted in accordance with the interests of the European powers (Findley 2010, 102).

This era was characterized by growing foreign influence. Capitulations and exemptions from local laws were provided to traders and businessmen from the West in order to increase trade and, thus, customs revenues. Such exemptions evolved into measures impairing sovereignty over time: foreigners obtained monopolistic rights for several products in the Ottoman Empire, and on many occasions, they also received more favorable treatment in respect to taxes than did local businessmen (Kuran 2011, 209). The treasury crisis after the Crimean War forced the Ottomans state to take foreign (English, French) loans in 1854. By the 1870s, this debt had become unmanageable, and in 1875, the state went bankrupt: the Ottoman Empire could not meet its payment obligations, which had risen over 50 percent of its revenue (Birdal 2010, 168).

To manage the tax crisis—as visible proof of strong foreign pressure—the Ottoman Public Debt Administration (OPDA) was established in 1881. The seven-member board of the OPDA was comprised of representatives of the main lending nations (Great Britain, France, Italy, the Netherlands, Austria). This organization entailed direct foreign intervention into the economic affairs of the country. For the sake of debt repayment, it managed over one-third of state revenues; for example, it managed the revenues of the salt monopoly, as well as the tax and duty revenues from stamps and alcohol (Echia 2010, 9). At the same time, however, the OPDA enforced the implementation of several modernization measures that improved economic performance. It forced the empire to consolidate its financial management, and it contributed to the creation of the modern system of state enterprises. The measures of the OPDA, which was interested in increasing revenues, also facilitated an increase in the competitiveness of the country and the amount of state revenue it brought in. Many Turks, however, see parallels between the effects and perception of the OPDA and later that of the IMF, as both institutions have facilitated the modernization of economy but at the same time serve foreign interests (Birdal 2010, xvii).

After its creation in 1923, the modern Turkish state was torn away from many of the territories it had once ruled for many decades. Atatürk saw Europe and the comprehensive import of European civilization as a means to modernize Turkey. As Abdullah Cevdet, one of the Turkish intellectuals who influenced Kemal Atatürk said, "there is only one civilization, and that is the European civilization. It must be imported with its roses and its thorns" (Lewis 1965, 231). The establishment of modern Turkey was the result of the breakup with the previous Ottoman Empire and a break with the empire's Muslim traditions. The new state intended to implement a clearly Western-style modernization program.

In the beginning of the twentieth century, the Muslim/Turkish bourgeoisie was created from above, through the active role of the state. As a result of this, the relationship between the state and the Turkish bourgeoisie was strong, and the latter played a subordinated, dependent role in the state.

The role of the state in the economy fluctuated in the decades that followed (division by Ayse Bugra, cited by Ahmad [1998]):

- between 1923 and 1929 the aim was to create a modern economy based on private enterprise;
- the period between 1930 and 1946 was characterized by the state's increased intervention in the economy under the principle of etatism;
- between 1946 and 1960, a more liberal economic system came to the fore;
- between 1960 and 1980, the state experimented with planned economy again;
- 1980 marks the beginning of extensive liberalization, which continues to today.

After the fall of the Ottoman Empire, the new Turkish nation-state faced serious problems. The economically most prosperous parts of the empire broke away, and the Turkish economy could only count on its agricultural products. One of the first steps taken by the new government was the distribution and allocation of land to penniless farmers.

Besides economic recovery, social reform was the biggest challenge for the new nation-state. Starting in the 1930s, the Turkish state did not tolerate any alternative ideologies besides Kemalism. In their interpretation, technology and culture stem from the same roots; thus, industrialization meant the simultaneous adoption of Western standards as well.

Kemalism was fundamentally based on etatism, which considered the state as the standard-bearer of modernism. Its presence in the economy became more and more obvious after the Great Depression when, in the beginning of the 1930s, the market for Turkish agricultural products collapsed. In 1934, the Turkish government introduced planned economy following Soviet patterns (Findley 2010, 274). At this time in the Soviet Union, and thus in Turkey, economic and modernization strategy was based on the development of heavy industry. The program saw some success in its attempts to establish the foundations of heavy industry, but the one-sided concentration of resources caused serious damage to other economic sectors. Instead of market coordination, the state that controlled investments and encouraged the development of capital-intensive sectors in a country that was otherwise capital poor and lacked skilled labor for such development, while at the same time, the low-skilled labor force hardly had any jobs. Large state enterprises (KIT in Turkish) were established. Although the private sector did not disappear, private enterprises were heavily dependent on the benevolence and support of the state (274).

After World War II, the country received strong support from the United Sates within the framework of the Marshall Plan and the Truman doctrine, and at the same time, it joined NATO, the IMF, and the OECD. Further, in the years after the war, a more liberal approach was taken in both the political and in the economic system. A multi-party system was created, and when the Democratic Party, which relied on support from the peasantry, came into power in 1950, focus was shifted to state support of the agricultural sector instead of industrial development. In the beginning of the 1950s, demand rose for Turkish exports (especially agricultural products), which had a positive effect on the economic growth of the country. By the end of the decade, however, with the decline of their export prosperity and because of less favorable weather, the economy slowed down. In order to maintain its voting base, the government decided in favor of even higher subsidization of agricultural products instead of cutting costs. The result of this policy was hyperinflation and shortages of products in markets, and because of the increasing economic problems, political differences re-emerged (Akça 2014).

In order to manage the political and economic crisis, the military intervened, and starting in the 1960s, the central power began to tighten its grip on the economy again. In 1963, that is, at the start of the first five-year plan, state intervention in the economy significantly increased; this move, however, had widespread popular support: besides the governing, etatist Republican People's Party, large manufacturers, and international organizations (e.g., the OECD) supported the introduction of development planning (Pamuk 2007).

Like other developing countries, Turkey's economic development policy was based primarily on import-substitution industrialization. According to macro figures, progress was impressive: GDP grew by an annual average of 7 percent, and industrial production showed an even quicker growth of an average of approximately 10 percent per annum between 1963 and 1976 (Aydın 2005, 38). Subsidies and development resources in the private sector were also dependent on the State Planning Office, which resulted in the strengthening of public-private patronage networks and dependency on the state. The agricultural sector, however, was basically left out of the plans, and resources were only rarely allocated to its development. Industrial development focused on supplying the domestic market while exports in the manufacturing industry were almost non-existent: exports accounted for 4 percent of GDP, and almost two-thirds of these were agricultural products. Increasing remittances sent by Turkish workers living abroad and loans from European money markets played an important role in maintaining the balance of payment of the country.

During the seventies and as a result of the oil crises, like most OECD countries, Turkey had to reorganize its economic structure. Reform delays and forced import-substitution strategies only aggravated the crisis.. The Economic Stabilization Program announced in January 1980 brought a fundamental change to the previous, primarily state intervention- and seclusion-based economic strategy. Among the goals of the government's Reagan-style program led by Prime Minister Özal were reducing the state's role in production, prioritizing market conditions, replacing import substitution with an export-oriented strategy, and strong incentives for foreign investments. Accordingly, the government strongly supported production for export by taking over 30 percent of the export costs on behalf of enterprises and giving them discounts on energy and transport costs.

The progress that began in 1980 was more convincing than the results achieved in the previous two decades. As a result of opening the economy, private enterprise began to flourish, and there was a boom in tourism and foreign investment.[1] In the period between 1980 and 1983, when total world trade decreased by 10 percent, Turkish exports almost doubled. During the same period, account deficits decreased from 4.9

---

[1] As Turgut Özal put it, "It's a luck that we don't have oil, because this way we have to work hard for our money" (Akyol 2006).

percent to 3.2 percent of GNP, and inflation from 110 percent to 30 percent (Krueger 1995).

One of the most important consequences of this economic liberalization was the switch to an export-oriented economy. Exports increased from $3 billion in 1980 to around $150 billion by 2015, which accounts for almost 20 percent of GDP. Primary growth was realized mainly by the textile industry, steel industry, automotive industry, and other manufacturing sectors, which together accounted for 90 percent of exports. The so-called *Anatolian tigers*, the relatively small but (externally) competitive enterprises that prospered under liberal economic conditions without state subsidies, played a key role in production. New industrial districts developed in areas that were previously relatively economically underdeveloped and focused on agricultural production and traditional handicrafts.[2] Industrial traditions provided the workforce, and at the same time, the lack of trade unions permitted lower wages. Most enterprises began as family businesses without state subsidies and foreign investment.[3]

In the second half of the eighties, the signs of imbalance intensified as a result of the quick growth in domestic demand and the failures of economic management. Because of incompletely implemented structural reforms, huge amounts of money were spent on financing unprofitable state enterprises, a result of which was a constant increase in the state budget deficit (from 3.5 percent in 1986 to 8 percent in 1990). Inflation was permanently above 50 percent, and economic progress slowed down significantly (Krueger 1995).

To ease the situation, in 1989, large-scale liberalization started again, and this framework made the freer inflow of foreign capital possible. This helped finance the deficit, but the influx of new short-term capital (so-called hot money) made the country vulnerable in times of external crises (Öniş and Şenses 2009).

It is not by accident that setting Turkey on a steady path of progress failed time and again for decades. Between 1970 and 2001, GNP per capita increased on average by 2 percent annually, which was far behind the growth of 4.3 percent in eastern Asia. The differences become even more stark if we consider the deviation from the average: this was 2.2 percentage points lower than eastern Asian growth indictors, which suggests

---

[2] Gaziantep, Denzili, Kayseri, Malatya, Konya, etc.
[3] At the same time, the capital transferred home by migrant workers working in Europe provided funds for these businesses, see below.

large fluctuations in growth. Characteristically, after a couple of years of dynamic progress came a setback, and in the decade after capital liberalization in the beginning of the nineties, there were three such setbacks (1994, 1999, 2001) that resulted in the decrease of GNP by 5 to 10 percent during these years. The development of crises was also fuelled by the deficiencies of Turkish financial institutions and the poor operation of the banking system[4] (Cizre and Yeldan 2005).

Starting in the 1980s and moving into the 1990s, the Turkish modernization process was increasingly—and openly—questioned. This partly took the form of a crisis in the legitimation of the "strong state." Since the establishment of the modern Turkish republic, the state had been the standard-bearer of modernization. In the 1990s, new players and a new language of modernization appeared in the Turkish political sphere. The traditional state was less and less able to meet modern social and economic challenges, and its legitimacy gradually decreased.

At the same time, the possibility of alternative methods of modernization emerged, which appeared not only at the level of theory, but were backed up by genuine and empirical social trends, among others, the return of Islam to public life. This alternative modernization vigorously criticized the overly secular-rational approach of previous modernization efforts based on Kemalist values, which, however, did not necessarily mean it embraced anti-globalist or anti-capital positions (Keyman and Koyuncu 2005).

Islamist Government and Neoliberal Reforms

The creation of the modern Turkish state in 1923 deliberately suppressed Islam in public life, and exclusively relegated it to the private sphere. When the Justice and Development Party (in Turkish Adalet ve Kalkınma Partisi, or AKP) came to power in 2002, it resulted in a growing appreciation for the role of Islam in public life.

By the end of the nineties, at the time of the reorganization of the economic and political spheres, fundamental changes took place within Turkish Islam, which had previously been strongly opposed to the EU and

---

[4] The state bank primarily funded the budget deficit, but private banks also funded the government with the help of foreign loans. There was no monetary control, either; although money supply was increased, this was used by the government only to finance governmental expenditures.

globalization. The group emphasizing the advantages of integration into the EU became more and more powerful among Islamists. The economic groups that formed the basis of this movement were interested in economic reforms, and the opening of European markets widened their export opportunities. Also, from the point of view of politics, the democratization requirements of the EU were advantageous for them. Such requirements limited the possibility of military intervention in political processes, and respect for freedom of speech and human rights allowed Islamists to have a more powerful public presence (Atasoy 2009, 109).

One of the secrets of AKP's success was that it was able to gain supporters among both the winners and the losers of the neoliberal globalization process. Actually, it was more like a middle-of-the-road modern social democratic party that emphasizes the advantages of the market and advocates for the reorganization of the state into a regulatory rather than an intervening-developer state that also cares about social justice (Öniş 2012). At the same time, however, Turkish Islam has special features. As opposed to many radical Islamist trends, Turkish Islamists do not fundamentally reject Western-style modernization; what is more, several elements of the Kemalist heritage (e.g., Turkish nationalism) have remained key elements of their ideology. Likewise, since the dominant part of the social groups forming the basis of the party are among the primary beneficiaries of the globalization process, they see globalization as more of an opportunity rather than a process that threatens their identity (Atasoy 2009). This was also reflected in the economic policy of Islamist forces.

P. Kemal Derviş, an official at the World Bank who was recalled and appointed as minister of the economy by the government preceding AKP, is credited with the recovery from the great crisis of 2001 and the launch of necessary and inevitable reforms. However, the implementation of the plan developed in collaboration with the IMF was continued by the governing AKP, and consequently, the results have been credited to them politically, and the results have been significant.

Economic success and the spectacular improvement in competitiveness were based on several factors. The political environment went through an advantageous change. Despite the centralization of the political institutional framework, political divisions and weak coalitions in previous years made it impossible to consistently implement any political program. The new single-party government formed in 2002 was backed by a two-thirds majority in parliament and was capable of more efficient control.

The strict fiscal and monetary policies and the floating exchange rate increased trust in Turkey, which was also reflected in the decreasing risk premiums of state bonds. The stabilization program following the 1999 crisis applied a fixed exchange rate that completely lost its value 2001, and therefore, after 2001, they switched to a floating exchange rate (Öniş and Şenses 2009). This allowed the National Bank to concentrate on price stability, which also brought its results. After decades of unsuccessful attempts, inflation finally was reduced to single digits.

These structural reforms (primarily in the monetary sector and in the public sector) improved economic conditions significantly (Öniş and Şenses 2009). Besides the extremely expensive bank consolidation,[5] the financial institutions managed by the state were merged, rationalized, and, in part, privatized. Requirements for bank reserves were raised, and, through other regulatory changes, banks were compelled to clean up their profiles and merge with each other. Growth was generated by the private sector, while the consumption and investments of the public sector decreased due to strict fiscal policy.

Productivity significantly improved. Although the strengthening of the Turkish Lire later completely eliminated the favorable effects the massive 2001 devaluation had on export prices, the favorable competitive position was maintained through the improvement of productivity. High value-added and technology-intensive products (vehicles, electric, and electronic products) carried increasingly significant weight in total exports.

After years of modest inflow of foreign direct investment (FDI), 2005 was the year of protrusion largely because of the start of privatization. In 2005 alone $19 billion of FDI came into the country, partly within the framework of privatization, but large amounts were also invested in the banking sector and as greenfield investments. The relatively high level (around $10 billion annually) of capital flowing into Turkey was maintained the years that followed.

The implementation of reforms was facilitated by the extended credit line of the IMF,[6] but also fundamental was increasing political support from the EU. In 2002, Turkey received a promise to achieve candidate status within two years, which increased the influence of the EU and Turkey's determination to implement reforms. The goal of EU accession

---

[5] The banks owned by the state (primarily Ziraat Bank and Halk Bank) had a massive amount of bad loans. During the crisis of 2000–1, the state executed a bank rescue program amounting to almost 30 percent of GDP, which led to a significant increase in state debts (Şimşek and Şimşek 2010, 171–2).

[6] Between 1999 and 2003, the IMF provided $20.4 billion in loans. See Yeldan (2008).

strengthened forces in Turkey that favored reforms, which the IMF had never been able to achieve (its reform requirements had a much smaller base of support and their effects were far more temporary).

To manage the problems caused by the 2008–9 global economic crisis, just like the case of other troubled "emerging markets," for example Hungary, the idea of getting help from the IMF emerged. However, the Turkish government wanted to avoid this for several reasons. In 2008, Turkey had been in a continuous relationship with IMF for more than a decade (since 1998), and the last $10 billion agreement had just expired in May 2008 (Yeldan 2008). According to official Turkish commentaries at the time, Turkey was now an adult, and it did not need any help maintaining its economic balance because it had learned its lesson. Turkey managed to stay on stable footing without the help of IMF, although in the short term it was weakened, while in the long term, this strengthened the image of the Turkish economy overall. All of this, of course, required strict fiscal policies, which also meant austerity measures similar to an IMF-package but with different areas of focus.[7]

The Changing Role of the State in the Economy

State enterprises were the center of gravity in the Turkish enterprise system for a long time. In the 1930s, the private sector was weak, and the state could influence most economic sectors through newly established state enterprises. Following World War II, a few larger conglomerates (a group of enterprises performing industrial, commercial, and sometimes banking functions) organized on a family basis were also organized and played an increasing role in the Turkish economy. Starting in the 1960s, the state dominated again, and in this golden age of industrialization, state enterprises were seen as motors of economic development. During this era, these enterprises accounted for almost half of the manufacturing output of the country. Later on they became an increasingly heavy burden and the main source of state deficits, and their role and significance in production was downgraded. The main sources of problems were high concentration and the lack of competitors and, therefore, low productivity (Aydın 2005, 40).

---

[7] For details see Öniş and Güven 2011.

Attempts were made during the 1980s to reform the unprofitable state sector, but such attempts were rather limited and proved to be ineffective. Subsidization of the large number of state enterprises cost a huge amount of money, and because of the loose fiscal policy, the country's budget deficit was always around 8 to 10 percent of GDP. There was an attempt to regroup some of the subventions so as to improve the market opportunities for flexible small and medium enterprises capable of export, instead of financing unprofitable large enterprises.

Table 1
Number and economic share of employees of state enterprises (1985–2015)

	Number of enterprises	Share within GDP, %	Total number of employees	from this, public servants
1985	48	6.24	653,066	187,276
1990	49	5.18	642,058	27,074
1995	50	4.75	496,352	13,085
2000	41	3.47	434,655	10,329
2005	32	2.01	247,262	7,012
2010	28	1.82	186,137	6,307
2015	26	0.91	119,452	4,431

Source: National Treasury of Turkey. See http://www.treasury.gov.tr/en-US/Stat-List?mid=744&cid=14&nm=829.

The number of state enterprises has been reduced by half since the 1990s; their share of GDP and the number of their employees have been reduced to a fraction. For the time being, enterprises still owned by the state produce less than 1 percent of the GDP and employ a little more than 100,000 employees, which is negligible in a country with a population of eighty million. The following is an overview of the main characteristics of the privatization of the public sector.

Privatization

The reforms of the 1980s considered privatization and the reduction of the state's ownership share of enterprises a fundamental element of the reorganization of the economic structure. The process of privatization that began at the beginning of the 1980s had moving very slow, and it only accelerated in the era following the 2001 crisis under the AKP government. Between 1985 and 2014, 270 enterprises were affected by privatization (in 194 of these companies, state ownership was eliminated completely), as well as almost 1,500 properties, several state monopolies (e.g., gambling), and infrastructural assets (two bridges, eight motorways, and six ports).[8]

The state withdrew completely from several industries that had been previously dominated by companies owned by the state (for example the concrete and milk industries), and significantly reduced its share in tourism, the iron and steel industry, the textile industry, sea freight, and meat processing. The state privatized the most important ports and oil refineries as well. Within the framework of bank bailouts after the 2001 crisis, several smaller banks owed by the state (Sümerbank, Etibank, Denizbank, Anadolu Bank) were sold.

Diagram 1
Income from privatization in Turkey (1985–2014) in billions

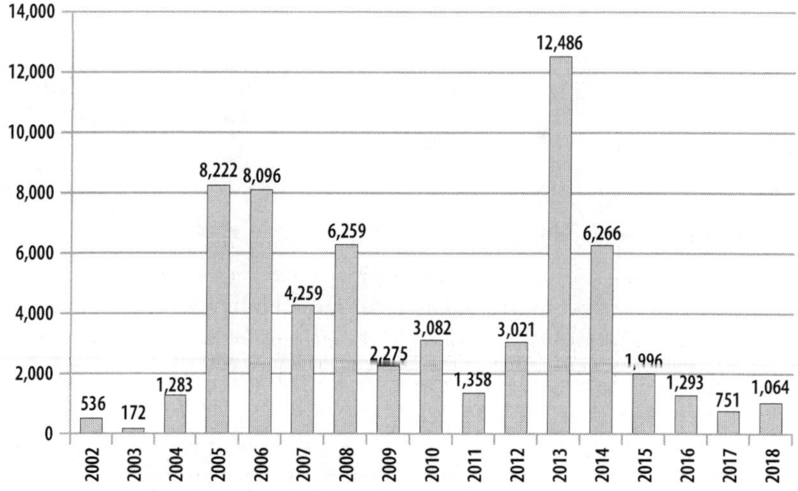

Year	Value
2002	536
2003	172
2004	1,283
2005	8,222
2006	8,096
2007	4,259
2008	6,259
2009	2,275
2010	3,082
2011	1,358
2012	3,021
2013	12,486
2014	6,266
2015	1,996
2016	1,293
2017	751
2018	1,064

Source: https://www.ceicdata.com/en/turkey/privatization-revenues?page=2

Out of the almost $75 billion the state acquired through privatization between 1985 and 2018, it received $8.4 billion during the period between 1985 and 2000, $33.6 billion in the period between 2001 and 2010, and a further $32 billion between 2011 and 2018.

---

[8] The source of this data is the Turkish Organization for Privatization (http://www.oib.gov.tr).

The preferred method of privatization was the so-called block sale; more than half of privatization income came from these. In such cases, the state enterprises were sold as one unit to a privately owned enterprise or consortium, which indicated a preference for maximizing income and achieving quick results. At the same time, however, this may not have been the best choice from the point of view of future competition, as state enterprises that had dominant positions in the markets were transformed into private enterprises in dominant positions. That is, the imbalance of the market structure was not necessarily corrected through this form of privatization. Another disadvantage of this method is that the possibility of corruption, especially sales below market value, is also much higher than for public sales. Nevertheless, stock sales involving the broader public amounted to a much smaller proportion of privatizations, and these were primarily sold after their initial public offering on the Istanbul stock exchange (Atiyas 2009).

The most significant privatizations were in the oil and chemical industry (Petrol Ofisi, Tüpras, Petkim), transportation (Turkish Airlines), telecommunications (Türk Telekom), tobacco (TEKEL), and financial services (Halk Bankasi). The buyers were partly foreign corporations (British Tobacco, Azerbaijani SOCAR, Austrian OMV, Saudi Oger Telekom) and partly consortiums of domestic and foreign companies, but overall, the majority of state corporations were purchased by domestic capital.

Turkish Airlines was one of the first enterprises designated for privatization. Shares of the airline were gradually offered to the public on the Istanbul stock exchange between 1990 and 2006, and since 2006, the state has been a minority owner (holding a 49 percent ownership share), but with a so-called golden share, it has control over strategic decisions. Although the idea of selling further state shares has come up several times, no shares have been offered to the public on the stock exchange since 2006.

Fifty-five percent of Türk Telekom shares were sold in 2005 to the Saudi Oger Telekom for $6.5 billion, while in 2008, a further 15 percent of shares were offered to the public on the Istanbul stock exchange, while 30 percent is still under state ownership.

Fifty-one percent of the Petrol Ofisi oil company was acquired by the Turkish Doğan Holding in 2000, and then in 2006, the Austrian OMV purchased a 34 percent ownership stake for $1.05 billion. In 2010, OMV also acquired the shares of Doğan. Thus, it now owns 95 percent of the company, which owns oil refineries and three thousand petrol stations.

In 2008, the Azerbaijani oil company SOCAR together with the Turkish company Turkas PetroKimya purchased 61 percent of the Petkim petrochemical group for $2.04 billion. Then, in 2011, when SOCAR bought out Turkas's shares, it became the majority owner. The state retained 11 percent ownership of the company, and the rest was sold on the stock exchange.

The privatization of Tüpras, an enterprise operating oil refineries, started in 1991, when 2.5 percent of shares were offered to the public on the stock exchange. Through secondary public offerings, this ratio rose to 49 percent. In 2009, the consortium of Turkish Koç Holding (75 percent), Aygaz (20 percent), Opet (3 percent), and Shell (2 percent) acquired the remaining 51 percent for $4 billion.

Tekel is the leading enterprise in the alcohol and tobacco industry, which was created in 1925 through the nationalization of the enterprise (Régie) that had a monopoly under the Ottomans and was partly under foreign control. British American Tobacco acquired the enterprise in an auction for $1.72 billion in 2008. This was partly due to the fact that its competitors (Philip Morris, Japan Tobacco) were already market players made a low offer because they would have acquired a dominant position through the sale, which could be challenged by the competition authority. Tekel holds a 36 percent market share in Turkey. In the spirit of reorganization, Tekel closed twelve factories and fired ten thousand people, which led to serious union protests not only against the new owner, but also against the AKP government that sold the company.

In the case of Halk Bankasi, the first 25 percent was privatized for $1.8 billion through the Istanbul stock exchange in 2007. Then, after the uncertainty caused by the crisis, the next 24 percent of shares were sold for $2.5 billion on the stock exchange in 2012. The ownership ratio of the state is currently 51 percent, which the state also wanted to privatize. But because of their violation of the sanctions against Iran, the company experienced serious attacks in the years leading up to the sale. The sale of the insurance companies owned by the bank is also on the agenda.

In 2015, the income generated by privatization was around $10 billion, and according to plans, further significant privatizations are expected in the upcoming years. Current privatization plans include motorways, bridges, power plants, and ports, as well as twenty-five sugar factories, five machine factories, the Turksat telecommunications enterprise, and the enterprise operating the BOTAS oil and gas pipeline network. The state-owned companies in the gambling sector (Spor Toto and the enterprise for horse race betting) are to be privatized as well, which by themselves may generate an income of around $10 billion. In the case of the Turkish electrical works (Türkiye Elektrik Iletim) and the Turkish oil company (TPAO), the sale of the 49 percent minority ownership share is planned.

According to Öniş (2011) all of the motivations behind the massive privatization mentioned in the literature were present in Turkey:

1. The government's need for income;
2. A centralized and strong executive power; and
3. Powerful influence from external players.

After a major crisis (as the examples of Mexico or Argentina show), a significant change in economic policy may occur. It was also typical in the case of Turkey that, after 2002, groups that had previously opposed certain economic reforms—for example, privatization—weakened, while those in favor of such reforms strengthened. Because of the crisis and its management (e.g., bank consolidation), the government's need for income increased as well. The role of certain external actors in favor of privatization (the IMF and, to a lesser extent, the EU) was also revaluated.

According to Öniş (2011), however, a few additional factors also played a central role in the acceleration of the privatization process. One such factor was the presence and participation of domestic capital in privatization, as privatization carried out only with the involvement of foreign capital often generates resentment in the people. Among those opposing privatization—as was demonstrated by several Turkish examples (Tüpras and Erdemir)—the presence of "national capital" reduced resentment. The favorable legal and institutional framework, and the positive demonstrative effect of privatizations carried out in other countries in the beginning of the decade also contributed to successful privatization.

The State and the System of Private Enterprises

The erosion of state capitalism also entails the strengthening of oligarchic capitalism (Karadağ 2010). A special relationship with the political-economic decision makers is an important part of economic life that results in the strengthening of traditionally strong political patronage networks. Liberalization, therefore, does not necessarily result in a liberal market economy in the Western sense, that is, where market players compete under the same regulations formulated by an impartial state bureaucracy. As a consequence of the Turkish reforms of the 1980s, the fragmentation of the political sphere, the weakening of the cooperative social system, and the formation of a new, closed political-business elite were fundamental elements of the new oligarchic capitalist system.

At the same time, starting in the late 1970s and early 1980s, privately owned large enterprises have come out more firmly against excessive state intervention, support schemes dependent on the state, and overregulated economic management.

The Association of Turkish Industrialists and Businessmen (TÜSIAD), established in the beginning of the 1970s, has advocated economic liberalization from the very beginning. It supported the military coup in 1980 because it saw it as guaranteeing the execution of economic reforms. Today, however, it advocates European-style democratization and respect for human rights; these principles dominate recent publications of TÜSIAD as well. In addition, TÜSIAD encourages the exploitation of opportunities created by globalization, and it also favors EU accession (e.g., it publishes full-page advertisements in European papers to build support for Turkish membership). TÜSIAD is the Turkish spokesman of Western-style modernization and the liberal economic-social model. It rejects excessive state intervention in the economy, and it does not oppose elements of globalization that influence the perception of market players (style, taste, outlook, a consumption-oriented approach).

The enterprises left out of the aristocratic "white-Turkish" TÜSIAD established several organizations to represent their interests in the beginning of the 1990s.

MÜSIAD is the short version of *Mustakil iş adanleri derneği*, that is the Association of Independent Businessmen, but many suspect that Muslim rather than Mustakil (independent) is the concept behind the name. Indeed, the association is fundamentally based on Islamic values, and the relationship of trust is quite strong among member enterprises, which together form a network within the Turkish economy. It is also because of the strong bonds among members that MÜSIAD questions the former leading role of TÜSIAD in the Turkish corporate sector in contemporary Turkey.

The strongest institution in the economic heartland of Islamists is MÜSIAD (Özcan and Turunç 2011). MÜSIAD is a good example of the compatibility of modern Western economic rationality with the values of Islam and the harmonic coexistence of free market capitalism and Muslim identity. Its goal is not only economic but, in a wider sense, social and also moral: economic and technological progress also has to be accompanied by advancement in a spiritual sense, since both Western-type capitalism and Kemalist modernization have neglected this side of progress. It builds on the values of Islam, and thus, trust, solidarity, and the prioritization of community interest over personal interest are fundamental (Lorasdaği 2010). MÜSIAD also supports the EU accession of Turkey, primarily on economic grounds. It values the positive effects of globalization, like economic openness and better foreign trade opportunities, because they provide a basis for the development of Muslim economic players. Business enterprises based on Islamic foundations are very active in the Balkans and in Central Asia (Losdaği 2010).

The Muslim capitalism represented by MÜSIAD is therefore different from the liberal capitalist concept of TÜSIAD. The basic interests of the two economic interest groups are, however, the same: a stable government, EU membership, and good relations with their main market: the West. Such similar business interests override the differences between the two groups.

Public Procurement and Crony Capitalism

Public procurements, or government purchase, comprise substantial shares of a government's expenditures, and this is the activity in which the state and private sector interact most intensively. Thus, the regulation and practice of public procurements effectively mirrors state involvement in economic interactions. Public procurement may be a policy device to support small and medium enterprises, but it is also a powerful tool to build up and finance clients. In Turkey, a new Procurement Law was enacted in January 2003; it was primarily based on international standards of transparency, accountability, and competitiveness set by the UN and agreed upon by the EU. While the AKP government initially supported the regulation, the business groups behind AKP opposed the new law. They wanted previous unjust practices to continue because they were now the privileged clientele (Gürakar 2016, 5). Consequently, the government gradually changed the procurement law, exempting several public institutions from the law, and introducing a "restricted procedure" instead of open tenders.[9] Public procurement, thus, became an influential tool to both promote the electoral success of AKP and build up its own loyal elite.

Corruption has been a widespread phenomenon in Turkey and continues to be a major problem in the country. Some rents were allocated to the construction industry: an extensive number of permits to contrac-

---

[9] While in 2005, 71 percent of procedures were open auctions, in 2014, only half of them were (Gürakar 2016, 6).

tors with strong political ties turned Turkey to a construction site[10] (Kentel 2016, 140). According to a new regulation adopted in 2012, any buildings that did not pass the state's inspection with respect to earthquake safety standards would be subject to "emergency nationalization" and redevelopment through government tenders. A new government-enabled real estate market was born, and hundreds of urban renewal projects have been initiated through the implementation of these laws (El-Kazaz 2015, 6). The new policy was not without contradictions: in December 2013, many officials from the Housing Development Administration (TOKI), and high-level figures related to a number of important government ministers were detained for illegal construction permits they had given to firms in exchange for bribes[11] (Ulusoy 2014, 2).

Competitiveness and Developmental State

The program followed by AKP made economic growth and restructuring top political priorities. This also entailed the improvement of the investment environment. New Turkish politics were, therefore, highly oriented to promoting competitiveness.

Ünay (2012) examines the 2002–2012 period of Turkish development based on the theory of the "competition state."[12] Its elements are: 1. neoliberal monetarism instead of expansionism with inflation; 2. micro- instead of macro-economic governance; 3. setting strategic goals instead of resorting to extensive intervention; 4. innovation and profitability instead of well-being maximization; and 5. economic diplomacy and market share instead of geo-strategy and national security.

After the early 2000s, the "post-Washington" competitiveness factors gained strength in Turkey. The reforms of the 1980s were unsuccessful because of hasty financial liberalization and the lack of fiscal discipline. Özal's reforms were frequently based on direct governmental interventions that circumvented the legislature, and this had negative repercussions on

---

[10] It also explains the 2013 Gazi Park protest against the "neoliberal arrogance" of the government (Kentel 2016, 148).
[11] Erdoğan accused Islamic community leader Fetullah Gülen of being behind the investigation and began a revenge campaign targeting followers of the Gülen community.
[12] The theory of the "competition state" primarily refers to the work of Cerny (2008; 2010).

fiscal discipline. For the sake of growth, he also found monetary easing acceptable, but the high rate of inflation greatly impaired growth potential in the long term. Starting in the second half of the 1990s, the dual external pressure (EU, IMF) forced the adoption of several institutional reforms in Turkey that resulted in the independence of the central bank and the strengthening of bank and competition supervision.

Micro-economic interventions are the most impressive in the fields of regulation, industrial policy, and employment policy. Especially in these early days, the specific vision for industrial policy was also missing, and besides external pressure (from the EU, IMF, and WTO) and because of it, economic subventions were typically applied in a sector-neutral way based on horizontal politics. According to Unay (2012), setting a target for industrial development strategy is still quite nascent even today, although recently there have been some shifts in this regard (see below).

Instead of (or rather in addition to) the populist, national well-being maximization program and policy (full employment, provision of widespread public services), the promotion of an entrepreneurial culture and innovation may be considered the economic goals of Turkey today. In previous years, despite the active role of the state, a European-style welfare state was not established; it may rather be defined as a minimalist and direct social system based on payments by employers and employees, with very low contributions from the state (Özdemir and Yücesan-Özdemir 2008, 470). The increasing deficit of the system (mainly the pension system), however, was increasingly becoming a serious problem,[13] and the crises of the 1990s kept the necessity for systemic reform continuously on the agenda. Social security reform by AKP reflected the neoliberal/conservative orientation of the party and the expectations of the external players (the EU and IMF): instead of state involvement, they were based on the strengthening of self-care and the introduction of market-based systems (e.g., a funded pension system). After coming into power, AKP tried to follow the post-Washington consensus, which tried to simultaneously satisfy the demands of the business sector and the needs of the broader society. According to Öniş (2011), however, on the whole, business priorities prevailed over social aspects in Turkey. In addition, on the basis of its own ideological beliefs based on the Islam, AKP reinforces a social policy based on traditional social structures (family orientation; husband as

---

[13] The annual deficit of the system amounted to 5–6 percent of GDP, which had to be supplemented by the central budget.

breadwinner) (Grütjen 2008, 112). Furthermore, in addition to direct state intervention, the role of religious caritative organizations (also supported by the state) strengthened.

Compared to the past, the challenges of globalization and preparations for the EU accession process have brought a change in foreign policy. Turkey's new position after the end of the Cold War also contributed to these changes: while previously Turkey used to be peripheral to the Western alliance, in the new geopolitical structure, it has gained regional power positions in the Balkans, Caucasus, the Middle East, and Central Asia. It was clear that the economy and trade were given more weight when setting priorities (Turkey as a "trading state"), although at the same time, the revaluation of regional geopolitics was also becoming increasingly important. In the case of AKP, globalization and nationalism are not mutually exclusive; rather the ruling party promotes and enforces national interests in global relations (Öniş 2012).

Despite quick growth after the crisis in 2001, the international competitiveness of Turkey still lags behind expectations. After the integration of China and India into world economy, the strategy of increasing competitiveness through its cheap workforce could not remain the key to Turkey's economic success. To increase competitiveness, effective market mechanisms, an attractive investment environment, and institutional structures need to be created.

In the period following World War II, many countries managed to advance to the category of middle-income countries relatively quickly. But in the end, only a few of them became high-income economies. Typically, the initial phase of swift growth was followed by a sudden deceleration of growth and production; this phenomenon is referred to as the "middle income trap" in the literature.[14]

Turkey is well aware of this threat. As the Turkish minister of finance, Mehmet Şimşek, emphasized in his article published in the *Wall Street Journal* (2014), Turkey, despite its quick progress, faces several challenges, and there are many things to do if the country wants to break from the group of middle-income countries. In order to succeed, it needs an appropriate economic policy, additional structural reforms, and a supportive international economic environment. The most important priorities of

---

[14] According to the estimates of the World Bank, out of 101 middle-income countries (data from 1960), only thirteen became high-income countries by 2008 (Agénor, Canuto, and Jelenic 2012).

Turkish reforms are improving the quality of the workforce by improving the quality of education; enhancing labor market flexibility; and improving productivity through technological development.

Accordingly, Turkey intends to implement a strategy based on the strengthening of sectors and factors that are in part trendy, and in part necessary for progress. By 2023, the centennial of the establishment of the Turkish Republic, the country intends to become one of the ten largest economies in the world with a GDP of two trillion dollars (this means a GDP of $25,000 per capita), and it wants to increase employment by ten percentage points and increase the value of exports to $500 billion through the manufacture and export of automobiles, airplanes and satellites.

In terms of specific plans, according to the long-term vision of the Document on Turkish Industrial Strategy, Turkey has to become the center of Eurasia in terms of the production of main high-tech products.[15] Additionally, the general goal of the strategy is the following: "Increasing the competitiveness and efficiency of the Turkish industry, restructuring the industry in a direction that facilitates for Turkey that its share be increased within World export where Turkish export mainly consists of high-tech products and products with high added value, to have well-trained workforce, while it is sensitive to environmental and social challenges" (Ministry of Industry and Trade 2010, 49). Among the strategic goals are increasing the weight of enterprises and high-tech industries and introducing products with high added values in low-tech fields.

The strategy named eight fields of industry: the amelioration of the investment and business environment, international trade and human resources, the expansion of the financial opportunities of small and medium enterprises, the technological development of enterprises, and infrastructural sectors including telecommunications, energy, transportation, environmental protection, and regional development. Priority sectors are the car industry, machinery manufacturing, household products, electronics, the textile industry and clothing, the food industry, and the iron and steel industry.

According to Yilmaz (2011), only a selective industrial policy that supports specific sectors can be successful. This is the basis of the economic success of Japan, South Korea, and Brazil, and developed countries have also applied this strategy; it is also, once again, becoming popular and accepted. The non-selective (neutral) policies that are promoted by neoliberal economic policy are ineffective according to Yilmaz. Strong economic

---

[15] According to the Ministry of Industry and Trade (2010).

foundations (macro-stability, markets operating properly) do not necessarily lead to the transformation of the economic structure; for industrial development, appropriate and supportive industrial policy is also a must. This is affirmed by Rodrik (2007, 23), although he puts his emphasis not on a traditional, selective industrial policy based on direct state subsidies but rather on the participation of a state that actively fosters the process of industrialization.

As Akan (2018, 164) points out, the AKP government began to transform the country's dependent institutional and industrial structures by launching the entrepreneurial state paradigm and focusing on industrial transformation programs. It partly failed in large part due to imperfections in the systemic functioning of the Turkish developmental regime.

A Security-Based Approach and Its Economic Consequences

In recent years, there have been substantial changes to the international environment of Turkey, which have given rise to the need reset foreign policy and partly internal policy priorities. The Arab Uprisings in 2011, followed by the civil war in Syria, and the strengthening of ISIS and Syrian Kurdish forces have produced unprecedented security challenges for Turkey (Keyman 2017, 59). In a more instable and insecure region, Turkey had to confront existential threats to its national security. The desecuritization of the Kurdish issue initiated by AKP in 2009 was quickly reversed (Noi 2016, 71). In Turkish foreign policy, this meant a shift away from a multi-layered, multi-actor, multi-dimensional, and soft power approach toward a more focused, selective, globally limited, and hard power policy orientation (Keyman 2017, 62).

In internal politics, corruption allegations against Erdoğan's circle in December 2013 were an important turning point for the regime. The government accused the Gülen (or Hizmet) Movement of creating a "parallel state" with increasing influence in state institutions, especially the police and judiciary (Noi 2016, 68). The coup d'état in July 2016 marked a new period in Turkey's political history. The Turkish government blamed the failed coup attempt on Fethullah Gülen and his followers. A state of emergency was declared, and the government started a systematic purge of state and media institutions. Currently, there are over ten thousand people in detention and allegations circulating about their ill-treatment in custody.

An economic consequence of the political changes has been AKP's shift toward security-oriented decision-making and away from their decade-long prioritization of the economy. The idea of a trading and competition state has started to fade.

The state of emergency has a clear, negative effect on business interests. The Europeanization process that defined the early 2000s helped promote the de-securitization of Turkish domestic policy, and it contributed to the economic successes of the country. A return to the democratization process is vital for the economic well-being of Turkey. The rule of law and strong commitment to democracy stands at the core of a predictable and favorable business environment (Noi 2016, 73).

Though the yearly growth rate of the GDP has remained high (7.4 percent in 2017), the fragility of the Turkish economy and the weaknesses of neoliberal economic reforms became increasingly visible. Turkey's "economic miracle" during the previous decade was partly based on revenue acquired through the privatization of public assets (Balkan, Balkan, and Öncü 2015, 3). Growing domestic demand was fueled by consumption and investments. However, in terms of investments, these flowed less to the manufacturing sector, and more to the less productive construction and housing sectors. The country's current account deficit has widened to 5.5 percent of GDP (2017), and its economic growth is largely dependent on access to new loans, that is, new capital inflows. Current political developments in Turkey and the unpredictable business environment have substantially heightened the uncertainty for many foreign investors.[16] Furthermore, the government's (and especially Erdoğan's) intention to exert pressure on the Central Bank to prevent a rise in interest rates (despite international and domestic conditions) has created even greater risks for foreign capital.

Despite hopeful structural reforms in the country, Turkish macroeconomic conditions have become increasingly worrying: with its current massive deficit, weakening currency, and double-digit inflation rates, Turkey has become one of most fragile economies in the world.

Conclusion

Modern Turkey is changing, and the role of state has also changed substantially in the last decades. Kemalist modernization was characterized by an etatist, state-led reform process with large-scale state involvement in the

---

[16] These concerns are especially important in case of Germany, one of Turkey's most important foreign investors (Szabó 2018, 8).

economy. Most of the important industrial firms were state-owned, while private enterprises were highly dependent on the support of the state. With the neoliberal economic opening of Turkey starting in the 1980s, the *Anatolian tigers*, a relatively small but competitive group of enterprises emerged, which were able to prosper without state subsidies in the new liberal economic conditions. These firms had strong ties to the socially conservative, Muslim middle-classes.

After the millennium, the electoral win of the AKP brought an Islamist party to power. Despite initial skepticism, the new government pursued successful economic reforms, and it has also continued the Europeanization process. The new regime made attempts to harmonize traditional Islamic values and neoliberal-type responses to the challenges of globalization, and it was able to execute neoliberal reforms with relatively strong support from the broader Turkish society. However, similar to many other developing countries, the reforms in Turkey have also been executed in the spirit of the post-Washington consensus, marked by a changing, but not necessarily decreasing, role for the state in the economy.

The Turkish state withdrew completely from several industries that had been previously dominated by state-owned companies and reduced its presence in others. The erosion of state capitalism, however, entailed the strengthening of oligarchic capitalism. A special relationship with political-economic decision makers is still an important part of business life that results in the strengthening of traditionally strong political patronage networks. Liberalization, therefore, did not result in a liberal market economy.

Regarding the future role to be played by the state, policies aimed at the improvement of competitiveness are clear priorities that require the state to formulate an active industrial and technological policy. Though the AKP governments have experience launching the entrepreneurial state paradigm and in focusing on industrial transformation programs, the results are still not convincing. Moreover, the shift of government policy from an economy-oriented to a security-oriented approach in recent years has substantially worsened the chances of the continuation of successful (or even EU-compatible) political and economic reforms in Turkey.

REFERENCES

Agénor, Pierre-Richard, Otaviano Canuto, and Michael Jelenic. 2012. "Avoiding Middle-Income Growth Traps." Economic Premise 98. The World Bank,

Poverty Reduction and Economic Management Network (PREM). http://documents.worldbank.org/curated/en/422121468155111398/Avoiding-middle-income-growth-traps.
Ahmad, Feroz. 1998. "The Development of Capitalism in Turkey." *Journal of Third World Studies* 15 (2): 137–44.
Akan, Taner. 2018. *The Complementary Roots of Growth and Development: Comparative Analysis of the United States, South Korea, and Turkey*. Basingstoke, Hampshire: Palgrave Macmillan.
Akça, İsmet. 2014. "Hegemonic Projects in Post-1980 Turkey and the Changing Forms of Authoritarianism." In *Turkey Reframed: Constituting Neoliberal Hegemony*, edited by İsmet Akça, Ahmet Bekmen and Barış Alp Özden, 13–46. London: Pluto Press.
Akyol, Mustafa. 2006. "'Islamic Capitalism' Faces Secular Challenge in Turkey." *Turkish Daily News*, December 18.
———. 2007. "Is Islam Compatible with Capitalism?" *Turkish Daily News*, February 19.
Atasoy, Yildiz. 2009. *Islam's Marriage with Neoliberalism: State Transformation in Turkey*. Basingstone–New York: Palgrave MacMillan.
Atiyas, İzak. 2009. "Recent Privatization Experiences of Turkey: A Reappraisal." In *Turkey and the Global Economy: Neo-liberal Restructuring and Integration in the Post-crisis Era*, edited by Ziya Öniş and Fikret Şenses, 101–22. London; New York: Routledge.
Aydın, Zülküf. 2005. *The Political Economy of Turkey*. London; Ann Arbor: Pluto Press.
Balkan, Neşecan, Erol Balkan, and Ahmet Öncü. 2015. "Introduction." In *The Neoliberal Landscape and the Rise of Islamist Capital in Turkey*, edited by Neşecan Balkan, Erol Balkan, and Ahmet Öncü, 1–12. New York; Oxford: Berghahn.
Birdal, Murat. 2010. *The Political Economy of Ottoman Public Debt: Insolvency and European Financial Control in the Late Nineteenth Century*. London; New York: I. B. Tauris.
Cerny, Philip G. 2008. "Embedding Neoliberalism: The Evolution of a Hegemonic Paradigm." *Journal of International Trade and Diplomacy* 2 (1): 1–46.
———. 2010. "The Competition State Today: From *raison d'État* to *raison du Monde*." *Policy Studies* 31 (1): 5–21.
Cizre, Ümit, and Erinç Yeldan. 2005. "The Turkish Encounter with Neo-Liberalism: Economics and Politics in the 2000/2001 Crises." *Review of International Political Economy* 12 (3): 387–408.
Echia, Stefania. 2010. "The Economic Policy of the Ottoman Empire (1876–1922)." MPRA Paper 42603. Munich Personal RePEc Archive. https://mpra.ub.uni-muenchen.de/42603/.
El-Kazaz, Sarah. 2015. "The AKP and the Gülen: The End of a Historic Alliance." Middle East Brief 94. Crown Center for Middle East Studies, Brandeis University.
Findley, Carter V. 2010. *Turkey, Islam, Nationalism, and Modernity: A History, 1787–2007*. New Haven; London: Yale University Press.
Grütjen, Daniel. 2008. "The Turkish Welfare Regime: An Example of the Southern European Model? The Role of the State, Market and Family in Welfare Provision." *Turkish Policy Quarterly* 7 (1): 111–29.

Gürakar, Esra Çeviker. 2016. "Introduction and Overview." In *Politics of Favoritism in Public Procurement in Turkey: Reconfigurations of Dependency Networks in AKP Era*, edited by Esra Çeviker Gürakar, 1–11. New York: Palgrave Macmillan.

Karadağ, Roy. 2010. "Neoliberal Restructuring in Turkey: From State to Oligarchic Capitalism." MPIfG Discussion Paper 10/7. Cologne: Max Planck Institut für Gesellschaftsforschung.

Kentel, Ferhat. 2016. "The Right to the City during the AK Party's Thermidor." In *The Turkish AK Party and its Leader: Criticism, Opposition and Dissent*, edited by Ümit Cizre, 132–65. London; New York: Routledge.

Keyman, E. Fuat. 2017. "A New Turkish Foreign Policy: Towards Proactive 'Moral Realism'." *Insight Turkey* 19 (1): 55–69.

Keyman, E. Fuat, and Berrin Koyuncu. 2005. "Globalisation, Alternative Modernities and Political Economy of Turkey." *Review of International Political Economy* 12 (1): 105–28.

Krueger, Anne O. 1995. "Partial Adjustment and Growth in the 1980s in Turkey." In *Reform, Recovery, and Growth: Latin America and the Middle East*, edited by Rudiger Dornbusch and Sebastian Edwards, 343–68. Chicago: University of Chicago Press.

Kuran, Timur. 2011. *The Long Divergence: How Islamic Law Held Back the Middle East*. Princeton: Princeton University Press.

Lewis, Bernard. 1965. *The Emergence of Modern Turkey*. Oxford: Oxford University Press.

Lorasdağı, Berrin Koyuncu. 2010. "The Relationship between Islam and Globalization in Turkey in the Post-1990 Period: The Case of MÜSIAD." *bilig* 52 (Winter): 105–28.

Ministry of Industry and Trade. 2010. *Turkish Industrial Strategy Document 2011–2014: Towards EU Membership*. Ankara: Ministry of Industry and Trade, Republic of Turkey.

Noi, Aylin Ünver. 2016. "Challenges of Democracy in Turkey: Europeanization, Modernization and Securitization Revisited." In *Challenges of Democracy in the European Union and its Neighbors*, edited by Aylin Ünver Noi and Sasha Toperich, 45–73. Washington D.C.: Center for Transatlantic Relations SAIS.

Önder, Nilgün. 2016. *The Economic Transformation of Turkey: Neoliberalism and State Intervention*. London; New York: I.B. Tauris.

Öniş, Ziya. 2006. "The Political Economy of Islam and Democracy in Turkey: From the Welfare Party to the AKP." In *Democratization and Development: New Political Strategies for the Middle East*, edited by Dietrich Jung, 103–28. New York: Palgrave Macmillan.

———. 2011. "Power, Interests and Coalitions: The Political Economy of Mass Privatisation in Turkey." *Third World Quarterly* 32 (4): 707–24.

———. 2012. "The Triumph of Conservative Globalism: The Political Economy of the AKP Era." *Turkish Studies* 13 (2): 135–52.

Öniş, Ziya, and Ali Burak Güven. 2011. "Global Crisis, National Responses: The Political Economy of Turkish Exceptionalism." *New Political Economy* 16 (5): 585–608.

Öniş, Ziya, and Fikret Şenses. 2009. "The New Phase of Neo-Liberal Restructuring in Turkey: An Overview." In *Turkey and the Global Economy. Neo-lib-*

eral *Restructuring and Integration in the Post-Crisis Era*, edited by Ziya Öniş and Fikrat Şenses, 1–11. London; New York: Routledge.

Öniş, Ziya, and Umut Türem. 2002. "Entrepreneurs, Democracy and Citizenship in Turkey." *Comparative Politics* 34 (4): 439–56.

Özcan, Gül Berna, and Hasan Turunç. 2011. "Economic Liberalization and Class Dynamics in Turkey: New Business Groups and Islamic Mobilization." *Insight Turkey* 13 (3): 63–86.

Özdemir, Murat-Ali, and Gamze Yücezan-Özdemir. 2008. "Opening Pandora's Box: Social Security Reform in Turkey in the Time of the AKP." *South-East Europe Review* 11 (4): 469–83.

Pamuk, Şevket. 2007. "Economic Change in Twentieth Century Turkey: Is the Glass More than Half Full?" Working Paper 41. The American University of Paris.

Rodrik, Dani. 2007. "Industrial Development: Some Stylized Facts and Policy Directions." In *Industrial Development for the 21st Century: Sustainable Development Perspectives*, edited by UN DESA, 7–28. New York: United Nations Publications.

Şimşek, Mehmet. 2014. "How Turkey Will Escape the Middle-Income Trap." *The Wall Street Journal Europe*, September 30.

Şimşek, Hayal Ayca, and Nezval Şimşek. 2011. "Has the Turkish Economy Been Less Affected by the 2008 Global Crisis: A Macroeconomic Perspective." *Research Journal of International Studies* 22 (December): 168–87.

Szabó, Stephen F. 2018. "Germany and Turkey: The Unavoidable Partnership." Turkey Project Policy Paper 14. Brookings Institute, Washington D.C.

Ulusoy, Kıvanç. 2014. "Turkey's Fight against Corruption: A Critical Assessment." *Global Turkey in Europe Commentary* 19 (November): 1–5.

Ünay, Sadik. 2012. "Domestic Transformation and *Raison du Monde*: Turkey's Nascent Competition State." *Emerging Markets Finance and Trade* 48 (Supplement 5): 7–18.

Yeldan, A. Erinc. 2008. "Turkey and the Long Decade with the IMF: 1998–2008." Retrieved February 23, 2013. http://www.networkideas.org/networkideas/pdfs/turkey_imf.pdf.

Yilmaz, Gökhan. 2011. "Resurgence of Selective Industrial Policy: What Turkey Needs." Discussion Paper 2011/3, Turkish Economic Association, March.

CHAPTER 13

Strong State Influence in the Brazilian Economy: Continuity or Change?

JUDIT RICZ

Introduction

The paper analyzes the changing role of the state in the Brazilian economy and its development. We argue that the Brazilian case is a useful example of how state influence in the economy has changed over the last three decades. Brazil, like most Latin American countries, has a long history of state capitalism, best described as "hierarchical market economies" (Schneider 2013) and "state-permeated market economies" (Nölke et al. 2015) that differ substantially from other more advanced countries (mostly analyzed in the Varieties of Capitalism scholarship and throughout this volume). While the emergence of the state-owned sector in Brazil has followed a similar path as in most countries around the world,[1] looking at the overarching, complex nature and persistence of state influence, Brazil substantially differs from the experiences and practices of more advanced countries. This makes Brazil a "good laboratory to study SOEs" (Musacchio and Lazzarini 2014a, 1).

Throughout this paper we argue, that despite decades of liberalization and privatization, the state continues to play an important role in the Brazilian economy, and this can be illustrated by the strategy of national champions, the activities of the BNDES, the National Development Bank, and the interventionist style of the Rousseff government in the years leading up to 2016. After the millennium, new developmentalist (neode-

---

[1] After World War II, governments owned and operated oil, gas, electric, water, and telecommunications companies, as well as railways, shipping companies, and businesses in other sectors of the economy (mainly related to extraction of natural resources or infrastructure).

sarrollista) tendencies have emerged throughout Latin America, especially in Brazil, where this approach to macro-economic and social policies was brand new. However, looking at complementary micro-economic reforms, and especially industrial policies and development financing, continuities with the *old* developmentalist model prevailed. Thus, we argue that the overall picture (and economic structure) is still dominated by institutional and political continuities with old developmentalist practices and the old developmental state paradigm in Brazil.

The biggest South American economy (as most other emerging economies) differs from other mainstream examples of the more developed world, as state influence was already strong (albeit altering and taking different forms) before the recent crisis in 2007–2009 and more importantly the global financial crisis (GFC) has not provoked large changes in this regard (at least not immediately). The direct effects of the crisis were relatively mild in the Brazilian economy. After the immediate sigh of relief and outstanding economic growth results in 2010, the profoundly changed *external context* (with lower global economic growth rates, especially slower growth in China—the major trading partner of Brazil; lower commodity prices; higher interest rates and worsening credit ratings), and the also altered domestic political context, have resulted in significant changes, and led to an economic crisis (with important social and political dimensions), thus by 2016 Brazil has arrived to a new crossroad in both economic and political terms.

The state has played a substantial and far-reaching role in modern economic development in Brazil, and economic literature on the old and new developmental state (its achievements and failures) is extensive.[2] A good illustration of the over-sized state in Brazil is provided by Winiecki (2016, 184–91), by highlighting the size of taxation and public expenditure, as well as the intrusive regulatory environment, both of which impede economic growth and productivity on the longer term, We, how-

---

[2] The recent article of Amado and Rollemberg Mollo (2015) provides a good overview on developmentalist thinking in Brazil, while the "classic" literature on new developmentalism in Brazil is mostly linked to Bresser Pereira's (2006, 2011, 2012) work. On the new DS is Brazil see Wylde (2012), Massi (2014), Ricz (2016), Schneider (2015).

ever, do not aim to reveal the complexity of state influence[3] in the Brazilian economy, as it would be a "mission impossible" within the framework of this paper. We aim to concentrate on the SOEs sector and argue, that changes within this sector illustrate well main trends in the changing role of state in the Brazilian economy. Our preliminary hypothesis runs as follows: state influence in Brazil has changed its forms and channels, but (though some ups and downs) remained relatively strong (compared to other capitalist countries) over the decades before and after the millennium.

The paper is in four parts: after this short introduction, a historical overview is provided to present the emergence and the fall of the state as entrepreneur model in Brazil. The third part is devoted to the processes since the millennium, more concretely to the emergence of new developmentalism á la Brazil and its dismantling. Finally, we conclude.

Historical Overview of the Emergence and Fall of State as Entrepreneur Model in Brazil

During the twentieth century state ownership took different forms in Brazil (Table 1). Though certain cyclicality can be revealed, we argue, that the role of the state in economy has been relatively strong throughout the examined period. During the time of market-oriented (neoliberal) reforms direct state-ownership and direct state interventions have been on the retreat, but indirectly (in different, often new and innovative forms and channels) the state has in several cases and areas maintained its influence over the economy (with Kerstenetzky [2014, 174] words "state-led governance by the market"). After the Millennium even this restricted neoliberalism has been reversed and a new wave of developmentalism emerged. Since 2016 a new turnaround change is going on in Brazilian economic policies and the aim to cut back the role of state in development has been put on the top of the development agenda.

---

[3] During the last century (or at the latest since 1940) the state has played a very multifaceted role in economic development in Brazil. Besides state ownership this influence took forms of tariff protection, subsidized credit, government contracts, research support, just to name a few direct means, while other more indirect forms and political influences were also widespread.

Table 1
Historical overview of the role of state in Brazilian economy

	Features of state ownership	Examples
1880s–1930s	State as accidental owner	Railways, shipping, banking
1930s–1980s	State as entrepreneur	Energy production, mining, petroleum extraction, railway, utilities, tele-communications
1980s–1990s	Fall of state as entrepreneur	Privatization waves (see Table 2)
2000–2016	State as majority or minority investor, other (indirect) forms of state influence	State ownership in strategic sectors, role of BNDES, strategy of national champions and internationalization of Brazilian enterprises
2016–	State on the retreat	New privatization wave, freezing federal government spending for twenty years

Source: own constructions based partially on Musacchio and Lazzarini (2014)

THE STATE AS ACCIDENTAL OWNER

Though first Brazilian SOEs were founded in the imperial period (such as the Bank of Brazil (BB) in 1808 and the Caixa Econômica Federal (Caixa) in 1861), between 1880 and 1930 the state owned enterprises emerged mostly as a consequence of bailouts. Early infrastructural projects (already in the second half of the nineteenth century) were mostly undertaken by commercial enterprises (railways, banks and shipping companies). The main task of the government by that time was to insure against failure, and after a series of bailouts and takeovers the government ended up as (residual) owner. State ownership did increase gradually, but rapidly in the first half of the twentieth century, but this was at least initially not a conscious decision, nor did it follow a specific grand plan (or ideology, at least until the 1930s), it happened rather accidentally (Musacchio and Lazzarini 2014a, 4).

THE STATE AS ENTREPRENEUR

The second stage of state interventionism (1930s–1980s) started after World War I with the explicit aim to use state ownership to overcome market failure, coordinate large sectors of the economy and push forward the economic development of the country. This golden age of state ownership relates to the import substitution industrialization (ISI) period (also called old developmental state). The "*state as entrepreneur*" model is best documented by Trebat (1983), describing a period, when SOEs were completely controlled and run by the state. SOEs served as direct tools to promote a big push to industrialization and economic development of the country, and the state invested directly in sectors in which private capital had no interest in or lacked the financial capacity (in line with the argumentation of the industrial policy view). Sometimes of course other, mainly social aims led the state to step in, for example to directly control supply or prices of public utilities (in line with the social view of SOEs).

The creation (or takeover) of many SOEs dates back to the presidencies (both authoritarian and democratic) of Getúlio Vargas and the establishment of the "Estado Novo," and took place mainly in sectors that were considered strategic for economic development or for national security reasons[4]. In this first period of ISI, the Brazilian state focused mainly on developing basic infrastructure and providing basic inputs for the industrialization, but did not dominate the whole economy. In line with the industrial policy view, the state played key role in sectors considered as being crucial for industrialization (and for economic development), such as mining, metallurgy and steel, public utilities and petroleum, but even in these, state ownership was at around 70 percent (Trebat 1983). Meanwhile in other sectors of the economy the private sector remained the dominant player.

The next wave for the expansion of the SOE sector dates to the military regime from the 1960s to the mid of the 1980s, and was mainly related to sectors such as transport and telecommunication[5]. The number of SOEs exploded during the presidency of Geisel (1974–79), who was a strong supporter of the ISI model and allowed foreign participation only when it was unavoidable to obtain the foreign technology.

According to Trebat (1983, 15) by 1975, the public sector was responsible for 17 percent of the total gross capital formation in the country (equalling to 4,3 percent of GDP), with around 25 percent of

---

[4] For example the National Steel Company (CSN) in 1941, the famous iron ore mining firm Vale do Rio Doce Company (Vale) in 1942, the manufacturer of buses, trucks and cars, called Fábrica Nacional de Motores (FNM) founded in 1943, the Brazilian national bank of economic development BNDE in 1952 (BNDE in Portuguese, later changed to BNDES when "social development" was added to its mission in 1982; for the sake of simplicity we use the current name, BNDES throughout this paper), and the national oil company Petrobrás in 1953, to mention just the largest ones.

[5] For example Embraer (aircraft manufacturer) was launched actually in 1969 but based on the results from previous state-led investments in aeronautical engineering and military technology. Other example of this period could be: Embratel (telephone), Correios (mail), and Radiobrás (radio, TV, and other telecommunications) or Embrapa (the National Agricultural Research Company).

those investments coming from large SOEs (and this ratio prevailed roughly until the end of 1990s). The (end of) 1960s and 1970s is often called in economic literature *the heyday of state capitalism* in Brazil. The expansion of the state-owned sector was not only underlined ideologically, but it was accompanied with very high GDP growth (especially during the years between 1967–73, the so-called economic miracle period in Brazil with economic growth rates above 10 percent on annual average). Part of this growth could be explained with the structural transformation of the economy (masses of labour relocating from agriculture to manufacturing), but rapid capital accumulation has also played a key role.

To sum up we can see that state ownership was mainly related to the state induced process of industrialization in Brazil, and large public investments were made initially in energy production, mining, petroleum extraction, while later also in infrastructure (railway and utilities) and telecommunications. However, we can note that by the end of the 1960s mechanisms to support domestic private entrepreneurs through subsidized credit (for example through BNDES) already existed in Brazil,[6] so there would have been alternatives of state ownership to promote and coordinate investments in risky or strategic sectors of the economy. Nevertheless, the extensive state ownership was needed to serve multiple (mainly economic, social and political) objectives of the government, like guaranteeing sufficient coverage, directly influencing prices, or even capturing expected profits. In line with the ISI model the political desire to avoid foreign control of "strategic assets" was also a key motivation.

During this period the creation of SOEs, and the explosion of their number was neither a planned phenomenon, nor a pure ideological answer, rather an uncoordinated process and according to Pinheiro (2011, 254–55) mainly resulting from the following, different processes: developmentalism (steel and highways); concerns for "national security" (mining and oil); regulatory failures (communication, electricity and railways); verticalization and diversification of activities of large SOEs (occupying "empty spaces") and nationalization of bankrupt companies (hotels, sugar mills, publishing companies, etc.).

This uncoordinated growth of the state sector was accompanied by poor monitoring and control over the actions of SOEs. In 1967 govern-

---

[6] On the role of the national development bank (BNDES) in (mainly long term) financing of private companies see Massi, 2014, Pinto and Reis 2017 and Cavalcante 2018.

ment decentralized the control of SOEs among different ministries (with the aim to improve execution), resulting that the government had lost all control on the number of SOEs and the kind of subsidiaries each of these firms had. To end this chaotic situation an explicit plan to count and control federal SOEs began in 1979 with the creation of the Secretary for SOE control (called SEST). Above the ministries three agencies[7] were in charge to coordinate actions of SOEs, however according to Musacchio and Lazzarini (2014a, 12) in practice SOEs responded to their ministries, which in line with the political (institutional) view, were obsessed with growth of the firms, or with Trebat's (1983, 52) words with "empire building" (thus preferred to have larger firms with more jobs than concentrating on efficiency or profitability)—a story well-known from the experiences of East Asian developmental states.

As a result of the old developmentalist model (from 1930–1980/85) by the end of the 1980s state influence over the economy was widespread in Brazil: the state has owned (or was minority shareholder in) a large number of companies; it had monopoly rights in many industries and large companies in "strategic sectors" such as oil, gas, steel, petrochemical, mining and defense sectors.

THE FALL OF STATE AS ENTREPRENEUR MODEL

The ISI development model, and its intrinsic characteristic, the expansion of SOE sector was (at least partly) made possible by favorable external context, mainly based on cheap credit available in the 1960s and early 1970s on the world financial markets. This external context has changed profoundly and the second oil shock in 1979, or at the latest the unfolding debt crisis in 1982 have marked the end of an era.[8]

---

[7] The Council for Economic Development, the Council for Social Development and the Ministry of Planning.
[8] The end of the "harmonious coexistence between private and state capital," as Castelar Pinheiro (2011, 256) has put it, was already conceived in 1974 when businessmen and the political opposition started a "campaign against nationalization" and against excessive state participation in the economy, in some instances comparing even the Brazilian style of state-led capitalism to state influence under the communist regimes. Still, it has to be added that main dissatisfaction of the business sphere by that time, was their exclusion from decision-making forums, like the CDE (Economic Development Council, Conselho de Desenvolvimento Econômico) from 1974 onwards.

Brazilian SOEs during the ISI tended to finance their current expenditures with foreign debt, in the early 1980s however with depreciating currency (and simultaneously rising inflation) and rising global interest rates most SOEs have experienced sharp increases in their financial expenditures. At the same time governments pushed to use these SOEs for social purposes, so as to secure lower prices and lower unemployment. These two main trends have led to quickly deteriorating financial situation of the SOEs, and finally to a dramatic fall in gross capital formation. Even though these worsening conditions and in line with the social view of SOEs, employment was increased in most state-owned companies (to artificially press down unemployment) after the crisis, when comparable private firms downsized their employee base (Musacchio and Lazzarini 2014a, 18). According to the political view poor performance of SOEs can (besides the above mentioned trends) also be explained by the dynamics of patronage, the use of SOEs positions to compensate political allies, cronies and to build coalitions. Though this practice has been traditionally present in Brazilian politics, Musacchio and Lazzarini (2014b) find no negative effect of having a political CEO on the performance of the SOE, however they did not analyze lower level managers, where the practice of hiring politicians has been also widespread.

To put it short, with the deterioration of external (global) and internal (domestic) conditions it became more and more difficult to financially sustain the multiplicity of (social and political) objectives aimed to pursue via the SOEs, conflicting with profitability, and finally the old development model (and with it the state as entrepreneur model) collapsed. The upcoming decades (mainly the 1990s) were dominated by the adoption of liberal policies, liberalization and deregulation of markets and privatization of SOEs. These policies were in line with the Washington Consensus (as well as the conditions posed by the international financial institutions, in particular the International Monetary Fund) and followed the main trends of other countries around the world.

During the years and decades after the debt crisis, most economic policy interventions aimed at *economic stabilization*: chronic fiscal imbalances and hyperinflation were the two main challenges. High inflation was an inherent feature of the Brazilian economy. Lasting operation of the economy under high and persistent inflation was made possible by institutional solutions (indexation mechanism), however counterproductive ones (Burlamaqui et al. 2006, 13). Accelerating inflation threatened to destroy the economy, while social unrest has risen and endangered political stability. Between 1985 and 1994 the Brazilian economy was subject to six heterodox stabilization plans[9]. The common element of all these plans was the use of price controls and currency reform to abruptly reduce inertial inflation to one-digit levels. After all the way towards less state intervention and more market-friendly economic policies was paved.

This is the main context in which the *process of privatization* has to be understood in Brazil. Thus Cardoso's main privatization strategy aimed not only at transferring state assets to the private sector, but also at breaking up with state monopolies and opening of many industries to domestic and foreign private capital (Massi 2014, 186).

Table 2
Waves of the Brazilian privatization process

Period	Political administration	Main features
1980s	Figueiredo, Sarney	small in scope and scale, BNDESPAR reorganization
1990–1995	Collor de Mello, Franco	incl. SOEs in productive and strategic sectors
1995–2002	Cardoso	incl. SOEs in services and infrastructure
2012–	Rousseff, Temer, Bolsonaro	mainly infrastructure (transport, energy, mining and sanitation)

Although the first wave of privatization is mostly associated with Collor de Mello and Cardoso, the idea of privatization dates back to the late 1970s. Already by the end of 1970s there were some worries of the huge size of the (uncontrolled) SOEs sectors, and even plans of "coordinated privatization" existed (as that of Marcos Vianna, the President of BNDES).[10] Though these were not implemented, with the words of Musacchio and Lazzarini (2014a, 14) these, have "set the stage for the privatization process and the subsequent model of state investment in which Leviathan is a minority investor and in which BNDES became a central actor as a lender and shareholder."

Under the Presidency of Figueiredo in 1979 the first national plan to privatize state-owned companies that were not essential for national security was announced, and the first wave of privatization started in 1981. Though the Special Committee on Privatization identified 140 SOEs suitable for privatization, out of these 50 were listed for sale and only 20 was

---

[9] The Cruzado plan of 1986; the Bresser plan of 1987; the "Summer" plan of 1989; the Collor I plan of 1990 and the Collor II plan of 1991; and the Real plan of 1994.
[10] See Massi (2014, 186–87).

sold, one rented and 8 were incorporated into other public institutions or enterprises. This first privatization (1981-84) phase did not include any of the large SOEs, and total revenues reached only 190 million USD (Pinheiro, 2011:259).

The unfolding debt crisis has pushed forward the privatization agenda: the crisis was increasingly associated with the huge size and inefficiency of SOEs or at least the perceptions regarding these. Some restrictions were put in place in 1985 to curb the growth of the public sector. However main former principles of privatization were maintained during the Sarney administration (1985-1990): foreign capital participation remained excluded and privatization remained subordinated to the national security and to nationalist-statist principles (thus large SOEs vital for national security and infrastructure or in sectors where the state hold monopoly was excluded). Two main lines of change can still be revealed: first, some institutional changes were put in place (Inter-ministerial Council on Privatization, and some transparency, evaluation and auditing measures were introduced) and second, a new legal structure for privatization was introduced in 1988. Previous concerns related to national security and market reserves for domestic enterprises were side-lined, and new instruments, such as concessions to private capital to provide public and infrastructure services and others to break up with the monopoly rights of large state-owned enterprises, were introduced. Fiscal motives also came in to play a role: privatization became an instrument to reduce public debt.

Despite all these changes, privatization under the Sarney administration remained small in its scope and scale.[11] As most commentators (Pinheiro 2000, 11; Massi 2014, 189) highlight privatization between 1985 and 1990 in fact was the financial reorganization of the BNDESPAR, the investment subsidiary of BNDES, and was mostly limited to small and medium enterprises. Still there were few exceptions to this, and the privatization of a few large and important industrial firms[12] has set precedents for the future.

Pinheiro (2011, 260) has highlighted three special circumstances that have contributed to the fact, that first wave of the Brazilian privatization remained small in scope and scale: 1. SOEs still showed relatively

---
[11] The World Bank (1989) has even concluded that the first wave of privatization in Brazil was a „classic example of failure" (cited in Castelar Pinheiro, 2011:260).
[12] Including the largest producer of ferro-alloy (Sibra) and the only electrolytic copper producer (Caraibas Metais).

good operation performance; 2. the argument of national security was still widely accepted in Brazil; 3. privatization was mainly seen as a process of denationalization and the increased presence of foreign investors was considered to be against the national interest. As an additional aspect Schneider (1988–89, 1990) emphasizes political reasons resulting in restricted privatization: as Sarney lacked support base in the Congress, the distribution of positions within the state sector (SOEs) was instrumental to strengthen his governing capacity. Also, domestic private sector was not heavily pushing forward the privatization agenda, while showing support at least rhetorically for privatization, many of the private companies depended on SOEs in their operation and were not in favor for a more drastic privatization program.

Inherent changes during the end of the 1980s have altered however the context of privatization in Brazil. First of all, SOEs (mostly incapable to generate fiscal surplus or to borrow from abroad) relied in terms of long term credits mainly on domestic public funding, for political and legal motives (see too-big-to-fail argumentation by classic developmental states) were however not enforced to pay up their bills. When due to fiscal problems public banks by the end of 1980s also ended to finance the activities of SOEs, the only viable way remained the privatization of state assets to private investors. As a second motive raising support for privatization in Brazil in the early 1990s was the deterioration of economic performance of SOEs (Pinheiro 2011, 262). During the second half of the 1980s in most SOEs management positions were politically appointed mostly for short periods and rarely rewarded on the basis of economic performance. Lack of management technical skills and economic incentives as well as the already mentioned soft budget constraints led to the further losses in terms of economic efficiency. At the same time changes in economic model, most importantly processes of trade liberalization have made these shortcomings even more evident.

The second wave of privatization, in fact the most important period of it in Brazil started in 1990 with the National Privatization Program (PND) of Collor de Mello.[13] It broke up with the former privatization schemes

---

[13] To set the context of this second wave of privatization one must however refer to the new constitution of 1988, which was rather of a nationalizing character, establishing public monopolies in oil and distribution of gas, telecommunications, and constructing barriers to foreign investors in mining and electricity. The results achieved under Collor de Mello (though limited) have to be regarded in the light of these constitutional restrictions.

in several ways: expanded its scope, addressed SOEs in productive and strategic sectors (such as steel, petrochemicals and fertilizers), and linked the process to macroeconomic stabilization. The BNDES became a major actor, and it was explicitly aimed to depoliticize the process of privatization. The failure to stabilize the economy finally led to the failure of the overly optimistic PND, and only 16 SOEs were privatized until 1993 (summing up to revenues at around 3,9 billion USD (BNDES, 2002).

Between 1993 and 1995 despite some changes and the rather developmentalist ambitions of Itamar Franco, the schedule and practices set up by the PND were mostly kept in place and 17 additional firms[14] were privatized, leading to revenues up to 4,7 billion USD.

With the start of the Cardoso era in 1995 the Brazilian privatization reached a new milestone. Fernando Henrique Cardoso (FHC) expanded the program and decided to break up with the monopoly rights of SOEs in services and infrastructure,[15] and also allowed for local governments to develop their own privatization programs (that was considered as means to raise revenues at local level). In the first three years of the privatization under FHC 80 SOEs were sold, with total revenues of 60,1 billion USD in receipts and 13,3 billion in debt transfers (Pinheiro 2011, 264).

Reasons leading to rapid expansion of the privatization program were manifold ranging from the stabilization of macroeconomic environment, through political support in Congress and fiscal motives on federal and state level, to demonstration effects of past privatizations—that have led to increased firm-level efficiency and investments capacity (Castelar Pinheiro, 2011, 264–67). Economic analysts tend to agree, that privatization played a crucial role in the whole stabilization process (as revenues were used to reduce public debt, and incoming FDI linked to privatization was also significant).

By 1995 previous concerns for national security and fears of denationalizing the economy lost importance in public debates. This change in perception and attitude towards privatization can largely be credited to the transition from military to civilian rule, the process of democratization, but was also supported by changes in the external context (the end of the cold war). Even though some protests from unionist and leftist groups remained, masses of population were mostly indifferent to the privatization

---

[14] Including CSN, the National Steel Company created by Vargas back in 1941.
[15] The circle of SOEs to sell was widened from industrial firms to incorporate public and financial services as well as concessions in transportation, highway, sanitation, telecommunications and electricity generation sectors.

program and heavy critic and opposition was linked rather to single cases and related to the selection criteria of SOEs to sell (considering the sale of efficient and profitable firms), the minimum price set for sale (whether it was below market value), the impact on the quality of public services and the role of BNDES played in the process.

During this main phase of privatization in Brazil the importance of improving regulation was also recognized. Emphasis has been put on the introduction of competition[16] in almost each sector, and the aim to strengthen regulation before privatization was present (although with different grades of success and in cases of failure mostly concessional contracts contained important regulatory clauses). The most important success story of privatization with regulatory reforms relates to the telecommunication sector, while in electricity provision the processes were less well coordinated and executed, and least progress in regulation and privatization has been achieved in water and sewage services.

The figures above summarize most striking features of the privatization process in Brazil between 1990 and 2002. With total revenues of around 87 billion USD the Brazilian privatization was among the biggest ones in the world (BNDES 2002) and meant the transfer of 170 SOEs to the private sector. These revenues have helped to reduce public debt by an amount approx. equaling to 8 percent of GDP (Carvalho 2001). While empirical studies in line with economic literature have proved not just country-, but also firm-level gains from privatization (positive effects on performance of privatized firms).[17]

Most authors agree that the privatization in Brazil was in fact a *pragmatic answer* to macroeconomic challenges in the 1990s[18] and it was tolerated by the electorate mainly due to the—correct—perception that it contributes to achieve the main developmental objective (by that time): macroeconomic stability (and also allows for increased investments). The Brazilian privatization was in fact a result of threefold changes (Pinheiro 2011, 272): 1) changes in politics, as foreign investment was no longer considered as a threat to national security; 2) a shift in the focus of devel-

---

[16] Often supported by vertical and horizontal separation of SOEs before privatization.
[17] Pinheiro, 1996; Anuatti-Neto et al. 2005
[18] In contrast to other systemic or tactical initiatives to privatization, where the former adjective refers to deep and ample objectives to reshape economic and political institutions (like in UK, New Zealand, or Chile), and the latter one mostly focuses on short term political aims (Castelar Pinheiro 2011, 252).

Figure 1
Accumulated results, annual evolution and sectoral composition of Brazilian privatization (1990–2002)

Accumulated Result   US$ million

Period	Sale Proceeds	Transferred Dept	Total Results	
1990–1994	8,608	3,266	11,874	11.2%
1995–2002	78,614	14,810	93,424	88.8%
Total	87,222	18,076	105,298	100.0%

Annual Evolution

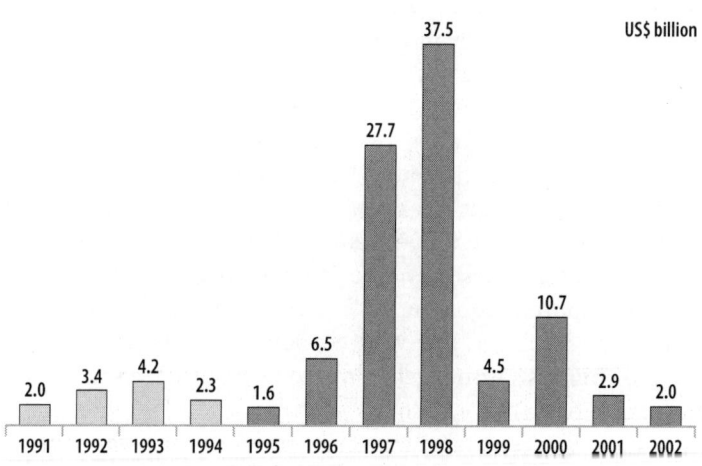

Participation by Sector

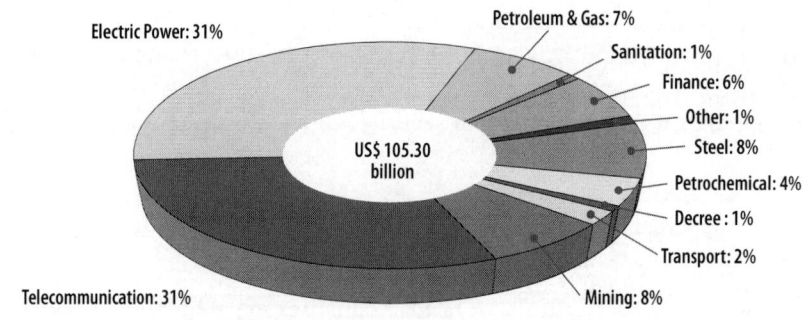

Source: Adapted from BNDES 2002

opment policy away from (forced) capital accumulation towards economic efficiency; and last but not least, 3) close linkages between privatization and macroeconomic policy. In the case of Brazil, however, this third argument is considered to be the most important factor.

Another often emphasized feature in the Brazilian case is, that even though twenty years of privatization experience, large masses (and even political fractions) in Brazil did not change their ideological views regarding the role of state in economy,[19] thus the Brazilian privatization process has to be considered much more as a pragmatic than as an ideological process.

Despite all the facts and numbers of Brazilian privatization, an additional aspect regarding the role of state or the degree of state influence should be added, mainly based on the logic presented by Evans (1995) and Schneider (2013): big business and the state has been traditionally interconnected in Brazil, and in fact privatization did not change much the degree of state influence, it rather changed its channels and forms. The best illustration could be the example of Vale, privatized in 1997, but in fact remaining under (hidden) state control ever since (via the ownership of state pension funds and the BNDES and other less explicit forms of state interference).

Having all these arguments in mind, it should not come as a surprise that after a privatization peak in 1997–98 economic policy priority given to privatization declined, as fiscal motives became less relevant and foreign direct investment (apart from privatization also) increased. A few years later, with economic indicators improving after 2004, the macroeconomic (and fiscal) imperative to support the privatization has further weakened, and in line with political changes (the turn to the left) the expectations towards the swinging back of the pendulum (to an economic model with increasing state influence) were curbed high.

New Developmentalism: New Forms of State Influence Emerging

By late 2002, political rhetoric regarding privatization has been changed to negative, as the Working Party (PT, Partido dos Trabalhadores) historically opposing the program has won the elections in Brazil.

---

[19] See for example successive public opinion surveys by latinobarometro or Alston et al. (2016).

Luiz Inácio Lula da Silva (from now on Lula) took office under stormy circumstances in January 2003: the context of external crisis, low growth and uncertain domestic political arena all led to speculative attack on real, and its devaluation. The first Lula government has had thus first to restore the confidence of the markets,[20] and continued (in contrast to all expectations among his allies as well as opponents) with the macroeconomic policies of his predecessor concentrating on the fight against inflation and public indebtedness. With the focus on macroeconomic issues, and as a result of more favorable international circumstances (such as global economic growth and the reversal of declining terms of trade, mainly due to increased Chinese demand towards basic Brazilian export products) economic indicators started to improve from 2004.

Lula continued with orthodox, conservative macroeconomic management (even after the immediate crisis management and in relative good economic times between 2003 and 2007), but at the same time, being a left-wing candidate also showed strong commitment to social issues. New and innovative social policies (like the often highlighted Bolsa Família Program) together with the expansion of the social frontier (hand in hand with sound macroeconomic policies) became the trademark of the new economic policy model of Brazil.

The third leg of this new economic policy-mix under Lula was made up of complementary micro-economic policies, mainly related to the Growth and Acceleration Program (PAC)[21]—a government infrastructural investment program—and the revival of industrial policies and with it an increased (albeit modified) role of state.

New industrial policies, though innovative in some aspects,[22] maintained or revived linkages, in terms of institutions and practices to the old

---

[20] "Letter to the Brazilian People" (Carta ao pavo brasiliero) issued during the electoral campaign in June 2002 and the institutionalization of the promises made in this letter by the agreement with IMF meant in practice the continuity with Cardoso's (neoliberal or orthodox) economic policies.

[21] The PAC (in original) was launched in 2007 and constitutes to be a cornerstone of Lula's policies to promote economic growth as an umbrella term for a complexity of infrastructural projects in areas such as sanitation, sewage, water, electricity, road and housing construction. The first phase of the program called for 346 billion USD, while the second phase (extending from 2011 to 2014) investments were estimated to reach 526 billion USD.

[22] For example, by linking the promotion of industrial production to foreign policy and export-orientation (see also Almeida and Schneider (2012) and Massi (2014).

DS model. Continuities can be revealed in its selectivity, concentration on a small number of sectors and in fact (and in contrast to all rhetoric) mainly leading to preserving the existing industrial sector. Related to this issue, one has also to refer to a discontinuity with the Cardoso era in terms of state—business relations. While Cardoso tried to insulate economic policy decisions from the business sector, Lula in contrast reopened channels of communication and negotiation and pursued a much more consultative approach (see for example Boschi 2011), but at the same time and in the light of the rather "fuzzy" political system (in terms of party and campaign financing rules and practices and the overly fragmented party system and Congress) these new "flexible" institutional arrangements often also lead to the (re-)politicization of state-business relations.

To sum up under the Lula administration a new form of developmentalism[23] emerged, representing some degree of continuity with the old developmentalist approach, such as building on the old corporativist structures (although improving and modifying those) and the revival of an "old-new" industrial policy, but innovative in several areas, such as in social policies and in terms of a more pluralistic and comprehensive (inclusive) institutional model. In the following section we turn towards analyzing changes in the state-owned sector, and in more general terms new forms of state influence.

THE STATE AS MAJORITY OR MINORITY INVESTOR, AND OTHER (INDIRECT) FORMS OF STATE INFLUENCE

State ownership has been transformed during the last decades in Brazil. Beyond some wholly-owned large state-enterprises mainly related to the sectors of oil, electricity and banking (Petrobras, Eletrobras, Caixa Econômica Federal), where the government continues to be majority shareholder, other forms of government control emerged and gained weight. State influence on private enterprises can take the form of minority equity investment, but also other channels of support exist: subsidized loans from development banks, equity and debt purchases via sovereign wealth and pension funds, local content requirements, to name just a few. The practice of picking national champions to support the strategy of internationalization (and the wider aim of transforming Brazil into

---

[23] For this see Boschi (2011); Wylde (2012); Amann-Barrientos (2014); Massi (2014); Ricz, (2017).

a global player in the world economy) is a good example of new forms of state influence while maintaining continuities with or similarities to the old developmental state model.

The main cycle of privatization ended in 2002 and with the new political cycle commencing in 2003 (the Lula administration) some fears regarding a new nationalization threat appeared. However, in contrast to expectations[24] Lula did not reverse the privatization process, but rather tried to encourage qualitative changes in public-private partnerships and to attract private investment into the Brazilian infrastructure systems. Some changes in the focus of privatization has started even before Lula came into power. This is best signaled with the big sale of Petrobrás shares[25] in August 2000 on the Brazilian Stock market (Bovespa) and the explicit aim to use privatization to strengthen the domestic capital market and attract foreign capital. Concessions granted to private actors were a new element under the Lula administration, such as in the case of the highway system and the airports[26], where the lack of investment was most apparent and urging (also taking into account the new infrastructure needs in the light of the 2014 Football World Championship and the Summer Olympic Games in 2016). To certain extent these processes can be even regarded as the continuation of the privatization process (although not called like this in Brazil, mainly due to political, or ideological, reasons).

At the same time Lula attacked regulatory models adopted during previous decade, especially in the oil and gas sector, and significantly weakened established regulatory agencies, by mostly giving responsibilities and final decision rights (back) to ministries, and with it implicitly increasing the (discretionary) role of the state. The new wave of "regu-

---

[24] It was feared by foreign investors, mainly based on the former PT's stance towards privatization and on their experiences in some other Latin American countries (like Argentina or Venezuela). As Amann and Barrientos put it (2014:4) Lula was so heavily committed to transform the Brazilian economy into a competitive global player that he even turned in some aspects against his own party and its priorities.

[25] With 337.000 individuals buying shares of the Brazilian oil giant, Petrobrás, possibly resulting in a record sale in the history of the Bovespa, the Brazilian stock market (Castelar Pinheiro, 2011, 273).

[26] These steps have to be regarded within the Latin American context, where in parallel some more radical leftist regimes started programs of (re-) nationalization (in contrast to Lula, who also came to power as a leftist candidate and after an electoral campaign criticizing neoliberal reforms, incl. privatization—and still went on with it in certain areas).

latory reforms" leading to an increased the role of political interventions under Lula was most apparent in the electricity sector, but also affected other sectors. During the second administration of Lula (2007–10) even attempts to establish new SOEs (e.g. in manufacture of drugs and fertilizers, or provision of broadband services) could be observed, while another form of increased state influence took the form of allocating public loans (mainly via BNDES) on a more politicized and interventionist way. A good example is the creation of "national champions" via the merger of large companies, and made possible by BNDES financing, such as in paper pulp, petrochemicals, telecom and food processing (Pinheiro 2011, 274). This initiative was in line with new foreign economic policies of internationalization and the aim of "Brazil going global." This type of state interventionism was partly "justified" by the GFC in 2007–2009, as a compensatory means, or anticyclical economic policy, but we will see, that it did not decreased subsequently, and became even more pronounced during the following years, under the governance of Dilma Rousseff.

State ownership in the twenty-first century in Brazil according to DEST data (cited among others by Musacchio and Lazzarini [2014a, 20]) was relatively extensive: by 2009, 47 SOEs were under federal government control, and 49 SOEs under state-level control, with assets equaling to USD 626 billion and USD 66 billion respectively. These are however only SOEs directly controlled by the government, and do not include a host of subsidiaries of state-owned holding companies. There are no exact numbers of the latter, but according to estimates direct and indirect state ownership sums up to 757 billion USD in total assets equalling approx. to 43–45 percent of GDP. While enterprises remaining under state control concentrated in "strategic" sectors, such as oil (Petrobras), electricity (Eletrobras, Cesp), sewage, water (Sabesp) and banking (BNDES, Banco do Brasil, Caixa Econômica Federal, Barisul).

The largest SOE's are traded in the Brazilian Stock Exchange (Bovespa), although these compromise only 58 percent of the SOEs under federal and 68 percent under state level control. Listing at least in principle results in better corporate governance practices, better mitigation of agency problems and better protection of minority shareholders. In most cases it happened also with Brazilian SOEs, though there are some exceptions from more recent years (see next section), where government still aims to overwrite profitability criteria or minority stakes. To commit to higher governance practices was however not just a pre-condition and result of listing, it also aimed to attract external funding, private capital. This latter constitutes to be an urging pressure in the Brazilian case if we take into consideration the constrained revenue raising capacity of the state and the low levels of domestic saving (leading also to low levels of gross capital formation).

This new-type of state-ownership was the "state as majority investor model" (Musacchio and Lazzarini 2014a), meaning that the state remains controlling shareholder, but at the same time accepts to follow certain rules to attract private investors as minority shareholders.[27] One of the best illustration for the model of state as majority shareholder is the case of Petrobras, the state-owned oil giant in Brazil, which is a perfect example of remaining and even strengthening government interventions up to most recent years (with all of the ups and downs of the company economic performance and political interference).

According to some estimates the state has equity interests in companies representing about 35 percent of Brazil's stock market capitalisation, while adding up companies with borrowings from the BNDES this number would increase to about 70 percent (FT, 2015). Investors in these companies were used to and have traditionally tolerated some state interference. However, during the recent years interventionism has grown more intense (starting already under Lula, but particularly extended under Rousseff) and also due to the new ICT media its controversies became more visible for the society, providing more accurate ground for social protests against discretionary (ad hoc) state interference.

Despite all direct state-ownership still represents only a part of state influence in Brazil. As we have argued earlier state control in Brazil remained very strong (compared to European or Western norms) even after large waves of privatizations, and state influence on the economy goes well beyond ownership of large enterprises like Petrobrás or BNDES. These indirect and hidden forms of state influence are very hard to reveal and quantify.

It is mostly highlighted that strong external regulations (also backed by insulation from political appointments) would be needed to prevent SOEs with majority state control to pursue outright government intervention. The problem thus in Brazil is twofold: on the one hand, regulatory bodies are relatively weak (and at the same time politicised, leading to missing checks-and-balances against discretionary government interventions), while on the other hand, due to an overly fragmented political party system, CEO and other manager positions in SOEs are part of political deals leading to widespread practices of patronage. Both result in heavy threats against perfor-

---

[27] For unintended consequences of this model in the Brazilian case see Pargendler (2012).

mance and profitability of SOEs, best illustrated by recent corruption scandals related to Petrobras (and other big Brazilian firms).

Recent Brazilian experiences with the state as majority (or even minority) investor shed light on the fact that the effective functioning of this model would require relatively developed capital markets, not only to attract private capital, but also to provide external monitoring and transparency (with both being rather in their infancy in Brazil). Even if the state is only a minority shareholder, other objectives than pure profitability criteria (such as political or social aims) might come to fore and work as incentives towards state intervention—this was often the case during the last one and a half decade in Brazil.

A striking example how state influence over the Brazilian economy has changed recently could be illustrated by the case of BNDES that besides its long-term, financing activities recently also gained weight as minority shareholder (Massi 2014; Musacchio and Lazzarini 2014b; Pinto and Reis 2017).

Lula and also Rousseff have expanded the reliance on direct transfers from government to finance activities of BNDES, and went beyond the former model of relying on forced savings—mainly from corporate taxes. This has led increasing public debt and tax burden, both high already in Brazil. Looking at Mazzucato's (2013) "entrepreneurial state" argumentation state induced financing (such as via BNDES) could work, if state would address private firms with clearly constrained or limited borrowing opportunities (firms that possess latent capabilities but lack resources or opportunities to borrow). In line with this thinking, however, if capital markets develop, and opportunities for firms widen to borrow (as new potential lenders, investors step in), then the state should curb back on his activities, step back, and exit. Looking at the changes in the activities and practices of the BNDES in Brazil exactly the opposite happened.[28]

The cases of Vale and Embraer can also serve as examples of *state as a minority investor*, with capital from pension funds and especially BNDES. In these cases, more autonomous governance and funding has developed

---

[28] These shortcomings are well-known by the management of the BNDES, and the BNDES would in principle aim to widen its activities towards building competitive advantage in high technology sectors (and there are even some examples of financing in the electronics sector). However, the statement of the former BNDES vice-president, currently one of its directors, João Carlos Ferraz is telling: "...the Bank would finance a technology-based company's project if one were presented to the Bank" (cited by Massi 2014, 223).

better technical capabilities and led to better implementation of performance-enhancing growth strategies (however also containing the risk, that enhanced autonomy leads to growth-obsession, e.g., when SOE managers engage in empire-building). The classical lesson from East Asian developmental states' experiences is valid also in this case: the operation in competitive foreign markets might impose the needed discipline on SOE managers. In the case of Embraer it was only after its privatization in 1994 that the company became truly competitive, with new product lines for regional routes such as the ERJ-145 and, more recently, the so-called E-Jets.

To sum up Lula has increased the role of government in economy via multiple channels. A striking example is the raising government control over regulators by shifting policy-making decisions away from independent industry regulators to government ministries. The politicization of regulations has opened the door for government appointees to discretionary political meddling and has among others finally led to destroying stability and with it to deterring investments. These dynamics have contributed to economic troubles under the Rousseff period, to which we turn in the next section.

CRISIS MANAGEMENT AND SOME TRENDS AFTER THE GLOBAL FINANCIAL AND ECONOMIC CRISIS

Before turning to the most recent trends regarding state influence in the Brazilian economy, we provide a short outlook to GFC, including its context, management and effects in Brazil.

During the first decade of the twenty-first century (mainly corresponding with the Lula administration period between 2003 and 2011) the Brazilian economy seemed to be on a positive track both in economic and social terms. Economic growth was mainly driven by external factors: increasing demand from Asia (mainly China) towards main Brazilian export products, and the rise in commodity prices led to significant surpluses in current account balance (between 2003 and 2007). Economic growth was accompanied by social achievements, mainly due to new policy approach (called socially inclusive policies or extension of social frontier): poverty and inequality decreased, and other social indicators, such as formal employment, minimum wage, social protection coverage, educational attainments improved.[29]

---

[29] Not just in media, but also in economic literature the period of Lula is often referred to as the second or new economic miracle period (see, e.g., Amann-Baer 2012).

Within this economic and social context, the GFC at least on the short term had a relatively mild impact on the Brazilian economy: the GDP after a 0,33 percent decrease in 2009 has risen in 2010 by an astonishing rate of 7,53 percent (WDI, 2015). On the medium term, however, the effects and consequences of global economic crisis and the following changes in the external environment turned out to be more severe for Brazil. Before turning to these most recent trends, we first sum up most important (anticyclical) measures of the Brazilian crisis management in the wake of the GFC according to Boschi (2011, 53–54):

- above-inflation real increase of minimum wage and adjustment of other benefits beyond minimum wage to maintain their purchasing power;
- expansion of directed (and subsidized) credit, especially through BNDES;
- introduction of two new individual taxes to raise government revenues;
- expansion of the circle of beneficiaries of the Program Bolsa Familia[30] (reaching additional 1,3 million people);
- increased efforts to implement the government's infrastructure program (PAC);
- reduction of the annual primary budget surplus target (from 4,3 percent to 2,5 percent);
- launching a new housing program (Minha Casa, Minha Vida) providing 1 million new homes and a great impetus for the construction sector and
- reducing the tax on industrialized products (IPI[31]) in several sectors (e.g. automobile industry).

There are some critics regarding economic policies afterwards the crisis, some highlight for example that the implementation of the PAC, the government's infrastructure program after 2008 was in fact put to serve the Brazilian crisis management, and concentrated much less on its formerly laid down principles (such as social inclusion and improving productive

---

[30] The Program Bolsa Familia (PBF) is a conditional cash transfer programme dating back to the Cardoso era (1990s), but it was extended and institutionally reformed under Lula. The PBF provides financial aid to poor Brazilian families, if they ensure that children attend school and are vaccinated.

[31] In Portuguese: Imposto sobre Produtos Industrializados.

capacities). Still there is a consensus that the anticyclical policies in the wake of the crisis had a positive impact concerning employment, industrial production (mainly in construction and automobile sector), household consumption and (at least) on the short term rescued Brazil from economic recession. Brazil's quick recovery from the crisis was awarded also by credit rating agency's promoting Brazil to investment grade.

However, after the short period of post-crisis adjustment and the accompanying euphoria regarding the overly optimistic Brazilian future, economic indicators started to deteriorate and within a five year period Brazil has sunk into one of the most severe economic (and political) crises since the 1930s, with significant social consequences. After a deteriorating trend of GDP growth rates since 2010, the Brazilian economy has actually stagnated in 2014 (0,25percent GDP growth rate), and has declined by more than 3 percent on yearly average in 2015 and 2016 (WDI, 2018). It is out of the scope of this paper to analyse the dimensions and symptoms of the most recent overarching and multifaceted crisis in Brazil (for this, see the next subchapter below and Nagy and Ricz 2018), instead we concentrate on the changes regarding the role of state in economy, especially via SOEs and BNDES.

CRISIS IN BRAZIL: POLITICAL (INSTITUTIONAL), ECONOMIC, AND SOCIAL DIMENSIONS

Compared to the Lula period (2003–2010) Dilma Rousseff, and the Brazilian economy has faced a much less favourable external context, with the deceleration of Chinese economic growth and demand, with deteriorating commodity prices. These external changes together with inherent internal (political and economic factors) have resulted that the Brazilian economy has been first decelerating after 2010, and turned into recession by 2014, and seems to get stabilized in 2017 (with an economic growth rate around 1,1 percent). Deteriorating exchange rate and fiscal indicators, increasing levels of inflation and unemployment just to name a few factors that added up to the crisis in Brazil and resulted in downgrading the Brazil's sovereign debt by all the three main credit rating agencies by 2016. Deterioration of economic performance was however preceded, accompanied and even reinforced by an unfolding political crisis, mainly (but not exclusively) related to corruption scandals (e.g., the Petrobrás case), the internal struggles within the Working

Party (PT) and the new governance style of president Dilma Rousseff. The political crisis has many dimensions and far-reaching consequences, and finally led to the impeachment process against Dilma (and the PT). According to the Brazilian constitution the former vice-president took the power in September 2016, Michel Temer (PMDB) and has formed his new (right-wing) government.

Political and economic difficulties have resulted in severe social dissatisfaction, and led to country-wide social demonstrations and protests, first already back in 2012, then against the Football World Cup in 2014 and Summer Olympic Games in 2016 (and the public spending connected to these events), followed by demonstrations against the new government of Temer and its austerity measures.

Main social achievements in Brazil under the Lula era were at least partly the result of promoting democratic values and institutions (in line with the "new" Brazilian constitution of 1988) and deliberate pro-poor public policy interventions. However, Brazil's social progress was accompanied by a deindustrialization of the economy, a "re-primarization" of exports, and a newly emerging dependence on China. Thus, Lula's new developmentalist model was clearly not sustainable—especially not in a less favorable external context, and with the exhaustion of the domestic-demand-led model based on significant increases in private-sector indebtedness. Regarding the role of state in development, however we also have to draw attention to the fact that the consecutive PT administrations (both under Lula and Dilma) have failed to succeed in reforming the political system—which according to most analysts, such as David Fleischer (2011, 2016)lies at the root of all corruption cases—as well as in initiating deeper running structural reforms, such as related to the educational, health or pension systems. In this vein the Lula period can be much more regarded as the era of lost opportunities, instead of the rise of the new Brazilian model of development, as it is often cited.

RISING INTERVENTIONISM AND THE FALL OF NEW
DEVELOPMENTALISM IN BRAZIL (2011–16)

Crisis management is always about the extension of state interventions in the economy, the question is whether after the crisis the level (scale and scope) of interventions is on the retreat. In the case of Brazil the answer is a definite no, the retreat of the state did not happened (at least not immediately, not until 2016), on the contrary, state interventions remained on the agenda, and served as an important tool in economic policies. It is out of the scope of this paper to one-by-one illustrate this new reliance of Dilma Rousseff on mainly ad hoc state interventions (mostly introduced on discretionary manner), as they were mostly related to single decisions, and took new forms (instead of state ownership, rather other forms dominate). Most cases have been extensively recorded by domestic and international media, here we only try to list some examples and reveal main trends that illustrate these recent changes.

The above presented context in which Dilma Rousseff took office in 2011 and has been forced to govern, has implied severe fiscal constraints to finance investment in infrastructure, which is considered traditionally as one of the most important constraint to economic growth in Brazil. The urgent need for infrastructural investments was even more pronounced in the light of the international mega-sports events in 2014 and 2016 hosted by the country. Rousseff has also realized the need for private investments and this constituted to be an important incentive or driving force for the government to go on with privatization of highways and airports (incl. concessions for building new facilities, but also aiming to transfer the operation of some existing facilities to private firms).

These aims were however less welcomed by the public, and even less by her electorate. The PT has been traditionally opposing privatization back during the Cardoso period, and it still does not fit into its political discourse. So Dilma Rousseff has had to protect her plans, by explaining that "this time it was different" by not "selling off state assets to raise cash" (Bloomberg, 2012) and stating that it is a new type of program to outsource government functions to be financed by private firms.

Even though this political and social resistance, and mainly due to the economic motives to revive economic growth[32] it is not much of a surprise that in 2012 the Brazilian government announced to sell state assets to private investors through long term concession deals, guaranteeing the right to operate roads, rails, ports and airports (many of these once built by the government while also containing some greenfield projects). The total amount of the proposed projects was estimated to be around 45 billion USD within five years. However, several adjustments had to be made

---

[32] Leading to struggles from quarter to quarter during 2012 to revive economic growth in the Brazilian economy, as the government has forecasted a yearly growth rate of 4 percent, and finally the economy grew with less than 2 percent in 2012.

to the original plans to offer adequate returns to potential private investors, and this led to delays in implementation in most of the projects. The media has been writing about a "new privatization wave in Brazil" mainly related to logistics infrastructure.[33]

The second round of this most recent privatization phase in Brazil is related to some of the remaining primary airports to be privatized by long-term concessions, with two peaks, one prior the Football World Cup in 2014 and the other one in 2015 (preceding the coming Summer Olympic Games in 2016).

Together with some other concession programs announced in June 2015, to attract private investment in productivity enhancing investments the government plans envisaged projects summing up to 25 billion USD within the period between 2015 and 2018. These plans were overly optimistic and neglected the role of some important complementary reforms, such as to enhance competition, reduce the administrative red tape and eliminate rigidities in the labor market to get closer to those targets. Federal interventions during the last years of the Rousseff government forced utilities companies (such as in electricity sector) to accept lower prices as a condition to renew their contracts, and these acted towards further discouraging investors.

Regulatory changes continued to be in line with the practice of Lula, thus mainly aimed at supporting the implementation of economic policies in Brazil. Ad hoc and discretionary use of regulations has flourished under both terms of Dilma Rousseff and once again one of the best the illustration is the example of the Petrobras and the pre-salt regulations.

The move towards more interventionism in the economy can also be well illustrated by the "meddling" with prices, in particularly in the energy sector (e.g., artificial repression of petrol prices and energy tariffs) to dampen inflation and by other industrial policy interventions (such as special taxes levied on certain industries). Since the Rousseff administrations (especially since 2012) the Brazilian government often used SOEs to directly control consumer prices (in order to support "higher objectives" such as to control inflation). Examples for government regulated prices (mainly due to macroeconomic motives) are numerous, while the most often highlighted cases are related to the oil and energy sector. The Brazilian government has repressed electricity prices by 30 percent, urban bus fares by 20 percent and gasoline prices by 15 percent between 2011 and

---

[33] For example, Forbes 2012.

2014 (Bloomberg 2014), and items subject to price controls accounted for approx. 20 percent of the inflation index. According to some estimates just the fuel subsidy costed an estimated 19 billion USD during the first term of Dilma Rousseff (2011–2014).

In more general terms, however, the policies of 'meddling with prices' have serious consequences, going much further than just their direct costs and effects on the fiscal balances: depression of private investment, distortion of resource allocation, encouraging excessive private consumption due to lower consumer prices, etc. Instead of further detailing these spillover effects, we just highlight two other aspect: 1. most subsidies benefitted the higher-income households and thus reinforced inequality (traditionally an urging social problem in Brazil) and 2. and artificially capped oil prices as well as energy subsidies artificially promoted capital-intensive industries (reinforcing distortions in production sector), while at the same time reduced incentives for investment in renewable resources, and accelerated the depletion of natural resources (hurting sustainability).

To drive back government's discretionary interventions checks-and-balances would be needed along strong, independent regulatory agencies—the ones that have been weakened and politicised under Lula, and even more so under Rousseff. Discretionary government interventions inherently raise uncertainty, and with it destroy business confidence, which might have long lasting detrimental effects on an economy, where one of the most important constraints to economic growth is lack of investments. A good-working regulatory system could ensure external monitoring and transparency, and with it a more rules-based government policy-making, while also providing more stability, even if SOEs serve some social objectives and are not only subject to profitability criteria.

Finally, on the one hand it could be argued that nothing new under sun, privatization came back to agenda in Brazil due to macroeconomic motives, as the government has desperately needed fiscal revenues, this is almost echoing the Cardoso period. On the other hand, looking at changes in the regulatory system, the opposite is true, a significant discontinuity with the reforms period of the 1990s, though the (re-)politicization of the regulatory schemes started already under Lula, and was continued and moved forward by Rousseff. The micro-managing of the industry is not new in Brazilian economic history, however it has been raised to new levels under Rousseff and lead to misuse of the anyway scarce resources in the twenty first century's Brazil.

To sum up we highlight that economic growth had already started to decelerate during the first Dilma term (beginning in 2011), but certain clear and deliberate (though often overlooked) policy choices also date back to the Rousseff government, and thus to the era of the PT and the leftist coalition. Serrano and Melin (2015) referred to these policies already as "Brazil's Neoliberal U-Turn," as they were explicitly aimed at reducing the direct role of the state in the Brazilian economy, even though important social policies remained in place.

It is worth to recall that in Lula's new Brazilian development model, the public sector (including SOEs and public banks) was clearly the major actor which would stimulate aggregate demand and generate supply-side structural change, mainly by means of investments. At the end of 2010, there was a clear economic-policy shift, an attempt to respond to the intensifying criticism coming from Brazilian corporations, banks, the media, and the conservative opposition, all of whom claimed that the Brazilian state had been intervening too much in the economy. The "ideology" behind the (rather ad hoc) economic-policy decisions which followed was the belief that the state could withdraw from its leading role in the economy, and that the private sector would immediately step in. The government started to offer incentives for private investment, mainly in the form of (unconditional) tax cuts; it also tried to reduce traditionally extremely high interest rates (though this policy was quickly reversed) and oversaw a significant exchange-rate devaluation of the Brazilian real (Serrano and Melin 2015, 2).

Even though all economic indicators pointed out the ineffectiveness of this new economic-policy direction, Rousseff's government continued to pursue its market-oriented (or rather, Brazilian-type selective business-friendly) strategy even into her second term, which began in 2015. By then, its primary aim was tackling the unfolding economic crisis, mainly by means of austerity measures such as cuts in public spending, interest-rate hikes, increasing utility prices, and reducing the availability of credit. By 2018, it was clear that these measures had contributed to or even aggravated the worst crisis in Brazil's modern economic history.

In the light of the recent corruption scandals and worsening economic outlook, economic analysts tend to agree, that the role of SOEs in the Brazilian economy should be reduced to increase transparency. Privatisation of SOEs (incl. state-owned banks) is essential, but should be preceded by the improvement of the rules of the game to ensure equal footing between the public and private sectors and local and foreign investors. Furthermore, the apparent political ties in SOEs remind us on the crony capitalism arguments in classic DS literature, and it seems that Brazil has not learnt yet the lessons resulting from the Asian crisis and the demise of the classic paradigm of DS in the 1990s.

THE NEW NEOLIBERAL TURN (2016–)

On top of all these described processes the new government of Michel Temer among its first economic policy steps[34] announced a large privatization program, and a twenty-years public spending cup (in form of a constitutional amendment, called PEC 241 or more recently PEC 55) indicating the commitment the neoliberal economic policy turn and the aim to radically drive back of the role of state in economy in Brazil (with immense social costs and threats lying however outside of the new government's focus).

The "Project Growth" was announced as the new ambitious privatization plan containing 32 infrastructural projects mainly in transport, energy, mining and sanitation sectors, with an expected income of 24 billion USD until 2018. To attract the much needed private (and foreign) investors several procedural and technical changes have been made, however often with debatable content (see e.g., the easing and speeding up of environmental licensing procedures). It is, however, straightforward to see the continuity with Dilma Rousseff's privatization plans presented above (the underlying economic and financial pressures and the overly optimistic estimates also remained unchanged).

Finally, public spending cup approved on 13 December 2016 has frozen most federal expenditures (and its structure) in real terms for the next 20 years (via constitutional amendment, such as to be revised the earliest in ten years). The proponents of this extremely divisive measure mostly highlight the need to regain market confidence and to cut budget deficit and keep inflation under control to avoid a future debt crisis. However, this spending cap might not be effective as it does not include the social security system (that currently covers more than 40 percent of the mandatory government expenditures). What is maybe more important, and lies also beyond the mass social protests across the country throughout the last years, is the fear that this measure harms the poor, who disproportionately rely on services provided by the government. At the same time, it

---

[34] It might be worth to note that as a first political step of Michel Temer the new (by then interim) cabinet after the removing from power Dilma Rousseff via the impeachment process in May 2016 was put together by exclusively white, elderly men (with a rather conservative stance). This has resulted heavy criticism, as Brazil is an ethnically and culturally very diverse and mixed country, and many social groups felt not to be represented by an all-men, all-white cabinet for which nobody has voted. Even the legitimacy of such a government was and is still currently questioned by many social groups and movements.

also harms future economic growth prospects by freezing up expenditures on the anyway underfinanced educational and health systems in Brazil.

Without going more into details with these recent economic policy measures and plans (such as reforms of the social-security system and pension system), we highlight the swinging of the pendulum, first towards more explicit and extended role of the state in economy and development between 2003 and 2016, and most recently back towards more neoliberal reforms and the retreat of the state. These recent economic policy measures are still at a very initial phase, and have to be realized in the aftermath of a severe economic and political crisis, which poses high uncertainties regarding their results and sustainability.

At the same time the elections in autumn 2018 have resulted in an even more explicit economic and political shift. The election of the former military officer and far-right nationalist Jair Bolsonaro represents a comeback for the traditional political elites and interests in Brazil (and this is an often overlooked difference if comparing to Donald Trump and the US), while his financial and economic super-minister Paulo Guedes, is a free-market economist form the Chicago school and thus strongly committed to cut back the role of the state in Brazil and transform its economy according to the Chilean model. The power balance within such a "strange marriage" (of Bolsonaro and Guedes) and its effects for the Brazilian economy are yet to be seen, though some potential threats and negative consequences on the society and environment are already emerging. The composition of the final socio-economic outcome (pros and contras) is still an open question, and depends also on the fact, whether this new (illiberal and radical) political regime will be a lasting one.

Conclusions

Throughout this paper we have argued that despite significant achievements in the Brazilian political economy during the last century (such as the transition to a competitive and pluralist democracy, privatization, deregulation, and macroeconomic stabilization), important structures and modes mainly related to the interconnectedness of the state with the private sector, as well as those related to developmental and productive activities have remained in place in (or have returned to) Brazil by the beginning of the twenty-first century. We have presented a rather strange combination of pragmatic privatization and intensified state economic intervention in Brazil during the 1990 and early 2000s.

We have also argued that privatization has depended more on political factors and economic (fiscal) pressures and much less on ideology. With the new, right-wing governments, first coming to power via the impeachment process in 2016, and then in the presidential election in autumn 2018 with the resounding (but not outright) victory of Bolsonaro, an ideological turn is taking place in high-level Brazilian politics. However, the electorate and Brazilian society more broadly is rather divided (as the share of votes during the election has also shown, 55 percent for Bolsonaro and 45 percent for Haddad). At this early stage of the new era it seems that the rhetoric and new governance style of the acting president tends to deepen these divisions and hurt social cohesion. Whether this will lead to a reversal in the Brazilian electorate's value-system and its rather rigid ideological views is yet to be seen and would require further research.

Like Boschi (2011), we have argued in favor of the existence of strong continuity with the old Brazilian developmentalist model, although Boschi put more emphasis on the preservation of a strategic bureaucratic nuclei and the mostly unchanged patterns of business-state relations. In contrast, we did not consider this as a comparative advantage in the post-GFC period, but rather argue that these continuities have also contributed (as one important cause) to the recent political and economic crisis in Brazil, and have led to severe social consequences and dissatisfaction, well demonstrated by the continuous public demonstrations over the past few years (especially since 2013), and ended up producing the unexpected election results in autumn 2018, where the majority of the electorate voted for change.

The adoption of emergency anti-cyclical policies after GFC has strengthened the revival (or, in the case of Brazil, rather the reassertion) of an activist and interventionist state, and a new era in Brazil, which began under Lula has "flourished" even more under Rousseff and has differed fundamentally from the experiences of other, more advanced countries. At the same time, we have argued that this new interventionism maintained its roots and links with the old DS model from the ISI period, and by 2014 at the latest, it proved to be unsustainable in economic and fiscal terms as well as socially and politically.

Finally, we have stressed that transforming SOEs through corporatization and public listing (the model called for the state as majority investor) requires a well-developed domestic capital market to attract private capital and to increase external monitoring and transparency (not least to develop rules that protect minority investors, whose stakes have often been violated in twenty-first-century Brazil).

The Brazilian experience has shown that a government's temptation to intervene is high (both in models where the state as a majority or minority investor). We have argued that, especially since 2011 (the Rousseff administration), a move towards more interventionism (though e.g., price controls for things like gasoline and electricity go back to 2006) and the strengthening state influence can be observed, and this happened on an ad hoc basis and via discretionary measures, which more often than not hurt minority stakes and undermined private investors' confidence. Weak and (re-)politicized regulation and strong state influence have resulted in missing or unsatisfactory checks and balances in the Brazilian SOE sector. Furthermore, discretionary governmental decisions and actions have continued to pose serious threats to the performance of SOEs and have destroyed investors' confidence and, more generally, the Brazilian business climate.

Finally, one of the most important lessons from the Brazilian model of the state as minority investor, derived from the activities of BNDES and is, above all, in line with the relatively new strain of scholarship on the entrepreneurial state (Mazzucato 2013). According to this view, the state (via e.g., state-owned development banks) might play an active role in financing private economic activities if selected firms have latent growth capabilities, but are constrained by a lack of financial resources. The practice of BNDES financing, however, was exactly the opposite, what the entrepreneurial state model would suggest: it provided hidden subsidies to the largest firms in Brazil, which clearly did not lack opportunities to borrow on the market.

The Brazilian explanation for BNDES subsidized credit, is, for example, the need for investment in a relatively new sector promoting infrastructure financing related to low consumer prices set by the government. However, this is a tautology: more stable rules and market prices could have encouraged private investors to step in, and (scarce) state capital could have been used in cases where the social externalities are outstandingly high, or in sectors private capital avoids for other reasons (such as high risk or overly long horizons of return, which is in line with Mazzucato's argument).

The creation of national champions has also been a costly experiment, not just directly, but also indirectly through the preservation or even the further distortion of the natural resource based economic structure of Brazil. This has strained the results of the BNDES equity arm (an important source of earnings lately in the BNDES budget). This can also be regarded as the reiteration of old DS practices and assumptions that have already proven to be wrong and outdated (both in practice—see the experiences of east Asia—and in theory—see the latest literature on DS).

It was out of the scope of this paper to deeply analyze the complexity of state-business relations in Brazil. We have only explored its main roots, which go back to the long-term institutional development of Brazil and are also deeply embedded in its political system, which used to allow private funding during electoral campaigns until 2016. The degree and varieties of state influence in Brazil may be also illustrated by case study analysis, but this was outside of the scope of this paper (though some of these are already covered by existing economic literature on companies like Vale, Embraer, Petrobras, or BNDES). All of these cases underline the scholarship of Schneider (2013, 2015) and Nölke et al. (2015), who argue that a distinctive institutional foundation of capitalism emerged in Brazil with different degrees and modes of state influence than in other, more developed parts of the world, which is best captured in the concept of a hierarchical or state-permeated market economy.

Our most important conclusion is that the role of the state as well and the degree of state influence in the economy increased in Brazil in the first decade of the new millennium. While state interventionism became even more pronounced in the Rousseff era between 2011 and 2016, the focus has shifted from pro-poor policies towards a more business-friendly approach. State influence has changed forms and channels (compared to the old developmentalist period of the ISI), but below the surface, state control survived and has heavily influenced everyday economic life in Brazil. The best proof of the strong interconnections between the political and economic spheres is provided by the ongoing Petrobras scandal (and the Car Wash Operation), in which almost the entire political elite is involved. Implicitly since 2016 and more explicitly since 2019, a new economic policy direction is emerging (first under the Temer government, and more recently under Bolsonaro's cabinet), however the implementation of this market-friendly agenda and its socio-economic effects will yet to be seen in the coming years.

REFERENCES

Almeida, Mansueto, and Ben Ross Schneider. 2012. "Globalization, Democratization, and the Challenges of Industrial Policy in Brazil." In *Industrial Policy*, edited by Campos Wonghyuk Lim and Richard Locke. Washington, DC: World Bank.

Alston, Lee J., Marcus André Melo, Bernardo Mueller, and Carlos Pereira. 2016. *Brazil in Transition: Beliefs, Leadership, and Institutional Change.* Princeton, NJ: Princeton University Press.

Amado, Adriana Moreira, and Maria de Lourdes Rollemberg Mollo. 2015. "The 'Developmentalism' Debate in Brazil: Some Economic and Political Issues." *Review of Keynesian Economics* 3 (1): 77–89.

Amann, Edmund, and Werner Baer. 2012. "Brazil: A New Economic Miracle?" *Brazilian Journal of Political Economy* 32 (3): 412–23.

Amann, Ed, and Armando Barrientos. 2014. "Is there a Brazilian Model of Development? Are There Lessons for Countries in Africa?" Working Paper 134. United Nations University World Institute for Development Economics Research (UNU-WIDER), Helsinki, Finland. https://ideas.repec.org/p/unu/wpaper/wp2014-134.html.

Anuatti-Neto, Francisco, Milton Barossi-Filho, Antonio G. de Carvalho, and Roberto Macedo. 2003. "Costs and Benefits of Privatization: Evidence from Brazil." Research Network Working Paper R-455. Inter-American Development Bank, Latin American Research Network, Washington, DC. https://www.joserobertoafonso.com.br/attachment/6096.

Brazilian Development Bank. 2002. "Privatization in Brazil: 1990–1994, 1995–2002." http://www.bndes.gov.br/SiteBNDES/export/sites/default/bndes_en/Galerias/Download/studies/priv_brazil.pdf.

Boschi, Raul. 2011. "State Developmentalism: Continuity and Uncertainty." In *The Brazilian State: Debate and Agenda*, edited by Mauricio A. Font and Laura Randall, 37–58. Lanham, MD: Lexington Books.

Bresser Pereira, Luiz Carlos. 2006. "The New Developmentalism and Conventional Orthodoxy." *São Paulo em Perspectiva review* 20 (1): 1–35.

———. 2011. "An Account of New Developmentalism and its Structuralist Macroeconomics." *Brazilian Journal of Political Economy* 31 (3): 493–502.

———. 2012. "The New Developmentalism as a Weberian Ideal Type." In *Macroeconomics and Development: Roberto Frenkel and the Economics of Latin America*, edited by Mario Damill, Martin Rapetti, and Guillermo Rozenwurcel, 373–83. New York: Columbia University Press.

Burlamaqui, Leonardo, Jose A. P. de Souza, and Nelson H. Barbosa-Filho. 2006. "The Rise and the Halt of Economic Development in Brazil, 1945–2004." Research Paper 81. United Nations University World Institute for Development Economics Research, Helsinki, Finland.

Carvalho, Marco Antonio S. 2001. "Privatization, Public Debt and Deficit in Brazil." IPEA Working Paper 847. Institute of Applied Economic Research (IPEA), Directory of Macroeconomic Policy and Studies (DIMAC). http://papers.ssrn.com/sol3/papers.cfm?abstract_id=304681.

Cavalcante, Luiz Ricardo. 2018. "The Brazilian Development Bank." In *The Oxford Handbook of the Brazilian Economy*, edited by Edmund Amann, Carlos Azzoni, and Werbner Baer, 177–97. New York: Oxford University Press.

The Economist Intelligence Unit. "Brazil." Accessed November 14, 2015. https://country.eiu.com/brazil.

Evans, Peter B. 1995. *Embedded Autonomy: States and Industrial Transformation.* Princeton, NJ: Princeton University Press.

Fleischer, David. 2011. "Political Reform: A Never-Ending Story." In *The Brazilian State: Debate and Agenda*, edited by M. Font and L. Randall, 129–44. Lanham, MD: Lexington Books.

———. 2016. "Attempts at Political Reform (1985–2015): Still a 'Never Ending Story.'" Presented at 13th International Congress of Brazilian Studies Association, Providence, RI March 31–April 2. http://www.brasa.org/wordpress/wp-content/uploads/2015/07/David-Fleischer.pdf.

Gaitán, Flavio, and Renato Boschi. 2015. "State–Business–Labour Relations and Patterns of Development in Latin America." In *New Directions in Comparative Capitalisms Research: Critical and Global Perspectives*, edited by Matthias Ebenau, Ian Bruff, and Christian May, 172–88. Basingstoke: Palgrave Macmillan.

Leahy, Joe. 2015. "Eletrobrás Ruling Exposes Impact of Brazil's Heavy Hand." *Financial Times*, July 14. https://www.ft.com/content/ddd514d2-29f5-11e5-acfb-cbd2e1c81cca

Kerstenetzky, Celia Les. 2014. "The Brazilian Social Developmental State: A Progressive Agenda in a (Still) Conservative Political Society." In *The End of Developmental State?*, edited by Michelle Williams, 172–96. New York: Routledge.

Massi, Eliza. 2014. "The Political Economy of Development Finance: The BNDES and Brazilian Industrialisation." PhD dissertation. Department of Development Studies, SOAS, University of London.

Mazzucato, Mariana. 2013. *The Entrepreneurial State: Debunking Public vs. Private Sector Myths*. London: Anthem Press.

Musacchio, Aldo, and Sergio G. Lazzarini. 2014a. "State-Owned Enterprises in Brazil: History and Lessons." Paper presented at the OECD Workshop on State-Owned Enterprises in the Development Process, Paris, April 4.

———. 2014b. *Reinventing State Capitalism: Leviathan in Business, Brazil and Beyond*. Cambridge: Harvard University Press.

Nagy, Sándor Gyula, and Judit Ricz. 2018. "Economic Crisis in Brazil: Its Roots, Causes and Scenarios." KKI Studies T-2018/04. Institute for Foreign Affairs and Trade, Budapest.

Nölke Andreas. 2015. "State-permeated Capitalism in Large Emerging Markets." Paper presented at conference The Role of State in Varieties of Capitalism (SVOC), Institute of World Economics of the Centre for Economic and Regional Studies, Hungarian Academy of Sciences and Center for EU Enlargement Studies, Central European University, November 26–27.

Nölke, Andreas, Tobias ten Brink, Simone Claar, and Christian May. 2015. "Domestic Structures, Foreign Economic Policies and Global Economic Order: Implications for the Rise of Large Emerging Economies." *European Journal of International Relations* 21 (3): 538–67.

Pargendler, Mariana. 2012. "The Unintended Consequences of State Ownership: The Brazilian Experience." *Theoretical Inquiries in Law* 13 (2): 504–23.

Phillips, Dominic. 2014. "Brazil Inflation Really at 8% Without Rouseff Fiddling." *Bloomberg*. http://www.bloomberg.com/news/articles/2014-07-08/brazil-inflation-really-at-8-without-rousseff-fiddling-economy.

Pinheiro, Armando Castelar. 1996. "Impactos microeconômicos da privatização." *Pesquisa e Planejamento Econômico* 26 (3): 357–98.

———. 2002. "The Brazilian Privatization Experience: What's Next?" Working Paper CBS-30-02. University of Oxford, Centre for Brazilian Studies.

———. 2011. "Two Decades of Privatization in Brazil." In *The Economies of Argentina and Brazil: A Comparative Perspective*, edited by Werner Baer and David Fleischer, 252–78. Cheltenham: Edward Elgar.

Pinheiro, Armando Castelar, and Fábio Giambiagi. 1994. "Brazilian Privatization in the 1990s." *World Development* 22 (5): 737–53.

Pinto, Luiz, and Marcos Reis. 2017. "Long-Term Finance in Brazil: The Role of Brazilian Development Bank (BNDES)." In *The New Brazilian Economy: Dynamic Transitions into the Future*, edited by E. C. Grivoyannis, 155–76. New York: Palgrave Macmillan.

Rapoza, Kenneth. 2012. "Brazil Opens Roads to Privatization." *Forbes*, August 10. https://www.forbes.com/sites/kenrapoza/2012/08/10/brazil-opens-roads-to-privatization/#255cd42b4ca5.

Reuters. 2015. "Brazil's Rousseff approval rating hits new low, poll shows." August 6. https://uk.reuters.com/article/brazil-rousseff-poll/brazils-rousseff-approval-rating-hits-new-low-poll-shows-idUKL1N10H0HK20150806

Ricz, Judit. 2017. "The Rise and Fall (?) of a New Developmental State in Brazil." *Society and Economy in Central and Eastern Europe* 39 (1): 85–108.

Schneider, Ben Ross. 1988–89. "Partly for Sale: Privatization and State Strength in Brazil and Mexico." *Journal of Interamerican Studies and World Affairs* 30 (4): 89–116.

———. 1990. "The Politics of Privatization in Brazil and Mexico: Variations on a Statist Theme." Conference paper, no. 23, Columbia University–New York University Consortium Series, Columbia University, New York, New York.

———. 2013. *Hierarchical Capitalism in Latin America. Business, Labor, and the Challenges of Equitable Development*. New York: Cambridge University Press.

———. 2015. "The Developmental State in Brazil: Comparative and Historical Perspectives." *Revista de Economia Política* 35 (1): 114–32.

———, ed. 2016. *New Order and Progress: Development and Democracy in Brazil*. New York: Oxford University Press.

Serrano, Franklin, and Luiz E. Melin. 2015. "Political Aspects of Unemployment: Brazil's Neoliberal U-Turn." http://www.excedente.org/wp-content/uploads/2015/12/Serrano-Melin-U-Turn.pdf.

Trebat, Thomas J. 1983. *Brazil's State-owned Enterprises: A Case Study of the State as Entrepreneur*. Cambridge: Cambridge University Press.

Vasconcelos, Erick. 2014. "How Privatizations Created New State Companies in Brazil." Center for a Stateless Society, September 9. https://c4ss.org/content/31544.

Winiecki, Jan. 2016. *Shortcut or Piecemeal: Economic Development Strategies and Structural Change*. Budapest–New York: CEU Press.

Wylde, Christopher. 2012. *Latin America after Neoliberalism: Developmental Regimes in Post-Crisis States*. Basingstoke: Palgrave Macmillan.

Concluding Remarks and Further Research Agenda

Miklós Szanyi

When the research program for this book was designed in 2014, clear changes in the size and depth of state economic involvement was already evident. At that time, the political impacts of these changes were less clear. The hypothesis of the research expected different economic and political impacts of increasing state intervention depending on the quality and embeddedness of democratic political and liberal economic institutions. The hypothesis expected that countries with less embedded or fewer institutions would be less able to withstand the political opportunities (temptations) of greater state influence. This hypothesis was largely proved by the research. However, since then, important changes have occurred in the global economy and politics. Later development in world economy and politics showed that the apogee of the neo-liberal concept reached a geographically wider area and produced further, rather serious changes in the status quo of the Great Moderation. Brexit, the American trade war, and the electoral success of various populist parties in Europe showed that countries with deeply embedded institutional systems of the competitive state were also seriously challenged in the post-crisis period. It is, therefore, highly relevant to also include developed countries in the scope of research on business-polity interactions and the role of state ownership in them.

The overall picture of the uses of increased state ownership supports the initial hypothesis. Traditional market economies tended to maintain their specific social institutional systems, the differences of which also affected state ownership patterns. In the French economy, the state has played important role in the stimulation of the economy, especially high-tech sectors, since the seventeenth century. Nationwide infrastructure systems together with their support industries have been also largely under state influence. It is important to mention here that direct state ownership is frequently complemented by indirect forms of control (partial ownership with special voting rights for example). Overall control may be much larger than what the analysis of state ownership may indicate (see Somai on France in Chapter Two, Körösi on Austria in Chapter Four, and Kozarzewski and Baltowski 2016 on the example of Poland). In Chapter One, Voszka also showed that state ownership, together with special features of market regulation, should be observed in order to grasp the full impact of state control over various industries or the economy as a whole.

Germany returned to its previous reduced ownership pattern rather quickly after the necessary nationalizations that took place after 2008. The orientation and stimulation of the economy used the traditional strong institution of the tri-party system's social consensus. The German economy recovered very quickly using the increased sales of exports in the manufacturing industry, which was supported by flexible labor market solutions rather than increased direct state intervention.

The Austrian case is more peculiar. Austro-Keynesianism prevailed well beyond its heyday in the second half of the twentieth century and produced a successful growth pattern for the country. It has always been bound to high level of direct state intervention partially based on state ownership. The socio-liberal governments continued this tradition after 2008. Ownership control was even strengthened and centralized in 2015 with the establishment of ÖBIB (Chapter Four). But after 2017, a new, right-wing, and to some extent populist government announced significant changes in traditional Austrian economic policy trends. The new policy package puts significant emphasis on the monetary stimulation of the economy, supports for innovation, and family businesses. These goals are, of course, not new, but their primacy in economic policy reflects neoliberal ideas combined with the potential scaling back of direct state intervention.

The three case studies focusing on developed market economies revealed major differences in traditional institutional systems and economic policy patterns that were not streamlined in a uniform direction after 2008. Varieties of capitalism remained vivid in the post-crisis period. Concerning the ownership policies of developed countries, Voszka concluded in Chapter One that (mostly reluctant and covert) nationalizations and privatization continued to occur simultaneously. This means that states as owners changed their corporate portfolios according to specific governmental (and perhaps social) goals. An important goal may also be making profits, and this aspect is not restricted to sovereign wealth funds (which, at their origin, have tended to be regarded mainly as business entities), but also manufacturing companies and service providers. Many of the large German, Italian, and French companies are not distinguishable from their private competitors in terms of their behavior (see the French case in Chapter Two but also similar policies in Poland, Chapter Six, and Brazil, Chapter Twelve). The state as owner trades with their securities and participates in their control as ordinary stakeholders. Many times state has only partial ownership in publicly traded joint-stock companies as a form of hybrid ownership.

Throughout the book, special attention has been paid to the role of state ownership in the shaping relationships between businesses and polities. These links, of course, also exist in developed countries. In the case of modern Western economies, moderate forms of corruption like favoring political allies and red-carpet treatment for state representatives in the management and on corporate boards may be observed (see the Austrian Proporz-system). State companies, however, were more likely to serve political goals, which were usually labeled as social goals, like maintaining employment levels (Boycko, Shleifer and Vishny, 1996). In all these cases, the costs of politically determined corporate goals may be traced back. Effective social and political control over government agents and state property, as well as the control of capital markets set limits on political and individual rent-seeking. Voszka also indicated that instead of nationalizations, governments sought to increase control through regulatory measures and limitations on property rights through the "expropriation of incomes."

Yet major political changes occurred in many Western countries after the crisis. Of course, the climax of the European migration problem contributed largely to the demise of traditional program parties and the advance of new "business firm" parties (populist parties). The two largest economies of the EU (France and Germany) hardly escaped the victory or at least significant political impact of populist parties in the 2017 elections. In Italy and Austria, they won elections. It is not very easy to foresee what policies these parties will pursue, since they are not traditional, ideologically driven political movements, but rather "parties of the people," that promise to say and do whatever voters would like to hear and see. Nevertheless, the Austrian Kurz government's program has some solid theoretical and practical grounding, but this cannot be said about the new Italian government. The picture is a blur.

The transition economies of ECE had much weaker or basically no tradition of political democracy and a liberal economy. All the necessary political, economic, and social institutions were imported, and these institutions had just started to become embedded when the 2008–9 crisis hit. The populations and also policymakers lacked a firm commitment to the values of the Western world that were reinforced in these countries also institutionally by the laws of the European Union after 2004. The weak underpinnings of the competition state concept were discovered by several empirical surveys (for example, on the social rejection of privatization, see Denisova et al. 2010). This also meant that the risks of deferring the institutional system in ways that enhance personal and political rent-seeking were much larger in this region than in more established market economies. Rolling back democratic political institutions and the safeguards of free competition in the economy already began in Hungary before the crisis. An important area of retreat was increasing state property.

Our analysis in Chapter Five proved that increased state ownership in the countries of ECE served markedly different purposes than in most of the more developed market economies. The demise of the neo-liberal concept weakened the factors that reinforced the merger of the region into the competitive state system. International institutions became aware that the suggested institutional solutions might become counterproductive in unfamiliar (to them) social environments and were discouraged. Pressure from the EU also softened after the successful accessions. Bourgeois economic patriotism spread across the ECE region. Under the umbrella of economic patriotism, a new system of patronage was established. Favoritism was not used generally towards inhabitants or firms of "patriae," but was selectively addressed to political clients. In this realm, state property played an important role. Besides the previously described "traditional" rent-seeking opportunities, SOEs could be effectively used for corruption. Against this background, the expanding state sector can be interpreted as the reversal of the political and institutional goal of privatization. This is no less than an attempt at widening the channels of rent-seeking and corruption, and it could be implemented because of the lack of solid political and social control and social disappointment.

Less private and more public property in itself should not cause problems. After all, the size of the state sector in many established market economies is still larger than in Poland or Hungary. The problem is caused when it is used or plays an increased role in political rent-seeking and corruption. Another related problem is the method of expanding state property as opposed to privatization. In many cases, property expropriation occurred, if not through outright theft or robbery (see the Russian practice of corporate raiding in Viktorov 2013), then through regulatory capture. In any case, many of the nationalizations were bound to the violation of private property rights. As such, basic institutions of the free market economy and the principle of competition state have been weakened. This tendency paralleled the outright rolling back of democratic political institutions in Hungary and Poland. Similar attempts in other ECE countries were less successful.

After giving a general overview of transition-related privatization process, ECE country case studies concentrated on issues that were typical and distinct to the given country. The highlight of the Polish case study was the successful combination of privatization and the development of capital markets (especially the Warsaw Stock Exchange). This topic naturally leads to corporate governance issues, since, in many cases, state control is exercised with partial state ownership. The exposure to competition on the capital market helped increase efficiency and transparency that in turn put limits on political objectives. Despite this positive feature, the interdependence of politics and the economy has remained strong in Poland. Much of the space for rent-seeking and corruption has remained in place. Most current events were the result of the deceleration of the privatization of remaining state property after 2011 and the new 2015 program of increasing Polish (state) ownership in the economy, called "re-Polonization." These steps were also taken in the name of economic patriotism. However, there is growing evidence that the transactions mainly served political rent-seeking purposes.

The Slovenian case in Chapter Seven clearly demonstrated the political stakes of privatization versus nationalization. The Slovenian transition process had long enjoyed a very good image because of the relatively strong macroeconomic performance and seemingly deep and quick advances in institution building and privatization. As we saw however, privatization was, in many cases, only surface privatization, and state ownership was retained, albeit in indirect forms largely through state-owned financial intermediaries. Moreover, incumbent management generally remained in place. This meant that the political goal of using privatization to replace the old nomenclature went unfulfilled (see Frydman and Rapaczinsky 1994), and important tasks of the neo-liberal agenda were not realized. This failure came back to haunt the state in the 2000s, when the new elite wanted to accomplish political transition and wanted to remove incumbent management from directly or indirectly state-controlled companies. Macroeconomic imbalances increased when the financial results of the mismanagement of quasi-privatized firms were realized.

Chapter Five clearly describes the various goals of privatization in the transition process in ECE. Poland stood out with a relatively slow, albeit very transparent privatization process that enjoyed social consensus. Hungarian privatization was quick and deep and built largely on the involvement of foreign direct investments. In both countries, political tasks, such as eliminating communist party officials' political and economic power, were failures. Yet, various political and business elites were confronted over the distribution of economic positions. These confrontations were also politically interwoven: the comprador elite serving foreign firms' interests was to be pushed back in business (together with "their" foreign firms). This has been one of the main arguments of populist Polish and Hungarian governments since the mid-2010's. In Slovenia, multinational businesses did not participate in the privatization process, hence it was not the comprador but the incumbent elite that had to be removed. The clash of various political and business elites may create macroeconomic problems, but, even worse, it also damages market institutions.

The Hungarian chapter described the process by which the Hungarian government rolled back important institutions in order to eliminate control over rent-seeking and corrupt transactions. The study also highlighted changes in the source(s) of rents. After joining the EU, the primary source of rents became EU financial transfers from structural funds and the agricultural fund. State-owned enterprises played an important role in political rent-seeking: in the reduction of utility prices and by providing financial support for various politically motivated programs. Corruption (that can be also legal) mainly targeted public procurement tenders that used EU funds. At the same time, the economic patriotism mantra was used to legitimate massive attacks against foreign business mainly in the service sector and trade. Foreign firms' market positions were to be captured either by state-owned companies (in public services in order to slash prices to buy election votes) or by partisan firms (e.g. in retail, trade, and banking). At the same time, the Hungarian government continued to support foreign manufacturing investments. Foreign investment attraction in certain segments of the economy remained very strong. The structure of the economy and especially exports became highly concentrated in the automotive industry and electronics, which increased vulnerability as was evidenced during the 2008–9 crisis.

Studies on the ECE region are also important from the perspective of developed countries. Negative anomalies of business and polity interactions in the old EU member states were not clear yet. An important reason for this are the relatively solid political (regular, free elections) and social controls (watchdog institutions). But major changes occurred in core Europe's party system as well! Business firm parties were established well before their advance in ECE. Silvio Berlusconi's political career or Jörg Haider's election victory preceded Viktor Orbán's second or Jarosław Kaczyński's first governments in Hungary and Poland respectively. Further damage to the traditional parties in core Europe may easily lead to similar dangers that we are witnessing now in ECE.

Emerging market economies are especially important fields of observation regarding the impact and applicability of classic democratic political institutions and liberal market economic principles in different cultural, historical, and political backgrounds. In fact, some countries on the peripheries of Europe and the US (Turkey, Mexico, and Russia) have repeatedly attempted Western-style modernization during their history. Chapter Eleven provides a brief overview of the latest Turkish attempts. The modern history of that country can be interpreted as the competition between social and political groups favoring Western modernization and those that call for a more traditional developmental course with strong Islamic features. The very long story of Turkey's association with the EU and the clumsy negotiations over membership reflects the fundamental difficulties of fitting the country into an alliance of such culturally diverse countries. The current popularity of President Erdoğan, and his successful policy of rolling back barely established democratic institutions, shows the declining impact of Western competition on the state's principles. Turkey's departure from European values worries the European Union but obviously not the majority of Turkish society. It is not yet clear if the presidential system and new economic policies will bring prosperity or decline.

There are also other countries with non-traditional economic models that proved to be successful, at least in some periods. Singapore's model has been regarded as a true success story (Chapter Ten). Nevertheless, the family of a charismatic leader has dominated the economy, state, and social life. Economic success was not bound to political competition. State-owned firms virtually meant the personal property of the ruler. Very specific circumstances, among others the strategic location of the tiny country and the British military presence, which provided exceptional opportunities that were cleverly utilized. Hence, the Singapore success story is rather unique, despite the fact that it is regularly mentioned as part the East-Asian developmental state model, together with other, equally distinctive Asian success stories (Taiwan, South Korea).

Chapter Nine deals with the issue of the revival of the developmental state concept. New statist approaches are applied to support the catching-up process of emerging market economies. These new attempts, however, must be different, not only because of the variety of countries' socio-economic models, but also because the operating environment has changed. Globalization redesigned the international division of labor with an outstanding role for large multinational companies that operate in global value chains of international corporate networks. This makes the development of new global players based in emerging market economies extremely difficult. Global free trade and many multilateral agreements limit the possibilities for traditional infant industry protection. Clift and Woll (2012) described the process of reinventing control tools over open markets as new forms of protectionism.

Other important differences stem from the altered structure of production and employment. Today, developmental success must be based on strengthening national participation in current dynamic sectors, most importantly in services, rather than the industrialization process of mid-twentieth-century national success stories. This focus also means different social impacts. In Chapter Nine, Ricz argues that today's typical employment structure focuses on highly paid knowledge intensive services and badly rewarded interpersonal services. The social impact of this specialization pattern is growing polarization. This stands in contrast to the industrialization process fifty years ago, which was based on massive labor reallocation from poorly paid agriculture to better paid industrial jobs with little wage inequality. Today's development pattern produces growing inequality, which may seriously undermine the political sustainability of such growth patterns. The case studies in the volume could not find convincing policies that improved the inclusiveness of economic development.

Although new developmental state concepts emphasize the role of enabling policies, there are many examples of a strong state sector presence tasked with the facilitation of national development goals. Singapore as an archetype is clearly such an example, although, most recently, when the development goals have been achieved, few SOEs were privatized. The other interesting case is Brazil (Chapter Twelve). Prevailing traditions of a less successful developmental state experiment contributed to recent political and economic crisis and social dissatisfaction, especially after 2014. The 2008–2009 crisis strengthened the reassertion of the activist state that has maintained its roots in the old type developmental state model after a period of less intensive state involvement (in the management of SOEs), which has also been earmarked by privatization transactions. This attempt proved to be unsustainable both in economic and fiscal terms, and politically and socially. The Brazilian government's temptation was too high to directly intervene in the management of SOEs. These interventions were sometimes unsuccessful and hurt private minority shareholders' interests. Weak and politicized regulation and strong state influence undermined the effects of checks and balances in Brazilian SOEs. Discretional government decisions posed serious threats to the performance of SOEs, destroyed investors' confidence, and weakened the business climate. This was also reflected in the privatization process through public listings, as investment opportunities in majority state-owned companies did not attract sufficient private capital.

The chapters in this volume analyzed direct economic interventions by the state mainly through state-owned firms. The primary aim was to distinguish different patterns of involvement in countries with different cultural and political backgrounds and development levels. The hypothesis that more stable institutions will resist the temptation of using increased state ownership after the 2008–2009 crisis has been proven. However, more detailed analysis revealed the fact that institutions' long traditions of and relationships with the institutions of the competition state will not provide full immunity from the temptations for more developed countries. The rolling back of democratic institutions has started in many emerging market economies as well as in some of the new EU member countries, with the potential threat of undermining the whole European institutional system. Potentially, these practices can be exported to core Europe as well. The state sector has played important roles in supporting various political goals in most of the countries analyzed here. Some of these goals were not economically rational. Although we discovered practices in harmony with the concept of the entrepreneurial state (Mazzucato 2013), more often, state intervention increased and often lacked business considerations. Actions of political rent-seeking discouraged private investment in publicly traded companies. Forced nationalizations and encroachments undermined the rule of law and the institutions of the competition state.

Based on the results of the analysis of direct state actions in the economy, we can continue our research on other areas of business polity interactions. The two areas should be simultaneously analyzed in an appropriate theoretical framework. Kornai (2000, 2016) has carried out simultaneous research on economic and political processes that have theoretical relevance. His concept of the system paradigm can be used as analytical tool in comparative studies. Most countries in the contemporary global economy can be treated as hybrids standing between the two major economic and political systems: capitalism and socialism (communism). Moreover, the demise of the neoliberal concept produced a major shift from the liberal-democratic pole of Kornai's dichotomy to the authoritarian-illiberal pole. This is reflected in the latest political events in various countries (Putin's Russia, Erdoğan's Turkey, Orbán's Hungary). Traditional Western democracies' institutional systems were largely maintained until now, but there are question marks in several countries (e.g., in Italy). We can therefore check whether it holds in any developed country if increased state economic involvement is not about the efficient allocation of economic resources, but about maximizing political control over society and the economy (Acemoglu and Robinson 2012).

Kornai explored the two main economic systems above as two ideal types of existing socio-political formations. Allowing for a wide range of actual implementation, Kornai (2000, 2016) described the fundamental characteristics of the two regimes as a dichotomy. Primary (decisive) system-specific characteristics were identified as determining the two systems as a whole. They are differentiated from secondary (reactive) features that modify the actual appearance. The three primary aspects that differentiate socialist and capitalist systems are the following: 1) the relation of the political sphere to property forms and economic coordination mechanisms, 2) the dominant form of property, 3) the dominant economic coordination mechanism. These main characteristics influence six secondary characteristics: 1) power relations between the two sides of the market for goods and services, 2) power relations between the two sides of the labor market, 3) the speed and qualitative features of technical progress (innovation), 4) the resulting income distribution, 5) the softness/hardness of firms' budget constraints, 6) the main direction of corruption.

Kornai (2016) distinguished three types of political categories: the two traditional politico-governmental forms; democracy and dictatorship; and a third form: autocracy. However, in Kornai's words (2016, 566) "autocracy, in this paradigm, is no blurred 'middle way' between democracy and dictatorship, but a sharply identifiable type in the sense Max Weber termed an 'ideal type.' It is a theoretical construct that in my approach is distinct from two other types: democracy and dictatorship."

In order to label one or another existing regime according to the three big politico-governmental forms, one has to first look at the following four primary characteristics: 1) the possibility of removing the government through peaceful and civilized procedure; 2) the existence and strength of institutions that jointly guarantee the conditions of removing the government; 3) the existence of legal parliamentary opposition and a multi-party system; 4) the existence of terror and/or other means of coercion applied against political adversaries. In the background of these main attributes, the following six areas have to be analyzed as secondary characteristics: 1) the use of repressive means against the parliamentary opposition; 2) the strength and independence of institutions functioning as checks and balances on political power; 3) the dominance of the ruling political group's appointive practices; 4) the strength of civil society and the legal constraints against civil protest; 5) levels and practices of participation (in decision making); and 6) freedom of the press legally and in practice.

These dimensions of economic and political systems can be verified, and therefore, they seem to be suitable for timely international comparisons. Cross-section analysis has to be supported by ample evidence gathered from case studies as well. The task is urgent, because the global economy and global politics change very quickly. Complex research on the economic and political drivers of the processes support and promote a better understanding of these changes.

REFERENCES

Acemoglu, Daron, and James A. Robinson. 2012. "Is State Capitalism Winning?" *Project Syndicate*, December 31.

Boycko, Maxim, Andrei Shleifer, and Robert W. Vishny. 1996. "A Theory of Privatisation." *The Economic Journal* 106 (3): 309–19.

Clift, Ben, and Cornelia Woll. 2012. "Economic Patriotism: Reinventing Control over Open Markets." *Journal of European Public Policy* 19 (3): 307–23.

Denisova, Irina, Markus Eller, Timothy Frye, and Ekaterina Zhuravskaya. 2010. "Everyone Hates Privatization, but Why? Survey Evidence from 28 Post-Communist Countries." *Journal of Comparative Economics* 40 (1): 44–61.

Frydman, Roman, and Andrzej Rapaczynski. 1994. *Privatization in Eastern Europe: Is the State Withering Away?* Budapest–New York: CEU Press.

Kornai, János. 2000. "The System Paradigm." In *Paradigms of Social Change: Modernization, Development, Transformation, Evolution*, edited by Waltraud Schekle, Wolf-Hagen Krauth, Martin Kohli, Georg Elwert, 111–33. Frankfurt and New York: Campus Verlag–St. Martin's Press.

———. 2016. "The System Paradigm Revisited: Clarification and Additions in the Light of Experiences in the Post-Socialist Region." *Acta Oeconomica* 66 (4): 547–96.

Kozarzewski, Piotr and Baltowski, Maciej, 2016. "Formal and Real Ownership Structure of the Polish Economy: State-owned versus State-controlled Enterprises." *Post-Communist Economies* 28 (3): 405–19.

Mazzucato, Mariana. 2013. *The Entrepreneurial State: Debunking Public vs. Private Sector Myths*. London: Anthem Press.

Viktorov, Ilja. 2013. "Corporate Raiding in Post-Soviet Russia." *Baltic Worlds*, October 29.

Contributors

EVA OZSVALD, retired senior research fellow, Institute of Economics, Center for Economic and Regional Studies, HAS, Budapest

ISTVÁN KŐRÖSI, associate professor, Pázmány Péter Catholic University, Budapest; senior research fellow, Institute of World Economy, Center for Economic and Regional Studies, HAS, Budapest

ZSÓFIA NASZÁDOS, junior research fellow, Institute of World Economics, Center for Economic and Regional Studies, HAS, Budapest

JUDIT RICZ, research fellow, Institute of World Economics, Center for Economic and Regional Studies, HAS, Budapest; assistant professor, Institute of World Economy, Corvinus University of Budapest

MIKLÓS SOMAI, senior research fellow, Institute of World Economics, Center for Economic and Regional Studies, HAS, Budapest

MIKLÓS SZANYI, director, Institute of World Economics, Center of Economic and Regional Studies, HAS, Budapest; professor, University of Szeged

TAMÁS SZIGETVÁRI, associate professor, Institute of International Studies and Political Science, Pázmány Péter Catholic University, Budapest; senior research fellow, Institute of World Economics of the Center for Economic and Regional Studies, HAS, Budapest

ÉVA VOSZKA, professor, head of the PhD school in economics, University of Szeged, Hungary

KATALIN VÖLGYI, research fellow, Institute of World Economics, Center for Economic and Regional Studies, HAS, Budapest

Index

A

Africa, 4–5, 238–39, 243, 252, 256, 267, 291
Albania, 151
Atatürk, Kemal, 297, 299
Athens, 42
Australia, 275, 291, 237
Austria, 10, 15–22, 26, 34, 79, 101–102, 104–134, 138, 199, 206, 213, 237, 298, 309, 364–65
Austro–Hungarian Monarchy, 114, 215
Azerbaijan, 42, 309

B

Balkans, 4, 201, 313, 316
Belgium, 16, 18–19, 21, 25, 28–29, 37, 45, 102, 124, 127
Berlin, 81, 94, 111
Berlusconi, Silvio, 369
Bismarck, Otto von, 79–82, 97
Bolsonaro, Jair, 333, 355
Brazil, 9–10, 238–39, 241–43, 263–64, 317, 325–28, 330–58, 365, 370–71
Brussels, 101–102
Budapest, 157, 178, 214–15, 229
Bulgaria, 29, 39, 151, 154, 194

C

Cardoso, Fernando Henrique, 242, 333, 336, 340–41 347, 350, 352
Central and Eastern Europe, 3, 33, 115, 129, 137, 169, 177, 190, 215, 237–38
Central Asia, 291, 313, 316
Cevdet, Abdullah, 299
Chile, 138, 337, 355
China, 5, 8, 21, 31, 88–89, 113, 163, 238–41, 249, 252, 261, 263–64, 278–79, 288–90, 316, 326, 346, 349
Colbert, Jean-Baptiste, 16, 54
Croatia, 194, 199, 206
Czech Republic 145, 151, 154, 222
Czechia, 73, 101, 137, 190
Czechoslovakia, 215

D

Denmark, 16, 21, 26, 29, 101–102

E

East Asia, 7–8, 10, 239, 241, 246, 249, 251–52, 258, 267, 269, 331, 346, 358, 369

Index

East Central Europe, 127, 137-138, 148, 191
Erdoğan, Recep Tayyip, 314, 318–19, 369, 372
Estonia, 39, 151, 194–95
European Central Bank, 41, 202
European Commission, 24, 26, 28–29, 37, 39, 41, 202, 203, 205
European Union, 2, 4, 27, 36, 39, 101, 119–20, 123, 127, 134, 156, 180, 185, 190, 366, 369
Eurozone, 25, 29, 42, 44, 102, 129, 197, 199, 208, 237

F

Finland, 16, 18, 21, 44, 73, 101–102, 243
France, 2, 4, 10, 15–16, 18–21, 25, 27, 29, 31, 32, 34, 40, 43–45, 53–61, 63–67, 69–73, 79, 82, 102, 124, 138, 163, 199, 226, 243, 298, 364–65

G

German Empire, 79, 81
Germany, 10, 14–22, 25–26, 29, 34, 40, 44–45, 64–65, 79–84, 87, 89–93, 95–96, 98, 118, 120, 124, 127, 133–34, 138, 199, 206, 215, 237, 319, 364–65
Great Britain, 2–3, 20, 79, 81–82, 86, 124, 226, 239, 298. *See also* United Kingdom
Greece, 21, 25–26, 29, 38-43, 45, 129, 202, 240–41
Guedes, Paolo, 355

H

Habsburg Empire, 79, 213
Haider, Jörg, 369
Hamburg, 81, 83, 96
Hong Kong, 238, 240–41, 243–44
Hungary, 4, 8, 91, 101–102, 133, 137–40, 144, 146–48, 151–57, 179–80, 194, 213–23, 225–27, 232–34, 306, 366–67, 369, 372

I

India, 5, 238–39, 242–43, 252, 276–78, 288–89, 316
Indonesia, 238, 243–44, 277–78, 288–89
International Monetary Fund (IMF), 41, 44, 202, 275, 286, 293, 300, 304, 305–306, 311, 315, 332, 340
Ireland, 16, 21, 25–26, 28–29, 39–41, 45, 127, 237, 240, 243
Italy, 14, 16, 18, 20–22, 34, 39–41, 44–45, 64, 66, 73, 132, 138, 199, 206, 298, 365, 372

J

Jackiewicz, David, 181–82

K

Kaczyński, Jarosław, 171, 181
Keynes, 1–2, 35, 118–19, 131, 267
Kohl, Helmut, 86–88, 90
Kurz, Sebastian, 132, 143, 365

L

Latin America, 3, 88, 239, 241–42, 250, 252, 256, 263, 291, 325–26, 342
Latvia, 29, 151, 194
Lithuania, 29, 151, 194
Louis IX, "the Saint," 54
Louis XI, "the Prudent," 54
Louis XIV, 16, 54,
Lula da Silva, Luiz Inácio, 9, 340-49, 351–53, 356
Luxemburg, 28–29, 37, 39, 127, 206

M

Malaysia, 238, 243–44, 277–79, 284, 288
Mexico, 138, 311, 369
Middle East, 241, 289, 291, 316
Morawiecki, Mateusz, 183, 185

N

NATO, 191, 300
Netherlands, 16, 18–21, 26, 28–29, 40, 44, 64, 73, 256, 298
New Zealand, 237, 291, 337
North America, 32, 288–89, 291
Norway, 6, 163

O

OECD, 96, 163, 173, 176–79, 184, 191, 196, 202, 207–208, 300–301
Orbán, Viktor, 140, 151, 369, 372
Ottoman Empire, 297–99
Özal, Targut, 301, 314

P

Poland, 4, 40–41, 43, 45, 73, 137–40, 142, 145, 147–48, 151, 153–54, 156–57, 163–67, 169–70, 172–75, 177–86, 194–95, 222, 232, 364–67, 369
Portugal, 15–16, 18–21, 29, 39–41, 45, 202, 240–41
Prague, 178
Prussia, 79–80
Putin, Vladimir, 372

R

Reagan, Ronald, 3, 301
Romania, 151, 154, 194, 215,
Rousseff, Dilma, 325, 333, 343–46, 348–54, 356–58
Russia, 3, 9, 28, 79, 80, 154–55, 196, 206, 238, 366, 369, 372

S

Schröder, Gerhard, 93
Schüssel, Wolfgang, 107
Singapore, 6–10, 32, 88, 238, 240–41, 243–45, 263, 275–94, 369–70
Slovenia, 25, 29, 137, 151, 154, 189–208, 367–68

South Korea, 9, 163, 238, 240, 243, 245, 317, 369
Southeast Asia, 3, 124, 238, 243, 246, 249, 252, 276
Soviet Union, 84, 91, 105, 112, 117, 137, 144, 215, 300
Spain, 16, 18–21, 25–26, 29, 40, 45, 64, 240–41
Sweden, 15–16, 18–19, 21, 40, 45, 101–102, 237
Switzerland, 102, 120, 127
Szydlo, Beata, 180–81

T

Taiwan, 238, 240–41, 243,
Temer, Michel, 333, 349, 354–58
Thailand, 6, 238, 243–45, 276, 369
Thatcher, Margaret, 3, 86
Third Reich, 97, 82–84
Trump, Donald, 355
Turkey, 10, 241–43, 263, 297, 299–302, 304–308, 310–20, 369, 372
Turkish Republic, 303, 317
Tusk, Donald, 140, 153, 172–74, 185

U

United Kingdom, 15–16, 18–19, 21, 25, 29, 40, 54, 64, 275. See also Great Britain
United States, 3–4, 23–25, 37, 56, 88, 111, 145, 239, 241, 247, 267, 279, 293

V

Vietnam, 288–89
Visegrád countries, 130, 137, 155–56, 232

W

Washington, 42, 314-315, 320
Western Balkans, 4
Western Europe, 18, 116, 118, 129, 191, 288

World Bank, 33, 167, 173, 193–94, 231, 240–41, 244, 286, 304, 316, 334
World Trade Organization (WTO), 249, 315

Y

Yeltsin, Boris, 3, 144
Yugoslavia, 189–90, 193